THE STORY OF
FOOD

THE STORY OF FOOD

AN ILLUSTRATED HISTORY OF EVERYTHING WE EAT

Contents

 Penguin Random House

Jacket Design Development Manager Sophia M.T.T.
Jacket Editor Claire Gell
Associate Publishing Director Liz Wheeler
Art Director Karen Self
Publishing Director Jonathan Metcalf

DK LONDON
Senior Art Editor Ina Stradins
Senior Editor Janet Mohun
US Editor Megan Douglass
Team Assistant Briony Corbett
Managing Art Editor Michael Duffy
Managing Editor Angeles Gavira
Producer, Pre-Production Jacqueline Street
Senior Producer Alex Bell
Jacket Designer Mark Cavenagh

DK DELHI
Senior Art Editor Chhaya Sajwan
Senior Editor Dharini Ganesh
Project Art Editor Vikas Sachdeva
Art Editors Roshni Kapur, Meenal Goel
Editor Riji Raju
Assistant Art Editors Simran Saini, Amrai Dua, Monam Nishat
Senior Managing Art Editor Arunesh Talapatra

Senior Managing Editor Rohan Sinha
Senior Picture Researcher Surya Sankarsh Sarangi
Picture Researcher Deepak Negi
Picture Research Manager Taiyaba Khatoon
DTP Designers Jaypal Chauhan, Nityanand Kumar, Vijay Kandwal
Senior DTP Designer Harish Aggarwal
Production Manager Pankaj Sharma
Pre-production Manager Balwant Singh
Jacket Designer Suhita Dharamjit
Jacket Editorial Coordinator Priyanka Sharma
Managing Jackets Editor Saloni Singh

SCHERMULY DESIGN CO. LTD.
Project Editor Cathy Meeus

Grains, Cereals, and Pulses

Dairy and Eggs

Sugars and Syrups

Oils and Condiments

Herbs and Spices

First American edition, 2018
Published in the United States by DK Publishing
345 Hudson Street, New York, New York 10014

Copyright © 2018 Dorling Kindersley Limited
DK, a Division of Penguin Random House LLC
18 19 20 21 22 10 9 8 7 6 5 4 3 2 1
001-293637– May/2018

Published in Great Britain by Dorling Kindersley Limited

A catalog record for this book
is available from the Library of Congress.
ISBN: 978-1-4654-7336-3

Printed and bound in China

A WORLD OF IDEAS:
SEE ALL THERE IS TO KNOW

www.dk.com

Contributors
Josephine Bacon
Alexandra Black
Liz Calvert Smith
Jane Garton
Jeremy Harwood
Patsy Westcott

Consulting editor
Jill Norman

Foreword

When I was a small boy of maybe ten or eleven, my dream breakfast was a bowl of Coco Pops with a little muesli mixed in, full cream milk, and then a light dusting of Ready Brek on the top, like newly fallen snow. The powdery oat cereal would fill out the crunchier chocolate mouthfuls, while the raisins and oats at the bottom fattened gradually in the browning, chocolatey milk. Oh, what heaven, to blend so many good things and to make something wholly new, wholly mine. What a delicious expression of my nascent self.

Except I never did. It remained forever a breakfast enjoyed only in my dreams. Because my parents, who were very strict about food, would not allow it. No mixing of cereals in one bowl. I don't know why. I was told only "because." Because food rules and the story of food are like that: shrouded in mystery but strongly believed in. Because we all think we know everything about food, when in fact we mostly know nothing.

Take Galen, the hugely influential classical Greek physician, who, I discover from the pages of this extraordinary book, thought fruit was linked to "cold, wet humours" and gave you diarrhea, thus condemning generations of Europeans to scurvy from vitamin C deprivation. Or the Chinese who thought carp turned into dragons when they spawned. Or the Germans who tied frisky horses to raspberry canes to calm them (the horses, not the raspberries). Or the American scientists of the 1950s who falsely linked coronary heart disease with a diet high in animal fats, creating the carb-heavy diet full of sugary flavorings that has given us our current obesity crisis and threatens to lower life expectancy in the developed world for the first time since the Black Death.

I'm not sure if that last one is in here (it is a big book), but it bugs me. Ignorance. The ignorance that mistreats animals with bad husbandry, contaminates water tables with poorly administered chemicals, fills the seas with single use plastics (drink tap water, you lemons!) and over-exposes children to fast, colorful, nutritionally catastrophic foods that set in motion a lifetime of bad habits.

This book is an antidote to that ignorance. It is an essential contribution to the ongoing debate about how we eat now, and what and why and since when and for how much longer. It comes at this enormous subject in a multi-disciplinary blizzard of enthusiasm, like the great encyclopedias of the Enlightenment, attacking food from historical, political, cultural, scientific, and medical angles in ways that make it gripping as a sit down read,

compulsive as an idle browse, and indispensable as a reference tool. And if you're not a big reader, you'll learn more from a flick through the dazzling images that illustrate it than you would from a thousand articles in the daily food press (apart from mine!).

Find out how meat changed our brains, why having a walnut for a brain is no bad thing in Afghanistan, and what the drains in Pompeii tell us about eating giraffes.

But first I think it is time for what Winnie the Pooh called "a little smackerel of something"—Coco Pops and muesli I think, with just the lightest scattering of Ready Brek …

GILES COREN

Feeding the masses
Traditional markets such as in Durbar Square, Kathmandu, Nepal, hark back to ancient ways of bartering produce. Like their modern supermarket counterparts, however, they serve a function as old as the human race: providing food for hungry mouths.

Introduction

From prehistoric hunter-gatherers to modern culinary superstars, food has occupied a prominent position in the human psyche. As a species, we depend upon food for survival, but how it is obtained, prepared, and consumed has shaped us as much as our quest for it has shaped plants, animals, and the environment.

Over the course of human history, food has become a potent topic, assuming enormous social, environmental, and commercial significance. The production of food has evolved into a massive global enterprise, and for the majority of people in the developed world, a trip to the supermarket is all the effort required in order to obtain the calories and nutrients needed to survive.

Hard-wired for nutrients

The ancient hunt for sustenance is mostly gone, but the quest for it is in our DNA, and our relationship with food remains as complex and vital as it ever was. From the time early humans learned how to harness the power of wild foods and began to make the right tools for hunting and butchering, cultivation and domestication, the process of evolution gained pace, allowing them to get enough nourishment not just to survive, but to thrive.

△ **Painted records**
Cave paintings depict animals that early humans hunted for food in prehistoric times. In France's Lascaux caves, horse was on the menu—at least until riding them proved more beneficial

Researchers believe that between 2 million and 3.9 million years ago a shift took place in the diet of early humans in Africa, which propelled them to exploit new sources of food and forced them into different environments as a consequence. When paleontologists examined the tooth enamel of several species of early humans found in Ethiopia, they discovered that some of them had added new types of plant foods to their diet. These plants, such as tubers, succulents, cabbage, and maize were especially nutrient- and energy-dense, and this new source of food channeled more calories into brain development. In the process, our taste receptors evolved to detect poisons in plants, distinguishing between foods that tasted bitter and were deadly, those that tasted slightly less bitter and were nutritious, and others that tasted sweet and would provide a fast-acting energy boost.

Food meant the difference between life and death—between a growing, prosperous population and a struggling one—and it assumed great social, religious, and cultural significance. The quest to find, hunt, and grow food forced people to cooperate, to arrange society in such a way that it maximized food production. On a hunt this meant that different members of a community assumed specialist roles in order to ensure the best chances of a kill.

Once herding and grain agriculture became established, more complex forms of organization and cooperation were required, pushing communities to innovate, invent, and become efficient not only at food production but at storing, transporting, and trading it. A surplus of food also allowed more children to survive to adulthood, triggering a population explosion. Thus a subsistence existence gave way to a thriving society with many different aspects.

Along with archaeological and anthropological finds, such as cave paintings, utensils, bones, and chemical traces of foodstuffs, much of what anthropologists and historians know about early food production and consumption comes from a limited number of texts, such as early recipe books and trade accounts. From these

Ashes found in a South African cave reveal that early humans were using fire to cook food 1 million years ago.

sources we now know that our ancestors were deep-sea fishing for tuna in southeast Asia, for example, as well as making cheese in Poland, and keeping bees in ancient Egypt.

How meat-eating affected the brain

Eating more meat was another crucial dietary change that provided further fuel for the expansion and evolution of the human brain. And as our ancestors' brains developed, so, too, did their ability to innovate. Developing tools with cutting edges gave groups the ability to hunt cooperatively, enabling them to bring down large game instead of scavenging the kills of other predators. This progression occurred over a long period of time, beginning with the use of basic scraper tools around 2.6 million years ago, which allowed meat to be butchered, to the creation of thrusting spears, the earliest of which date back approximately 500,000 years.

How cooking changed the world

Once humans had harnessed fire, they began to cook their food, a development that heralded the beginning of a love affair with culinary experimentation, commentary, and, eventually, the art of entertaining. Most importantly, however, cooking unlocked different nutrients in certain foods by breaking down proteins, carbohydrates, and fats to make them easier to digest. It also killed germs that caused food poisoning, and even eradicated poisons from some plants. Only when a potato is cooked, for example, does it release its starches in a form that can be efficiently absorbed by the human gut.

It is believed that all of these factors contributed to our biological development in many different ways. Cooked food led to smaller jaws and smaller intestines, while increased calorie consumption led to bigger brains, but the changing relationship between humans and their food supply was also the catalyst for social and technological advances.

Fine dining in the ancient world

The 3rd-century CE Greek writer Athenaeus of Naucratis provides modern readers with a fascinating glimpse of food in ancient times in his encyclopedic *Deipnosophistae*, otherwise known as *The Sophists at Dinner*. Essentially a collection of quotations from various dinner parties, Athenaeus captures fashionable talk about food, obesity, diet, recipes, condiments, and gravies, among other topics.

A century or so later, *De re coquinaria* (*On the Subject of Cooking*) provided a collection of 400 recipes used in imperial Rome; it is more commonly known as *Apicius*, after decadent epicure Marcus Gavius Apicius, who was famous for his lavish 1st-century banquets. A cookbook for the cognoscenti rather than the common citizen, *Apicius* emphasized the importance of good ingredients, and most of its recipes are for dishes that were richly flavored with herbs, spices, and sauces.

Expanding food trade

The great variety of spices available hints at the trade routes that were being established at various times in the Roman Empire—the conquest of Egypt in 30 BCE, for example, resulted in a flow of exotic spices such as pepper and cumin from India, and silphium from North Africa. It was not long before this early globalization of food

◁ **Pictogram beer record**
Records of food and drinks were being kept as early as 3100 BCE in Mesopotamia. This tablet records the allocation of beer in a community using pictograms created by pushing a wooden stylus into moist clay.

△ **Well-traveled route**
When Marco Polo left Venice for China in the 13th century, he was
following a long-established trade route between East and West,
which had transported foods into both parts of the world.

accelerated beyond the wildest dreams of the ancient Romans. By
the time the Venetian merchant Marco Polo began his explorations
in the 13th century, the flow of goods between East and West
along the network known as the Silk Road was already hundreds
of years old, and the migration of culinary traditions already
inevitable. Some sources claim that the noodles of China and the
pasta of Italy may both have originated from the Arab technique of
making dried pasta from durum wheat flour—knowledge that
traveled eastward to China, Japan, and Korea, then westward
to the Mediterranean.

A similar exchange transpired between the Old World and
the New World when potatoes, tomatoes, cocoa, and tobacco
were introduced to Europe, Africa, and Asia, while in the other
direction, olives, rice, wheat, and cattle were imported to Central
and South America. And not only foodstuffs made the journey.

Cooking styles, for example, changed dramatically in Latin
America where, before the arrival of the Spanish, frying was
virtually unknown, but later became commonplace.

Mealtimes in Mesopotamia

One of the oldest written records about food dates from around
1650 BCE in the form of a recipe collection, complete with other
culinary information, engraved on clay tablets from Mesopotamia.
Originating from a region of the Middle East that equates to
modern-day Iraq, Kuwait, Syria, and southeastern Turkey, these

tablets provide an insight into how food was prepared in this ancient Middle Eastern region. These cuneiform tablets hint at the variety of food available, listing 20 kinds of cheese, 100 different soups, and 300 types of bread. They also indicate how important mealtimes were to social organization, as well as to religion.

Researchers deciphering these tablets have deduced that the social elite ate a main meal in the morning and one in the evening, with two smaller snacks during the day, while laborers ate just two meals. At royal banquets, guests were seated according to a strict hierarchy arranged by profession, ethnicity, and status at court. Food was also a central part of religious rituals, with four meals a day served to the gods at local temples, where any "leftovers" were eaten by temple attendants, royal staff, and possibly needy townspeople.

Social and religious customs

The principle of social or religious groups eating together—whether as entire communities, members of a particular clique, or families—provides a practical approach to communal food preparation. Yet it is also a way of bonding, providing a forum for sharing information and oral history, giving advice, and reinforcing particular beliefs.

A study by the University of Oxford, UK, shows that the more often people eat together, the happier they are.

In the Middle Ages, the Christian Church preached the importance of eating at regular times to discourage gluttony and reinforce a sense of discipline. In ancient China, too, eating excessively was frowned upon, and at the dinner table children were instructed to eat only until they were three-quarters full. Business deals were cemented in the coffee houses of 17th century London; gossip was shared, marriages planned, and domestic manipulation plotted over afternoon tea in the polite society of 18th-century Europe; and political alliances were forged over dinners in 1950s Communist Beijing. Criminals and their victims found reconciliation, and communities brokered peace in the Middle Eastern tradition of *mumalaha* (breaking bread)—a practice echoed in the bipartisan breaking of bread begun in 1987 in the US Senate prior to the presidential State of the Union address.

Mealtimes have functioned in this way since the earliest times and continue to exert a powerful influence in many societies. In France, lunch is rarely consumed on the go or as street food— employees take an hour for lunch and go out to eat. In many Southeast Asian cultures, street food is an essential element of daily life. Eating together in public places is a fundamental part of seasonal and religious celebrations around the world. One example is Japan's custom of *hanami*, picnicking under blossoming cherry trees every spring. At a domestic level, modern psychologists say that children who eat meals with their parents at least a few times a week are much more likely eat healthily, have fewer problems with drugs and alcohol, and perform better at school than children who do not have regular mealtimes with one or both parents. Our ancestors clearly knew the powerful effects of sharing food.

△ **London coffee house**
In 17th- and 18th-century London, trade agreements and financial deals were often conducted over coffee, tea, or chocolate in coffee houses. Such places provided a clear-headed environment for business.

The future of food

While examining the history of food reveals many interesting facts, it also leads us to think about the future of food, especially in the face of environmental issues such as overfishing and deforestation for crop planting and political issues such as genetically modified foods and intensive animal farming.

Agriscientists are exploring new technologies and new approaches to growing food that will help conserve precious resources such as energy, land, and water. Among their predictions are an increase in urban agriculture, with innovations such as rooftop vegetable gardens and beehives, and vertical farms that take crop growing sky high to preserve precious woodland. In vitro meat production is another possibility that is already being realized, although it may be a challenge to convince consumers to buy laboratory-produced animal products.

One technique at the forefront of future food production is aquaponics, which combines crop-growing and fish-farming. Hydroponics—growing plants indoors in water rather than soil—is an already well-established practice that supplies the majority of salad leaves, tomatoes, and cucumbers in supermarkets in some parts of the world. Aquaponics, however, goes one step further. It involves no chemicals, uses energy-saving LED lights, and is typically set up in disused buildings in dense urban areas with a ready-made local customer base. In fact, the idea of companion farming fish and crops has been practised since Aztec times, but it was not until 2010 that the concept was moved indoors.

The revival in the West of "nose-to-tail" eating, which involves consuming every part of an animal, is another example of modern generations discovering how efficient food production once went hand in hand with social needs, culinary creativity, and a deep respect for nature. The past continues to inspire the future of food, and with it, our future a species.

▷ **In the pink**
Hydroponic techniques—cultivating plants in a soilless, indoor environment— are helping to boost food productivity in sites otherwise unsuitable for growing food. UV lights create a pink glow.

Nuts
and Seeds

Nuts and seeds

Nuts and seeds were a perfect food for our ancient hunter-gatherer ancestors. Consisting of edible kernels in a hard outer shell, nuts were particularly nourishing and sustaining, providing fat, carbohydrate, protein, and fiber in varying quantities, depending on the species. Unlike roots and tubers, which required digging out, they were easy to gather, kept well, and could be moved from one place to another without great difficulty or loss.

Gaining knowledge though observation

Like many other animal species, the earliest humans ate whatever they could find growing readily available. Over the centuries, they steadily increased their knowledge of which plants were most beneficial to eat, which should be avoided, and which provided the most energy. These early humans were observant, often ingenious, and were acutely aware of their surroundings. They noticed that nut-tree harvests varied from year to year, and also discovered that the trees growing deep in the shady forest interior were usually less productive than the ones growing around the forest edge. This knowledge, coupled with an increasingly sophisticated variety of tools, eventually inspired them to clear away undergrowth and smaller trees to foster greater nut harvests, giving rise to the beginnings of what we now call cultivation. Hunting and organized crop-raising came later.

The first nutcrackers

Nut remains and "nutting stones"—flat or slightly concave rocks bearing traces of nuts and seeds—have been found at archaeological sites all over the world, providing evidence of the importance of these foods in prehistoric diets. These primitive nutcrackers typically have a shallow depression in the center, showing where the nuts had been placed and then cracked with another stone—the same technique that has been observed among many primate species today. At Gesher Benot Ya'aqov, close to the Dead Sea in Israel, 50 pitted stones of this type were found and given an estimated date of 780,000 years old. Among the nut remains were acorns, almonds, and pistachios.

△ **Hunter-gatherer feast**
The types of foods our earliest ancestors ate are reflected in nomadic tribes today. For the Penan people of Brunei, nuts and seeds form an integral part of a tribal feast.

◁ **Autumn harvest**
Harvesting nuts was an important part of the medieval year. Among the most common were almonds, which were used in cooking, ground for flour, and mixed with water to make "milk."

△ **Stone age essential**
Grinding stones were central to Neolithic people's existence and were used to grind some roots and vegetables as well as seeds, nuts, and many types of grains.

Some nuts could be cracked and eaten but others needed processing to become edible. Acorns, for example, were put into woven baskets and suspended in running water in a stream to remove their bitter tannic acid. They were then dried or roasted and ground into meal. Acorns and anything made from them have very good storage qualities, and new scientific techniques that can identify microscopic traces have shown that acorns were much more important than previously thought. This is shown in writings from ancient periods such as in those of 1st-century Roman naturalist and chronicler Pliny the Elder, who wrote that the oak was the "tree which first produced food for mortal man." It is now believed that nut consumption in general has been widely underestimated, mainly because the evidence for them had disappeared: the nuts were all eaten, while the shells were burned in fires as extra fuel.

Hoards of hazelnuts

Hazelnuts are the most commonly found nut excavated at archaeological sites worldwide. Their shells are especially hard; many that formed millennia ago have survived intact to this day. They probably reached Italy and Greece from Asia Minor, and have been found at prehistoric lake-dwelling sites in Switzerland and at least one Neolithic site in Sweden. At Colonsay in the Scottish Hebrides, hundreds of thousands of burned hazelnut shells from 7000 BCE were unearthed in a shallow pit, evidence of hazelnut

storing on an epic scale. In addition to protein and other nutrients, the high fat content of nuts meant that oil could be produced from them; this was also true of seeds. Ancient Egyptians used a variety of seeds to produce oil, including radish, flax, moringa, and sesame; the latter was also used in King Nebuchadnezzar's palace in Mesopotamia. Seeds, like nuts, were easily transportable and useful as a ready source of energy.

> In the Middle Ages, pine nuts were thought to quench thirst, alleviate heartburn, and stop stomach pain.

Seeds as early breath mints

In medieval times, seeds were coated in layers of sugar—an expensive and time-consuming process—and eaten as sweetmeats and breath-fresheners. Generally, however, seeds were not consumed as much as nuts, although sunflower seeds became popular in Russia in the early 18th century when Peter the Great introduced the plant there. Poppy seeds were used in spice mixtures in India where the Indian poppy's pale seed is ground and used as a thickener.

△ **The nature of nuts**
One of the first recorded naturalists, Pliny the Elder, mentions acorns and hazelnuts as important sources of food. The hazel is thought to have been an import from Asia Minor.

◁ **Mechanized marzipan**
In the 19th and 20th centuries, machines took over the arduous task of nut-grinding—and sweets such as marzipan, from ground almonds, were no longer exclusively a treat for the rich.

△ **Candied delights**
Marrons glacés, or glazed chestnuts, have been enjoyed in France and Italy since the 16th century. The process involves shelling, then boiling the nuts in a sugar syrup.

Almond harvest old-style
Dervishes at Qand-i Badam, in the Fergana Valley in present-day Tajikistan, gather their almond crop in baskets and sacks in this 16th-century illustration.

Almonds good luck charm

Considered a fertility charm by the ancient Romans, this sweet-tasting nut has provided the basis of desserts and cakes for centuries. It is also the source of oil and flavorings for a host of foods and drinks.

For thousands of years, almonds have been regarded as a symbol of hope, rebirth, and good fortune. One of the oldest mentions in literature appears in the Bible's Book of Numbers, where Aaron's rod blossoms and produces ripe almonds. Almonds were a popular food in ancient Egypt and ancient Greece, while the Romans regarded it as a Greek nut calling it *nux graeca*.

In fact, wild almond trees are native to the Middle East and western Asia, but cultivation quickly spread from there to the Mediterranean. They were taken by Phoenician traders to Spain, and by the

◁ **Pretty and pink**
The almond tree has delicate pink flowers that appear in early spring. Many countries have festivals to mark the almond blossom season.

Sweet almonds have myriad uses. Available shelled and unshelled, whole, flaked, or ground, they can be eaten raw, blanched, or as a salted snack as well as featuring in numerous dishes both savory (such as trout with almonds) and sweet. They are the main ingredient in marzipan, a thick paste consisting of sugar and finely ground almonds sometimes bound with egg. This originated in the Middle East and became popular in Europe in the Middle Ages.

△ **Fuzzy fruit**
Almond fruit, like their relative the peach, have a fuzzy skin. When ripe, the outer flesh peels away to expose the nut.

Origins	Middle East, western Asia
Major producers	US, Spain, Italy
Main food component	15 percent fat
Source of	Iron
Non-food use	Cosmetics
Scientific name	*Prunus dulcis*

> Nearly one million beehives are trucked to California annually to pollinate the almond groves.

8th century were being widely cultivated in the south of France, from where they spread to Italy and the rest of Europe. Almonds played an important role in early Arab and medieval European cooking. They were taken to North America by Franciscan friars in the 1700s, but it was not until the early 20th century that the almond industry became firmly established in California, now the world's largest producer.

Pastries, cakes, and cookies

Almond paste is used as a pastry filling in many cuisines, from the Portuguese *tarte de amândoa* to the traditional British Bakewell tart. Ground almonds are also the basis for many cookies, including macaroons. Almond-flavored cakes and cookies are especially popular in Spain, including the famous *pan de Cádiz*, a confection of marzipan and dried fruit. And in Sweden, cinnamon-flavored rice pudding with an almond hidden inside is a special Christmas dish.

▽ **Shaking things up**
A specialized harvesting machine shakes ripe almonds off the tree ready for collection.

Sweet or bitter

Almonds are not true nuts, but rather seeds encased in a hard outer layer or hull. Two varieties are cultivated today. Sweet almonds are typically eaten as nuts and used in cooking or as a source of almond oil. The oil of bitter almonds is included in flavoring extracts for foods and liqueurs such as Italy's amaretto. However, bitter almond oil contains prussic acid (hydrogen cyanide), which has to be removed by heating to make it safe to eat.

Walnuts

Jupiter's nut

Known to have been eaten by humans in the Neolithic period, walnuts remain one of the most popular nuts for snacking and cooking.

Archaeological excavations in the Aquitaine region of France have uncovered fossilized shells of roasted walnuts dating back to the Neolithic era more than 8,000 years ago. It is known from inscriptions on clay tablets discovered in Mesopotamia that the walnut was also part of the diet of ancient civilizations of the Middle East. These writings suggest that walnuts were being cultivated in the Hanging Gardens of Babylon (in present-day Iraq) around 2000 BCE.

Association with the ancient gods

Encased in thick, green husks, walnuts have finely ridged shells and are the rounded, single-stoned fruits of trees belonging to the genus *Juglans*, the most widely

> The Afghan name for the walnut means "four brains," referring to its brainlike appearance.

cultivated being the common walnut (*Juglans regia*), thought to have originated in Central Asia. The species name is a reference to the Roman god Jupiter (Jovis or Jove) and the word for nut in Latin (*glans*). Jupiter was believed to have eaten walnuts when he lived among mortals. In Greek mythology, Carya, a mortal beloved by the god Dionysus, was transformed into a walnut tree. On hearing of this Carya's father ordered a temple to be built in her memory, with columns in the shape of nymphs of the walnut tree, called caryatids.

◁ **Barrels of nuts**
In this depiction of a late 18th-century rural market, a trader scoops walnuts out of a barrel to sell to an eager customer. This would have been a familiar autumnal scene in southern Europe.

△ Ground down
Throughout southern Europe, walnuts are sold in ground form for making pastes and sauces. Here, shelled nuts are poured into a traditional mill.

In the Middle Ages, walnuts were traded along the Silk Road between Asia and the Middle East, and in later centuries were spread by seafaring traders around the rest of the world. The walnut was brought to North America by Spanish missionaries, who settled along the Californian coast in the 1800s. Today, California remains among the world's leading producers of walnuts, although China tops the list.

Snacks, soups, and sauces

In Europe and America, walnuts are mostly eaten as snacks and are used in cakes and sweet dishes from ice cream to baklava. They also appear in savory dishes such as French walnut soup, pasta sauces in Italy, and in eastern European and Middle Eastern meat dishes. Walnut paste is widely used in the cuisines of countries in the Caucasus Mountains. Walnut oil was traditionally used in France, Switzerland, and northern Italy for cooking and in salad dressings, but is less popular now due to its high price.

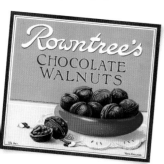

△ Chocolate covered
By the early 20th century, walnuts covered in chocolate had become a favorite sweet snack in the UK.

Origins
Central Asia

Major producers
China, Iran, US

Main food component
67 percent carbohydrate

Source of
Iron, potassium

Scientific name
Juglans regia

Hazelnuts
elegantly flavored nut

The fruit of the hazel tree, which grows throughout the northern hemisphere, hazelnuts are now one of the world's favorite nut crops.

△ Nuts and catkins
Hazelnuts form from flowers that have been pollinated by the long, yellow pollen-bearing clusters known as catkins.

This common nut was undoubtedly a favorite of our Neolithic ancestors. Archaeological digs have unearthed charred fragments of hazelnut shells in many Neolithic sites in several parts of northern Europe. The hazelnut would have been a ready source of food in autumn for these early people. The nut grows on a wide shrub with toothed leaves and yellow catkins that flower in spring. The grape-size nuts appear from late August to October.

Classical sustenance

There are mentions in Greek literature from the 1st century BCE of hazelnuts being brought to Greece from the shores of the Black Sea (present-day Turkey). The 1st-century CE Roman historian Pliny the Elder writes of hazelnuts being gathered for food, although with the fall of the Roman Empire it is probable that cultivation slowed. By the early 17th century, however, cultivation appears to have restarted in Italy and also in England. In 1629, early settlers in North America started to import hazelnuts from England and probably began growing them locally around this time, too.

Today, hazelnuts are grown on a commercial scale in many parts of the world. As well as being eaten raw, the nuts are used, chopped or ground, in baking and candy making. Hazelnut flour adds aroma and nuttiness to cakes and pastries, and hazelnut oil adds its flavor to salad dressing. Chocolate and hazelnut spread is enjoyed worldwide.

Origins
Europe, western Asia

Major producers
Turkey, Italy, Spain

Main food components
12 percent fat, 12 percent carbohydrate

Source of
Calcium, iron

Scientific name
Corylus avellana

▷ Medieval harvest
In the 14th century, collecting hazelnuts may have been an enjoyable activity for wealthier families, as this illustration suggests.

Brazil nuts jungle nut

Originating in the Amazon Basin, Brazil nuts are a favorite snacking nut and recently have become valued for their nutritional value as an unrivalled source of selenium.

Origins
Amazon Basin
Major producers
Bolivia, Brazil
Main food component
67 percent fat
Source of
Selenium, calcium
Non-food use
Cosmetics
Scientific name
Bertholletia excelsa

Brazil nut trees grow wild in the Amazon rainforests of South America, where they usually tower over their neighbors; a mature tree can be as tall as 165ft (50m). They cannot be grown in plantations outside the rainforest because the flowers need to be pollinated by native bees and the resulting seeds—the "nuts"—are dispersed solely by agoutis, large rodents that live on the forest floor.

◁ **Inside the shell**
The Brazil nut consists of a spherical, hard, rough-textured shell, enclosing the individual "nut" segments.

Look out below!

With a hard, thick, woody shell, the Brazil nut tree's fruit is similar in size to a coconut and contains 12–24 seeds arranged like the segments of an orange, each with its own woody covering. Because the trees are too tall to climb, the nuts cannot be harvested until the fruit pods fall to the ground, reaching speeds of up to 50mph (80kph). The weight of the fruit, which can be as much as 5lb (2.3kg), makes this a potentially lethal event, and at harvest time the locals wear hard hats for protection and avoid gathering the pods on windy days.

Brazil nuts have been a good source of nutrients for Amazonian tribes for many thousands of years, but they were unknown elsewhere until Portuguese and Spanish explorers first came across them in the 16th century. However, it was Dutch traders who introduced the nuts to Europe, in 1633, and they didn't reach North America until the 19th century.

Today, the US is the largest importer of Brazil nuts, most of which come from Bolivia, the world's largest exporter of the nuts. In Brazil, Bolivia, and Peru, the trees that bear the nuts are highly protected and logging is prohibited by law.

Hard times

Brazil nuts are available to buy shelled or unshelled, although they are a hard nut to crack. They can be eaten raw, blanched, or roasted as a snacking nut. They are also an ingredient used mainly in the candy industry. In Brazil, they feature in the popular Brazil nut cake.

A mature Brazil nut tree can produce 250lb (113kg) of nuts a year.

◁ **At the tree top**
The fruit of the Brazil nut tree are borne on branches high up in the forest canopy. The tree is deciduous, dropping its leaves in the dry season.

▷ **Loads of nuts**
Brazil nuts are big business and a significant commodity for Brazil, which exports around 41,888 tons of the nuts each year.

Pecans

North America's own tree nut

The only tree nut native to North America, the pecan and its eponymous pie have become inextricably linked with American celebrations, notably Thanksgiving.

Despite its name, rather than being a true nut the pecan is actually a drupe, like its relative the walnut. However, unlike a walnut, a pecan has a smooth shell. Although its kernel has a similar wrinkled appearance, it is darker brown and has an oilier, milder flavor.

A type of hickory, pecan trees are native to the southeastern US and a few Mexican river valleys. Wild pecans were a valuable food source for American Indian tribes, who would gather and eat the nuts during autumn. Pencans were also used to make a nut milk by fermenting powdered pecans into a, possibly intoxicating, drink known as *powcohicora*.

Hard graft

Pecans may have first been cultivated by the American Indians, who traded their crop with early European explorers. Certainly, Spanish colonists planted pecan trees in northern Mexico in the late 16th or early 17th centuries, then other colonists followed suit in Long Island in the early 1770s. The US pecan industry gathered momentum and by 1805 advertisements in London were branding the pecans as meriting attention as a cultivated crop. There were still, however, great variations in the size, shape, and flavor of pecan nuts until the mid 19th century, when a Louisiana slave named Antoine worked out how to graft wood from superior wild trees onto seedling stocks. Pecans are used mainly in sweet dishes, such as pecan pie and candy.

Origins
North America

Major producers
US, Mexico

Main food component
72 percent fat

Source of
Iron, zinc, vitamin B3, vitamin E, vitamin K

Scientific name
Carya illinoinensis

▷ **Pecan types**
In 1912 the US Department of Agriculture published an illustrated guide to the main varieties of pecans grown in the US at the time.

Peanuts the underground nut

First cultivated more than 7,000 years ago in South America, peanuts have since conquered the world. Once considered mere animal feed in the US, they are now an integral part of the American diet, a universal snack food, and an important component of African and Asian cuisines.

△ **Roasted peanuts**
Americans eat 6lb (2.7kg) of peanuts per person per year, although half of that is as peanut butter, while Europeans tend to munch roasted peanuts with drinks.

Fossilized shells from the Nanchoc Valley in northern Peru reveal that peanuts were grown and eaten by indigenous people from around 5600 BCE. As the species was not one that grew naturally in the area, peanuts must have been farmed earlier elsewhere, probably in Bolivia. Research has revealed that the cultivated peanut, *Arachis hypogaea*, was the product, by selection, of two wild South American species.

Despite the name, peanuts—also known as groundnuts, monkey nuts, and goobers—are not true nuts but legumes, members of the pea or bean family. The seeds, or peanuts, have a substantial oil content, so are easily ground into a thick, nutritious paste. The earliest Peruvian peanut-farming communities were probably the first to enjoy some form of peanut butter and may also have roasted the nuts.

A passion for peanuts

Evidence of the peanut's long-standing popularity is found in artefacts from the Moche civilization, which flourished in Peru between the 1st and 8th centuries CE. These include ceramics molded into peanut forms or illustrated with peanut designs, gold peanut pod-shaped jewelry, and funerary offerings of peanut-filled vases. Centuries later, the Incas also farmed peanuts, transporting their harvest of nuts on llamas.

Spanish explorers took peanuts back to Spain in the late 16th century, the Dutch took them to the Dutch East Indies, and they also traveled via the Pacific to China. The Portuguese introduced peanuts to Africa and India. Despite the proximity of South America, the peanut is said to have traveled to the US with slaves from Africa as late as the early 18th century. Slave traders stocked up on the crop because it traveled well and was cheap and nutritious.

Americans initially regarded peanuts as animal fodder or food for the poor. It was only in the 1800s that peanuts started to be grown commercially in Virginia. Dr. John H. Kellogg, who with his brother Will later created corn flakes, patented peanut butter—

△ **Growing underground**
Peanuts grow in the ground on trailing stems within fruit pods containing up to seven seeds or "nuts."

now an integral part of the American diet—as a nutritious health food in 1898. Impressed with his teachings, Seventh Day Adventists in Australia imported peanut butter with some of his other health foods, popularizing peanut products there.

Enjoyed worldwide

The advent of labor-saving machines to plant and harvest peanuts boosted US production in the early 1900s and, when the boll weevil threatened cotton production, many Southern farmers turned to peanut-growing instead. With the encouragement of the botanist and inventor George Washington Carver, a staunch advocate of peanut-farming, the industry flourished. In the 20th century, the US was the largest producer of peanuts after India and China, and was also the world's largest exporter.

Whole and pureed peanuts are important ingredients in various Thai and Chinese noodle recipes. They are also used in Indonesia as dipping (satay) sauces for grilled meat and fish on skewers; in India's popular breakfast dish *poha*; and in West African stews, soups, cakes, and candy.

◁ **Cheap snack**
In the 1930s, Americans could treat themselves to a handful of peanuts for just one cent, dispensed by this innovative vending machine.

◁ **Food mountain**
Peanuts were, and continue to be, big business in the tropics. Here, heavy sacks of peanuts are carried across gangplanks at the foot of a great mound of peanuts awaiting export.

"Man cannot live by bread alone; he must have peanut butter."

JAMES A. GARFIELD, US PRESIDENT (1831–1881)

Origins	South America
Major producers	China, India, Nigeria
Main food component	39 per cent fat
Source of	Iron, vitamins B, E
Scientific name	*Arachis hypogaea*

Cacao food of the gods

Cocoa beans from the cacao tree have had a long and remarkable history, being used for everything from money to medicine and religious rituals, eventually becoming the basis of one of the world's favorite sweet treats.

Origins
Mexico, Central and northern South America

Major producers
Ivory Coast, Ghana, Indonesia

Main food component
57 percent carbohydrate

Scientific name
Theobroma cacao

Believed by the Maya and Aztecs of Mexico and Central America to be a gift of the gods, chocolate in those civilizations was only for the elite and for special occasions, served after feasts and drunk from gourd cups. In fact, it was thought to be an ill omen if an ordinary person drank it. For some rituals, it was mixed with blood, which was also seen as sacred. The name chocolate comes from the Aztec word *xocolatl*, which means "bitter water." Carl Linnaeus, the 18th-century Swedish naturalist, echoed early beliefs when he named the cacao tree *Theobroma cacao*—*theobroma* is Latin for "food of the gods."

◁ **Goddess of chocolate**
The earth goddess Ixcacao was revered as a protector against famine and the guardian of crops by the Mayan people.

The right conditions

Cacao trees, originally from tropical Mexico, Central America, and northern South America, grow in damp conditions, where they can be pollinated by midges and shaded by taller tropical trees. The trees shed all their leaves and die if the temperature falls below 60°F (15.5°C). Cacao seeds grow well when planted in ideal conditions and the trees will fruit by their third or fourth year. The cacao pods grow directly from the trunk and branches in an unusual way known as cauliflory. This was outside the knowledge of early botanical illustrators, so it was often drawn incorrectly in the style of more familiar fruit trees with pods shown hanging from the ends of branches. Three main varieties of cacao tree are cultivated today.

Although they can grow to about 60ft (18m) in height, they are usually restricted to 20ft (6m) or so in plantations for ease of picking, and the pods are harvested twice a year. The Criollo variety produces the finest beans and may even be the same ones that were harvested by the Maya and Aztecs. Although the flavor is considered to be outstanding, they are susceptible to many diseases, are difficult to grow, and produce fewer beans per pod than some other varieties. The more reliable Forastero is the major commercial variety, accounting for 80 percent of world production. The Trinitario is a natural hybrid that came about after a storm on Trinidad was assumed to have wiped out all the Criollo trees there. Forastero trees were planted, but natural hybrids occurred combining the best features of both varieties. The tree cannot disperse its own seeds, but needs intervention by humans or another agent to do this.

▷ **Poured from a great height**
Traditionally in Mexico and Central America the foam on the surface of a chocolate drink was created by pouring the liquid from one vessel into another.

▷ **Brewing up**
In this 17th-century artist's view of chocolate-making in Central America, indigenous people are shown preparing and serving cacao as a drink.

FROM AN ORIGINAL PICTURE IN THE POSSESSION OF THE PROPRIETOR OF

EPPS'S COCOA.

Day & Son (Limited) Gate Str. London, W.C.

Served old style

Archaeologists have found traces of cacao in drinking vessels dating back more than a thousand years in Honduras. However, it is impossible to say whether these are the remains of bitter cocoa beans or of the sweet pulp that surrounds them in the pod. The latter would have been fermented and made into an alcoholic drink, but the beans needed to go through several processes to become palatable. They were fermented for several days during which the pulp around them became liquid and drained off. After that they were dried for a week or two and then roasted for one to two hours. The final process was winnowing to remove the papery shell before grinding.

The chocolate the Maya and the Aztecs drank was very different from the drinking chocolate consumed around the world today—it was often served cold and sometimes eaten as gruel or porridge and mixed with chili, honey, vanilla, and various flowers. It is thought to have been served hot by the Maya and cool by the Aztecs, but was always poured from one vessel to another to produce a frothy head.

> The average Swiss person eats 20lb (9kg) of chocolate a year—the most per head of any country in the world.

The dissemination of chocolate to the wider world began with the Spanish conquest of the Americas. On his fourth and last voyage in 1502, the explorer Christopher Columbus chanced to meet with a large Mayan trading canoe from the Yucatán Peninsula. He captured it and on inspecting the cargo found only garments, foodstuffs, and cacao beans, which he didn't recognize. He described them as "almonds which in New Spain [Mexico] are used for money." Columbus, who was looking for gold, was not impressed. It is unclear when chocolate first reached Spain—one story is that it happened in 1544, when Dominican friars who had spent time in Guatemala brought a delegation

◁ **Exotic product**
Epps's Cocoa was Britain's leading brand of cocoa powder in the 19th century. This advertisement clearly shows the leaves, pod, and beans within.

◁ **Chocolate to go**
A street trader in 19th-century Paris sells hot chocolate from an insulated container carried on his back.

By 1773, it had been observed that chocolate was a useful way of masking the taste of poison and it is believed that Pope Clement XIV met his end in this fashion. His innocent confectioner served him chocolate, which the Pope said had a more bitter taste than usual. Somewhat surprisingly they still drank it all and both died soon afterward.

Chocolate had many virtues ascribed to it as a cure for all ills and as an aphrodisiac, too. There are references to chocolate having the same effect as hallucinogenic mushrooms. Bernardino de Sahagún,

△ **Luxury packaging**
Cocoa remained a luxury product in Europe throughout the 19th century, as proclaimed by the lavish design of this German brand.

"The superiority of chocolate … will soon give it … preference over tea and coffee in America."

THOMAS JEFFERSON (1785)

of Mayan nobles to meet Prince Philip II of Spain. They presented him with many gifts and with vessels of beaten chocolate. This may well have been the first time chocolate was seen in Europe, but there is no record of the reaction to it. It was not until 1585 that a whole shipment of beans finally reached Seville. The drink was well received by the wealthy in Spain for whom it was prepared very differently from the traditional way. They wanted no strong spices like chilis, preferring gentler additions like cane sugar, cinnamon, and honey.

Dangerously intoxicating

There are several theories as to how chocolate reached France. The most popular is that it was introduced to the French court as a gift from the Spanish royal family, associated with two marriages between French and Spanish dynasties in 1615, but there is no hard evidence for this. Another suggests it was through a French cardinal receiving it as a medicine from Spanish monks "to moderate the vapors of his spleen". It is known that chocolate had arrived in England by 1657. A London newspaper advertisement called it: "Chocolate, an excellent West India drink, sold in Queen's Head Alley, in Bishopsgate Street, by a Frenchman." Samuel Pepys, the famous English diarist of the period, recorded drinking with a friend, "Chocolate ready made for our morning draught," and again with his own haphazard spelling, "About noon out with Commissioner Pett, and he and I into a Coffee House to drink Jocolatte, very good!"

a Spanish Franciscan friar and assiduous chronicler, wrote: "This cacao, when much is drunk … makes one drunk … makes one dizzy, confuses one, makes one sick, deranges one." This has puzzled scholars, some of whom speculate that the chocolate the friar was served had been mixed with alcohol or another intoxicating substance.

Solid and sweet

Today, most chocolate is eaten in a sweetened form, made from a combination of cocoa powder, cocoa butter (or vegetable oil), and sugar. It is commonly consumed in the form of solid bars, sometimes with additional flavorings or fillings, or as a covering for different types of candy. It is a popular ingredient in cakes, desserts, and ice cream. It is also used in some savory dishes, notably in Mexico's *mole* sauce, which also includes chili peppers and is often served with turkey, chicken, and other meats on festive occasions.

▷ **Labor saving**
By the end of the 19th century, chocolate-making was becoming mechanized. Machines such as this mill had been developed to reduce the labor needed to grind the beans.

Expedition food

From the 16th century onward, keeping ships' crews healthy during voyages was a never-ending struggle. Fresh meat and dairy spoiled easily, as did fruits and vegetables; dried fruits like raisins were the exception. This meant that malnutrition was a huge problem. Scurvy, a disease caused by vitamin C deficiency, is thought to have killed approximately two million sailors between 1500 and 1800 alone.

Explorers on land had it slightly easier. When Meriwether Lewis and William Clark set off across the emerging US in 1804, they relied on the game they could shoot, net, and trap to augment their dried foodstuffs. These included flour, salt, coffee, pork, meat, corn, sugar, beans, and lard as well as a concoction they called "portable soup." This mixture was boiled until it turned into jelly, then left to harden. Its taste was unappealing, but it saved the expedition from starvation on more than one occasion.

Captain Robert Scott's ill-fated 1912 expedition to reach the South Pole was not so fortunate. Safe in a hut at Cape Evans, he and fellow expedition members ate well, but away from the hut it was a different story. The tractors Scott's team brought with them to haul their sledges broke down and their ponies died. Scott and his men had no alternative but to drag their sledges along as they began their attempt for the pole. For food, they mainly relied on pemmican: ground dried meat mixed with melted fat, which they boiled with water to make *hoosh*, a kind of stew. Otherwise, their diet consisted of butter, biscuits, cheese, sugar, and cocoa. Modern nutritionists believe the rations lacked fat as well as vitamins. At best, Scott and his men consumed 4,500 calories a day—well short of the 6,000 to 7,000 needed. On their laborious return journey, they simply began to starve to death.

◁ **Better food equals better times**
Russian dog driver Dimitri Geroff (left) and dog handler Cecil Meares cook provisions in 1902 during Scott's *Discovery* expedition.

▷ **Ripening fruit and nuts**
Only cashew nuts can be exported. The juicy apples, though considered a delicacy, are too easily damaged.

Cashews
an irritating nut

When Portuguese explorers first discovered cashew fruits in Brazil, they thought them inedible. But once they had learned how to extract the nuts, they enjoyed them as a tasty snack, and they have been eaten in Europe and beyond ever since.

Origins	Brazil
Major producers	Ivory Coast, Vietnam
Main food component	47 percent fat
Source of	Iron
Scientific name	*Anacardium occidentale*

Cashew fruit is unusual in that it has two distinct parts—the fleshy, oval, sweet-smelling cashew apple and the seed, or nut, encased in a hard double shell that hangs from it. The shell is difficult to crack and contains two highly irritant chemicals—cardol and anacardic acid. The native Tupi people of Brazil discovered that drying and roasting the shells made the nuts much easier to remove—a technique they passed on to the Portuguese, who also used cashew apple pulp to make wine.

Snacks and sauces
The Portuguese took cashews to the Indian coastal state of Goa around 1560. The trees thrived, and Indians soon began using the nuts medicinally and for food—consumed whole, ground into a paste to serve as the base of a sauce for curries, or used in powdered form in desserts. The popularity of cashews soon spread to Southeast Asia, and the trees were also found to grow well in Africa, where the nutritious nuts became an integral part of the local cuisine. The cashew was not popular in North America until the 1920s, but by 1941 some 20,000 tons (18,000 tonnes) were imported annually—not from their native South America, but from India. Today, the mild, delicate flavor of cashew nuts is enjoyed the world over, although they remain an expensive snack. The apples are sometimes eaten raw or made into jams and jellies.

▷ **Handle with care**
An Indian farm worker removes cashew nuts from the fruit by hand. Removal of the shells requires protection from the irritant chemicals released.

Chestnuts sweet and starchy

For thousands of years, sweet chestnuts were an important source of carbohydrate for many people and were dried and ground into flour. Today, they are still enjoyed as a hot winter treat or a candied delicacy.

Dedicated to the supreme Greek god Zeus, the sweet chestnut was introduced to ancient Greece from Sardis (present-day Sart in Turkey). Encased in prickly husks, sweet chestnuts are the seeds of a large hardy tree, *Castanea sativa*, and should not be confused with the inedible horse chestnuts of the genus *Aesculus*. The Greeks and Romans stored chestnuts in ceramic jars, preserving them with wild honey to impart a delicate sweet flavor.

△ **Easy to peel**
Sweet chestnuts have a soft outer shell, which can be removed by peeling, and a hairy inner skin.

Vital source of starch
By the Middle Ages, sweet chestnut trees were grown throughout Europe, mostly in mountain and forest regions where communities could not cultivate wheat for flour. Before the arrival of maize and potatoes from the Americas in the 16th

▷ **Hot nuts**
The cry of "hot chestnuts" used to resound around London in winter as street vendors roasted chestnuts on a brazier.

century, chestnuts, which contain less fat but more carbohydrate than other nuts, were one of Europe's main sources of starch. They were dried and ground into flour for baking and making into pasta, soups, and gruels, and in Italy sweet chestnuts were originally used to make polenta. In the US, the nuts of the towering American chestnut tree (*C. dentata*) were used medicinally and for flour by American Indians—long before chestnuts became popular as a winter treat, roasted on an open fire.

There are several species of sweet chestnut in Asia and they have been cultivated for thousands of years. The first written record of chestnuts as food in China is from the Zhou dynasty (1046–256 BCE). In Japan, candied chestnuts with mashed sweet potatoes is a popular New Year's dish.

On trend
The most expensive chestnut delicacy is the candied French marrons glacés, which dates back at least 400 years. Other sweet confections include nesselrode pudding—a Victorian favorite made from pureed chestnuts, cream, and maraschino liqueur that originated in Austria—and *crème de marrons de l'Ardèche*, a spread created by Frenchman Clément Faugier in 1885. Italians and Austrians still use chestnut flour for baking and, in recent years, the use of chestnuts in savory stuffings, soups, and mashes has become increasingly fashionable.

△ **How many?**
The prickly husks usually contain 2–4 kernels, or nuts, but some chestnut cultivars, such as Marron de Lyon, have just one large kernel.

Origins	Europe, Turkey
Major producer	Italy
Main food component	44 percent carbohydrate
Source of	Vitamin C, vitamin B6
Non-food use	Timber
Scientific name	*Castanea sativa*

"Chestnuts are … a lusty and masculine food for rusticks."

JOHN EVELYN, ENGLISH AUTHOR (1620–1706)

Pine nuts ancient aphrodisiac

The edible seeds of pine trees have been eaten in Europe, Asia, and North America since the Stone Age. Small, light, and easily transportable, pine nuts were carried by Roman soldiers on their campaigns.

△ **Forest food**
Pine nuts are a rich source of calories and nutrients for those dwelling in colder climates.

Pine nuts were a popular snack in ancient Greece and Rome, and the 1st century CE Roman author and philosopher, Pliny the Elder wrote of them being preserved in honey. They were also reputed to have aphrodisiac powers—Galen, a 2nd-century Greek physician, recommended eating them with honey and almonds on three consecutive nights to boost performance in the bedroom.

Northern food
Pine trees are a familiar sight in the northern hemisphere, but their edible seeds, or nuts, are gathered from only 18 of the more than 100 species. The most important ones include the Italian stone pine, Korean pine, North America's single-leaf piñon, and Colorado piñon. The actual nuts grow on the scales of the pine cones, which can take as long

▷ **Stone pine**
The stone pine, native to the Mediterranean region, is one of the few species that are cultivated for edible pine nuts.

as three years to mature. The green cones are then dried in the sun until they open; then the nuts can be extracted, a process often done by hand.

Pine nuts have myriad uses in the kitchen, notably in pesto—the Italian sauce made with pine nuts, garlic, basil, olive oil, and Parmesan—as well as in the popular Italian biscuit, *biscotti ai pinoli*. Pine nuts also feature in other Mediterranean and Middle Eastern dishes such as baklava, a Turkish pastry. In Tunisia they are sometimes added to tea. Lightly roasted to bring out their flavor, they can be added to sweet and savory stuffings and to salads for extra crunch.

KOREAN PINE

Origins
Eastern Asia

Major producers
China, Russia, Pakistan

Main food component
20 percent fat

Source of
Iron

Scientific name
Pinus koraiensis

Pistachios the smiling nuts

Belonging to the same family as cashew nuts, pistachios are the much-loved green nuts of a small, bushy tree. Their distinctive color and sweet taste have brought them fame beyond their native Turkey as a flavoring for ice cream.

Origins	Middle East and C. Asia
Major producers	Iran, US, Turkey
Main food component	45 percent fat
Scientific name	*Pistacia vera*

The ruins of Göbekli Tepe, a 12,000-year-old hilltop site in Anatolia (part of present-day Turkey), revealed that the people who lived and perhaps worshipped there ate pistachios. Pistachio trees are reputed to have grown some 8,000 years later in the Hanging Gardens of Babylon (in present-day Iraq).

Native to the Middle East and Central Asia, the pistachio tree bears clusters of reddish wrinkled fruits, similar in appearance to olives. Inside the stone of the fruit nestles the nut, or kernel, which is usually green.

> Pistachios are one of the only two types of nut mentioned in the Bible.

The kernel is further protected by a thin, ivory colored shell, which splits open at one end as it ripens—in Iran, pistachios are known as the "smiling nut." Pistachios were highly valued as a food by traders traveling along the Silk Road between China and the West. They are thought to have been introduced to Italy from Syria in the 1st century BCE.

Dyed red

Pistachios were taken to California in the mid 19th century where they became a common sight in vending machines, their shells often dyed red to hide imperfections and distinguish them from other nuts. Large-scale cultivation, however, only started in California in the 1970s. Today, the US is one of the chief producers, along with Iran and Turkey.

Pistachios are often used in Middle Eastern pastries or in savory dishes such as pilaffs. They are also a popular snack all over the world as well as being an important ingredient in ice cream. In India, pistachio *barfi* (a sweetmeat) and kulfi (Indian ice cream) are favorites among the sweet-toothed.

Pistachier en fruit

△ **Split shell**
The pistachio tree bears its fruit in clusters around its stems of dark green leaves. The shells naturally split when the "fruit"—the pistachio nut—is ripe.

Sunflower seeds

the staple that became a snack

A natural and nutritious food source traditionally enjoyed by the indigenous people of North America, sunflower seeds rank high as one of the world's healthiest foods.

Precisely when sunflower seeds were first harvested is uncertain. Some sources say that sunflowers were being grown by early American Indian tribes around 3000 BCE. Others believe that the sunflower plant was domesticated much earlier. Whatever the case, it is clear that by 2000 BCE sunflowers were not only being widely raised, but also that these early farmers knew how to get them to produce bigger seeds.

Food on the go

American Indians would parch or dry the seeds and then pound them to create a flourlike meal, and it was common practice to crack the seeds open and eat them as a snack. Sunflower seed

Origins	North America
Major producers	Ukraine, Russia, Argentina
Main food component	50 percent fat
Source of	Calcium
Scientific name	*Helianthus annuus*

> "Ah, Sunflower, weary of time
> Who countest the steps of the sun."

WILLIAM BLAKE, ENGLISH POET, (1757–1827)

balls, made from the meal, also served to provide sustenance for hungry warriors when hunting far from home.

The Spanish brought sunflower seeds to Europe in the early 1500s, but it was Russia that embraced sunflower cultivation in the 18th century. In 1891, American writer Thomas Stanley noted how, in Russia, "everybody, everywhere nibbles sunflower seeds." With their pleasant, slightly sweet taste, sunflower seeds now enjoy worldwide popularity as a snack and are added to bread, crackers, and other baked goods.

△ **Stripy seeds**
Newly harvested sunflower seeds are white with dark stripes along their length. Each flower can produce up to 2,000 seeds.

▷ **Seed collection**
A smallholder in Worcestershire, UK, removes the seeds from sunflower heads in 1946. Modern methods perform this task mechanically.

Pumpkin seeds

tiny packages of powerful nutrients

A readily available food with powerful medicinal qualities, pumpkin seeds were valued as a source of nutrition by the ancient civilizations of Mexico and Central America as long ago as 7000 BCE.

Origins	Mexico, Central America
Major producers	China, India, Russia
Main food component	47 percent carbohydrate
Source of	Iron, magnesium, zinc
Scientific name	*Cucurbita pepo*

△ **Treasure within**
Pumpkin seeds form in the center of the fleshy interior of the pumpkin, often attached to fibrous strands.

Especially popular in Mexico, where they are eaten roasted, fried, or salted, pumpkin seeds have a long history which may well date back to long before Aztec times. Archaeologists excavating tombs in the central region of the country have discovered preserved pumpkin seeds from the eighth millennium BCE. It is also known that pumpkins were being cultivated there 1,000 to 2,000 years later. More evidence of pumpkin seeds has been found at archaeological sites in Central and South America, and southwestern and eastern North America.

Bitter flesh

It is generally thought that pumpkin seeds were the only part of the plant ancient peoples consumed, since the flesh of most wild pumpkins was too bitter to eat. By the time of the rise of the Mayan and Aztec civilizations, however, palatable pumpkins were being widely cultivated. The Aztecs certainly liked the seeds, which they ate either raw or roasted as a quick, satisfying snack. They also used them to produce a sauce called *pipian*, which consisted of seeds, spices, and chili peppers. Pumpkin seeds even played a part in Aztec festivals. During Quecholli, the festival honoring Mixcoatl, one of the four creators of the world, young priestesses tossed handfuls of pumpkin seeds and colored maize kernels to the watching spectators.

Just two tablespoons of pumpkin seeds contain 74 mg of magnesium, a quarter of the daily recommended dietary allowance.

Today, pumpkin seeds have proved to be highly nutritious. They contain significant amounts of magnesium, iron, and zinc, and high levels of healthy fatty acids. They are processed as flour and added to baked goods, as well as being eaten roasted as a snack.

▽ **Without hulls**
Seeds from pumpkins grown for seed have soft, translucent hulls that do not need to be removed before eating or processing.

Origins
Africa

Major producers
Brazil, Vietnam, Colombia

Non-food use (caffeine)
Medicinal (stimulant)

Scientific name
Coffea arabica, Coffea canephora

Coffee the drink with a kick

No one knows for certain how or when coffee was first discovered, though legends abound. Of the two main species—"arabica" and "robusta"—the former tastes smoother and has a richer flavor than the latter.

Coffee is a drink with a kick thanks to the large amount of caffeine it contains. This is probably why, at certain times in the long history of this beverage, several attempts were made to ban its consumption. In 1675, Charles II of England not only ordered coffee houses to be closed, but also forbade the selling of "Coffee, Chocolet, Sherbett, and Tea." The ban, however, was never implemented. Public pressure forced the king to revoke it just two days before it was due to come into effect.

◁ **Hand-operated mill**
This large coffee mill from the early 1900s, probably from a shop selling coffee rather than a home, was used to grind beans into a powder.

By the time Rhazes was writing, coffee was being cultivated in Yemen, using plants that Arab traders had brought back from Ethiopia. The country's coffee plantations in the mountains at the southwestern tip of the Arabian Peninsula became famous throughout the Muslim world, and the type of coffee was called "arabica." Turkey was introduced to coffee in 1555 by Özdemir Pasha, the Ottoman Governor of Yemen, who brought sackfuls of beans back with him to Istanbul. The Turks originated a new way of preparing coffee: the beans were roasted before being ground to a fine powder, which was then slowly brewed in hot water.

> Coffee is the world's most popular beverage, with around 2 billion cups drunk every day.

Mysterious beginnings

The earliest known record of coffee is in the writings of the 9th-century CE Persian physician Rhazes, who described a beverage named *bunchum*, an infusion of a fruit called *bunn*, the Ethiopian name for a coffee berry. However, according to one legend, the credit for the discovery should go to a young Ethiopian goat herder called Kaldi. He noticed how, after eating the red berries and shiny leaves of a strange bush, his goats were so full of energy that they did not want to sleep at night. Some sources say Kaldi took some leaves and berries to a local monastery and presented them to the abbot, who concocted a drink from the berries, which he found helped to keep him awake through the long hours of evening prayer.

Breaking the monopoly

By the 17th century, coffee had spread to Europe and North America, although it was the hated tea tax of 1773 that spurred Americans to become a nation of coffee drinkers. As demand grew, Arabian coffee traders were determined to preserve their monopoly. To ensure that beans could not be germinated to create rival sources of the crop, they parched or boiled them before exporting them.

The Dutch, French, and Portuguese, however, soon found a way around this apparent impasse by illicitly obtaining coffee plants from different sources and transporting them to their respective colonies in Southeast Asia, the Caribbean, and Brazil. Today, in Vietnam, most of the coffee produced is the "robusta" variety, originally from Central and West Africa.

△ **Brazilian cargo**
By the 1830s, coffee had become Brazil's most important export. A decade later, the country was the world's largest coffee producer, a position it still holds today.

▷ **Ottoman coffee house**
After its introduction to the Ottoman Empire in the 16th century, coffee quickly became a favorite at the court of Suleiman the Magnificent, where the post of Chief Coffee Maker was established as a sign of the drink's importance.

Gathering the seeds
Women workers in Myanmar, one of the world's top producers of sesame seeds, gather and dry the harvest.

Sesame seeds lucky food

These tiny seeds and the oil pressed from them have been used in many cultures as far back as the first recorded civilizations. Today, they remain widely used in baked goods and for their flavor-rich oil.

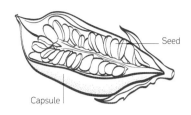

△ **Open sesame**
Sesame capsules "pop" spontaneously when ripe, making the seeds difficult and labor-intensive to harvest.

The sesame plant was disseminated widely thousands of years ago, long before there were any written records, but it appears likely that it was domesicated in Africa and then taken to India. Traces of the seeds dating back more than 4,000 years have been found in the Indus Valley, in present-day Pakistan.

Sesame plants are robust and drought tolerant. They grow 3¼–3½ ft (1–2m) in height with the seed capsules growing all the way down the stems. The capsules contain seeds that vary in colour from creamy white to yellow, brown, and black.

Seeds of youth and beauty

It is thought that the Babylonians of the second millennium BCE made cakes with the seeds and used sesame seed oil for cooking and as a base for perfumes. Babylonian women are said to have used the oil to stay young and beautiful. Sesame seeds

> The Chinese burned black sesame seed oil to make the ink blocks for writing and painting.

were certainly known in Egypt by 1500 BCE. A tomb painting from this period shows a baker putting what may be sesame seeds into bread dough, and seeds that look like sesame were found in the 2nd century BCE tomb of Tutankhamun. The ancient Egyptians are said to have prescribed the oil as medicine and it was used for ceremonial purposes in their temples.

Sesame seeds were also known in ancient Rome, where they were toasted and mixed with crushed figs or made into a kind of paste to put on bread. In the 2nd century CE, the Greek writer Athenaeus wrote of little cakes of honey and sesame in Sicily. The seeds are also mentioned in a collection of recipes published in the 4th or 5th century, attributed to Marcus Gavius

Apicius, a 1st-century Roman gourmet. Many legends are associated with these ancient seeds. Three thousand years ago, the Assyrians believed that their gods drank sesame wine before they created the Earth, and to this day in South Asia, to Hindu Brahmins, the seeds are a sign of good fortune and immortality. There are also associations with generosity, as in the Pakistani description for someone who is ungenerous that says there is no oil in his seed.

Conquest of the East and West

Sesame seeds spread eastward along the Silk Road to China, where sesame oil was is thought to have been used as long ago as the 2nd century BCE, and the seeds were used in various dishes. Today, sesame toast, made with a mixture of sesame and prawns, is a favorite appetizer in Chinese restaurants. Sesame was also grown farther south. In West Africa sesame was known as *benne* or *benni* seed. The same name is used in the southern US, where the seeds are thought to have been taken by slave traders.

Sesame seeds are now commonly added to bakery products in the West. In Turkey they are crushed to make tahini paste. Perhaps their most significant use is for their flavorful oil, used in stir-fries and dressings. In south India, it is widely used in cooking instead of ghee.

Origins
South Asia or Africa
Major producers
China, India, Myanmar
Main food component
50 percent fat
Source of
Calcium, iron, zinc
Scientific name
Sesamum indicum

▷ **Sun lover**
The warmth-loving sesame plant has pointed oval leaves and pale tubular flowers. The seed capsules each contain up to 100 seeds roughly ⅛ in (4mm) in length.

Vegetables

Vegetables

Paleolithic humans foraged for vegetables as part of their subsistence diet, but they were nothing like the plump domestic varieties we know today. Instead, most were small and generally bitter-tasting. Carrots were scrawny, corn was a straggly grass bearing tiny bundles of kernels in a rock-hard casing, and peas had to be roasted and peeled before they were remotely palatable. In addition, wild vegetables were often potent and poisonous, so eating them was a gamble—some beans, for example, were naturally laced with cyanide.

Our ancestors' plant-rich diet

Few plant remains exist from the Paleolithic era. In 2016, however, excavations in one Stone Age site along Lake Hula, west of Israel's River Jordan, revealed more than 9,000 types of edible plants. By examining these fossilized plant remains, archaeologists identified that almost 800,000 years ago people living in the area were eating grapes, blackberries, figs, celery, grass seeds, ribwort, plantain, and even reeds and rushes. Eventually, around 10,000

years ago, people made the long transition from this kind of Paleolithic subsistence living to the more settled lifestyle of the Neolithic age. The change was made possible by agriculture, and agriculture was made possible, in part, by humans learning to fashion more precise, refined tools.

The beginnings of cultivation

It was from this point on that vegetables as we would recognize them began to emerge. Anthropologists believe that agriculture probably began with the cultivation of wild vegetables; instead of simply finding the wild forms where they grew and storing them for later, people gathered the seeds and planted them in a dedicated place close to home. As time went on, however, people learned how to create new and improved versions of their favorite food crops. They probably first observed natural genetic mutations—a larger tomato than usual, for example, or a plant that gave a higher yield than others—and saved the seed from these exceptional individuals to plant the following season.

▽ **The first farmers**
During the Neolithic age, which began around 10,000 BCE, humans created settlements and began cultivating crops using simple ploughs pulled by oxen.

△ **Way of life—and death**
By 1200 BCE, Egyptians depended on cultivation. This tomb fresco from Deir el-Medina shows a craftsman called Sennedjem ploughing in the afterlife.

▷ **Pioneering planter**
Botanist Luther Burbank, who created hundreds of new plant varieties, began his career by planting the seeds of just one potato in his own garden.

Generation by generation, agricultural communities experimented with vegetable varieties, changing them one characteristic at a time. The process of transforming wild plants to the highly cultivated vegetables we are familiar with today took place over hundreds—and sometimes thousands—of years. Corn cobs, for example, are now 1,000 times bigger than they were in the Neolithic age and contain about six times the amount of natural sugars that give them their sweet flavor. One of the main traits of domesticated vegetables was their taste. Wild vegetables would have seemed quite bitter to modern palates, but cultivated versions became far more pleasant to eat—especially green, leafy vegetables such as salad plants.

> Celibate priests in ancient Egypt were forbidden from eating onions which were thought to be an aphrodisiac.

Manipulating taste and resistance

The selective breeding of vegetables gained pace from the 17th century onward, in line with expanding scientific knowledge on botanical life. However, it was not until the following century that the biology of selective breeding was understood more fully, and the first hybridization experiments—crossing one plant with another to produce a completely different plant—began in earnest. One example of this is Franz Achard's cross-breeding program for sugar beets, conducted from 1786 until around 1820. Achard, a German chemist with an interest in biology, carried out a systematic selection process on beets used for animal fodder, in which he looked for specimens with a particularly high sucrose content. By continually crossing these sweeter beets, he eventually created a new beet cultivar with consistently higher sucrose levels than any other type.

One of the great selective-breeding pioneers was US botanist Luther Burbank, who generated 800 or more new plant cultivars between 1870 and 1920, including the Burbank and Russet potatoes. During the 50 years he devoted to this endeavor, he also made improvements to numerous vegetables, from artichokes to celery to squash. Burbank was particularly focused on commercially viable vegetables, and his work laid the foundations for the seed-industry giants of the 20th century, who became intent on creating disease-resistant produce. This was achieved through breeding for resistance, as well as growing tactics such as crop rotation and, most controversially, the use of pesticides. In recent years, awareness of the health risks and environmental damage caused by pesticides has sparked an interest in organically grown vegetables and heritage varieties.

▽ **Organic revival**
Modern consumers are choosing more vegetables grown by organic methods. Organic farming is more labor-intensive, but poses fewer health risks.

◁ **Waterwheel wonder**
Circle irrigation, created in 1940, waters a circular area around a pivot. Innovations like this allowed crops to be grown on a vast scale.

△ **Aerial pest control**
In the 1920s, aerial application of pesticides, or crop-dusting, began in the US. Today it is also used to fertilize crops from cabbages to salad leaves.

Brassicas stalwarts of the vegetable garden

Originating from a wild species of straggly weed, the brassica family of leafy green vegetables includes cabbages, cauliflower, and broccoli. Through cultivation over millennia, it has evolved into one of most widely eaten groups of vegetables.

The brassica family, which today includes more than 3,500 species, evolved from a single species of leafy weed with yellow flowers, known as the wild cabbage or mustard plant. In its most primitive form, wild cabbage (*Brassica oleracea*) is thought to have originated in what is now Turkey. The edible parts of modern brassicas, depending on the type, include the leaves, flowers, stems, and roots. The group encompasses some of the most common vegetables in both Eastern and Western cuisine, including green and white cabbage, broccoli, cauliflower, kale, Brussels sprouts, kohlrabi, pak choy, pe-tsai, and gai lan. Cabbage itself is a terminal leaf bud (the part that grows at the top of the plant), while kale and collard greens are leaf brassicas, meaning they are cultivated exclusively for their leaves. Chinese gai lan is eaten for both its stalks and leaves.

△ **Italian breeding**
A street seller in mid-19th century Rome is laden with baskets of purple broccoli. The variety was developed in Italy and became known in English as "Roman" broccoli.

Valued in the ancient world

In the 4th century BCE, Greek philosopher Theophrastus of Eresus wrote a description of cabbage, and two centuries later Roman author Cato the Elder noted that, "Cabbage surpasses all vegetables. Eat it either cooked or raw. If you eat it raw, dress it with vinegar. It aids digestion remarkably." The Romans, who it is thought were responsible for developing many different varieties of brassica, also used cabbage leaves for bandaging battle wounds. Modern scientific research has shown that this practice was not misjudged—cabbage leaves have antibacterial properties that counter infection.

Diverging traditions

While the ancient Mediterranean civilizations were growing cabbages with soft heads of loosely packed leaves, the hard-headed (or white) cabbage was being developed further north. Celtic marauders from the northern fringes of Europe in the 7th century BCE are credited with breeding the cooler-climate white cabbage after bringing the vegetables back to Ireland from Asia Minor (part of modern-day Turkey) or the Mediterranean from their raiding voyages. Widespread cultivation of cabbages in northern Europe probably dates from that time. From about the 10th century, because of its ability to withstand harsh winters, cabbage became a familiar and vital ingredient of the peasant diet, providing nutritional benefits throughout the winter, when most other vegetables were lacking.

Patterns of consumption

The culinary uses of cabbage varied according to region. In Russia, it was made into *schchi*, a nutritious soup. In Germany, it was preserved as sauerkraut, and peasants are said to have eaten as many as three to four servings a day. Cabbage rolls, comprising pickled or boiled cabbage leaves wrapped around fillings of meat or grains, had been part of Middle Eastern cuisine and a traditional Jewish dish for many centuries before becoming widespread in Europe, especially Scandinavia and Eastern Europe.

Unfashionable food

Notwithstanding its key role as a staple food of the poor of Europe, the upper classes, particularly in England, preferred not to eat cabbage, thinking it

▷ **Amazing variety**
Selective breeding over many centuries has created an astonishing diversity in the brassica family, from leafy greens to succulent stems and flavorful flowers.

Corned beef and cabbage, a New England favorite, was on the menu for President Lincoln's inaugural lunch in 1861.

malodorous and unpalatable. In his book *The Anatomy of Melancholy* (1621), English clergyman Robert Burton wrote that eating cabbage "caused trouble-some dreams and sends up black vapours to the brain." Possibly as a way of countering its poor reputation, English chef Robert May included a recipe for cabbage boiled in milk (to remove any bitterness) in his 1660 cookbook *The Accomplisht Cook*. Whatever

◁ **Found in a cabbage patch**
This early 20th-century French illustration depicts the widespread myth that babies were born under a cabbage leaf.

their perceived disadvantages, brassicas remained an important part of the Central and Northern European diet.

Multiplicity of forms

By the 13th century, Brussels sprouts—in essence, tiny cabbages harvested from a central stem—were being cultivated in what is now Belgium. However, the first written reference didn't appear until the 16th century in the writings of the Dutch physician and botanist Rembertus Dodonaeus. The miniature cabbage buds were only later given the name Brussels sprouts after the Belgian city.

Kohlrabi (from the German *Kohl* for cabbage and *Rabi* for turnip), first described in 1554, was selectively bred in northern Europe to increase the size of its thick bulbous stem. Other forms of brassica were cultivated

---

SAVOY CABBAGE

Origins
Northern Europe

Major producers
China, India, Russia

Main food component
6 percent carbohydrate

Source of
Vitamin C

Scientific name
Brassica oleracea

to emphasize different edible parts. Both broccoli and cauliflower had been grown since Roman times, the result of breeding programs to develop the flower as the edible portion. The sprouting forms of broccoli may have been introduced to France in the 16th century by the Italian-born Catherine de' Medici. Her influence helped to popularize broccoli and other brassicas among the French middle and upper classes after she became queen of France in 1549.

From Europe to Asia

Cauliflower, like its relative broccoli, emerged from the Mediterranean and spread to other parts of Europe during the 16th century. The English referred to cauliflower as "Cyprus Kale," indicating that the first seed stock may have come from the island of Cyprus.

> "I want death to find me planting my cabbages."

MICHEL DE MONTAIGNE, FRENCH ESSAYIST, 1571

These early cauliflowers were the direct antecedents of the group known today as Italian cauliflowers, which includes Romanesco and several colored varieties. In the 17th and 18th centuries, cauliflower breeding in Germany, the Netherlands, and England produced many local varieties. The new types were better suited to cooler climates, but they were still highly sensitive to frost, limiting their growing period. A further diversification took place in the 19th century when the British brought cauliflower seeds to India. Suited to growing in the tropics, Indian (or Asian) cauliflowers provided a year-round supply for domestic consumption—cauliflower is a key ingredient of the popular Indian dish *aloo gobi*—and for global markets.

◁ **Gigantic cabbage**
Cabbages can grow to an enormous size. The weight of the world's heaviest cabbage, grown in 2012, was nearly 138lb (63kg). This young girl was photographed with a huge cabbage in 1931.

◁ **A heavy load**
By the 19th century cabbages were being grown on European farms in "industrial" quantities, both for consumption as a fresh vegetable and for pickling. In Eastern Europe, the popularity of fermented cabbage—sauerkraut—added to the demand.

Brassicas in China and beyond

Although some brassicas developed from wild forms in East Asia in a similar way to western cabbages, recent evidence suggests that Portuguese traders also brought some kinds of cabbages and kale to China in the 17th century. The Portuguese Tronchuda cabbage was cultivated there to produce gai lan. In turn, Chinese travelers took gai lan to Japan, Laos, Vietnam, Malaya, and other parts of Asia. Today, Westerners know this Chinese staple as Chinese kale or Chinese broccoli.

Domesticated brassicas first arrived in the New World with the French explorer Jacques Cartier, who planted cabbages in Canada in 1541. By the 18th century, cabbage was being grown by American Indians as well as by colonials in North America. Brussels sprouts, brought by French settlers, had also been grown there since the 18th century. Within a hundred years, Bernard McMahon, an Irish-American horticulturist, listed more than 20 different varieties of cabbage being grown in the United States in his *Catalogue* (1804), as well as two kinds of cauliflower, green and purple varieties of broccoli, several types of kale including green curly and brown curly, and common Brussels sprouts.

Taken to America's heart

Irish immigrants helped to popularize cabbage in the United States with their traditional dish of corned beef and cabbage, which became a New England favorite. German settlers also took cabbage seeds with them and continued to make sauerkraut. Another European cabbage dish taken to heart by Americans in the 20th century was coleslaw, originally brought by Dutch settlers. Now a standard side dish in fast food outlets around the world, coleslaw, based on white cabbage, was also integrated into Japanese cuisine as a result of the influence of American forces stationed there after World War II.

From the 18th century onward, broccoli was also popular with Americans, especially those with an interest in horticulture. In John Randolph's *Treatise on Gardening*, written around 1765, the author advised boiling broccoli and cauliflower in a clean cloth and serving them simply with butter. President Thomas Jefferson, who was also a keen gardener, had Randolph's book in his library, and was inspired to plant ornamental rows of purple, white, and green broccoli on his terrace.

Brassicas today

Today, vegetables of the brassica family are grown in approximately 150 countries throughout the world. China is the largest producer, while other countries that produce brassicas on a significant scale include India, Russia, and Korea. Four times as much cabbage is grown as broccoli and cauliflower combined.

▽ **Seeds of size**
This 1888 advertisement for "Dutch" cabbage from an American seed merchant indicates the importance given to the potential size of the cabbage. This variety stores particularly well.

◁ **Winter stalwart**
A hardy winter vegetable, Brussels sprouts taste much better if harvested after being frosted—although some people don't like the taste of them at all.

Lettuce
soporific salad green

Despite demanding irrigation requirements making it expensive to cultivate, lettuce is enormously popular, and has become one of the top-selling vegetables in the world.

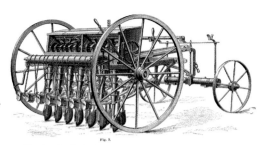

△ **Mechanical planter**
Invented by English agriculturalist Jethro Tull in 1701, the mechanical seed drill made planting seeds far more efficient and enabled a plentiful supply of lettuce to markets.

The ancient Greek physician Hippocrates considered cos lettuce—which is named for the island of Kos, where he was born—to be a narcotic and used it to treat sleep disorders. Modern science has confirmed this soporific effect is due to terpene-based alcohols found in the plant's milky white sap, which are also responsible for lettuce's bitter taste. When cut, lettuce oozes this sap, hence its botanical name *Lactuca sativa*, from the Latin "lactis" (milk) and "sativa" (common).

The ancient Sumerians of southern Mesopotamia (modern-day southern Iraq) were the first to cultivate lettuce, in irrigated beds, around 4000 BCE. These early plants grew to about 3ft (1m) in height. Around 2000 BCE, the ancient Egyptians grew a lettuce that was a distant relative of the modern cos, or romaine, lettuce. They used the bitter-tasting leaves mostly as a love potion and pressed the seeds into culinary oil. Hippocrates later mentioned this lettuce in his diet and nutrition treatise *On Regimen in Acute Diseases* in 400 BCE. The Romans adopted lettuce from the Greeks, and Pliny the Elder mentions nine types in his *Naturalis Historia* of 77–79 CE.

Valued in Europe and beyond
By the 16th century, lettuce was being cultivated across Europe. In 1597, English botanist and herbalist John Gerard noted that eight types were grown in England, where it was served dressed with vinegar, oil, and a little salt to stimulate the appetite and calm delicate stomachs. The French, however, cooked lettuce, probably to remove any bitterness and kill bacteria. Cultivation boomed, and by 1866 a survey

▷ **Street trader**
In the centuries before supermarkets, lettuce was sold at markets or by street traders, who carried their produce in large wicker baskets fashioned like backpacks.

found 65 different types being grown. These included oak leaf lettuce (cut young for salads), the waxy-leaved early Dutch butterhead, and the sweet-tasting black-seeded simpson, which is still a popular garden variety.

Lettuce began to flourish in China from around the 7th century. The Chinese also developed their own variety: stem or asparagus lettuce. They considered raw lettuce unsafe to eat, so they stir-fried it, steamed it, or simmered it in soups. Today, China is the largest producer of lettuce in the world.

A cold traveler
In the 1940s, the creation of the hardy iceberg variety, which could withstand refrigerated transport, triggered a boom in lettuce consumption worldwide. Iceberg lettuce quickly became the second most popular vegetable in North America (after potatoes). Often eaten as a wedge, drizzled with blue cheese dressing, or as a vessel to hold hot, piquant meats in Asian cuisine, iceberg accounted for more than 90 percent of global lettuce consumption in the latter half of the 20th century.

△ **Thirsty vegetable**
Lettuce has a shallow root system and therefore needs a strict irrigation routine, like this crop in Imperial Valley, California, where most of America's salad leaves are grown during the winter.

COS LETTUCE

Origins
Egypt

Major producers
China, Spain, US

Main food component
3 percent carbohydrate

Source of
Potassium, vitamin A, vitamin K, folate

Scientific name
Lactuca sativa

A taste of the country
Fresh salad leaves were
mainstays of city markets.
Paris's legendary Les Halles,
for example, provided lettuces
to urban dwellers who would
never have seen one otherwise.

Garden of plenty
A gardener carries a basket of spinach on her head in a scene from a 16th-century Italian volume.

Spinach iron-packed vegetable

One of the rare green vegetables that lends itself to raw and cooked dishes with equal ease, spinach has provided inspiration to home cooks and chefs for centuries and has become a grocery staple.

◁ **In flower**
This hand-colored copperplate engraving of flowering spinach is from Wilhelm's *Encyclopedia of Natural History*, published in Germany in 1811.

Known in 7th century CE China as the "Persian vegetable," spinach is thought to have originated in the region that is now Iran (formerly Persia). It was not known outside that area until traders introduced it to India. It is recorded that in 647 CE the Nepalese king presented spinach to the Tang Emperor in China. Of all the leafy greens, spinach has proven the most versatile, and the most productive. Today it is found the world over in a wide array of dishes.

Unusually, spinach was unknown in ancient Greece and Rome, and it was only when the Arab invaders brought the bright green leaves to Spain in the 11th century that Europeans had their first taste of it. Despite the fact that spinach generally does not fare well in hot conditions, it seems to have thrived thanks to ingenious irrigation systems devised by the Arabs. In his 12th-century agricultural encyclopedia, agronomist Ibn al-'Awwam referred to it as the "chieftain of leafy greens."

French and Italian favorite

From Spain, spinach was taken to southwestern France. Here it became entrenched in the local cuisine, and was an essential plant in the Provençal garden. It quickly became the region's favorite vegetable. Spreading to Italy, spinach became an integral part of cooking in Florence, Venice, and Rome, where spinach and ricotta cheese were used to stuff pasta.

By the late Middle Ages, cultivation of spinach had spread throughout Europe. In England and other cool climates, it became an indispensable food source because it could be harvested in early spring when other vegetables were scarce and it yielded three crops a year. In France, when Florence-born Catherine de' Medici was crowned queen in 1547 she brought her

Origins
Central and Western Asia

Main producers
China, US, Japan

Main food components
4 percent carbohydrate

Source of
Iron, vitamin B9 (folate)

Scientific name
Spinacia oleracea

> ## "To make a tarte of spinage … take Spynage and perboyle it."
>
> **A PROPER NEWE BOOKE OF COKERYE (1545)**

passion for spinach to the court, apparently eating it at every meal. Dishes served on a bed of spinach were, and still are, referred to as "Florentine" in her honor. Spinach reached North America by the 18th century and flourished there thanks to the recently developed heat-tolerant varieties.

The Popeye connection

What the early growers of the vegetable had not known is that spinach is packed with iron. The high iron and protein content of spinach is one of its exceptional features, a fact first identified in the late 19th century and later much publicized thanks to the Popeye comics of the 1930s, prompting a notable increase in spinach consumption in North America. In the 21st century, spinach remains a hugely popular vegetable in many countries throughout the world as both a salad leaf and as an ingredient in cooked dishes.

▽ **A full basket**
Chinese spinach, with its flat serrated leaf, is harvested by hand in Lijiatuo, China, which is the world's top producer of all spinach varieties.

Origins	Afghanistan
Major producers	China, Russia, US
Main food component	10 percent carbohydrate
Source of	Vitamin A, vitamin C
Scientific name	*Daucus carota*

Carrots a root of many colors

A true chameleon of the food world, the carrot has been transformed over thousands of years from white to purple to orange and from an unpalatable weed to one of the world's favorite vegetables.

The familiar orange carrot owes its vibrant color to a genetic accident. Although the original wild carrot was white, domestication in western and Central Asia around 3000 BCE led to a purple variety that became the standard for many centuries, until a mutant yellow variety triggered a 17th-century breeding program that changed both the color and flavor.

From medicine to food

Early cultivation can be traced to present-day Afghanistan. From there, the plant seeds were carried along trade routes to the Middle East and beyond. At this stage the primitive cultivated carrot root was virtually inedible, but the leaves and seeds were used for medicinal purposes. The ancient Romans used

▷ **All chopped up**
During the 19th century, all kinds of machines were invented to peel and chop vegetables. This machine was designed to slice carrots.

carrot seeds as an antidote to unspecified poisons. But they employed them, too, as an aphrodisiac. The Romans also began to refine the root into something more palatable, developing garden varieties for eating. Roman literature of the 1st century BCE made a clear distinction between the wild carrot and the cultivated carrot, and many Roman recipes included raw carrots as a main ingredient.

Traveling East and West

After the 5th century, carrot development moved to the Arab world where, over the next few hundred years, the carrot family was expanded to include reds as well as yellows and purples and the taste was further refined. Traders carried the carrot east along the Silk Road to India, China, and Japan, and west to Europe. When the new, sweeter Arab carrots made their way to Europe, they became an important part of the diet, with the 8th-century Holy Roman Emperor Charlemagne including carrots in his list of vegetables recommended to be cultivated in his empire. By the 13th century, carrots were widely grown in Western and Central Europe and the preferred yellow variety became the basis for a major transformation. In the 17th century, Dutch growers had established a breeding program to produce a sweeter, more uniform vegetable. The result was an orange carrot that resembles the modern varieties. French horticulturists took breeding further in the 19th century, producing the Nantes and Chantenay varieties still available today. Carrots are one of the ten most important vegetable crops in the world.

▽ **Healthy crop**
In the Middle Ages, carrots were valued primarily for their medicinal properties. This 11th-century illustration is from *Tacuinum Sanitatis*, a health book of the period.

"The day is coming when a single carrot, freshly observed, will set off a revolution."

PAUL CEZANNE, 19TH-CENTURY FRENCH ARTIST

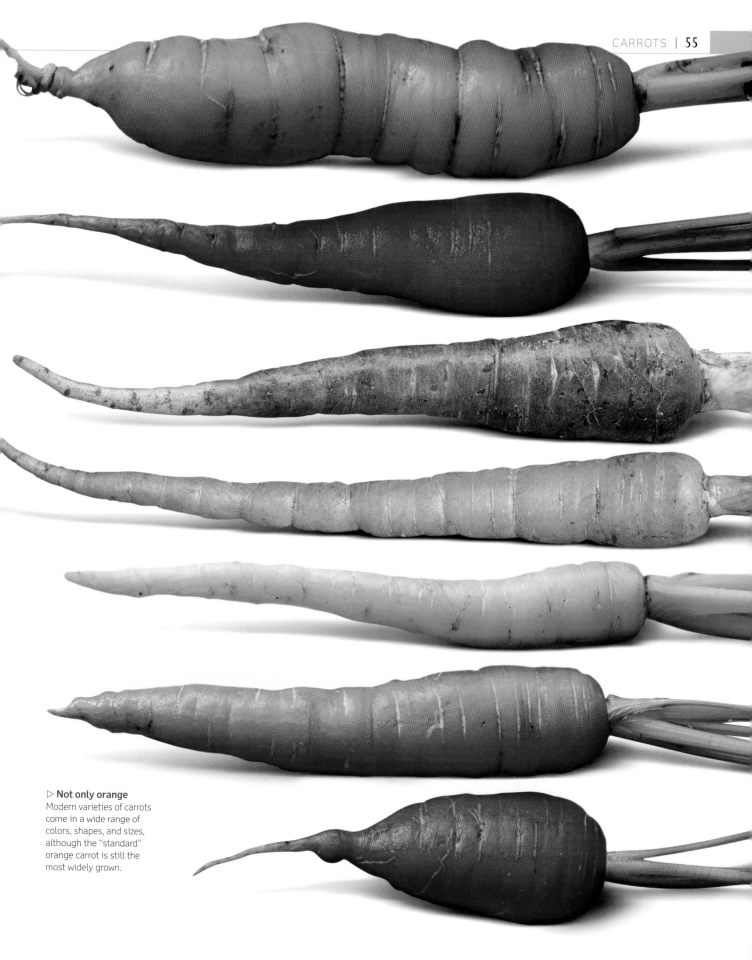

▷ **Not only orange**
Modern varieties of carrots
come in a wide range of
colors, shapes, and sizes,
although the "standard"
orange carrot is still the
most widely grown.

Seaweed manna from the ocean

Harvested and eaten by coastal cultures around the world from the Arctic to the southern Pacific, seaweeds are not only some of the world's oldest vegetables, they are thought to be among the world's oldest living plants.

A truly global food, seaweeds are the most diversely located of all vegetables. They are found washed up on shores as far north as Greenland and as far south as New Zealand. Seaweeds were among the first plants to emerge on Earth. Fossils found in China of simple seaweeds have been dated at between 580 million and 635 million years old. Of the 10,000 or so species of seaweed that occur worldwide, which are divided into three groups—brown, red, and green—only around 150 are used as food.

Seaweed was probably first eaten in China from around 2700 BCE. The Chinese writer Sze Teu sang its praises around 600 BCE, and more substantial references to seaweed appear from the 6th century CE, particularly as a medicine. The father of Chinese medicine, Sun Simiao, recommended seaweed as a cure for the thyroid complaint goiter.

Japanese varieties

Seaweed has formed part of the Japanese diet for millennia. Wakame, a present-day staple of Japanese cuisine, has been eaten in Japan for thousands of years, with traces of it found in pottery dating from around 3000 BCE. Another Japanese seaweed, nori—best known today as the thin wrapping for sushi rolls—was eaten raw in Japan as early as the 7th century CE.

△ **Sweet seaweed**
Sugar kelp grows around the coasts of Britain and Ireland. The name comes from the sweet-tasting powder that coats the fronds when dried.

▽ **Kelp collection**
Fishermen collect dried kelp from bamboo poles on the coastal mudflats of Xiapu in China's Fujian province, where harvesting takes place from March to May.

Nori was originally consumed in paste form, but in the mid-18th century new paper-making techniques led to the production of the crisp, wafer-thin nori sheets commonly used today. Kombu, which is native to the Japanese coastline, is used to make a flavorful stock.

Ancient seaweed traditions of the north

Northern Europe, from Scandinavia to Brittany, France, has a long history of eating seaweed. In Ireland and Scotland, seaweed was collected from at least the 1st century CE. St. Columba, a native of Donegal,

▽ **Famine relief**
Seaweed provided a vital—and free—source of nutrients after the failure of the potato crop in Ireland from 1845 to 1852.

Seaweed extracts are used in the making of ice cream, toothpaste, beer, and baby food.

Ireland, referred to the practice in a poem of 563 CE. A red seaweed known as dilisk, or dulse, was often mixed into butter and then spread on bread, while carrageenan, another type of red seaweed, was used as a thickener and jelly.

In Wales, purple laverweed has been eaten for over a thousand years, traditionally mixed with oats to make laver bread (*bara lawr*), and from the 18th century it became an essential element of the diet of the poor. Icelandic sagas from the 10th century detail regulations about sea vegetable rights. In both Iceland and Norway, dulse was traditionally eaten with potatoes or turnips, or added to porridge.

In the modern world, many of the local traditions surrounding seaweed consumption survive. But seaweed is also finding a new popularity in fashionable restaurants, providing both flavor and nutrients.

WAKAME

Origins
Japan, Korea, China

Major producers
Japan, Korea

Main food component
9 percent carbohydrate

Source of
Iodine, sodium, calcium, omega-3 fatty acid

Non-food use
Cosmetics

Scientific name
Undaria pinnatifida

Food markets

For as long as humans have traded together, food markets have flourished. The earliest were probably established in ancient Persia and spread from there throughout the Middle East and eventually into Europe. In England, the Domesday Book recorded the existence of 50 markets at which food was sold, although many historians think this is a very conservative estimate. By the 13th century, that number had risen to 356, and a hundred years later it had reached 1,746.

Elsewhere in Europe, the well-to-do of ancient Rome frequented the *Marcellum*, a luxury food market located in the Forum, where prized specialities such as red mullet were on sale. Medieval Venice's food market was especially well known, due both to its size and the variety of foodstuffs that could be found there. Matteo Bandello, a 16th-century Italian writer, praised it for its *abbondanza grandissima d'ogni sorte di cose da mangiare*—"the great abundance of everything possible to eat."

In modern Germany, Christmas markets are renowned for peddling sizzling bratwurst (a sausage made of pork combined with spices and herbs), mulled wine, gingerbread, and toasted almonds, but the origins of these markets stretch back at least as early as the 15th century. Founded in 1434, Dresden's Striezelmarkt is said to be the country's oldest, although Munich, Bautzen, and Frankfurt also lay claim to the title.

In the Far East, Thailand is famed for its floating markets, where produce is bought and sold from hundreds of small boats, floating stalls, and piers. Probably the most celebrated is in Damnoen Saduak, near Bangkok, where local farmers paddle wooden canoes rammed with fruit, flowers, and produce along the city's ancient canals. Nearby Amphawa's floating market, more popular with locals, specializes in seafood, selling everything from shellfish to squid.

◁ **Holding steady**
Produce and flower sellers grab onto each other's canoes to maintain their positions at a floating market in Thailand.

Garlic the pungent bulb

Spice, food, and medicine compressed into one bulb, garlic has long been prized by the poor, but frequently shunned by richer people because of its pungent aroma, which was associated with the peasantry.

△ **Bulbs and cloves**
Each bulb of garlic consists of separate cloves, each enclosed in a papery skin.

In its wild form, garlic originally grew across a swath of Central Asia, from western China to northeastern Iran. It was cultivated in ancient Egypt and fed to slaves building the pyramids to boost their health and stamina. Garlic was eaten by Olympic athletes in ancient Greece to enhance performance, and it was also popular with Greek and Roman soldiers. Archaeological evidence of its use includes a recipe written on a Babylonian tablet, dating from around 1750 BCE, for a meat pie flavored with pounded garlic. An even older Asian cooking method (from Korea) suggests roasting garlic slowly for up to a month until it blackens and caramelizes to produce a sweet, mellow taste.

◁ **Garlic seller**
Braided strings of garlic hang around the neck of a young man selling his produce in the northwest Italian city of San Remo in the early 20th century.

Roman poet Horace called it "the essence of vulgarity," claiming it would drive one's lover to the other side of the bed. It was banned from many religious buildings, and the Qu'ran urges worshippers not to attend the mosque if they have recently consumed it. In 1818, the English poet Percy Bysshe Shelley wrote home from Naples, declaring: "What do you think? Young women of rank eat—you will never guess what— garlick!" In Bram Stoker's 1897 novel *Dracula*, Van Helsing uses garlic to repel the vampire, and this "fact" has since entered Western folklore and been used in countless novels and films.

Origins
Central Asia

Major producers
China, India

Main food component
33 percent carbohydrate

Non-food uses
Medicinal (lowers blood pressure and cholesterol)

Scientific name
Allium sativum

Ungodly smell

Garlic's pungency offended some, however, especially the upper classes. Aristocratic Romans abhorred its smell and may only have used it medicinally. The

△ **Powered by garlic**
An ancient Roman mosaic depicts gladiators in action. These fighters are thought to have had a diet rich in garlic, which was believed to boost their aggression in the arena.

"Do not eat garlic … their smell will reveal that you are a peasant."

CERVANTES, *DON QUIXOTE*

Fresh honors for the "stinking rose"

However, in smart 19th-century French households, dishes with a base of sautéed garlic, such as *coq au vin*, were becoming a fixture. Boeuf bourguignon became haute cuisine when Auguste Escoffier published his recipe for it in 1903. Later, the food writer Julia Child brought garlic-infused Mediterranean dishes to a new audience in North America.

In the 1990s, with greater promotion of its health benefits, the so-called "stinking rose" became highly fashionable. Chefs served up whole roasted garlic bulbs, garlic-themed restaurants sprang up, and recipes for cooking the long stems (scapes) appeared. In a few decades, consumption of garlic worldwide tripled, banishing forever its tainted image as peasant food.

▷ **Braiding bulbs**
After harvesting, garlic is traditionally braided ready for drying and storage. Strings of garlic are often displayed and sold in shops and markets throughout southern Europe.

Onions a vegetable to make you cry

Distinctive for their pungent flavor and capacity to produce tears, onions—edible bulbs of the Allium group—have been cultivated for at least 5,000 years, becoming an essential component of soups, stews, and curries worldwide.

△ **Large and small**
Onions vary in size, color, and flavor from the large and mild-tasting varieties to those that are small and strong-tasting. The skin color can be brown or purple.

Among the ingredients listed in the world's oldest cookbooks—Babylonian cuneiform tablets from around 1750 BCE—onions were probably first grown in Central Asia. In ancient Egypt, they were an everyday food and were also used medicinally and ritually. A papyrus dated to 1500 BCE prescribes them for scurvy—and as a source of vitamin C, they were probably effective. Onions were widely used in funeral rites and set in and around mummified bodies to help the deceased in the journey beyond. Their spherical and concentric form was said to represent eternal life. This idea possibly persisted—the name "onion" is thought to stem from the Latin word *unus*, meaning "one," referring to the unity of onion layers.

From everyday food to fashionable fare

The 1st-century Roman author Pliny the Elder wrote of Egyptians swearing oaths by onions and garlic as if they were deities. He also described different varieties of onions and their medicinal and culinary uses in Pompeii. Many of the recipes in *Apicius*, the 4th–5th century Roman cookbook, use onions, both as a base and main ingredient; they include a forerunner of onion soup. The Romans introduced cultivated onions throughout the northern parts of their empire in the early centuries CE. By the Middle Ages, onions were a dietary staple of the peasant class throughout Europe. In later centuries, conquerors and settlers took them to the Americas, where wild species already grew. The city name Chicago is said to derive from the French pronunciation of an American Indian word *shikaakwa*, meaning "smelly onion," and thought to refer to plants of the onion family growing nearby.

> " … lest your kissing … be spoil'd, your onions must be fully boil'd."
>
> JONATHAN SWIFT, *VERSES MADE FOR FRUIT WOMEN* (c.1730)

Onions were always easy to transport; they kept well and could be dried and preserved. Pickled onions became a popular treat in Britain in the 1700s. In France, one particular dish elevated the onion to elegant fare. In his *Dictionary of Cuisine* (1873), the novelist Alexandre Dumas recounts how the Duke of Lorraine and former king of Poland, Stanislas Leszczyński, stopped at an inn en route to Versailles where they were served onion soup. Stanislas was so taken with the soup that he asked for the recipe and the dish was later named in his honour, "Soupe à l'oignon à la Stanislas."

▷ **Onions without tears**
An American serviceman at Camp Kearny, California, photographed in 1918, tries to avoid the tear-producing effects of onion fumes by wearing a gas mask as he peels onions.

Modern essential

Onions are now grown worldwide and are used in a wide variety of regional cuisines. They have become an essential base for a vast range of dishes, often those that involve slow cooking in a sauce, and are indispensable in many soups and sauces. In the Indian subcontinent, where onions have been a staple food for millennia, they are a key ingredient of curries.

◁ **On the quay**
Onions were traded by many countries. In this early 20th-century photograph, large baskets of onions wait to be loaded onto a ship at Galata Quay (now Karaköy), Istanbul, Turkey.

Origins
Central Asia
Major producers
China, India, US
Main food component
9 percent carbohydrate
Source of
Vitamin C
Scientific name
Allium cepa

Potatoes legacy of the Incas

Unknown beyond South America until the 16th century, the humble potato has since been on a bumpy journey from exotic curiosity to peasant lifeline to universal vegetable consumed by more than 1 billion people worldwide.

Origins	South America
Major producers	China, India, Russia
Main food component	17 percent carbohydrate
Source of	Potassium, vitamin C
Scientific name	*Solanum tuberosum*

A starchy tuber, the potato is the swollen underground stem of a dark green, slightly hairy-leaved plant with blue, pink, or white flowers. As a member of the nightshade family, it is related to tomatoes, peppers, eggplants, and tobacco, as well as to poisonous plants, such as mandrake and deadly nightshade. Potatoes themselves contain a poisonous compound called solanine, which is present in small, harmless amounts throughout the plant. However, the poison becomes concentrated in green potatoes—ones that have been exposed to light during storage—and in the sprouts that form when, for example, potatoes are chitted (prepared for planting).

Cool crop

Potatoes were first cultivated in the cool Andean highlands of Peru and Bolivia, possibly between around 8000 and 5000 BCE, although the earliest wild potato remains, found in southern Chile, have been dated to about 11,000 BCE. The tubers aided the colonization of mountain areas because they could grow at altitudes where maize crops, the staple food of most early South American peoples, failed. Different types of potato

◁ **Potato mother**
This pottery vessel from Peru (200–500 CE) features a female head on a potato-shaped body.

Peace offering
▷ This early 20th century Swedish publication depicts a fictional scene of a native South American offering potatoes to a Spanish conquistador.

were cultivated at different altitudes, and they soon began to vary greatly in size, shape, and color.

The Incas, whose Andean empire emerged in the 13th century CE, relied heavily on the potato and cultivated thousands of new varieties. Arriving in South America between 1510 and 1530, Spanish conquistadors reportedly witnessed Inca potato-planting ceremonies and soon realized the food value of the unfamiliar vegetable. The exact date of the arrival of potatoes in Europe is unknown. They were planted in the Canary Islands around 1570 and carried from there to Spain and then further around Europe, usually as an exotic gift or botanic curiosity.

Bad reputation
By the early 17th century, the potato was known, if not widely cultivated, in much of Europe, and it had even reached the North American colony of Virginia, where it was introduced by the English privateer Nathaniel Butler. Most farmers and cooks, however, did not embrace the potato immediately, dismissing it as fit only for animal feed and food for the destitute. The potato's reputation was not improved by its association with evil, possibly due to the similarity of its flowers and berries to those of deadly nightshade and mandrake, which were linked in folklore to witchcraft and the devil. Even as late as 1869, the English writer and social thinker John Ruskin damned the potato as "the scarcely innocent underground stem of one of a tribe set aside for evil."

▷ Knobby tubers
This 19th-century engraving shows the delicate leaves and flowers and the knobbly tubers of the potato plant.

△ All shapes and sizes
Potatoes have been cultivated to produce an extraordinary variety of shapes, sizes, and colors, with a range of flavors and cooking characteristics.

◁ Easy peeling

This machine from the 1900s was designed to wash, peel, and remove eyes and sprouts from potatoes. Such labor-saving devices were invaluable for the mass preparation of potatoes.

It took a former French army pharmacist, Antoine-Augustin Parmentier, to champion potatoes as a desirable and healthy food after being fed them while a prisoner of the Prussians during the Seven Years' War of 1756–1763. His subsequent research found that, contrary to popular opinion, potatoes were indeed nutritious, and he campaigned to convert the French to the food. He is even said to have persuaded King Louis XVI and his queen, Marie Antoinette, to sport potato flower buttonholes and set a new fashion. Such was his success that Parmentier's name lives on in potato dishes such as *pommes Parmentier* (diced potatoes fried in butter), and there is both an Avenue Parmentier and a metro station named after him in Paris. By the time the German naturalist and explorer Alexander von Humboldt made a five-year expedition to South America from 1799 to 1804, potatoes were seen as a positive contribution to European life, and he is quoted as saying: "The continent has given us one great blessing and one great curse: the blessing is the potato and the curse is tobacco!"

Food for the masses

New potato varieties had been developed that could flourish in the more temperate European climates. These made an invaluable addition to a peasant diet hit by a series of famines in the late 18th century. By the early 19th century, potatoes were being grown on a large scale, and, as people began to move from country to town during the Industrial Revolution, they became a cheap, easy-to-grow, and nutritious "convenience food." However, the potatoes grown in Europe and North America at this time contained a fatal flaw—inbreeding—and this led to a vulnerability to disease. The first hint of catastrophe came in 1844–1845, when the funguslike microorganism *Phytophthora infestans*, which causes a disease known as "late blight," devastated Europe's potato crop. In Ireland, where "the crop of all crops" made up 80 percent of the calorie intake for the poor, this was especially ruinous. Between 1845 and 1848 a million people died of starvation or disease, with a further million driven away from Ireland by the famine, most of them emigrating to North America.

However, it was in that continent where another pest of the potato emerged: the Colorado potato beetle (*Leptinotarsa decemlineata*). In its native Mexico, the beetle fed on buffalo bur (a relative of the potato

△ The potato state

The potato's adoption as the symbol of Idaho testifies to its importance to the economy of the state, where the first crops were planted in the mid 19th century. This decal dates from 1960.

plant) and caused little damage, but as the beetle spread to the US, it quickly adapted to the new food that it found planted in vast quantities. The beetle first began destroying potato crops in Nebraska around 1860. It rapidly spread eastward and by 1874 had reached the Atlantic Coast. From there, the Colorado potato beetle soon spread to Western Europe, where it also became a major threat to potato crops.

Worldwide versatility

While the popularity of the potato was spreading in Europe and North America, it was also becoming known further east. Early in the 17th century,

China grows around 100 million tons of potatoes a year—more than any other country—but exports less than 1 percent of them.

European sailors had taken the tubers on voyages to India, China, and Japan (they were a useful source of vitamin C). Colonial expansion and emigration over the next 200 years carried the potato to North Africa, Australia, and even back to South America.

The 20th century saw the potato emerge as a truly global food, aided by inventions such as the mechanical peeler, and the mass production of fast food, including the now ubiquitous "French fries." Today, potatoes are the basis of some of the most popular dishes and snacks all over the world, ranging from British fish and chips to *patatas bravas* (Spain), colcannon (Ireland), gnocchi (Italy), rösti (Switzerland), *hasselback* (Sweden), and *aloo gobi* (a popular potato and cauliflower curry commonly served in India and Pakistan).

Food for the future

Scientists are currently working on developing drought-resistant and blight-resistant tubers. In 1995, NASA astronauts successfully grew five small potatoes from seed tubers on the Space Shuttle *Columbia*, and the International Potato Center in Peru is investigating whether potatoes can grow under the atmospheric conditions of Mars.

◁ **Potato pest**
The colorful Colorado potato beetle wrought havoc on the potato harvests of the American Midwest in the mid 19th century.

▽ **Heavy work**
This 1878 painting by Jules Bastien-Lepage depicts the hard manual labor involved in harvesting potatoes before the advent of mechanization.

Wartime food

All the combatant powers in World War II faced food shortages, which was why, learning the lessons of the Great War, food rationing was introduced as soon as or shortly after hostilities broke out. In Britain, even before rationing officially started, the Ministry of Agriculture launched its "Dig for Victory" campaign. The aim was to encourage people to turn their gardens into vegetable plots, while, in towns and cities, parks and other green spaces were ploughed into allotments. Even the moat at the Tower of London was drained and planted with vegetables.

The campaign was a massive success. By 1943, it was estimated that home vegetable gardens were producing more than a million tons of produce. Many people also kept chickens for eggs and ducks and rabbits for meat. Potatoes were a staple crop, white flour gave way to whole grain National Flour, and people were encouraged to use powdered milk.

In the US, Victory Gardens, which had been a feature of World War I, made a reappearance. With the introduction of rationing in early 1942, Americans had an even greater urge to grow their own fruit and vegetables. In that year, roughly 15 million of them started Victory Gardens. By 1944, an estimated 20 million such gardens were producing 9–10 million tons of food a year. Americans ploughed up backyards, parks, and even baseball pitches. The lead came from the top; Eleanor Roosevelt had a Victory Garden planted on the lawn of the White House.

Rationing was also imposed in Germany. As meat was diverted to the armed forces, various ersatz, or substitute, foods were developed, such as "meat" made from vegetable flour, barley, and mushrooms. Rations were usually smaller in occupied countries— for example, the meat ration of industrial workers in France was one-third of that in Germany.

◁ **From playground to vegetable garden**
Americans embraced vegetable growing during World War II. These children are at work in a Victory Garden in a Manhattan park in 1943.

Cassava drought-resistant staple

Feeding some 800 million people worldwide, cassava is one of the world's most cultivated and consumed plants. It has the potential to become a popular food in all parts of the globe as well as remaining a staple of the poorest regions.

Cassava, otherwise known as manioc, tapioca, and yucca, is cultivated in 105 countries and is especially important as a staple in South America, Africa, and Asia. Both the spinachlike leaves and roots of cassava can be eaten, but the starchy roots are the part most commonly consumed. Each plant may provide up to 18lb (8 kilograms) of root. One of cassava's biggest advantages as a crop is its resistance to drought and its adaptability to poor soil and ability to thrive in a

wide range of environmental conditions. There are two main varieties of cassava—sweet and bitter. Sweet varieties can be peeled and eaten without much preparation, but bitter varieties require lengthy processing in order to neutralize significant levels of highly toxic hydrocyanic acid (cyanide) in the roots. The roots must be carefully peeled, grated, soaked, fermented, and sun dried or heated before becoming safe for consumption.

Origins
South America

Major producers
Nigeria, Thailand, Brazil

Main food component
38 percent carbohydrate

Source of
Vitamin C

Non-food use
Laundry starch

Scientific name
Manihot esculenta

A long history

Cassava has its origins in South America, where it has been cultivated for nearly 5,000 years. When Europeans arrived in the Amazon Basin in the 16th century, they discovered that the local name of one of the native tribes, the Aruak (or Arawak), translated as "people who eat the tubers" and that they had been growing cassava for centuries. Archaeological evidence of cassava cultivation dating back to 1785 BCE has been discovered close to Peru's Casma Valley, and ancient manioc griddles have been excavated in the Caribbean Islands of St. Kitts, St. Vincent, Antigua, and Martinique. In an early literary mention of cassava, Peter Martyr d'Anghiera, a 16th-century chronicler of the discoveries of the explorer Christopher Columbus, refers to "venomous roots" used to prepare breads.

> Since the 1980s, the area of cassava cultivation worldwide has doubled.

Cassava was subsequently introduced to West Africa by Europeans in the 16th century and in the succeeding centuries became a major food crop there and also in Asia. In Brazil, it became a staple of both coastal settlers and their slaves. The crop may also have had a role in ending slavery in that country, enabling runaway slaves to survive in remote and inhospitable areas where cassava grew in the wild.

Prepared for nutrition

With its high carbohydrate content, cassava is a highly digestible and cheap source of energy. It makes up 50 to 80 percent of all calories consumed in some African countries. Processing may increase cassava's nutritional value as research has shown that the action of fungi or microorganisms when it is fermented and ground may increase its protein content.

One common use for cassava in food is as tapioca—flakes made of casava flour. The root can be boiled or steamed and then deep-fried, or the cooked root can be made into purées, dumplings, soups, stews, and gravies. Prepared cassava is also ground into flour for breads, cakes, and biscuits.

In Brazil, detoxified cassava is ground and cooked to a dry, often crunchy grain known as *farinha*, which is used as a condiment, toasted in butter, or eaten alone mixed with water to make a gruel. In Central Africa, detoxified sliced "batons" of fermented cassava dough cooked in banana leaves are popular.

In West Africa, cassava flakes are traditionally boiled with water to form a porridge that is eaten as a snack, called *gari, garri, garry,* or *gali. Gari* may be served with sugar or honey, chunks of coconut, groundnuts, or cashew nuts, or it may be eaten with soups and stews. In other parts of Africa detoxified cassava is boiled and served hot. In West and Central Africa, cassava is called *fufu,* and *fufu* flour is widely available around the world in shops that sell African foods. Some indigenous peoples in South America use cassava to make alcoholic drinks.

△ **Tight squeeze**
This engraving, made in 1820, shows two Africans using a special press to squeeze excess liquid out of grated cassava root.

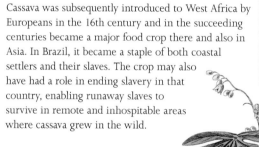

◁ **Plant and root**
Cassava is a tall, woody shrub with dark green hand-shaped leaves. The roots are up to 1ft (30cm) long.

Mushrooms
food of danger and delight

A familiar food that grows everywhere, mushrooms have nevertheless retained an air of mystery and magic since humans first sought out nourishment.

◁ **Specialized tool**
To prepare mushrooms for the table, tools such as this combined knife and brush have been developed.

For millennia, mushrooms have been feared for their toxicity. Some mushrooms contain the deadly toxin muscarine, which is what killed the Roman emperor Claudius in 54 CE, served up in a plate of fungi by his wife, Agrippina. About 20 percent of species are toxic, but only around one percent are deadly, with another one percent containing hallucinogenic chemicals. Although a high percentage of mushrooms are, in theory, edible, less than 5 percent of species have enough flavor to be classed as good to eat.

Mushrooms are fungi, a group of organisms that are neither plant nor animal. Edible mushrooms grow in the ground or on trees, and the part that is eaten is actually the fruiting body of a microscopic organism.

◁ **Smiling sacrifice**
In documentation of the Aztec culture, 16th-century Spanish cleric Bernardino de Sahagun shows sacrificial victims smile as they consume sacred mushrooms prior to their decapitation.

Mushroom mythology

The relative rarity of palatable wild mushrooms has made them highly prized through the ages. They were delicacies in the western Asian region of Mesopotamia by 1800 BCE, and in ancient Egypt they were associated with immortality and only pharaohs could eat them. They were believed to be "sons of gods," sent to Earth in bolts of lightning, which explained their ability, unlike plants, to grow with no roots. For the Mayan civilization of Mexico in the 1st century CE, it was the mind-altering consequences of eating mushrooms that made them a sacred part of their religious ceremonies. Ancient Greeks saw the medicinal potential of fungi, and both they and the Romans admired the taste of ceps (*Boletus edulis*), also known as porcini, which is used in Italian cuisine to flavor risottos and sauces.

In China, mushrooms have been used both as a food and medicine for thousands of years, and the Japanese have cultivated shiitake mushrooms (grown on logs) for at least 2,000 years. In most of Europe, however, the folklore and superstition that surrounded the mushroom, or "toadstool," particularly its toxic properties, meant that it was something to be picked only in the wild rather than cultivated as a food. As late as 1699, the English diarist John Evelyn described mushrooms as "malignant and noxious."

The French connection

That perception gradually changed as cultivation of mushrooms began to take hold in France. In 1600 the French agronomist Olivier de Serres described the

WHITE MUSHROOM

Origins
Europe, US

Major producers (all edible mushrooms)
China, Italy, US

Main food components
3 percent carbohydrate,
3 percent protein

Source of
Vitamin B2, vitamin B3

Scientific name
Agaricus bisporus

◁ **All shapes and sizes**
Mushrooms and edible fungi are found in a huge variety of forms. Knowing how to distinguish the edible from the poisonous varieties requires specialist knowledge.

cultivation of mushrooms in beds of earth mixed with manure. And they appeared in one of French cuisine's most influential cookbooks—*Le Cuisinier François* by Pierre La Varenne, published in 1651—albeit mostly in recipes for sauces and condiments.

Mass cultivation of the mushroom as an ingredient in its own right began almost by accident when, around 1650, a melon grower near Paris discovered fungi growing on the fertilizer he used for his crop. This new delicacy began to fill Parisian restaurants, where it became known as the "*champignon de Paris,*" which is still a name used for the simple button mushroom (*Agaricus bisporus*). Almost two hundred

"The truffle… makes women kinder, and men more amiable."

JEAN ANTHELME BRILLAT-SAVARIN (1825)

years later, around 1810, a Parisian gardener, called Chambry, is said to have discovered that he could grow mushrooms all year by exploiting the cool, moist, and dark environment in caves under and around Paris, and by 1880 there were hundreds of underground mushroom farms in the city.

Gardeners around northern Europe now found that the mushroom was an easy and cheap crop to cultivate, requiring only a little space and a plentiful supply of horse manure. From England, the cultivated mushroom was carried to the eastern US in the mid 19th century. At first, the old European poisoning stories surrounding fungi persisted, but the influence

△ **Underground activity**
Workers tend their subterranean crop in a mushroom cave at Montrouge, near Paris, France, in this illustration from *The Illustrated London News*, December 1869.

of French cuisine and mushroom-loving immigrants, such as the Italians and Chinese, grew such that by 1899 the American cook and naturalist Kate Sargeant was able to publish *One Hundred Mushroom Receipts* and say, "Soon public opinion will acknowledge that … the great majority of fungeses … is [sic] not only wholesome but highly nutritious." Today, only China grows more mushrooms than the US, with the state of Pennsylvania accounting for 60 percent of American production.

White gold
Around the world, mushrooms such as the button, chestnut, and portobello varieties are grown on an industrial scale and have become a cheap, readily available, and nutritious food. However, one kind of edible fungus—the truffle—has remained a highly expensive delicacy, which has to be "hunted" or sniffed out by dogs, or sometimes pigs, and dug from its underground habitat, up to 12in (30cm) below the surface, among the roots of trees such as oak, beech, and hazel. Its use as a food first appears in Sumerian inscriptions

△ **Truffle enemy**
Pictured in this 1880 engraving, the truffle beetle feeds on truffles and can cause huge damage to the "crop."

from around the 20th century BCE, and the truffle has been prized ever since by Romans, Greeks, Renaissance princes, and gastronomes. There are several varieties of this fungus: black truffles (*Tuber melanosporum* and *T. aestivum*) and the most expensive of all, the white truffle (*T. magnatum*), found mainly in Piedmont, northern Italy.

Eggplants
a gift from Asia

The shiny purple eggplant, typically thought of as a Mediterranean staple, has its origins much further east—in Asia, where many different types are found.

In medieval Europe, the eggplant, or aubergine, was thought to have aphrodisiac properties or to be poisonous. It belongs to the same family (Solanaceae) as potatoes, peppers, tomatoes, and deadly nightshade. Although used in cooking as a vegetable, eggplants are in fact the fruit of a tall shrub that has violet or occasionally white flowers. The fruit itself can range in shape, size, and color from the plump, dark purple

△ **Bumper harvest**
The 14th-century Italian illuminated manuscript *Il Libro de Casa Cerruti* (Book of the House of Cerruti) contains one of the earliest European depictions of eggplants.

type best known in the West to the red, yellow, and green eggplants found in India, the pink and white striped ones seen in Italy, and the long Chinese types. The name "eggplant" comes from an old variety with white fruit shaped like swan or goose eggs. Eggplants are thought to have first been domesticated from a wild plant in an area between present-day India,

Myanmar (formerly Burma), and China, but recent studies suggest the cultivation of eggplants may also have occurred separately in the area of Southeast Asia now known as Malaysia. They feature in Sanskrit texts dating back around 2,000 years and also in the 5th-century Chinese agricultural manual *Ts'I Min Yao Shu*.

In the 7th century, Arab armies returned from India and Persia bearing eggplants and took them to the Iberian Peninsula, from where in the succeeding centuries they spread to the rest of Europe and Africa and eventually to North America and the Caribbean.

Worldwide appeal
Today, eggplants are especially popular in the cuisine of southern Europe as well as the Middle East and Asia. Layers of sliced eggplant are a feature of the famous

> In West Africa, eggplants are called "garden eggs."

Greek dish moussaka, and in Italy's *melanzane parmigiana*. Stuffed eggplant dishes include the traditional Greek dish *papoutsakia* (which means "little shoes") and Turkey's *imam bayildi* ("the imam fainted"). Pureed eggplant is a key ingredient in *melitzana salata*, the dip found on every Greek taverna menu, while *baba ganoush* is a Middle Eastern dip made from smoked eggplant. Popular Asian eggplant dishes include Indian curries such as *brinjal bhaji* and the Punjab's *baingan ka bhurta*. The Japanese eat *nasu dengaku* (eggplant glazed with miso), and the Chinese often stir-fry the vegetable.

△ **Chef's choice**
The color of eggplants can vary. This white-streaked purple variety has a naturally sweet, delicate flesh, making it a favorite among chefs.

Origins
Southern Asia

Major producers
China, India, Egypt

Main food component
6 percent carbohydrate

Source of
Potassium

Scientific name
Solanum melongena

Sweet peppers mild-mannered chilis

Members of the *Capsicum* genus, these peppers are called "sweet" to distinguish them from chili peppers, their feistier cousins. A genetic quirk means that sweet peppers don't contain the chemical that gives chili peppers their heat.

△ **Distinctive shape**
The bell-shaped fruit of the sweet pepper is the source of its other common name, the bell pepper.

Like eggplants, sweet peppers belong to the Solanaceae family. Along with chili peppers, they belong to a branch of the family called *Capsicum*. Confusingly, pepper, chili, paprika, aji, and capsicum are all used interchangeably for plants in this group. However, sweet, or bell, pepper refers to the milder-tasting cube-shaped variety—the only one that does not produce the "hot" tasting chemical capsaicin.

A story of discovery

Archaeological excavations have revealed that ancient Central American civilizations cultivated an early form of sweet pepper. Although Genoese-born explorer Christopher Columbus found Caribbean islanders using hot capsicums (now called chilis), the first specific mention of the bell-shaped sweet pepper dates to 1699, when an English ship's surgeon and buccaneer, Lionel Wafer, wrote of seeing sweet peppers in Panama.

◁ **Green perfection**
This 1940s label is for peppers grown in Florida. The state remains a major grower of the vegetable.

Global appeal

While the history is unclear, it may be assumed that the sweet pepper was brought to Europe by Spanish, Portuguese, and other European colonists from the 16th century onward. In 1774, Edward Long, a British plantation owner in Jamaica, listed nine varieties of *Capsicum* as being under cultivation in Jamaica. He noted, "the Bell is esteemed most proper for pickling." Today, sweet peppers are found in nearly every cuisine around the world—used raw, roasted, in stews and casseroles, and stuffed. In Asian cuisine, sweet peppers are commonly included in stir-fries.

Origins
Central America
Major producers
China, Mexico, Indonesia
Main food component
5 percent carbohydrate
Source of
Vitamin A, vitamin C
Scientific name
Capsicum annuum

▽ **All strung out**
In many major sweet pepper-producing countries, much of the crop is dried for use when no fresh produce is available.

△ **Exotic curiosity**
In the 16th and 17th centuries, tomatoes
were seen as exotic plants and grown
ornamentally in gardens. This illustration
is by German botanist Basilius Besler.

Tomatoes the Aztec "golden apple"

A New World plant brought to the Old World by the Spanish, the tomato—though viewed with suspicion in Europe at first—changed the way the whole world ate.

The English word "tomato" derives from the Spanish *tomate*, which in turn is thought to have originated from the Nahuatl or Aztec word, *tomatl*. To 16th-century Italians, the tomato was *pomo d'oro* ("golden apple") and to the Provençals of southern France, *pomme d'amour* ("love apple"). However, whatever the vegetable—or, more correctly, fruit—is called, the tomato has become one of the most popular and versatile ingredients in almost every cuisine.

From New World to wide world

The tomato originated as a wild, weedy plant, a member of the same family as the potato and deadly nightshade, in the high Andes of South America, probably in Peru and Ecuador. From there, it moved northward and was domesticated in Mexico by around 700 CE, where it became an important crop for the Aztecs, the native people of the region.

When the Spanish conquistadors arrived in Mexico in the early 16th century they saw tomatoes of all shapes, sizes, and colors, piled high in the market of the Aztec city of Tlatelolco, as witnessed by Bernardino de Sahagún, a missionary priest and ethnographer who counted "… many different varieties … yellow tomatoes, red ones, and those that are very ripe."

Tomatoes arrived in Europe some time in the mid-16th century, brought by returning Spaniards. The fruit is mentioned in a 1544 herbal by Pietro Andrea Mattioli, an Italian physician and botanist, who described a new type of eggplant "flattened like red apples and composed of segments, green at first and of

△ **Huge variety**
There are 7,500 varieties of tomato, from small, sweet cherry types to large beef ones, in a range of shapes and colors.

◁ **On the cards**
Tomato cultivation in the south of France features on one of the famous collectable trade cards issued from 1870 to 1975 by the Liebig company, makers of meat extract.

Origins	South America
Major producers	China, India, US
Main food component	4 percent carbohydrate
Source of	Vitamin C, potassium
Scientific name	*Solanum lycopersicum*

a golden color when ripe." By the 1550s, tomatoes had reached Germany and the Netherlands, while, at the same time, Portuguese explorers took them to India, where they quickly became ubiquitous, appearing in typical Indian dishes, such as sambar, matar paneer, and vindaloo, from the Portuguese *carne de vin d'ahlo*, meaning "meat with wine and garlic." Perhaps

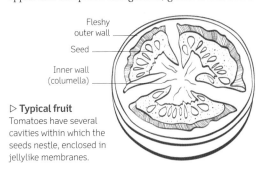

Fleshy outer wall

Seed

Inner wall (columella)

▷ **Typical fruit**
Tomatoes have several cavities within which the seeds nestle, enclosed in jellylike membranes.

> " … they yield very little nourishement to the body, and the same nought and corrupt."

JOHN GERARD, *HERBALL* (1597)

surprisingly, given its cuisine of salads, kebabs, and colorful sauces, the Middle East did not see the cultivation of the tomato until the early 19th century, after it was introduced by John Barker, who was British consul in the Syrian city of Aleppo and a keen horticulturist.

Treated warily

At first the tomato attracted less interest as a food than as a medicinal or ornamental plant, possibly because, like its relative the potato, it was initially thought poisonous. In his *Herball* of 1597, the English botanist John Gerard described the tomato as "of ranke and stinking savour," and this derogatory opinion persisted in northern Europe and in the North American colonies for the next two centuries. Around the Mediterranean, however, especially in Italy and Spain, a more conducive growing climate made the tomato a cuisine staple, where they were recorded as being boiled with pepper, salt, and oil. An early recipe for tomato sauce "*alla spagnuola*" (Spanish style) features in the cookbook *Lo scalco alla moderna* ("The Modern Steward"), written by the Italian cook and steward Antonio Latini and published in 1692.

> During *La Tomatina* held in Buñol, Spain, 100 tons of ripe tomatoes are thrown.

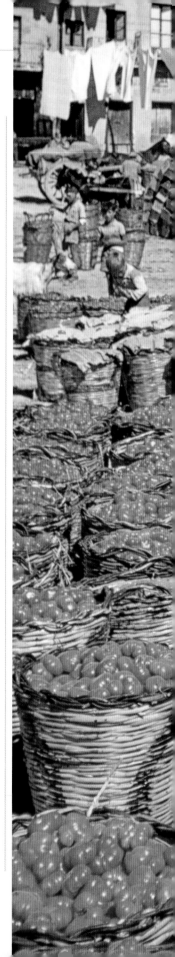

▷ **All in the sauce**
The Heinz company of Pittsburgh, Pennsylvania, launched its now-iconic octagonal glass bottle for tomato ketchup in 1890.

In Naples, the local tradition of adding tomatoes to flatbread developed during the 19th century into the street food we now know as pizza.

Presidential approval

In North America, Thomas Jefferson, the founding father and third President of the United States, recorded planting tomatoes in his famed Monticello vegetable garden in Virginia from 1809 until 1824. It was two American innovations in the processing of the tomato that were key to its journey toward worldwide popularity. The first tomato ketchup (or catsup) recipe dates from 1801, a time when Americans still did not eat fresh tomatoes. Then, in 1876, the Heinz food processing company introduced its tomato ketchup, which today commands 80 percent of the ketchup market share in Europe and 60 percent in the US. In 1897, the tomato was given a further boost, when former fruit merchant Joseph Campbell launched his condensed tomato soup.

In the modern world, tomatoes are eaten fresh as a salad ingredient, cooked in a wide variety of dishes, and processed into canned soups, juices, and myriad convenience foods. Tomatoes remain a staple of the Mediterranean diet, in iconic dishes such as Spain's gazpacho soup, Italy's spaghetti *pomodoro*, France's ratatouille, and Greece's *yemistes domates* (stuffed tomatoes). Even China, which until around 100 years ago did not cultivate tomatoes, has absorbed them into its cuisine, adding tomatoes to soups, salads, and stir-fries. China now produces more than 30 percent of the world's crop.

◁ **Mechanized harvest**
A machine that could harvest central California's huge tomato crop was invented by plant breeder Jack Hanna and engineer Coby Lorenzen in the 1960s, after many failed attempts.

Avocados fruit with Aztec roots

More than 10,000 years ago people in Mexico and Central America gathered and ate the fruit of wild avocado trees, and it didn't take long before they started to cultivate this high-fat, tasty food.

△ **Harvest time**
Choosing when to harvest avocados requires knowledge—if picked too early, the oil content will be low and the fruit won't ripen.

The name avocado is derived from an Aztec word, *ahuacatl*, which means testicle and refers to the shape of the fruit. The earliest evidence of avocado consumption by humans are the seeds, or stones, found in Coxcatlán Cave in the Tehuacán Valley, Mexico, which have been dated to around 8000 BCE. The high oil content of the avocado's green flesh would have made the fruit a valuable addition to the prehistoric diet. Domestication of the avocado soon followed, with the trees being cultivated in Mexico and Central America. By the time the explorer

Christopher Columbus reached South America in 1492, avocados were being consumed as far south as Peru. Today, Mexico is the world's leading avocado producer, and the fruit is also an important crop in the state of California, the Dominican Republic, and Indonesia.

Sweet or savory ingredient
With a subtle flavor, buttery flesh, and high nutrient content, the avocado has enjoyed a recent rise in popularity, and people continue to find innovative

Origins
Mexico, Central America

Major producers
Mexico, Dominican Republic, Peru

Main food component
15 percent fat

Source of
Vitamin E, potassium

Non-food use
Cosmetics

Scientific name
Persea americana

▷ **California dreaming**
San Diego County in California is the avocado capital of the US. Just one Californian avocado tree can produce around 500 avocados a year.

▷ **Fruit of friendship**
The Tlaxcalans in central Mexico greeted the arrival of the Spanish conquistadors in the 16th century with baskets of avocados and offerings of other local foods.

Old names for avocados include alligator pears and shell pears.

ways to enjoy it. It is perhaps most famous as the main ingredient of guacamole, but in Latin America avocados are still widely used to garnish Colombian *ajiaco* (chicken and potato soup) and in Guatemalan *chapin* (hot dog with cabbage and avocado cream).

Cucumbers
emperors' favorite

As a food first enjoyed by ancient civilizations, the history of cucumber cultivation extends back to antiquity, marked by rises and falls in popularity.

The cucumber is the fruit of a creeping vine that is native to southern India, where it has been cultivated for more than 3,000 years. Cucumbers were also grown in ancient Egypt, and in ancient Greece and Rome they were used to treat scorpion bites, bad eyesight, and frighten off mice. The Roman emperor Tiberius allegedly ate cucumbers daily.

The cucumber fell out of fashion in Europe after the Roman Empire fell in 476 CE, but it reappeared in the 8th-century court of the Holy Roman Emperor Charlemagne, who commanded it be grown on his estates. European trappers introduced the cucumber to North America, and the French navigator, Jacques Cartier, wrote of "very great cucumbers" being grown on the site of present-day Montreal, Canada, in 1535.

A taste of summer
Cucumbers were first introduced to England in the 14th century and during the 18th century sliced cucumber sandwiches became popular in British society. Today, cucumbers feature in salads, soups, and dips. They are often combined with yogurt in dishes such as the Persian *mast-o-khiar*, Indian raita, and Greek tzatziki. They are also popular pickled in either brine or vinegar, often with dill.

△ **In a pickle**
Around 1900, Heinz used to sell pickled cucumbers in huge quantities. In the US they were a popular accompaniment to cold cuts and cheeses.

Origins
Southern India

Major producers
China, Turkey, Iran

Main food component
4 percent carbohydrate

Source of
Vitamin K

Non-food use
Cosmetics

Scientific name
Cucumis sativus

◁ **Trailing glory**
This engraved illustration of a cucumber shows the plant's stem, leaves, flowers, fruit, and long tendrils.

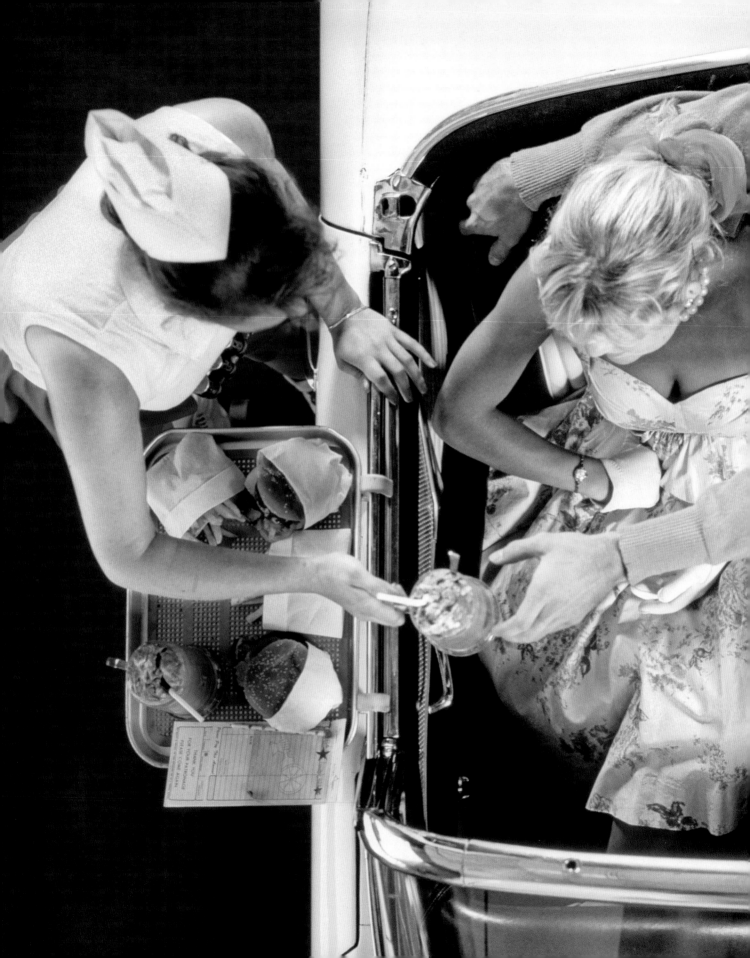

Fast food

Best defined as food that can be bought quickly, cheaply, and eaten on the fly, fast food is a modern universal culinary and cultural phenomenon. Its rise to global predominance began in 1921 in the Midwestern US, when Walt Anderson—who in 1916 had opened his first diner in a converted streetcar in Wichita, Kansas—partnered with Billy Ingram, an insurance and real-estate salesman, to set up the first White Star burger outlet. The two men soon expanded into other towns and cities, creating what was to become America's first fast-food chain. Records show that, by 1941, White Star had sold more than 50 million burgers at no more than 10 cents apiece.

Where Anderson and Ingram led, others followed. McDonald's dates from 1940, when brothers Richard and Maurice McDonald opened their first drive-in restaurant in San Bernardino, California. It was the start of what was to become the most instantly recognizable food brand in the world. Originally, McDonald's focused on barbecued food, but when the brothers saw that burgers were outselling everything else on their menu, they transformed their business. In 1948, they devised a streamlined menu offering a hamburger, a cheeseburger, French fries, and a choice of three soft drinks, as well as milkshakes, milk, and coffee. They had found a winning formula. McDonald's expanded rapidly, especially once it began granting franchises to other would-be restaurateurs.

Fast food swiftly spread its wings. Colonel Harlan Sanders began franchising his fried chicken restaurants in 1952. Burger King opened in 1953 in Jacksonville, Florida. Taco Bell popularized an Americanized version of Mexican food, while Pizza Hut and Domino's did the same for pizza. And Pete's Super Submarines eventually became Subway, which is now the world's leading sandwich chain.

◁ **Eating on the move**
Drive-in restaurants first opened in the US during the 1920s, hot on the heels of rising automobile use. By the 1960s, they were a feature of many fast-food chains.

Peas and edible pods

sweet green seeds of age-old versatility

Technically fruit rather than vegetables, peas and green beans were first cultivated by humans in the Middle East and the Americas, respectively. Today, they are grown and eaten on every continent except Antarctica.

Peas were among the first foods to be cultivated during the rise of agriculture in the Middle East. There is archaeological evidence of the common pea (*Pisum sativum*) being domesticated in Syria around 5000 BCE. Since wild peas have hard shells, or pods, that ripen over a long period, the edible seeds ripen at different times, making them difficult to harvest. New varieties with softer shells were selectively bred, which allowed water to permeate during the wet season and so encouraged the seeds to ripen at the same time.

The green bean story

In the Americas, another type of pod fruit had appeared—the green bean (*Phaseolus vulgaris*), which had both pod and seeds that were edible. Green beans were domesticated separately in the Andes of Peru (around 6000 BCE) and in Mexico (around 5000 BCE), then carried to other parts of the Americas with migrating Indian tribes. Christopher Columbus

GARDEN PEAS
Origins Middle East
Major producers China, India, Canada
Main food component 14 percent carbohydrate
Source of Vitamin A, Vitamin B6, Vitamin C, Vitamin K
Scientific name *Pisum sativum*

◁ **Mangetout**
The flat pods of mangetout contain tiny peas, and are eaten whole—raw or cooked—once the thick strings along the side are peeled away.

▽ **Popping from pods**
Garden peas grow in pods, which are not edible, unlike other podded types such as sugar snaps.

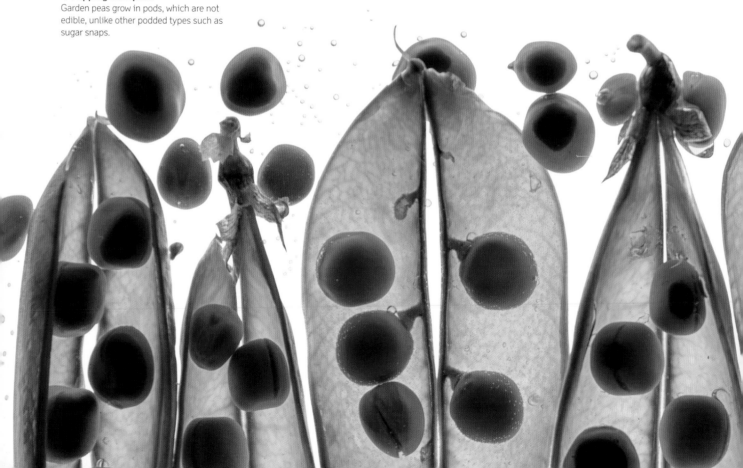

brought the green bean to Europe after his second voyage to the New World in 1493. It spread through the Mediterranean and by the 17th century was grown in Italy, Greece, and Turkey. When Europeans colonized North America, the new settlers included it in the first Thanksgiving meal in 1621.

From dried to fresh

For thousands of years, peas and beans were harvested and dried, rather than eaten in their immature green state. As a stored food, they provided crucial protein and vitamins during seasons when other crops were scarce. Pea soup, made using dried peas, was a popular dish in ancient Greece. The playwright Aristophanes refers to it in his play *The Birds* (414 BCE), making fun of the divine hero Heracles for breaking wind when he eats too much of it. In medieval Europe pea soups, such as pease pudding (England) and *ärtsoppa* (Sweden), became staples of peasant diets. The first references to eating fresh, or "green," peas appear around the 12th century, though

◁ **Making a frame**
A woman arranges branches in her vegetable garden to form what could be a support for growing peas.

they remained an expensive delicacy, as they had to be picked young. The 16th-century Italian-born French queen Catherine de' Medici is said to have introduced tiny green peas to France. These dainty *piselli novella*, or new peas, enchanted the French aristocracy, who renamed them *petit pois*. Another delicacy, developed by the Dutch in the early 17th century, was the edible pod pea in the form of the snow pea, or mangetout (meaning "eat all"). It was not until the development of new canning processes in the 19th century and the invention of food-freezing techniques by the American Clarence Birdseye in the 1920s that "fresh" peas became widely available and affordable.

△ **Selling seeds**
An early 20th-century seed catalog illustration draws on the idiom of a couple being like "two peas in a pod" in this humorous portrayal.

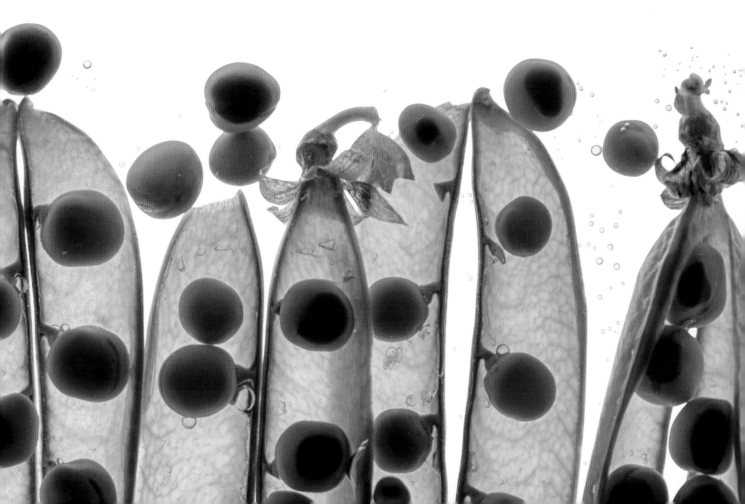

Sign of the times
Harvesting pumpkins is a familiar autumn scene in the United States, whether for use in pies, breads, and casseroles at Thanksgiving, or to carve into jack-o'-lanterns for Halloween.

Squashes

all-American symbols of survival

Mainstays of that great American celebration, Thanksgiving, squashes—including the pumpkin—have traveled far from their ancient Mexican roots to find popularity in savory and sweet dishes the world over.

△ **Food and culture**
A distinctive earthenware dish (c.600 BCE–600 CE) in shape of a squash shows the importance of the food to the Colima culture from Mexico.

Technically fruit rather than vegetables, squashes can weigh anything from 1oz (30g) to 44lb (20kg). They are members of the vast Cucurbitaceae family of vines, which also includes cucumbers, melons, and watermelons. More specifically, they are part of the relatively small *Cucurbita* genus, which nevertheless has produced dozens of cultivated varieties, especially of the *C. pepo* species, which includes the marrow; zucchini (courgette); and pattypan, sunburst, crookneck (summer squash), and spaghetti squashes. Other *Cucurbita* species include *C. maxima*, which originated in Bolivia and counts the largest pumpkins among its varieties, and *C. moschata*, which thrives in warm, humid parts of the world, such as the Central American areas of its origins, and includes butternut, winter crookneck, and cushaw squashes.

Squashes come in an array of shapes, sizes, colors, and patterns. They are grown all over the world, with the top international producers—India, Russia, Iran, US, and China—generating around 30 percent of the more than 25 million metric tons that are cultivated each year.

A rambling family tree

Squashes originated in southern Mexico and spread south into South America and north into the southern US. They are among the earliest foods to be domesticated. Remnants of *C. pepo* stalks and seeds were discovered in the late 1960s in a small prehistoric cave in the Valley of Oaxaca, in the western highlands of Mexico, which was occupied for almost 10,000 years. *C. pepo* thrives best in a cool, dry environment and it is thought farmers used the cave during the late rainy or early dry seasons. Archaeologists have found evidence of *C. moschata*

in Peru dating back to 4,000–3,000 BCE, and in Mexican sites from 1440 BCE. They have also discovered summer squash seeds dating back 5,000 years in the state of Missouri.

Three sisters

Along with corn and beans, squashes formed a trio of staple foods, known as "the three sisters," which were grown and eaten by American Indians before the arrival of Europeans. The three were grown together: the corn stalks providing a pole for the beans to climb up; the beans adding nitrogen to the soil for the other plants; and the sprawling squash leaves shading the soil, keeping it cool and moist and hindering the growth of weeds. At least five different squash species had probably been domesticated before the Europeans

"We have pumpkins at morning and pumpkins at noon ..."

VERSE OF THE PILGRIM FATHERS, c.1630

arrived on American shores in the late 15th century, and they were among the earliest plants to be cultivated in the New World. American Indians at the time ate squashes similarly to the way we do today—fresh, chopped into chunks and added to soups and stews, baked and eaten whole, sliced and dried in strips to be stored for winter, and also ground into flour.

◁ **Sprawling habit**
The pumpkin plant sends out sprawling stems from which the flowers and, ultimately, the fruit develop.

PUMPKIN

Origins
Mexico

Major producers
China, India, Russia

Main food component
8 percent carbohydrate

Source of
Iron, vitamin A

Scientific name
Cucurbita pepo

▽ **Into Africa**
By the 19th century, squashes were common in parts of Africa, for example, in Zululand, South Africa.

The flesh and sometimes the seeds were boiled and eaten, while the flowers are also thought to have been added to stews or dried for later use. The seeds were used as medicine, while the dried shells served as bowls and containers to store grain, beans, and seeds. The Patuxet tribe in Massachusetts taught the Pilgrim Fathers who colonized Plymouth in 1620 how to plant pumpkins, although the settlers found them too stringy at first. Early settlers also picked up on the word *asquutasquash*, meaning "eaten raw, or uncooked," used by the Narragansett, another New England tribe, and coined the name "squash" for this new food.

Spreading from the Americas

When squashes first reached Europe from the Americas in the 16th century, they were not seen as fit for human consumption and were used instead to feed pigs. The climate was too cool and the growing season too short for squash to be cultivated widely in northern Europe, but it gained popularity as a food crop in the warmer

> The heaviest pumpkin in history was grown in 2016 by a Belgian, Mathias Willemijns, and weighed 2,625lb (1,190.49kg).

▽ **All in the family**
This display of vegetables from the *Cucurbita* genus includes many different kinds of squash as well as marrows, which belong to the same family.

◁ **Bulky harvest**
Villagers gather their crop
of enormous squashes in this
19th-century farming scene.

climes of France, Italy, and Central Europe. Festoons of fruits, flowers, and vegetables, including the New World species painted by Giovanni Martini da Udine, adorn the walls of the Renaissance Villa Farnesina in Rome. Squashes, along with other American plants such as maize, chilies, and green beans, appear in the *De Historia Stirpium* herbal, published by the German physician and botanist Leonhart Fuchs in 1542, but as medicinal plants rather than food.

Portuguese sailors introduced the squash to the Far East in the 1540s. They named it *Cambodia abóbora*, but the Japanese then shortened this to *kabocha*. From there, squashes spread to China, with the Chinese creating their own hybrids, such as the spaghetti squash, which was developed in the 1890s and made the reverse journey to the Americas in the 1930s as seeds exported from Japan.

Squash cuisine

Pumpkins and other squashes have become a popular food across the world. The flesh can be roasted; steamed; boiled; sliced, battered, and fried, for example in *kabocha tempura* (Japan); stuffed; stir-fried; made into croquettes; added to stews and soups, such as *soupe au potiron* (France); made into savory pies such as *kolokotes* (Cyprus); and used to stuff ravioli (Italy). In India, the flesh is cooked with butter, sugar, and spices to make the popular *kaddu ka halwa*, and in the Guangxi region of China pumpkin leaves are eaten as a cooked vegetable or in soups.

Star of Halloween and Thanksgiving

Pumpkins have a special place in American culture. The name "pumpkin," usually used to described the large, orange fruit familiar from Halloween lanterns, comes from the Old English *pumpion*, which in turn derives from the old French *pompon*. The Thanksgiving favorite pumpkin pie, popular with early American settlers, consisted of a ripe pumpkin filled with fruit, sugar, spices, and milk—added through a hole cut in the top—and baked on the coals of an open fire. Records of the first Thanksgiving feast in 1621 reveal that the celebration meal, which lasted several days, included squash along with deer, waterfowl, turkeys, shellfish, eels, corn, and beans. The 17th-century French chef François Pierre La Varenne devised the earliest known recipe for a crusted pumpkin pie in his *Le Pâtissier françois* of 1653, but it was not until 1796 that a dessert similar to modern pumpkin pie was created in the US.

▽ **Tradition of the fall**
No American Halloween
celebration is complete
without a jack-o'-lantern.

Fruits

Fruits

Long before fruit was cultivated, prehistoric peoples picked wild berries and other fruits and ate them just as they found them. No one really knows when the cultivation of fruit began; archaeological remains are scant, and the main evidence at present comes in the form of fruit stones and pips. However, botanical archaeology in Borneo and other Asian countries has revealed indications of fruit cultivation dating from over 6,000 years ago. Although there is a great deal of debate about the nature of these early fruits and how sour they might have been, prehistoric people with no sugar in their diets would have tasted foods quite differently from the way modern humans do. Fruits growing in warm, sunny climates would have produced more natural sugars.

The first grafting begins

By the Bronze Age, which began in various parts of the world between approximately 3000 BCE and 1900 BCE, fruits such as grapes, figs, dates, and olives, which could be propagated from cuttings, were being grown around the Aegean Sea. Fruit trees grown from seed often vary greatly from their parent trees in terms of the taste of the fruit they produce, so grafting and pruning developed as a result of the human search for consistent flavor. Both practices seem to have been used in China and the Near East very early on, but were not common across Europe until classical times. Certainly cross-breeding was performed in Greece, according to Pliny the Elder, who wrote of the plum: "No other tree has been so ingeniously crossed." In addition, *Ceratonia siliqua*, the carob tree, was being grafted during the same period in Greece, where its pods were highly prized for the gummy syrup that they produced that was made into sweetmeats.

Persians made a kind of fruit jelly sweetmeat, the ancestor of Turkish delight, and gave added sharpness of flavor to their meat dishes by using apricots, lemons, and oranges—an idea that was copied by Arab tribes. Some fruits were preserved in honey, while others, like the grape, were dried in the sun. Zante currants, a type of raisin from Corinth, were obtained by drying a small grape variety that had been grown for over 2,000 years. They

▽ **Assyrian technology**
Sophisticated canal irrigation systems allowed the ancient city of Ninevah to cultivate vines, figs, and pomegranate trees beginning in the 9th century BCE.

△ **Wine from the Nile**
By around 3000 BCE, grape-growing flourished in Egypt's Nile Delta, which led to wine making. Residue from amphorae show much of it was red.

▷ **Pearls of Uzbekistan**
In Samarkand, melons have been sold for over 2,000 years. As well as quenching people's thirst, they provided energy-boosting fructose.

became increasingly popular as a trading item, and by the 15th century these "raisins of Corinth" were being mentioned in medieval manuscripts, named for the harbor city from which they were shipped.

A garden of orange trees

One of Europe's oldest surviving "city orchards" dates from around 982 CE, and is found in the Great Mosque Cathedral of Córdoba, located in the Andalusia region of southern Spain. Built as a Moorish mosque in the 8th century, the building's garden, the Patio de los Naranjos, or Courtyard of the Orange Trees, was noted for producing cultivated oranges just 200 years later. Monasteries grew various fruits, not only to eat but also for medical purposes, and monks played an important part in the development and cataloging of fruit varieties.

The "perils" of soft fruit

In Western Europe, wild berries were most likely the first fruits to have been domesticated by humans. Wild strawberry plants, for example, were removed from the forests and transplanted into gardens, where they began to be selectively cultivated. In the Middle Ages, however, many types of raw fruit were regarded with suspicion. Too much eaten at once made people ill, so instead of reducing the amount consumed, the fruit itself was deemed bad for digestion. This idea was based on the writings of ancient Greek physician Galen and was still prevalent centuries after his death. He stated that too much fruit could cause fevers; however, cooked fruit eaten in moderation was acceptable. Denying raw fruit to children was thus considered beneficial, until vitamins were discovered in the early 19th century.

> The oldest banana in the UK was discovered in a rubbish pit dating back to the mid 15th century.

Mysterious histories

Many fruits were transported around the world, but a traceable history for many species is often elusive. A mural found in the ruins of Pompeii at the base of Mount Vesuvius depicts a fruit that looks remarkably like a pineapple, yet the pineapple was unknown in Europe until much later. Many other fruiting species simply don't tolerate transplantation to different climates, so remained unknown outside their point of origin. While fruit was preserved by drying or in sweetmeats for hundreds of years, it wasn't until the 19th century that canning provided a longer-lasting form of storage, followed by freezing in the 20th century.

△ **Lasting misdiagnosis**
Greek physician Galen believed fruit was linked to cold, wet "humors" and caused fever and diarrhea. This prevented generations from getting crucial sources of vitamin C.

◁ **Sacred oranges**
The orange trees of Córdoba's Great Mosque-Cathedral were originally imported by Muslim Prince Abd al-Rahman I in the 8th and 9th centuries.

△ **Successful transplant**
Egyptians cultivated watermelons at least 4,000 years ago. No one knows when the fruit was first exported, but it was known in Italy by the 14th century and has been popular ever since.

Apples and pears

fruits with an illustrious history

One of the world's oldest fruits with a history dating back 4,000 years, an apple is delicious to eat and packed with nutrients. Its equally tasty cousin, the pear, has a similarly distinguished history.

The first apples, thought to have originated in the mountains of Kazakhstan in Central Asia some 4,000 years ago, were much smaller and more tart than modern types, but human intervention turned apples into something approaching the fruits we know today. The Roman statesman Cato the Elder described the process of taking cuttings (scions) from a good tree and grafting them onto a suitable rootstock in his 2nd-century BCE book *De Agricultura*.

Increasing variety

Apple cultivation gradually spread throughout Europe, but with the fall of the Roman Empire, knowledge of grafting was lost and was not rediscovered until the late Middle Ages. By the 16th century, the French, followed by the English, had started growing new, improved varieties. Classic examples include Pippins (so-named because they were originally grown from seeds rather than cuttings), Russets, and Reinettes.

British and Dutch settlers carried apple seeds with them across the Atlantic, while the French took them to Canada. Entirely new varieties were developed when

▷ **Cider press**
For centuries, cider presses such as this have been used to extract apple juice for cider-making.

the introduced apples were crossed with native crab apples. Cultivation spread, thanks in part to American John Chapman, a nurseryman who planted apple trees for making cider in large parts of the eastern US in the 1800s—today, he is known as "Johnny Appleseed."

The extended family

A cousin of the apple, the pear, also originated in Central Asia, spreading from there to places as diverse as Greece, Rome, and China. The ancient Greeks, in particular, favored the fruit. In around 300 BCE, the scholar Theophrastus described how to grow, graft, and cross-pollinate them. Three centuries later in Rome, Pliny the Elder described 41 varieties in his encyclopaedic *Naturalis Historia*.

△ **Fruit basket**
Pears resembling modern varieties, as pictured in this 3rd-century floor mosaic, seem to have been known and favored in ancient Rome.

APPLES

Origins
Central Asia

Major producers
China, US, Turkey

Main food component
14 percent carbohydrate

Source of
Potassium, vitamin C

Scientific name
Malus pumila

△ **Arkansas apple harvest**
The Ozark region in the state of Arkansas is famed for its apple orchards. The first apple trees were planted by settlers from further east in the early 19th century.

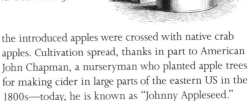

"There are only 10 minutes in the life of a pear when it is ready to eat."

RALPH WALDO EMERSON (1803–1882), POET

During the Middle Ages, pears found popularity in France and Italy. And in the 17th century Louis XIV was passionately fond of the fruit. The English settlers in New England matched this enthusiasm, and in 1629 the Massachusetts Bay Company began to import pear seeds from England. About 7,000 varieties are currently grown worldwide, roughly divided into the European varieties with green or pink skins and the Asian ones with their firmer flesh.

▷ **Apple varieties**
Five apple varieties are pictured in this 19th-century print. Even in those days, this would have been a small sample of what was available. Today, there are 10,000 apple varieties in the world.

1854.

23.

Peaches a symbol of opulence

From the time of its early cultivation in China 8,000 years ago, where it became a symbol of happiness and immortality, the peach, with its soft flesh and luscious juiciness, has had an enduring global popularity as a luxurious dessert fruit.

The peach is older than humankind. In 2015, scientists found fossilized peach kernels dating from the late Pleiocene Epoch in Kunming, southwestern China, proving that a type of peach was growing wild there at least 2.6 million years ago, long before the arrival of modern humans.

A member of the Rosaceae family, the modern peach tree can grow up to 30ft (9m) tall and 15ft (4.5m) wide. Its fruit is a drupe, with a seed inside a stone surrounded by sweet flesh and enclosed in a fuzzy pink-tinged white or yellow skin.

China has three types of peach (northern, north-western, and southern) and 495 varieties, testifying to its long history of cultivation. Peaches are mentioned in Chinese literature as symbols of indulgence and privilege, and were often depicted on Chinese porcelain. Chinese emperors served them at banquets. A domesticated form of peach was taken to Japan as early as 4700–4400 BCE and peaches later appeared in India c.1700 BCE. The peach was carried to the West along the Silk Road via Persia (modern-day Iran), where it had been easily cultivated, bringing about

△ **Sun-dried peaches**
The Ceres Valley in the Western Cape is one of South Africa's major fruit-growing areas. Here, pallets full of peach halves are laid out in the hot sun to dry.

Origins
China

Major producers
China, Italy, Spain

Main food component
10 percent carbohydrate

Source of
Vitamin C

Non-food uses
Flavoring, cosmetics

Scientific name
Prunus persica

the peach's botanical name, *Prunus persica*. It reached Greece around 300 BCE, arriving in Rome about two hundred years later, where people called them Persian apples. Under the Roman Empire peaches were taken to North Africa, Spain, and even into Britain. They were soon established throughout the Mediterranean region.

Adopted in America

In 1513, Spanish settlers began growing peaches in Florida, and they were also found growing in Mexico 50 years after the arrival of Spanish conquistador Hernán Cortés in 1519. In the succeeding centuries, the indigenous people of North America adopted the peach as their own, and many historical accounts of the so-called "Indian peach" exist. American Indians planted peaches as they moved northward into southern Canada and westward.

By the 19th century, US horticulturists hoping to reduce the South's reliance on cotton as a crop tried to encourage the cultivation of diverse soft fruits but only peaches flourished and remained viable there.

Chinese brides carry peach blossom at their wedding as a symbol of a happy marriage.

Today, peaches are grown in all temperate regions of the world. China remains the world's leading peach producer, with Spain, Italy, Greece, and the US trailing far behind.

The peach-fuzz problem

Since the last century, scientists and growers have attempted to resolve what was identified as the "peach-fuzz problem," the fruit's fuzzy skin. Eminent US botanist Luther Burbank stated in 1914 that, "a good many of us would about as willingly bite into a spiny cactus as a fuzzy peach." Two solutions seemed to be breeding fruit with reduced fuzz or using brushing machines to remove

◁ **Peach of immortality**
Peaches were believed to confer immortality in 17th-century China. The decoration on this porcelain vase shows "immortals" standing on clouds preparing to offer the peach of immortality to a favored mortal, usually the emperor.

it. Such machinery was used in the 1930s in the state of Georgia to reduce the fuzz, make the fruit shiny, and thereby increase sales since some people refused to eat fresh peaches as they found the fuzz itchy and irritating.

Fuzz-free delight

An answer to the problem of peach fuzz is provided by the nectarine (*Prunus persica* var. *nucipersica*), a genetic variant of the peach belonging to the same species. The trees are virtually indistinguishable. Nectarines have a smooth yellow skin with a dark-red blush. The flesh can be golden, white, or red and is slightly firmer than that of the peach. Nectarines, like peaches, originated in China, where their domestication began more than 4,000 years ago, and the ancient Romans may have known them. Europeans first encountered them in Persia, hence the botanical name, though they were rare in Europe until the 16th century. Today, nectarines are cultivated in warmer areas across the globe.

Wartime sustenance

While fresh peaches have always been a treat when in season, the invention of the canning process in the 1800s made the fruit available at all times of the year. Canned peaches became popular in Europe and America, particularly when fresh fruit was less abundant during the wars of the 20th century. Much of the crop is eaten as fresh fruit, but significant quantities are preserved by canning and, to a lesser extent, drying.

▷ **Peach peeler**
The invention of a peach peeler enabled the quick and efficient removal of the fuzzy skin so loathed by some people.

△ **Stone fruit**
Both nectarines and peaches have a large stone, or kernel, at their heart. Although inedible, the kernels can be used to make infused syrups or vinegars and oils.

Mangoes the friendship fruit

Native to the foothills of the Himalayas, the mango has been cultivated there for millennia and is grown today in most tropical and a few subtropical countries.

△ **Easy eating**
The flesh of a halved mango is often scored to create neat cubes for ease of eating.

△ **Essential condiment**
One of the best-known ways in which mangoes are eaten in India—and wherever curry is popular—is in the form of chutney, an essential accompaniment to many Indian dishes.

A gift of mangoes is a sign of friendship in India, where it is known from references in ancient Hindu manuscripts that this succulent fruit has been cultivated for more than 4,000 years. The Indian mango is native to northeastern India, Bangladesh, and the country that is now known as Myanmar (formerly Burma). It is an evergreen tree, related to the cashew and pistachio nut, which grows to a height of about 115ft (35m) and can live for several hundred years. The fruit contains a large, flattened seed, or stone, and the ripe flesh is bright yellow-orange, smooth, buttery, and aromatic.

By 400 CE, the mango had been introduced to East Asia, and it later spread to the Middle East and Africa. The name mango comes from the Portuguese name for the fruit, *manga*—an adaptation of the fruit's name in the Tamil language. Portuguese colonists introduced the fruit to tropical Brazil, where it has become an important export crop. Today, India is the world's largest producer of mangoes. They are also widely grown in Pakistan, Thailand, Malaysia, and China.

Consumed in many forms

A high proportion of ripe mangoes are eaten raw in their country of origin. In many regions, the fruit is sold as street food. The pulp is also drunk as juice or incorporated as a flavoring into drinks and ice cream. Green, or unripe, mangoes are cooked in stews, served as a vegetable, or made into chutney. Unripe, dried mango is also widely used as a spice in Indian cooking. Dried mango is a popular snack in many countries.

△ **Monkeys and mangoes**
This detail from an 18th-century Mughal hunting scene depicts langurs in a mango tree. The fruit is a favorite meal of these Indian monkeys.

Origins
South Asia

Major producers
India, China, Thailand

Main food component
15 percent carbohydrate

Good source of
Vitamin A, vitamin C

Scientific name
Mangifera indica

Apricots golden and fragrant

Origins
Central Asia

Major producers
Turkey, Iran, Uzbekistan

Main food component
11 percent carbohydrate

Scientific name
Prunus armeniaca

This stone fruit, native to Central Asia, has found a key role in the cuisine of the Middle East and in the store cupboards of Europe and America.

Highly nutritious and golden in color, the apricot packs a potentially poisonous punch in its stone, which contains minute quantities of cyanide. The apricot, a member of the Rosaceae family, probably originated in Central Asia near the present-day Russian-Chinese border. Unpruned, the tree can grow to 45ft (14m) tall and survive for over a century.

▽ **Flushed with pink**
The apricot is a drupe—that is, a fruit with a single stone. Its golden flesh is enclosed in a skin of a similar color, often with a pink tinge.

Carried by trade and warfare

The apricot was being cultivated as early as 5,000 years ago in the area encompassing modern-day Iran, Turkistan, Afghanistan, and western China. Alexander the Great took apricots to Anatolia (now part of Turkey) from Persia in the 4th century BCE, and even today Turkey remains a leading producer. The fruit was introduced into Italy and then to Greece during the Roman–Persian Wars (54 BCE–628 CE). Over a thousand years later, in the 13th century, it was introduced to Spain, and it was first cultivated in France in the 17th century under Louis XIV at Versailles. Most American apricots originate from seedlings taken to Californian monasteries in the late 17th century by Spanish missionaries. Today, apricots are enjoyed fresh, dried, stewed, or canned, and are also popular in preserves.

△ **Preserved in Australia**
Apricot jam has long enjoyed popularity in many parts of the world. This brand was marketed in Australia in the early 20th century.

"The only thing better ... is an apricot in Damascus."

TURKISH SAYING

Cherries bunches of sweetness

Wherever cherries were found growing, since prehistoric times humans have eaten them. Today, the fruit of this beautifully blossoming tree is a favorite fruit for snacking and cooking in both East and West.

Origins	Western Asia
Major producers	Turkey, US, Iran
Main food component	16 percent carbohydrate
Source of	Vitamin C
Scientific name	*Prunus avium*

The Japanese have been celebrating *hanami*, a ritual of viewing cherry blossoms and having picnics under the trees, since the 8th century CE, but the history of this tree and its edible fruit goes back much further. The cherry is believed to be indigenous to Asia Minor (part of modern-day Turkey) and from here spread throughout the Roman Empire.

Color and flavor

A member of the plum family, *Prunus*, the two main varieties of cherry are sweet (*P. avium*) and sour (*P. cerasus*). The sweet cherry tree can grow to 20ft (6m) in height and 27ft (9m) in width, while the sour cherry variety is slightly smaller. The color of the fruit varies from yellow shaded with red to bright red or purple. Cherry stones (known

◁ **Black, red, and yellow**
Cherry varieties have been cultivated to produce fruit in a range of colors and with different taste characteristics and keeping qualities.

as pits) contain minute quantities of cyanide and can be toxic if eaten in large quantities.

Fruit of battle

The first mention of the cherry is by the ancient Greek historian Herodotus in the 5th century BCE. He called it the "Pontic tree," Pontus being the ancient Greek name for northeastern Anatolia (in present-day Turkey). According to Pliny the Elder, the Roman historian and naturalist, Lucullus, who beat the king of Pontus in battle c.65 BCE, took the cherry to Rome. England's 16th-century King Henry VIII is said to have tasted cherries in the Netherlands and was so impressed he had them introduced into England. Today, cherries are grown in temperate areas all over the world, with Turkey being the world's leading producer.

Celebrated summer treat

Cherries are widely eaten in season in their natural state straight from the tree. They are also used in baked goods, ice cream, and in desserts. Stewed cherries are often combined with brandy to make cherry brandy and can be distilled into kirsch, a colorless liqueur. They are also used in *meggyleves* (Hungarian sour cherry soup).

△ **Walk in the woods**
Visits to orchards of fruit blossom remain a popular pastime in Japan. In this 19th-century Japanese print, crowds visit a plum orchard.

▽ **Ripe and ready**
The color of plums give little clue to their ripeness. They can be equally sweet and juicy whatever their hue.

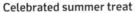

◁ **Symbol of sweetness**
In this 19th-century illustration a young girl carries a cloth filled with cherries. Her expression and the implied sweetness of the fruit create a sentimental image typical of the period.

Plums a fruit of East and West

One of the oldest cultivated fruits—evidence has been found in the remains of settlements of the Neolithic period—plums are still widely consumed today in a wealth of forms: fresh, dried, preserved, and even as an alcoholic drink.

The plum tree has been cultivated for so long that the original wild version has disappeared. Today, there are two main species of plum: *Prunus salicina*, originating in China, and now common throughout Asia; and *P. domestica*, from the region of the Caucasus Mountains and the Caspian Sea, the species most familiar in Europe.

Going West

The European plum was originally transported by traders traveling westward to ancient Greece and Rome. In the Middle Ages, probably as a result of the journeys of the Crusaders, plums were brought further west. Much later, in the 18th century, Spanish missionaries took plums to the American west coast, English colonists to the east coast, and the French to Canada.

Over the centuries hundreds of varieties of plums have been developed. They vary in size and color from small very dark damsons, to sweet green greengages, and large pink-red Victoria plums. The uses of plums are equally varied. As well as being eaten fresh, dried, canned, or cooked, plums are popular in preserves, baked goods, and in stews. In Eastern Europe, plums are made into the alcoholic drink *slivovitz* (plum brandy), while in France Agen prunes (dried plums) are a famous traditional sweet confection. In Asia, the native plum is often pickled or salted.

> "When the old plum tree blooms the entire world blooms."
>
> DŌGEN ZENJI (1200–1253), JAPANESE BUDDHIST PRIEST AND ZEN MASTER

EUROPEAN PLUM

Origins
Asia

Major producers
Serbia, Romania, US

Main food component
11 percent carbohydrate

Source of
Vitamin K

Non-food use
Medicinal (laxative)

Scientific name
Prunus domestica

Canning and preserving food

Finding an effective way of storing food while maintaining its flavor has preoccupied people since prehistoric times. From fermenting and pickling to salting, smoking, and drying, various methods were tried until the early 1800s, when Frenchman and chef Nicolas Appert invented a method of heat-processing food in glass jars. Appert's invention earned a 12,000-Franc prize from Napoleon's government, and also won him an international reputation.

Just how canning was invented remains a mystery. London merchant Peter Durand took out a patent for the first unbreakable tin can in 1811, but food historians say the original idea was not his, but Philippe de Gérard's, who, as a French national, was not allowed to take out a patent himself. What is certain is that the patent was sold to Bryan Donkin, a successful engineer who set up the world's first canned-food factory in 1813, in London. Once England's Queen Charlotte and the Prince Regent tried his canned beef and deemed it worth eating, Donkin was soon supplying cans to the Royal Navy.

Yet canned food was expensive, and the cans themselves were hard to get into. Before the invention of the can opener in the US in 1858, the only way of getting into them was with a hammer and chisel. American ingenuity not only solved this problem, its commercial savvy made canned food cheaper. Large-scale canning of tomatoes began in Pennsylvania in 1846, and soon, canned food of all types became something that even the poor could afford. Today, according to the Can Manufacturers' Institute, households in the US and Europe alone go through 40 billion cans of food a year.

◁ **Preserving more than food**
Canning not only provided a reliable way to store fruit and other edibles, it also created millions of jobs in the 19th and 20th centuries.

Mature palm
A full-grown male date palm can reach a height of 75ft (23m) and produce up to 155–310lb (70–140kg) of dates every season.

Dates sustainers of life in the desert

The classic symbol of an oasis, the date palm has played a vital role in the establishment of ancient human settlements in the deserts of the Middle East, North Africa, and northwest India, providing food and building materials.

△ **Sunshine fruit**
Some varieties of dates are golden yellow in color, but turn brown when dried. Others are red in their fresh form.

Dates have been a sweet source of sustenance for desert-dwellers for at least 7,000 years, and their significance in some cultures is reflected by frequent mentions in religious and other ancient texts. In the case of the Bible, academics have interpreted the Old Testament description of the Holy Land as "flowing with milk and honey" as referring not to honey from bees but from date syrup, which is still used as a sweetener in the Middle East.

Hot crown, wet roots

As a sturdy, shade-giving tree, both the date palm and the fruit it bears enabled ancient societies not just to survive, but to thrive in extremely hot, arid regions. As long as there is sufficient water around the tree's roots, the palm can survive in places with little or no rainfall and is therefore a reliable indicator of the presence of groundwater. Dried dates are easily transportable, so they can sustain people on long journeys across barren landscapes as well as being a commodity for trade.

The plant's precise origins are unknown, as date palms have such a long history of cultivation in the Middle East, northern Africa, and northwest India, and are now extinct in the wild. Date palms are known to have been grown in the ancient city of Babylon in Mesopotamia (modern-day Iraq) along the banks of the Euphrates and Tigris rivers. The Babylonian Code of Hammurabi—which was written c.1754 BCE—has four paragraphs dedicated to the planting of date orchards. They were also already being cultivated in ancient

▷ **Tree-top harvest**
Simple rope tackles were often used to climb date palms to gather the fruit. This 1876 engraving depicts workers in Ceylon (Sri Lanka).

Egypt at that time. Dates were taken to Spain from North Africa by the Moors in the 6th century CE and ten centuries later, Spanish missionaries planted the first date palm in the New World, in Baja California, Mexico. Over the past 300 years, date cultivation has also been taken up in hot, dry regions of South America, Australia, and southern Africa.

Turning syrup into wine

Today, there are more than 1,000 varieties of dates. The most popular are the light-brown Deglet Noor (Arabic for "date of light") and the Medjool ("unknown"—it was cultivated from an unidentified Moroccan variety). In his 10th-century work, *Kitab al-Tabikh* (Book of Cookery), Baghdadi writer Ibn Sayyar al-Warraq gave a recipe for *dadh*, a type of wine made using date syrup. An alcoholic drink made from dates are still produced in India today. However, in the Middle East and North Africa, dates are more frequently served stuffed, in salads or desserts, or used to flavor roast meats. In some Moroccan tagines, entire dates are cooked with lamb.

◁ **Anatomy of a date**
The date is an elongated oval shape. The pale brown flesh encloses a stone about 1in (25mm) by ¼in (7mm).

Stone (seed)

Skin

Edible flesh

Origins
Middle East, North Africa, northern India

Major producers
Egypt, Iran, Saudi Arabia

Main food component
75 percent carbohydrate

Source of
Iron, vitamin B3, vitamin B6

Scientific name
Phoenix dactylifera

In 2005, a male date palm, named Methuselah, was sprouted from a 2,000-year-old seed.

KING. GOLDEN QUEEN. LOUDON.

CUMBERLAND.

W. N. SCARFF

New Carlisle, OHIO,

SPRING 1904

MUNGER

CARDINAL.

Two Plants each of best Collection of Raspberries ever offered.
Post-paid, only 50 cents; 5 Plants of each, $1.00.

Raspberries fruit of kindness

From a plant of woodland clearings to a key crop of modern fruit farms, the raspberry has evolved to become a perennial favorite for jam-making and desserts, as well as being enjoyed fresh and unadorned.

Origins
Middle East
Major producers
Russia, Poland, US
Main food component
12 percent carbohydrate
Source of
Vitamin C
Scientific name
Rubus idaeus

The raspberry has been part of the human diet for tens of thousands of years. Archaeological evidence from present-day Israel indicates that humans during Paleolithic times (some 20,000 years ago) ate raspberries. The numerous species of raspberry all belong to the rose family and are related to blackberries. The fruits, which consist of a cluster of approximately 100 tiny "drupelets," grow on thin, thorny branches, commonly called canes, that can reach over 6ft (1.8m) in height. The red raspberry plant probably originated in western Asia and later became native to southeastern Europe.

> In Germany, raspberry canes were traditionally tied to frisky horses to calm them.

It is thought that the fruit we know today was cultivated by the ancient Greeks. According to the Roman naturalist Pliny the Elder, the Greeks cultivated raspberries on the slopes of Mount Ida. This association may be the origin of the scientific name of the species, *Rubus idaeus*. The Romans continued to grow the fruit, and were probably responsible for spreading the raspberry throughout their European empire as far afield as Britain, where raspberry seeds have been discovered in archaeological excavations of Roman sites. The berries continued to be cultivated during the medieval period and later. It is said that the 13th-century English king, Edward I, encouraged raspberry growing in England. In that period, the leaves as well as the fruit were highly valued, being used to relieve labor pains. Raspberries often appeared in medieval art to symbolize kindness, possibly linked to the blood-red color of the juice, which was associated with ideas of energy and nutrition. The juice was also sometimes used as a fabric dye.

Into the modern world

By the 18th century, raspberry plants had been introduced to North America by European settlers, and many new varieties were developed to suit conditions in the New World. Raspberries are now grown all over the world in areas with mild climates, and varieties have been cultivated that bear fruit in a wide range of colors from red to purple and gold.

The top producers globally are Russia, Poland, and the United States, where the native raspberry has been crossed with related species such as the blackberry and cloudberry to produce the olallieberry, loganberry, and youngberry. Boysenberries, another North American relative of the raspberry, are thought to be a cross between a raspberry, a blackberry, and a loganberry.

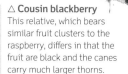

△ **Cousin blackberry**
This relative, which bears similar fruit clusters to the raspberry, differs in that the fruit are black and the canes carry much larger thorns.

▽ **Joint effort**
A family work together to pick raspberries at their farm in Minnesota in the early 20th century.

◁ **Colour spectrum**
This advertisement from an Ohio nursery shows some of the fruit colours available to US raspberry growers in the early 20th century. Several of the varieties advertised here are still grown.

Strawberries

synonymous with summer

Humans have been gathering wild strawberries since the Stone Age. However, the much larger garden strawberry, which is eaten in huge quantities around the world today, was bred in the 18th century.

△ **Favored in France**
The French have a long history of association with the strawberry and developed the first widely cultivated commercial variety.

When praising the strawberry in the 17th century, the English physician William Butler observed: "Doubtless God could have made a better berry, but doubtless God never did." Little did he know that less than 100 years later, humans would indeed create a better berry.

Lifting the spirits

The strawberries so loved by Butler would have been a variety of the wild strawberry, *Fragaria vesca*, which has small, deep red, intensely flavored fruits. A member of the rose family, the wild strawberry was used in ancient Rome as a cure for depression and other ailments. The

French were the first to cultivate the plant in kitchen gardens, a practice that spread among the aristocracy of northern Europe in the 14th century—France's King Charles V is reported to have had 1,200 wild strawberry plants specially grown to feed the royal appetite and that of his court. In the 15th century,

Origins
Central Europe and Chile

Major producers
US, Mexico, Turkey

Main food component
8 percent carbohydrate

Source of
Vitamin C

Scientific name
Fragaria x *ananassa*

▷ **Soft and seedy**
Strawberries are the only fruit that carry their seeds on the outside of the flesh. Each berry has about 200 seeds.

monks included illustrations of strawberries in their illuminated manuscripts. In medieval times, crushed strawberries or other berries were also used as ink, a practice that was rediscovered in the mid-19th century by some soldiers in the American Civil War, for whom berry juice was the only ink available for them to write letters to their loved ones back home.

New world, new strawberries

It was the wild strawberries found in the Americas that led to the eventual creation of the large garden strawberry, *Fragaria x ananassa*, widely grown today. The Mapuche and Huilliche Indians of Chile had cultivated a native variety, the beach strawberry (*F. chiloensis*), for hundreds of years. In the early 18th century, a French expedition brought some of the plants back to Europe, where they grew vigorously but produced no fruit as the plants had only female flowers.

Another strawberry species native to eastern North America, the Virginia strawberry (*F. virginiana*), is the subject of a well-known Cherokee legend involving the First Woman, who forgot her anger at her husband after eating strawberries. This species, introduced to Europe in around 1750, was first cultivated in a

the second largest producer of strawberries after China, the strawberry is a winter crop, fruiting as early as January. Spain is one of the world's largest producers of strawberries and is a top exporter of the fruit. A high proportion of the crop is destined for markets elsewhere in Europe, but in recent years it has also been exported to more distant markets in Asia.

△ **Berry hard work**
Fruit picking and packing has long provided work for seasonal laborers, many of whom were women.

"It's not a good idea to marry a girl who wants strawberries in January."

ALBANIAN PROVERB

botanical garden in Paris, France.

It was discovered that the pollen of the Virginia strawberry would fertilize the hitherto sterile Chilean plants and yield fruit. Plants grown from the seeds of these hybrids gave larger, more intensely flavored fruit and they soon found favor and began to be widely cultivated in Europe.

Conquering the world

Today, strawberries are cultivated in all temperate regions of the world and even some subtropical ones. The European strawberry season was once a short one, starting in May and lasting for only a month, but new varieties have been cultivated, extending the growing season until September. In the state of California,

The expansion of this trade has been made possible by development of new varieties able to remain in good condition during the longer transit times.

Love match

The classic combination of strawberries and cream is said to have been created by Cardinal Thomas Wolsey at the 16th-century English court of King Henry VIII. The British tradition has continued, with tens of thousands of tubs of strawberries and cream being ardently consumed by visitors to the Wimbledon tennis championships held in London every year.

In the US and elsewhere, strawberries are used in baking as toppings for dessert and as the eponymous filling in strawberry shortcake. The soft fruits are also used to make jam, syrup, wine, and as a popular flavoring for ice cream, yogurt, and milkshakes.

△ **Small and wild**
A variety of strawberry plant with very small berries is depicted in this drawing from John Gerard's *Herball* (1597). Larger fruits were only developed 200 years later.

▽ **Currant colors**
Out of hundreds of wild and
cultivated species of currant,
the most widely used as a
food are the white, black, and
red varieties.

Currants intensely flavored vitamin source

Black currants and their red and white currant cousins have a relatively short cultivation history but a long medicinal and culinary tradition in Europe. There the fruit is a favorite in pies, jams, and jellies, and as a vitamin-packed juice.

BLACKCURRANT

Origins
Europe

Major producers
Russia, Poland, Ukraine

Source of
Vitamin C, vitamin K

Scientific name
Ribes nigrum

Many species of currant grow in North America, but most Americans have no idea what they taste like. American Indians ate the berries and used them as a remedy for ailments, including snake bites, and edible cultivated varieties introduced from Europe in the 17th century soon became a popular crop. Currants, though, are a natural host of blister rust, a parasitic fungus that was accidentally introduced to the US in the 19th century. This fungal pest has another host, the white pine, the backbone of America's timber industry, and since the trees had no resistance to the disease it could destroy whole forests. In 1911, the US federal government banned the cultivation of currants and the gooseberry (a related fruit) in all but a small part of the country. Although the ban was lifted in 1966, some states still enforce it. Fresh currants and gooseberries cannot be bought in US supermarkets, and only canned fruit or preserves are on the shelf.

From medicine to food

Currants are unrelated to the small dried grapes also known as currants. The shared name is probably a corruption of "Corinth," a Greek city that was known for drying and exporting its grapes. Most currant production happens in Europe, where the berries were first cultivated around 500 years ago. The English plant collector John Tradescant imported black currants (*Ribes nigrum*) from the Netherlands in 1611, and it was the medicinal properties of the fruit and leaves that were first noted, such as in the botanist John Gerard's *Herball* of 1597. Like their dark cousin, red currants (*R. rubrum*) were also gathered

△ **Cordial company**
France has a long tradition of currant cultivation. The fruit harvested here may have been used for making the alcoholic black currant cordial known as *crème de cassis*.

originally in the wilds of northern Europe for their medicinal properties. Their juicy berries later made them a popular food, and sweeter red currants were cultivated in northern France, Belgium, and the Netherlands from the 17th century.

Vitamin booster

All varieties of currant, including the white currant (a sweeter variety of red currant), are rich in vitamin C. During World War II, black currants were the only

◁ **Currant liqueur**
A French poster advertises cassis, first made from the juice of blackberries in Dijon in 1841.

Two-thirds of black currants produced in Europe are used for juice.

homegrown source of the vitamin in Britain. From 1942, black currant cordial was given free to babies and young children to boost immunity. Even today, 90 percent of the British blackcurrant crop is used for juice. In France, the juice is also used to make *crème de cassis*, a syrupy liqueur, which is often mixed with white wine.

Blueberries an American hero

Originally prized by American Indians as a medicine and preservative, by the 21st century this humble berry of the eastern regions of North America had acquired an international reputation as a fashionable "superfood."

Blueberries are at the heart of many American Indian myths. According to one legend—possibly inspired by the star-shaped calyx at the base of each berry—the Great Spirit sent "star berries" to relieve hunger during times of famine. American Indian tribes used both the berries and leaves (infused as a tea) as medicine. Dried berries were crushed and powdered then rubbed into the fat and flesh of buffalo to make the dried meat known as pemmican. This had excellent keeping qualities so it could be taken on long journeys and could sustain them through the harsh winters.

Part of the American story

Dried blueberries also formed a key ingredient of a cornmeal pudding called sautauthig, which was later adopted by European settlers and may have formed part of early Thanksgiving feasts. During the Civil War of 1861–1865, blueberries were made into a drink to sustain the soldiers of the Union Army.

In from the wild

Blueberries begin to ripen from mid-summer onward, changing color from pale green to a dusty deep blue. They were originally harvested only in the wild, and were not grown commercially until 1911, when they were first cultivated in New Jersey by Elizabeth White, a farmer's daughter, and Frederick Coville, a botanist. The pair aimed to grow the berries on a large scale, and succeeded in bringing

△ **Blooming berries**
Blueberries typically have a dusty bloom on their outer skin and vary in size from ¼– ½in (5–16mm) in diameter.

◁ **Stamp of approval**
In 1980, a design featuring blueberries appeared on a 6-kopek stamp from the former Soviet Union.

ГОЛУБИКА
ПОЧТА СССР 6ᴷ

"I saw blueberries… as big as the end of your thumb."

ROBERT FROST, "BLUEBERRIES", 1915

their first crop of cultivated berries to market in 1916. By the 1940s, blueberries were being grown commercially in 13 states. Blueberries are now cultivated in temperate regions with plenty of rainfall worldwide, including parts of Europe, where they were introduced in 1930. Japan joined the ranks of blueberry-growing nations in 1951.

Today, blueberries are widely consumed as a fresh fruit. They are also processed into juice and used to make jams and preserves, or added to desserts. Numerous claims for the berries as a nutritional "powerhouse" and superfood have been made. These may be exaggerated, but blueberries remain one of the most popular berries in the US and Europe.

You say "blueberry," we say "bilberry"

The European relation of the blueberry, which grows wild only in northern Europe, is the bilberry (*Vaccinium myrtillus*). It produces single or pairs of dark purple berries on the bush, instead of the clusters produced by the blueberry. Bilberries are particularly popular in

Scandinavia, especially Sweden, and families often go foraging for them in forests. They are eaten fresh, but as the berries are fairly acidic, they are often cooked and made into pie fillings and desserts, jams, and even soups.

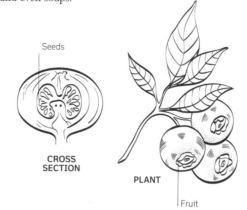

Seeds

CROSS SECTION

PLANT

Fruit

Origins
North America
Major producers
US, Canada
Main food component
14 percent carbohydrate
Good source of
Potassium, vitamin C
Scientific name
Vaccinium corymbosum

◁ **Fruit clusters**
The blueberry bush produces clusters of fruit and individual berries in a cluster may ripen at different times.

▽ **Crateloads of blueberries**
American farm workers pack blueberries into a wooden sorting device while another assembles crates in this 1940s photograph.

Eating outdoors

Outdoor eating means different things to different people. In Britain and the US, it usually means a countryside or seaside picnic, where hard-boiled eggs, sandwiches, and fried chicken are the standard fare. In Japan, however, picnics are held to celebrate *hanami,* the appearance of cherry blossoms. Traditional *hanami* food includes carrots cut in the shape of cherry blossom petals, *onigiri* (rice balls), and *sakuramochi*—pink rice cakes filled with sweet red bean paste and wrapped in pickled cherry leaves.

In medieval Europe, it became common practice for wealthy landowners to hold outdoor hunting feasts prior to the start of a hunt. In his 1387 *Le Livre de Chasse (Book of the Chase),* Frenchman Gaston de Foix described such an event where guests consumed vast quantities of pastries, hams, and baked meats as well as gallons of drink. Picnics remained reserved for the rich until the late 1700s. After the French Revolution of 1789 toppled the monarchy, royal parks were opened to the public for the first time and rapidly became popular meeting places. Visitors often brought food and drink with them, but picnicking really came into its own in Regency and Victorian Britain.

Victorian picnics, however, did not come cheap. In her *Book of Household Management,* Isabella ("Mrs.") Beeton, specified that, to feed 40, joints of roasted and boiled beef, two lamb ribs, four meat pies, four roast chickens, two roast ducks, four-dozen cheesecakes, and a large plum pudding were required, along with three-dozen quart bottles of beer, claret, sherry, and brandy. In her 1900 book *Queen of the Household,* US cookbook writer Mrs. M. W. Ellsworth gave similarly elaborate instructions, although she favored potted rabbit sandwiches and "bewitched veal."

◁ **Breakfast of champions**
In the 18th century, no self-respecting hunt could begin before fortifying the party with a hunt breakfast—the more lavish, the better.

Cranberries
bright bouncing berry of the bog

The famous berry of America, the cranberry—once a key to survival in the harsh northern winters—has adopted a new role as an essential accompaniment to Thanksgiving meals.

Origins
North America, northern Europe, northen Asia

Major producers
US, Canada, Belarus

Main food component
12 percent carbohydrate

Source of
Vitamin C, potassium

Scientific name
Vaccinium macrocarpon

△ **European relation**
A cousin of the cranberry that is native to Europe, the cowberry (*Vaccinium vitis-idaea*), has edible red and yellow berries.

Some argue that it is a gross injustice that the cranberry's beautiful appearance is not matched by its flavor. But the story of its rise in popularity tells a different story. The main cultivated species is the

"And they bought ... a pound of Rice, and a Cranberry Tart..."

EDWARD LEAR, "THE JUMBLIES," 1871

American cranberry (*Vaccinium macrocarpon*). Its natural home is the colossal sandy bogs in temperate zones on the east coast of the US and Canada, extending as far west as the Great Lakes and south to the Appalachians. The glowing scarlet berries grow on low, trailing vines that produce runners up to 6ft (2m) in length. In the growing season these vines form a dense mat over the top of a cultivated bed. Flooding the beds causes the cranberries to detach from the vines and float to the surface where they can be skimmed off. Through history, people have given cranberries an

A sea of berries
In today's world, cranberries are big business. Here, huge machines scoop ripe berries from a cranberry bog in British Columbia, Canada.

extensive list of nicknames. Indigenous people called them *atoca*. However, except for in Canada, this has been overtaken by the English name cranberry, itself a shortened form of "craneberry." This name derives from way the plant's pink flowers dip down toward the water, reminding the English settlers of the heads of the cranes they saw wading through the cranberry bogs. The ripe cranberry's ability to bounce when dropped also earned it the nickname "bounceberry."

Powers of preservation

The indigenous people introduced the early English settlers to cranberries in the 17th century. Some of the settlers were so impressed by the fruit's keeping qualities that they shipped 10 barrels back to Charles II as a gift. No records indicate if the fruit arrived or if the king liked them. Small cranberries were also carried on American and English ships and eaten by trappers in remote regions. On their explorations across the US, Meriwether Lewis and William Clark also ate dried cranberries, and at Thanksgiving in 1805 the two men made cranberry sauce from fruit supplied by Chinook women. We now know that cranberries contain a natural preservative—benzoic acid—and for

long journeys, Iroquois hunters were supplied with high-energy rations called "pemmican"—portable cakes of pounded fat, seeds, smoked game, and dried cranberries. Today cranberries are used for their juice, in preserves, in tarts, and even in a liqueur. Cranberry sauce is a traditional accompaniment to roast turkey.

△ **Hand scoop**
Before mechanization, special hand tools such as this scoop from Massachusetts were used to harvest the berries.

◁ **Good pickings**
In the early 20th century, cranberry picking could involve workers of all ages. This eight-year-old is carrying a harvest from Brown Mills, New Jersey.

Bananas a fruity staple

Originating in Southeast Asia, bananas now provide a nutritious staple in countries throughout Asia, Africa, and the Caribbean, as well as a popular snack, dessert fruit, and cake component in Europe and North America.

Origins   South Pacific Islands
Major producers   India, China, the Philippines
Main food component   23 percent carbohydrate
Source of   Vitamin B3
Non-food uses   Roofing, fiber (leaves)
Scientific name   *Musa* sp.

Surprisingly, botanically the banana is not a fruit but a berry. It forms in big bunches from a large, purple or red teardrop-shaped flower. The banana plant has large, flat leaves that are often used as thatching in the countries where it grows. The edible parts do not grow on the trunk of the bush itself but on a root structure, which technically makes the banana an herb, albeit a very large one.

◁ **Massive leaves**
The large leaves of the banana plant, used for shelter in some parts of the world, can clearly be seen in this engraving.

▷ **Emerging fruit**
Banana fruit develop in bunches from large cone-shaped flowers.

Global reach
Banana plants are believed to have originated in Southeast Asia, in the region stretching from India to Malaysia, Indonesia, and New Guinea. From there, bananas spread more widely to other parts of Asia and, by 1000 BCE, to Madagascar, which was probably the origin of banana growing in Africa. Bananas may also have been transported from Asia across the Pacific to South America by 200 BCE.

By around 1200 CE, Moorish invaders had brought bananas to North Africa and the Iberian Peninsula.

Following the discovery of the New World, a Spanish friar, Thomas de Berlanga, is reputed to have taken banana plants from Africa to Santo Domingo in the Caribbean in 1516. As the crop became established in Central and South America, bananas not only provided a convenient and cheap staple for the slave populations of the region, but also the plants themselves were useful to the colonists as a means of protecting other crops such as coffee and cacao. The advent of refrigerated ships in the 20th century meant that bananas could be transported throughout the world and ensured their enduring popularity.

It is likely that the famous Macedonian king Alexander the Great encountered bananas during his expeditions to India in the 4th century BCE and may have brought them back to Europe with him.

Top bananas
Today's predominant banana variety is the Cavendish, a large fruit named after the English William Cavendish, Duke of Devonshire, who in the 19th century successfully grew bananas imported from Mauritius in the hothouse on his estate. A cousin of the dessert banana, the plantain, has become a popular starchy staple in Central and South America, Africa, and parts of Asia. It is larger and more floury in texture than the dessert varieties and is not as sweet.

Bananas of all types are now grown in over 100 countries, and are ranked fourth among the world's staple foods in monetary value, after wheat, rice, and maize. Uganda has the highest consumption of bananas (mainly plantains) per person per year, with Americans a close second. The world's top producer of dessert bananas is India. Uganda is the largest producer of plantains.

◁ **Great discovery**
By the 19th century bananas were being used in commercial bakery products such as this brand of banana bread from around 1870.

"When bad luck is your companion, even a ripe banana can break your teeth."

AFRICAN PROVERB

△ **A journey begins**
Bananas often travel thousands of miles to reach their markets. Here a shipment of the fruit, probably bound for the US, is loaded at the harbor at Guayaquil, Ecuador (c.1955).

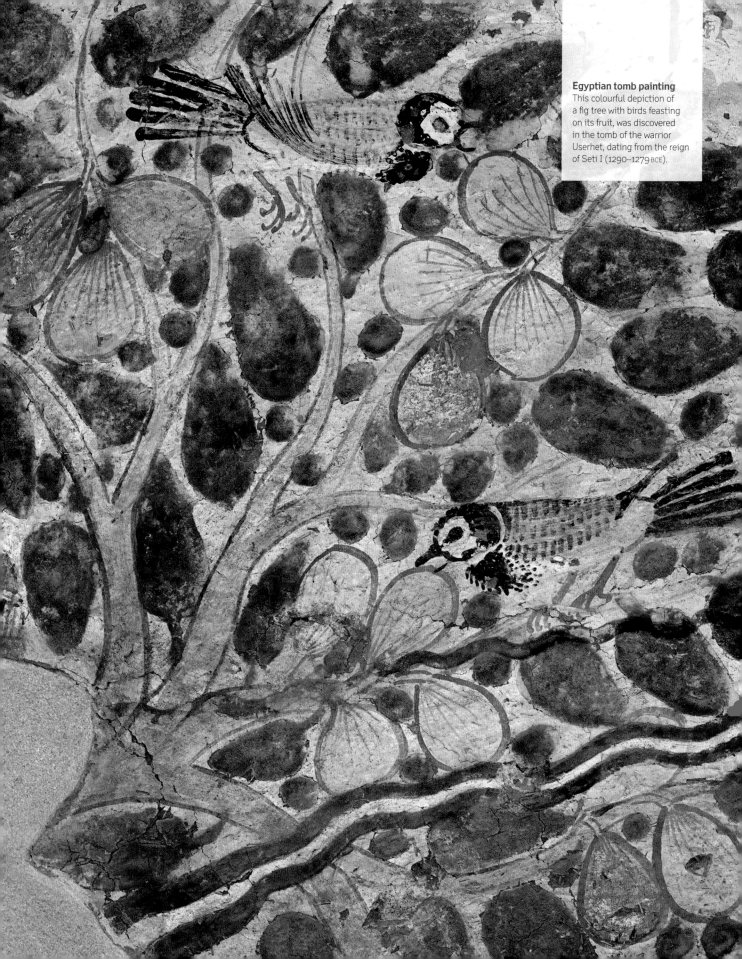

Figs sweet-tasting fruit of antiquity

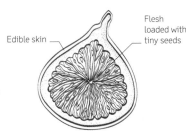

Edible skin

Flesh loaded with tiny seeds

△ **Seedy center**
The soft interior of the fig is filled with seeds embedded in reddish pink flesh. The whole fruit is edible.

The luscious "fruits" of the fig tree provided a sweet treat many thousands of years ago for the people of the ancient civilizations of the Middle East, a luxury that is enjoyed today by people around the world.

The fig is technically not a fruit but a syconium, a portion of the stem that expands into a sac containing flowers that grow internally. The "fruit" may be green or purple and rounded or cone-shaped at the stem end, and they contain a multitude of tiny seeds. The common fig tree has large, lobed leaves with branches that spread widely. It contains only female flowers and propagates without pollination, so the seeds are infertile.

◁ **Basket of plenty**
Figs are seen overflowing from a basket—a classic image of plenty—in this segment of a Roman mosaic from Utica, Tunisia.

Spreading from the East

The common fig originated in Asia Minor (present-day Turkey), but in prehistoric times spread to the eastern Mediterranean region and the Arabian Peninsula. Fossilized remains of figs, dated to around 9000 BCE, have been found during archaeological excavations of a village in the Jordan Valley in present-day Israel, making the fig one of the earliest domesticated crops. They are mentioned as a food in Sumerian stone tablets dating back to 2500 BCE. The cultivation of figs was common in ancient Greece, and was described by both the philosopher Aristotle and his successor,

Spanish missionaries. Their cultivation there was boosted in the 19th century by the introduction of new varieties from France and England. Today, Turkey is the world's largest producer of figs, accounting for about a fifth of global production. Other important fig-growing countries include Egypt and Morocco.

Fresh and dried

Throughout history figs have been enjoyed in their fresh state, but they are also popular dried. The ability to preserve the fruit easily in this way has made the fig an all-season food as well as facilitating its transport and storage. In the modern world, figs are enjoyed simply as a fruit, often as an accompaniment to cheese, and as an ingredient in desserts and pastries. The seeds are also roasted and used to flavor "Viennese coffee"—a custom acquired from the Turkish invaders, who occupied Austria in the 17th century.

Origins	Turkey
Major producers	Turkey, Egypt, Morocco
Major food component	19 percent carbohydrate
Source of	Potassium
Non-food use	Laxative (syrup)
Scientific name	*Ficus carica*

▽ **Traditional work**
In this late 19th-century postcard image from the fig-producing region of Smyrna (in modern-day Turkey), women are seen sorting figs for market.

"Here the blue fig, with luscious juice overflows."

HOMER, *THE ODYSSEY*, 8TH-CENTURY BCE

Theophrastus. The ancient Romans also valued the fig, and probably were responsible for spreading it throughout the Mediterranean parts of their empire.

By the 16th century, figs were also being cultivated in northern Europe. The English cardinal Reginald Pole grew fig trees in his London palace garden. Figs were brought to California in the 18th century by

Souvenir de Smyrne. Le Travail des Figues.

Grapes ancient food and drink

With their sweetness and natural capacity for fermentation, discovered over 9,000 years ago, grapes were possibly the earliest food that both nourished and inebriated humans.

The ancient Chinese enjoyed a drink of fermented wild grapes as long ago as 7000–6600 BCE. The first evidence of propagation, however, comes from *Vitis vinifera* grape pips dated to the early 6th millennium BCE, which were discovered in a Neolithic settlement in southeast Georgia, western Asia. Residues from clay jars indicate that winemaking soon followed.

Of grapes and gods

Over the next few thousand years, grape growing spread south and west across the Middle East, to Egypt and Europe. The fruit, fresh and dried, was part of

> More than 70 percent of the grapes grown in the world today are used to make wine.

Sumerian and Babylonian cuisine, with grape juice and raisins used as sweeteners. Only the royal household or the rich drank wine. In ancient Egypt, too, where vines were cultivated from around 3000 BCE, wine was enjoyed mainly by the elite and also played an important ceremonial role.

As nations traded their fruit and wine, grapes became economically important, but cultivating them demanded great care. This may be why, from around 1500 BCE, the Mycenaean Greeks began worshipping Dionysus, the god of the grape harvest. He was also known as Bacchus, a name later adopted by the wine-loving Romans, who enjoyed grapes in every form and even used raisins for bartering. In 75 CE, Pliny the Elder wrote about a dried, seedless grape exported from Corinth; the word "currant" comes from the city's name.

Raisins feature in recipes for veal and fish set down in *Apicius*, a 4th–5th-century CE Roman cookbook. Much later, in the 14th century, currants were often added to

a dish called frumenty—cracked wheat cooked in milk or broth—which was served with meat or fish and became popular across Medieval Europe. Christmas stollen, a moist fruit bread from Germany, can be traced back to around 1400, and similar sweet breads enjoyed around this time include *panettone*, from Milan, and *kulich*, a traditional Easter bread from Russia.

Foxy flavors

In eastern North America, the native grapevine is *V. labrusca*, a hardy species. Early European settlers found that the fresh grapes and their juice have strong, earthy yet sweet aromas, characteristically described as "foxy." The most common *V. labrusca* cultivar is the black-skinned grape Concord, which is used to make most of the grape juice and grape jelly sold in US stores. The *V. vinifera* grape was brought to the continent in the 1600s by Spanish missionaries, who brought cuttings with them so they could make wine. Today, there are more than 8,000 active wineries in North America. Mexico, Chile, and Argentina have also become important growers and wine producers.

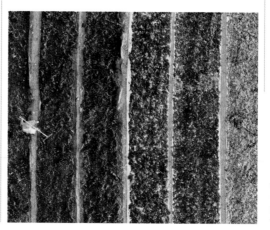

◁ **Drunken god**
The Greek god Silenus holds a bunch of grapes in this marble statue. Dubbed the god of drunkenness, Silenus was the companion or tutor of Dionysius, the god of the grape harvest.

Origins
Western Asia
Main producers
China, US, Italy
Main food component
18 percent carbohydrate
Source of
Vitamin K
Non-food use
Nutritional supplement
Scientific names
Vitis vinifera, *Vitis labrusca*

▷ **Grape offering**
The tree goddess makes offerings of beer, bread, grapes, and onions to the deceased in this scene in the tomb of Nakht on the banks of the Nile.

◁ **Grape drying**
Raisins have been popular since Roman times. Simple methods of drying seedless grapes in the sun are still used today in many grape-producing areas including this in Turkey.

Lemons and limes
ancient citrus twins

Closely related, but different in color and sharpness of taste, lemons and limes both emerged from India and the Far East to become vital ingredients and flavorings in many of the world's foods and drinks today.

Lemons and limes are thought most probably to have been cultivated first in the monsoon belt of Asia. The lemon is mentioned in Indian Sanskrit writing from around 800 BCE, and again by the Greek botanist and philosopher Theophrastus of Eresus in the 4th century BCE, who called it the "Fruit of Persia" and recommended its use as a perfume, insect repellent, and poison antidote. Roman traders brought citrus

15th century that lemons began to be cultivated on a large scale in Europe, along the Ligurian coast around Genoa, Italy. It was the Genoese-born explorer Christopher Columbus who carried lemon seeds to the Caribbean island of Hispaniola in 1493, an introduction to the New World that saw lemons spread to Central and South America as Spanish settlement increased during the 16th and 17th centuries.

The sweet and the sour
The earliest written evidence of still lemonade, in the form of freshly squeezed lemon juice sweetened with cane sugar, comes from Egypt in the 11th century, while the Mongols are believed to have enjoyed an alcoholic version during the early 13th century under the rule of Ghenghis Khan. A taste for non-alcoholic still lemonade developed in France during the 1600s, with *limonadiers* selling it on the streets of Paris. By the early 1700s, lemonade began to appear in bottles. Two hundred years later, in 1929, Charles Leiper Grigg of Missouri introduced his "lithiated lemon-lime soda" (later renamed 7 Up), which was made with carbonated water.

Lemons have always been prized for the sourness of their juice and the subtle perfume of the zest (the grated outer rind).
The earliest known lemon recipes were

△ **Mediterranean harvest**
Menton on the French Riviera has a long, proud history of growing lemons. This crop was being harvested c.1900.

fruits from India to other parts of the empire, and lemons are depicted in frescoes discovered in the ruins of Pompeii.

Gradual spread
The lemon appears in a 10th-century CE Arabic treatise on farming, and Arabs cultivated the fruit in Mediterranean areas such as Spain, Sicily, and Egypt. The Arabs used the words limun and lima for the lemon and lime, which formed the basis for the names in a number of Western languages. However, it was only in the middle of the

△ **Eye-catching label**
The invention of cheap color printing in the 18th century coincided with the winter export of citrus from the orchards of sunny California to the snowbound northeastern states.

◁ **Hot dogs, cold lemonade**
This enterprising street vendor in Manhattan offered his customers refreshing ice cold lemonade to wash down their hot dogs at 5 cents for a glass in 1936.

LEMON

Origins
Asia

Major producers
India, Mexico, China

Main food component
9 percent carbohydrate

Source of
Vitamin C, potassium

Non-food uses
Perfume, cosmetics,
cleaning products

Scientific name
Citrus limon

△ **Thin skin**
Limes usually have a green skin, although some varieties are yellow. The thin skin makes the fruit sensitive to cold so limes can only be grown in areas free of frost.

recorded in a 12th-century Egyptian treatise, *On Lemon, Its Drinking and Use,* written by Ibn Jumay, an Arabic-speaking Jewish physician. His method for preserving lemons in salt still plays a key role today in North African cuisines. Salted limes are often used in south Asian cooking. Lemons have become important ingredients in savory foods—such as the Greek *avgolemono* (egg and lemon) sauce, which is served with stuffed vine leaves or used to make a chicken soup—and sweet dishes—such as lemon tarts, cakes, sorbets, and ice creams.

A popular fruit

Limes have a high vitamin C content and were once carried on sailing ships to counteract scurvy. They are used in similar ways to lemons in cooking. Dried limes, sliced or ground, add piquancy to stews and soups in Iraq and Iran, while hot and spicy lime pickle is a popular Indian condiment served as an accompaniment to curries. The key lime, so-called because it originates from the Florida Keys, gave its name to the popular American dessert, key lime pie, which first appeared in the early 20th century. In the South American seafood dish ceviche, lemons and limes are often united, the preservative qualities of their combined juices used to marinade and "cook" raw fish and seafood.

"It's not until you squeeze the lemon, that you'll see its juice."

SWAHILI PROVERB

Oranges the sunshine fruit

A hybrid, cultivated for thousands of years, the orange has traveled gradually from East to West, following trade routes and colonial adventures, to become a year-round symbol of health and sunshine.

Origins
China (cultivated)

Major producers
Brazil, China, US, India, Mexico

Main food component
16 percent carbohydrate

Source of
Vitamin C, vitamin B1, vitamin B9, calcium

Non-food uses
Cleaning products (oil), perfume (oil), cattle feed

Scientific name
Citrus sinensis

Wherever winters are warm and dry and summers are hot, oranges can be cultivated. These perennially popular fruits have the advantage of ripening in the winter, when many others are unavailable in northern hemisphere countries. This seasonal bonus helps to make the sweet orange, which grows on a small evergreen tree, one of the most widely grown fruits.

The orange's origins in the wild are unknown, but the fruit was first cultivated in China as early as 2500 BCE. It was introduced to Europe in the late 15th century, probably by Portuguese traders. Today there are many varieties of sweet orange, including the *shamouti* or Jaffa orange, first grown by Palestinian farmers in the mid 19th century, and the late-ripening Valencia orange, developed in California, also in the 19th century. The smaller, sweet, thin-skinned oranges, such as the clementine, mandarin, and tangerine, are grown mainly in North Africa and the US.

The bitter or Seville orange was introduced to Spain by Moorish invaders in the 8th century. The Moors also brought the fruit to Sicily when they seized the island in the 9th century. Today, the bitter orange is used mainly in cooking, especially to make the tangy

In 1919, the California Fruit Exchange branded its oranges with "Sunkist," the first fresh fruit to carry a trademark.

▷ **Spanish bounty**
A group of women pack oranges in the marketplace of Seville in this 19th-century engraving. Today, the streets of the city are lined with more than 14,000 orange trees.

◁ **Marmalade maker**
An advertisement from the 1890s shows oranges flying from their source in Seville to London, where E & T Pink claimed to be "by far the largest manufacturer of marmalade in the world."

orange jam known in Britain as "marmalade," from the Portuguese *marmelada*, meaning "quince jam."

In turn, orange seeds were taken to the Caribbean on Christopher Columbus's second voyage, in 1493. Then, in the early years of the 16th century, Spanish and Portuguese settlers introduced the sweet orange to Central and South America. Spanish missionaries planted California's first orange seeds in 1769, but it was a surge in demand for oranges during the Gold Rush of 1849 that saw an early growth in cultivation. When transcontinental railways opened up the US starting in the 1870s, oranges were able to reach the big eastern markets such as Chicago and New York.

Your daily juice

The "sunshine state" of Florida is the other major US orange producer and the center of orange juice production, with 95 percent of its oranges turned into juice. As orange-growing boomed in the early 20th century, the adoption of the pasteurization technique of preserving food through heat treatment allowed orange juice to be canned and easily transported. Following World War II, the invention of frozen concentrated orange juice created a convenient, cheap fruit drink that was heavily promoted for its health-giving benefits, helping it to become a breakfast essential.

▽ **Orange harvest**
A team of workers picks fruit from an orange grove in Miami, Florida. Orange seeds were first planted in this state by Spanish explorers in the 16th century.

Food offerings

Offering foods to their gods was a way of life for ancient peoples throughout the world. They believed that the gods needed food to sustain them and trusted that the gods, in return, would help their crops to flourish. The gods also depended on people for their sustenance, through offerings; an early Egyptian text refers to humans as the "cattle" of the gods, denoting mutual interdependence. Some peoples believed that their ancestors needed food offerings, too, as they could cause crops to fail if they were allowed to become hungry.

In Egypt, when a haunch of beef was sacrificed, part of it was given to the priest in payment for his services. Breads, milk, figs, dates, grapes, salt, vegetables, grains, and wild fowl were all acceptable as sacrifices. Egyptians also believed that the god Osiris invented beer, so it was logical to present that libation as an offering as well. *Chicha* or corn beer was offered in the same way by the Incas of Peru.

Greeks, when sacrificing an animal, sprinkled it with holy water, causing it to shake its head so it seemed to have given assent to its sacrifice. The ascending smoke was said to take the spirit of the offering up to the gods. Similarly, the Incas burned llama meat as incense, and its blood was used for ritual purposes.

Generally speaking, people take the best and most elaborate food offerings to a temple, but such gifts can also be small and inconspicuous items proffered in the home. Balinese Hindus, for example, set out small daily *canangs*—simple square baskets made of coconut or banana leaves and filled with flowers, rice, and often a small banknote—in designated places as offerings of selfless gratitude to their deities. *Canangs* are also found on the streets of Bali for the same reason, topped with burning incense.

◁ **Towering offerings**
Balinese Hindus make daily offerings to their gods. Here a procession of women carry *banten tegeh*—tall towers of fruit, rice cakes, and various items—to a temple.

Grapefruit and pomelos

late arrivals on the world fruit stage

The two heavyweights of the citrus family, the grapefruit and the pomelo are related but come from opposite ends of the Earth and are separated in history by thousands of years.

GRAPEFRUIT

Origins
Caribbean islands

Major producers
US, South Africa, Israel

Main food component
9 percent carbohydrate

Source of
Vitamin C

Non-food uses
Medicinal

Scientific name
Citrus x paradisi

The grapefruit does not appear in cookbooks until the 19th century, for the simple reason that it was first recorded only in the previous century. In 1750, the Welsh naturalist Reverend Griffith Hughes came across a tree in Barbados that bore huge yellow fruits, growing in bunches like enormous grapes, which he described as "the forbidden fruit." A year later, the young George Washington, future first President of the United States, mentioned the forbidden fruit as one of the local offerings at a dinner party.

The grapefruit, the only citrus native to the Caribbean, is a cross between two citrus fruits. One is possibly an orange but more likely a citron, the first citrus fruit brought to the West from India via Persia around 300 BCE. The citron, like the grapefruit, has thick pith and bitter flesh. The other part of the cross is the pomelo, the largest of the citrus fruits, with smooth green and yellow skin, thick pith, and sweeter flesh

▷ **Segmented fruit**
Grapefruit and pomelos have the typical segments of all citrus fruit when cut open. The flesh can vary from pale yellow to pink.

than the slightly bitter-tasting grapefruit. The pomelo originated in Southeast Asia, had reached China by 2200 BCE, and then traveled west along the Silk Road to Europe. It was brought to the West Indies in 1696, allegedly by a Captain Shaddock on an East India Company ship, which is the origin of the fruit's alternative name, shaddock.

Today grapefruit is widely consumed both as a fresh fruit and in the form of juice. The US is the world's top producer, with China and South Africa also cultivating significant numbers.

◁ **Typically tropical**
Grapefruit are particularly suited to tropical climates and the only citrus native to the Caribbean, the scene of this 19th-century painting.

▷ **Celebrated in Rome**
Pomegranates were known and enjoyed in ancient Rome. In this Roman fresco from the 1st century BCE, birds perch on pomegranate trees.

Pomegranates

fruit of myth and legend

The very image of plenty, the pomegranate, with its mass of flesh-covered, jewel-like seeds, features in myths and legends of many cultures, and is still highly prized today.

According to Greek mythology, Hades, god of the underworld, tempted Persephone, his consort, with a pomegranate, and the jewel-like seeds certainly have a tempting appearance. The fruit has a tough pink rind, shading to yellow, that encloses the ruby-red juice sacs known as arils.

Rich in symbolism

The pomegranate is said to have originated in Persia or the Caucasus, and was first cultivated around 5,000 years ago. It soon spread throughout the ancient world, where it became the subject of myth. To the ancient Egyptians, who used the fruit mainly as a medicine, the pomegranate was a symbol of fertility and

△ **Red gems**
When a pomegranate is opened, hundreds of shiny deep-red juice sacs (arils) enclosed in bitter-tasting pith are revealed.

"With deeper red, the full pomegranate glows."

ALEXANDER POPE, *THE ODYSSEY OF HOMER* (1726)

prosperity. Pomegranates are mentioned many times in the Bible. The spies sent by Moses to perform reconnaissance in the land of Canaan brought back pomegranates from the Vale of Eshcol to show how fertile the land was, and the tops of the pillars of King Solomon's temple were carved to resemble pomegranates. Modern Jewish traditions include eating pomegranates on Jewish New Year to symbolize, through their many seeds, hopes for abundance to come. In the Qu'ran, the pomegranate is one of the rewards awaiting those who attain Paradise.

Pomegranates have long been important in the cuisines of the Middle East, and more recently have been adopted into modern Western cuisine. Today the fruit is grown in many areas beyond its traditional Asian and Middle Eastern strongholds, including Spain, Sicily, and California.

Origins
Western Asia

Major producers
Iran, US, China

Main food component
19 percent carbohydrate

Source of
Vitamin C

Non-food uses
Cosmetics

Scientific name
Punica granatum

Melons

thirst-quenching sweet-fleshed fruit

This group of juice-filled fruits have been enjoyed for millennia in lands and cultures as diverse as ancient Egypt, Moorish Spain, and the Pacific Islands.

Encompassing hundreds of varieties, melons are relatives of the cucumber, gourd, and pumpkin family. Melons grow best in warm climates, but demand large amounts of water. There are two types of melon, the muskmelon (which includes cantaloupe and honeydew melons) and the watermelon. All have a tough-skinned rind, either green or yellow; a thick pulp; and grow on an annual vine.

> ## "To taste a watermelon is to know what the angels eat."
>
> MARK TWAIN, 19TH-CENTURY WRITER

The ancient Egyptians were cultivating watermelons in the Nile Valley at least as far back as 2400 BCE. Watermelon seeds were found in the tomb of Tutankhamun, who died c.1323 BCE. There is later evidence of watermelons being eaten in Spain—in Córdoba in 961 and in Seville in 1158. The fruit reached India and China in the Middle Ages, and spread northward through southern Europe. By 1600, melons were listed in European botanical texts. Where climate allowed, Europeans cultivated melons extensively. Spanish colonists had taken watermelons to the New World in the 16th century, and they are recorded as being grown in Florida and the Mississippi Valley in 1576. Japanese scientists initially developed seedless watermelons in 1939, and they now account for nearly 85 percent of total watermelon sales in the US. China is the world's largest producer of melons.

▷ **Seeds of temptation**
An advertising sheet inside an 1890 American seed catalog promises the prospective grower a luscious crop of orange-fleshed melons.

Vicks Irondequoit Melon Lemon Cucumber Laxton Pe...

FOR DESCRIPTIONS AND PRIC... SEE PAGES 14 AND 15

△ **Street treat**
Watermelons were common in Italy by the 19th century. In this Naples street scene of the period, a watermelon seller plies his trade.

△ **Ridged skin**
The external appearance of melons is variable. Some melons, such as the cantaloupe, have ridged skin, others have colored stripes or textured skin.

MUSKMELONS

Origins
Middle East, North Africa

Major producers
China, Turkey, US

Main food component
8 percent carbohydrate

Source of
Potassium, vitamins A, C

Scientific name
Cucumis melo

Papayas a fruity powerhouse

The Mayans called the papaya plant the "tree of life," and they were right. The papaya is now known for its vast range of nutritional and medicinal properties.

Origins
Central America

Major producers
India, Brazil, Indonesia

Main food component
11 percent carbohydrate

Source of
Vitamin A, vitamin C

Scientific name
Carica papaya

The original wild papaya plants were spindly with nearly inedible fruits. However, over time the plant developed into the modern herbaceous shrub that grows as tall as 23ft (7m) and bears leaves nearly 3ft (1m) wide. The fruit, also known as pawpaw in South Africa, hangs in clumps below the branches. When ripe, a papaya has a thin, greenish-yellow skin and pinkish-orange sweet-tasting flesh. Most fruits resemble a pear in shape and size, though some can weigh up to 20lb (9kg) each.

Spanish explorers spread the love

The papaya first grew wild in the lowlands of Central America, from Mexico to Panama. Cultivation and deliberate selection by the indigenous people bred larger, more flavorful fruit. In the 16th century, Spanish explorers carried the seeds (which can survive for years when dried) first to the Caribbean and then to the Philippines. From there they were distributed to India, the islands of the South Pacific, and Africa. In the early 1800s, a new generation of Spanish seafarers introduced the fruit to Hawaii. Papayas are now grown widely throughout warm, tropical regions of the world.

All parts of the papaya are useful, including the young leaves (made into a tea said to protect against malaria), seeds (used as a mild spice when dried), ripe and unripe fruits, and juice. Most often papayas are peeled and served fresh with a wedge of lemon or lime. In South America, Asia, and Africa, unripe papayas are boiled and served as a vegetable, cooked in stews, or baked. In Southeast Asia young leaves are cooked and eaten like spinach. Green papaya contains enzymes that can tenderize meat.

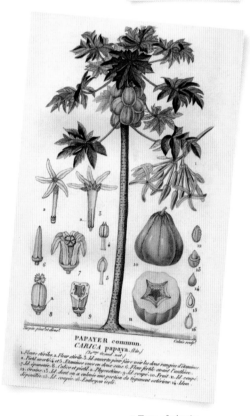

PAPAYER commun.
CARICA papaya (Min)

△ **Tree of plenty**
This illustration by Pierre Jean François Turpin from *Dictionnaire des Sciences Naturelles* (1816) clearly shows the large, lobed leaves and the pear-shaped fruit of the papaya tree.

◁ **Inside the skin**
The interior of the papaya consists of edible orange flesh and dark brownish-black seeds, which are not eaten.

Coconuts
food and drink in a shell

The coconut is probably the most useful plant known to humankind, providing food and building materials in most tropical regions of the world.

The tall, graceful coconut palm needs no human assistance to spread. The nuts float and are carried by ocean currents from island to island in the tropics. The trees can reach 100ft (30m) and bear up to 30 large, round or oval nuts encased in a soft gray-green husk. An inner layer consists of a hard brown shell covered in long fibers, which in turn encloses a layer of snow-white flesh. The hollow center contains a liquid known as coconut water. The flesh, the liquid that can be extracted from it (coconut milk), and coconut water provide sustenance to local populations and consumers further afield.

Pacific traveler

Fossils of ancestors of the modern coconut dating from up to 55 million years ago have been found in Australia and India, and it is generally accepted that the species originated in the islands of the western Pacific and the Indian oceans. It is mentioned in Indian documents that date back more than 2,000 years. From this time, it is likely that Arab traders spread the nut to the Middle East and East Africa. The tree was established in Egypt by the 13th century, when it was recorded by the Venetian explorer Marco Polo, and by the 16th century, Europeans had taken the coconut to West Africa, the Caribbean, and Central America. Today, coconut products are important as a food source in the regions where the tree is grown and are also valued elsewhere in the world.

△ **Reaching high**
The use of ladders and ropes, the traditional way to climb a coconut tree to harvest the coconuts, is still the method of choice in many parts of the world.

▷ **Two halves, two layers**
With the outer husk removed, the inner hard brown shell covered in long fibers and the interior white flesh are seen when the coconut is cut in half.

The name coconut may come from the Portuguese *cocuruto* (top of the head), because the base looks like a face.

Origins	Indian Ocean, Pacific islands
Main food component	33 percent fat
Source of	Iron, zinc
Non-food use	Matting
Scientific name	*Cocos nucifera*

Pineapples
taste of the tropics

The "king of fruits," the pineapple was, until the 20th century, a luxury outside its native regions. It only became widely available with the advent of canning.

Origins	South America
Major producers	Costa Rica, Brazil, the Philippines
Main food component	13 percent carbohydrate
Source of	Vitamin C
Scientific name	*Ananas comosus*

When first introduced to Europe in the 17th century, pineapples caused a sensation. Royalty and the aristocracy competed to grow the largest and best pineapples in their specially designed hothouses, and pineapple designs were often included to ornament gateposts of grand houses.

Unconnected with pines
The name "pineapple" refers to the fruit's resemblance to pinecones noted by the first Europeans to encounter the fruit. But the plant is in no way connected with conifer trees—it is a member of the bromeliad family, a group of flowering plants native to South America.

In spite of its appearance, the pineapple is not a single fruit but a collection of berries. Unlike many fruit, it does not continue to ripen after picking, so it must be harvested and sold in a 24-hour window. Originally cultivated by the indigenous peoples of Central and South America and the Caribbean, pineapples were shipped to Spain

◁ **Sharp-leaved fruit**
The leaves and the outer skin of the pineapple have spiky tips. The yellow slightly fibrous interior of the fruit is succulent and sweet, but sometimes somewhat acidic.

△ **Piles of pineapples**
Skill is needed to judge the precise moment when a pineapple is ready to be harvested—a job that is generally best done by hand as here in Tangail, Bangladesh.

in the 16th century following the expeditions to the New World by Christopher Columbus, and were later taken by European traders to Africa and Asia, where they became established. Today, they are widely grown in tropical countries throughout the world.

These sweet but sometimes acidic fruit are popular in their natural state as a dessert, but they are also preserved by canning, drying, and in candied form. Unusually, the fresh fruit contains an enzyme called bromelain that has meat-tenderizing properties, which is why fresh pineapple is often served with ham.

"Love is like a pineapple, sweet and undefinable."

PIET PIETERSZOON HEIN, 17TH-CENTURY DUTCH NAVAL COMMANDER

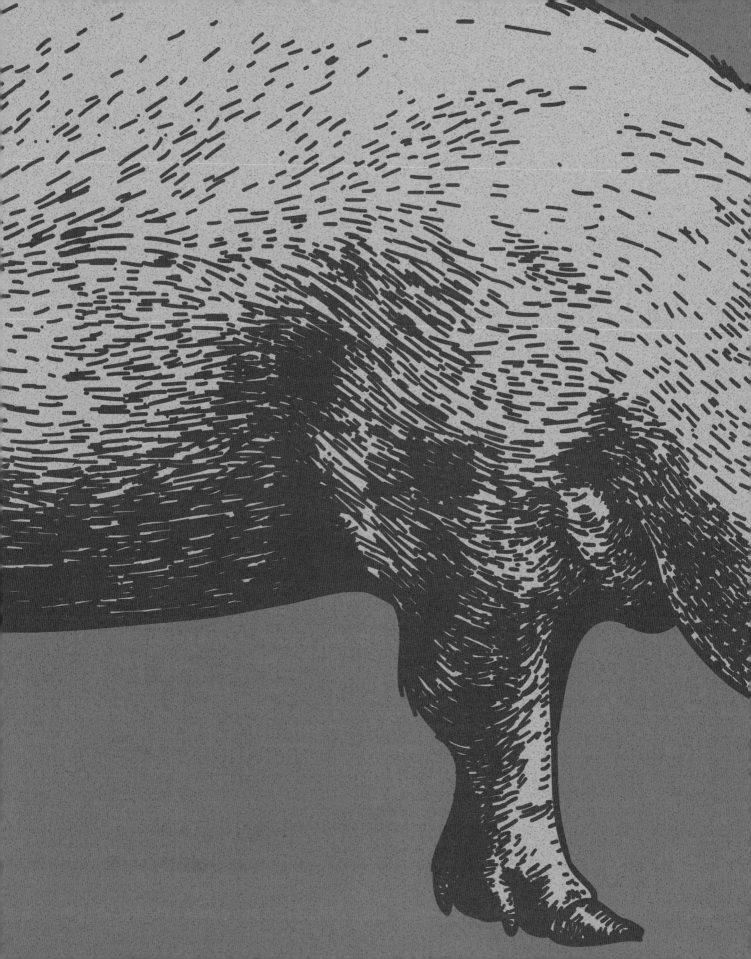

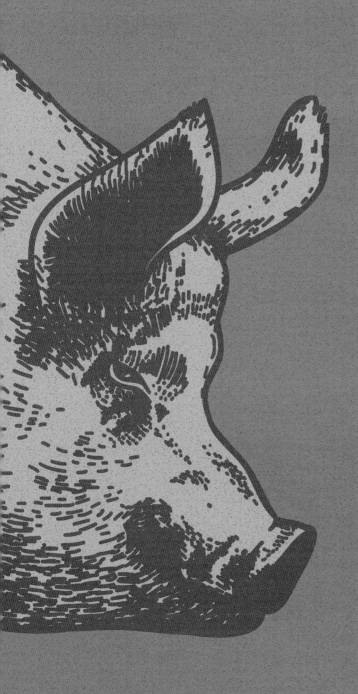

Meat

Meat

According to evidence found at Olduvai Gorge, Tanzania, and Lake Victoria in Kenya, our ancient human ancestors hunted animals for meat at least as early as 2 million years ago, and possibly longer. Anthropologists believe that primitive humans ambushed herds to kill antelope, gazelles, wildebeest, and other large animals. They probably isolated the most vulnerable animals from the herd in a strategy similar to that employed by the big cats of the African plains.

Meat played a part in the early human diet across most of the planet, with the exception of some coastal and island dwellings, where fish fulfilled the body's needs for complex proteins.

Hunting horses and bison

In Germany, archaeologists have also found evidence indicating that 400,000 years ago, wild horses were being speared and eaten. To manage this kind of feat required intelligence—not only tactical know-how but technological prowess as well. Another example of this type of hunting comes from the American

Indians, who hunted buffalo and bison on foot across the Great Plains and Canadian Prairies around 12,000 BCE. They developed spears with carved stone points, which archaeologists believe were capable of bringing down an animal the size of an African elephant.

How meat may have changed our brains

Once primitive peoples became successful at hunting and eating meat, anthropologists believe that this, in turn, fostered further advances in human development. This is due mainly to the fact that the complex proteins contained in meat are easier to metabolize, or make use of, in the body than the simpler proteins which are derived from vegetables and fruit. In addition, eating some protein helps slow the release of energy-giving calories from plant-derived foods, so a diet consisting of up to a third animal protein helped provide early man with a consistent supply of calories. Hunting also required cooperation, which accelerated the evolution of language and communication. It was only a matter of a few thousand years before prehistoric humans took their next

△ **Group effort**
Some prehistoric people hunted in groups to obtain meat, often from huge animals such as woolly mammoths. It is thought a high-protein diet may have led to increased height among hunters.

▷ **How the upper class ate**
Just as in most early cultures, meat was a sign of wealth in ancient Egypt. This relief from a princess's tomb at Saqqara, dated at around 2330 BCE, shows servants with a haunch of beef.

▽ **Hunting as status**
Although most meat in 1st-century Rome came from livestock, hunting remained a popular leisure pursuit of the elite. Killing a wild animal such as a boar linked the hunter with power.

great evolutionary step—domesticating livestock, either by rearing captured individual animals in fixed settlements or herding and controlling them as part of a nomadic lifestyle. However it occurred, a reliable supply of meat became a part of the human experience.

> Scraps found in drains in Pompeii have revealed that more well-to-do people ate exotic meats such as giraffe.

From what historians and scientists can piece together, raising livestock began about 10,500 years ago in the Fertile Crescent, the region we know today as encompassing Iran, Turkey, Syria, and Iraq. Sheep were among the first animals to be domesticated for meat, bred from wild sheep. Around the same time, and in the same region, goats were bred from the wild bezoar ibex, and cattle were domesticated from now-extinct wild aurochs. Cattle were traded in Europe about 6,400 years ago and in China, Mongolia, and Korea roughly 1,000 years after that. By this time, yaks had also been domesticated in Tibet.

On the other side of the globe, just 500 years after cattle domestication, the ancestors of modern chickens were bred from jungle fowl in Southeast Asia. A relative latecomer, the pig was first domesticated between 9,000 and 10,000 years ago in two places: what is now modern-day Turkey and in China's Mekong Valley. Pork has remained the most popular meat in China ever since. Most livestock was not primarily kept for meat, but for the production of milk or eggs. One exception was the pig, which is difficult to milk; another was the turkey, which lays far fewer eggs than chickens. But from the 18th century onward, farmers began to focus on raising animals for meat as much as for their by-products. English agriculturist Robert Bakewell was an innovator in the science of selectively breeding cattle and sheep for meat. In the mid-18th century, at his family farm in Leicestershire, he developed the Leicestershire Longhorn cattle, which were poor milk-makers but good meat producers, and the Leicestershire sheep, which boasted a high yield of succulent meat. Bakewell's efforts laid the foundation for modern meat production.

Post-war farming boom

After World War II, intensive farming of meat began in earnest, in part to compensate for shortages caused by the conflict. However, when bovine spongiform encephalopathy (BSE) broke out in British cattle in the mid-1980s, producers and consumers began to rethink some of the unsanitary and unsafe practices of the meat industry. This sparked a revival in traditional organic farming methods, as well as an interest in wild meats such as venison, game birds, and rabbit.

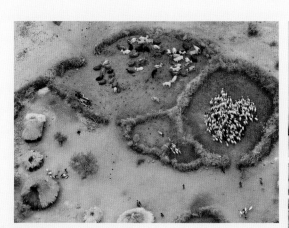

△ **Tried-and-tested protection**
Bomas, or livestock enclosures made of thorn bushes, are still used by Masai tribes in Africa. Similar corrals were used by the earliest herdsman to protect animals from nocturnal predators.

△ **Early breed management**
By selectively breeding Longhorn cattle, Englishman Robert Bakewell emphasized their meat-producing qualities and revolutionized stockbreeding.

◁ **Long pedigree**
DNA tests show that farmed pig breeds in China are direct descendents of the animals that were first domesticated there during the Neolithic age.

Beef most prized of meats

In their long history, beef cattle have proven to be one of the most useful of all domesticated livestock, providing meats for a rich variety of dishes, from the most tender filet mignon to a tasty hamburger.

In the caves of Lascaux in southwestern France, 17,000-year-old rock paintings depict the hunt for black aurochs, the extinct ancestor of today's beef cattle. Native to North Africa and Eurasia, the auroch was one of the earliest animals to be domesticated, and for good reason. Aurochs provided not only meat but milk, blood, and fat, as well as hides for clothing and hair, horns, hooves, and bones for making tools. In their domesticated form, they also doubled as beasts of burden to pull ploughs and carts.

In ancient times, the beef consumed would typically have been from animals that had reached the end of their working life, and required slow cooking in broth to break down the tough sinews. Cooks in medieval France held that roasting beef would dry it out whereas boiling beef would make it moist, laying the foundations for a culinary tradition of stews such as *boeuf bourgignon*. Prime cuts, which usually only the rich could afford, needed little cooking to produce a tender, flavorful result, and were therefore best served rare or

> ## "Bring the fattened calf and kill it. Let's have a feast and celebrate."
>
> THE PARABLE OF THE PRODIGAL SON, LUKE 15:23

medium rare. Steak tartare, first popularized in France in the 19th century, takes this idea to the extreme. A dish of raw chopped beef bound with a raw egg, it relies on the prime part of the carcass, the tenderloin—the least exercised muscle of the animal—from which filet mignon is also cut. The muscles of the legs and neck of the animal work the hardest, so the cuts from these parts, such as brisket and chuck steak, tend to be tougher and therefore require longer cooking. Animals younger than six months old are butchered as veal.

The quest for tenderness

The Japanese have a special approach to rearing beef cattle in order to achieve maximum tenderness. The animals are raised in small numbers on a grain diet, predominantly indoors, a method that echoes the ancient Egyptian practice of keeping beef cattle inside in stalls. The latter were fed by hand and mainly reared for religious sacrifice—beef for human consumption was considered an extravagant delicacy. *Tajima-gyu*, a strain of the famous Japanese Wagyu cattle breed, is the most expensive beef in the world. Raised under a strict protocol for at least 30 months, it must achieve a specific amount of fat marbling before

△ **Leg of veal**
The wealthy of ancient Sumeria (modern-day Iraq) and ancient Rome indulged in veal—meat from young male calves of dairy stock. In later centuries, it became popular in European cuisine.

Origins
Eurasia, North Africa

Major producers
US, Brazil, China

Main food component
21 percent protein

Source of
Iron, vitamin B3, vitamin B12

Non-food use
Leather goods

Scientific name
Bos taurus

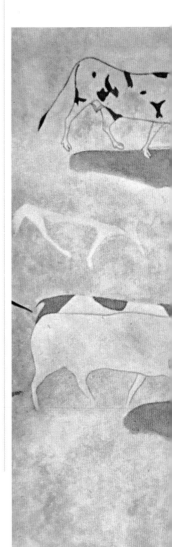

▷ **Texas beef**
Stockmen urge Texas-reared beef cattle to climb the ramp into a cattle truck, ready for transport on the Kansas Pacific railway to Colorado.

it can be approved as Wagyu beef. The finest grade of Wagyu beef is so tender that it is often served raw and finely sliced, sashimi-style.

Vying with Japan as a producer of premier-quality beef, Argentina lays claim to some of the best meat in the world, and its people eat more beef per head than any other nationality. Argentine cattle, descendants of cattle brought from Spain in the 16th century by conquistador Pedro de Mendoza, are raised on the grass that grows on the country's vast lowland plains.

Beef on a bun

By the 19th century, cattle were being raised for beef in Texas. They were fattened in feed lots before being sent north to Chicago for slaughter. Around the same time, one of the great American food traditions was born. Ground beef, extended with bread crumbs and onions, was served as a cheap meal to immigrants sailing from Hamburg in Germany to North America. Called Hamburg steak, the dish was reinvented on US shores. The most famous variation made its debut at the 1904 World's Fair in St. Louis, Missouri. Minced beef served on a bun, the hamburger quickly became an American classic.

▽ **Ancient cattle**
This ancient rock painting from Tassili n'Ajjer in the Sahara Desert depicts two breeds of cattle, one of which has the lyre-shaped horns of the now-extinct auroch.

Rearing meat

It is believed that humans started domesticating animals more than 10,000 years ago. As herd animals, cattle, sheep, and goats were the first to be reared for food, and cattle and sheep have remained main sources of meat for cultures all across the globe.

Cattle ranching in the Americas began in the early 16th century, when Mexican *vaqueros,* or cowboys, started herding longhorns imported by the Spanish. After Texas won its independence from Mexico in 1836, its cowboys took over from the *vaqueros,* and by 1865, around 5 million cattle roamed the open range. Thousands of them were herded along the Chisholm and Abilene trails to railroad hubs such as Abilene, Texas, and Wichita, Kansas. From there, the animals were shipped by rail to stockyards and slaughter-houses in Chicago and Kansas City. More meat was processed in Chicago than anywhere else on the planet, and by 1885, 35 "cattle barons" owned 1.5 million head of cattle.

Cattle ranching was also growing in many South American countries, notably in Brazil, Argentina, and Uruguay. In Australia, too, cattle became a way of life. The Kidman estate there, for example, remains the largest cattle operation in the world; one of its 11 "stations," is larger than Belgium.

What beef was for Australia, lamb became for New Zealand. In the late 1800s, sheep farming became the country's most important agricultural industry. Wool, already a valuable export, was joined in the 1880s by mutton and lamb when the first refrigerated ships came into service. Consumption has declined in recent years, however; in 2015, just 28.6 million sheep roamed the country, compared to 57.9 million in 1990.

◁ **Cattle drive**
Despite a decrease in available grazing, ranches like Arizona's Three-V still drove huge herds across miles of open range in the late 1940s.

Lamb and goat
the first domesticated meat

Sheep were the first animals to be domesticated for food, 11,000 years ago. Often herded alongside their close relative, the goat, they provided tender spring lamb and flavorful mutton in conditions where beef cattle could not thrive.

▽ **Mountain trail**
A young goatherd moves his charges to new pastures high in the Sierra Nevada mountains of Spain's Andalusia region.

The stories of lamb and goat are intertwined. In the Zagros Mountains of Iraq and Iran, archaeologists have found evidence of humans herding sheep and goats by 8000 BCE, and before that of humans hunting the wild animals. Goat and sheep herding spread through Africa and Asia because they could survive on the sparse vegetation of dry mountainous terrain.

From Babylon to Barbados
Three Babylonian clay tablets have been found in Iraq, inscribed with recipes written around 1700 BCE, among them lamb stew made with beer and onion. Ancient Egyptians cooked lamb with spices such as coriander, cumin, and garlic. The Romans preferred pork to lamb, and yet the Roman cookbook *Apicius*, compiled in the 4th–5th centuries CE, devoted an entire chapter to lamb. The practice of cooking lamb and goat with fruit became entrenched in the Middle East. The

△ **Head count**
This Sumerian clay tablet from Mesopotamia (present-day Iraq) dated *c.*2350 BCE is inscribed with the number of goats and sheep accounted for.

10th-century Middle Eastern cookbook *Kitāb al-Ṭabīkh* recommended roasted or stewed lamb and goat for spring. Some recipes were simple—pieces of lamb or goat threaded onto sticks and grilled as kebabs—while others were far richer. Arab invaders then brought their style of cooking to the Mughal Empire in India, where the influence is evident in cinnamon-infused lamb biryani and cardamom-spiced goat curry. That Arab influence was also felt in Spain in the Middle Ages, when the occupying Moors brought spices, citrus fruits, dried fruits, and nuts and used them in lamb dishes.

The Spanish introduced lamb and goat to Mexico, Central, and South America, and the British, French, and Dutch brought them to North America, while Indian immigrants took goat curry to the Caribbean. The British also took sheep to Australia and New Zealand, where today there are six sheep for every person.

LAMB

Origins
Middle East

Major producers
China, Australia, India

Main food component
20 percent protein

Source of
Vitamin B3, vitamin B12, selenium

Non-food uses
Wool, sheepskin

Scientific name
Ovis aries

◁ **Sacrificial lamb**
Lamb has great significance for Christianity. This 13th-century illustration of a butcher's market stall is from Ulrich of Richental's chronicle of Germany's Ecumenical Council of Constance.

▷ **The good shepherd**
Although they are hardy animals, sheep need the care of a shepherd and must be protected from predators.

New Zealand's first sheep were brought ashore by British explorer and navigator Captain James Cook in 1773.

Pork and wild boar

meat that divides cultures

Swine in their various forms have withstood the test of time, running the gamut from adored to reviled to become the most widely consumed meat on the planet. There are around 1 billion pigs in the world, roughly half of which are in China.

The story of pork is one of love and hate: enjoyed by billions over the centuries, but shunned by others for reasons of religion or health. Historically, pork meat was a staple food of peasants, since pigs could be fed on household scraps and required very little space—unlike cattle and sheep. They were also prolific breeders, and the meat preserved well, unlike chicken, a pig's nearest rival for household rearing.

◁ **Origin of the species**
The wild boar has a thicker, more bristly coat, larger head, and longer, straighter tail than its cousin and ancestor the domesticated pig.

Meat of mixed fortunes

The pig is descended from the wild boars that once roamed prehistoric Europe and Asia. They were hunted by early humans, but were first domesticated around 9,000–10,000 years ago in eastern Anatolia (now Turkey) and China, where a pig's high fat content enhanced the animal's value as it also offered cooking oil as a by-product. From Anatolia, the domesticated pig spread through Europe, the Middle East, and North Africa, and into eastern Asia from China, becoming a vital supply of meat for farming communities.

By around 1000 BCE, however, the rearing of pigs was in decline in the Middle East, as the chicken rose in popularity as an easy source of protein. Pigs require much more water than hens to produce the same volume of meat, so in a dry climate it made sense to favor chicken over pork. For Jews, the pig was damned as an unclean animal in the laws of Judaism, laid out particularly in the Old Testament book of Leviticus, written around 700 BCE. The Muslim religion then followed suit in the 7th century CE, with swine declared unclean in the words of the Qu'ran. Early Christians adhered to the Judaistic ban on pork until it was lifted at the Council of Jerusalem in around 50 CE.

The ancient Greeks and Romans had no such qualms about pigs. Like the Chinese, they valued the animal's fat content, especially the pork crackling that developed during roasting. Indeed, the 1st-century CE Roman gourmet Marcus Gavius Apicius, whose recipes were compiled three to four centuries later, described a crackling technique in which the skin is removed and placed over a layer of dough to improve the crisping.

The lure of the suckling pig

In 1539, when Spanish explorer Hernando de Soto landed at Tampa Bay in what is now Florida, he disembarked with 13 pigs in tow, among other animals brought from Europe. A few of the pigs escaped and ran wild—the ancestors of today's feral razorbacks—but the majority were contained and bred. Within a few years there was a herd of 700, the founding pigs of the American pork industry.

△ **Breeds on show**
British pig breeds include (clockwise from bottom left) the Large White, Small White, Berkshire boar, Tamworth sow, and Large Black. Specific breeds have gained in popularity.

DOMESTIC PIG

Origins
Turkey, China

Major producers
China, US, Brazil

Main food component
26 percent protein

Source of
Vitamins B1, B2, and B3, selenium, zinc, phosphorus

Non-food uses
Cosmetics, medicine (insulin), shoes (suede)

Scientific name
Sus scrofa domesticus

These pigs also found a new political role as peace offerings to Native Americans, who developed a fondness for succulent suckling pork, introduced from Spain, where it is called *cochinillo asado* and is a delicacy from the Castile region. The recipe calls for a piglet, between two and six weeks old, still being fed on its mother's milk before it is slaughtered, which is then cooked in a clay dish over an oak fire or on a spit over a charcoal fire. The recipe, which has its roots in ancient China and Rome, has remained a favorite among pork lovers, including the American writer Ernest Hemingway, who would devour suckling pig at his favorite Castilian restaurant in Madrid.

Hunted for sport and food

Even after its descendants were domesticated, the wild boar was still hunted. Romans used the hunt both for food and as a training exercise for battle. In the Middle Ages, hunting of wild boar was fashionable as a sport in many countries, including Persia, India, and Japan, where the pursuit of the boar—a symbol of both fertility and prosperity—was as culturally important as it was vital for surviving the winter.

Today, the wild boar is one of the world's most widespread mammals and is still commonly hunted. In England, where the wild boar was pursued to extinction by the mid 17th century, the animal was reintroduced in the 1980s and now numbers around 4,000. The boar is also increasingly bred in captivity for its meat, which is leaner than pork with a stronger, more gamey flavor.

△ **Japanese boar hunt**
Samurai warriors were renowned for their bravery and strength, and this woodblock print of a 16th-century Samurai warrior tackling a huge boar reinforces that ideal.

"The well-fed suckling pig did crackle, roasting."

ATHENAEUS, *THE DEIPNOSOPHISTS*, 3RD CENTURY CE

BACON

Origins
Worldwide

Major producers (bacon
and ham)
The Netherlands,
Denmark, US

Main food component
40 percent fat

Source of
Sodium, zinc, vitamin B3

Bacon and other cured meats _preserved for flavor_

From salted pork belly in China to air-dried beef in Lombardy, cured meats have sustained civilizations through lean winter months and tantalized the palettes of ancient and modern gourmets.

Before the days of refrigerators, freezers, and cold storage, meat either had to be consumed quickly, before it rotted, or somehow preserved to be eaten later. The preservation of flesh was particularly important to provide nourishment in the winter months, during periods of famine, or for peoples and armies on the move. The earliest farmers, about 10,000 years ago, simply used the drying properties of air, but also discovered that meat exposed to smoke lasted longer, the smoke sealing the flesh and acting

"The flesh of these hogs has nearly fifty different flavors."

PLINY THE ELDER, 1ST-CENTURY ROMAN WRITER

as a barrier to bacteria. Layers of fat also helped in the preservation process, so the pig, a fatty, easily reared animal, became the best source of cured meats.

The preserving power of salt

Using salt to preserve meats was pioneered by civilizations thousands of miles apart. In China, it was discovered that salt could provide the means of preserving all kinds of food. Layered with meat in earthenware pots, salt drew out the moisture and stopped the perishing process. The technique is still used in China.

Tribes of southern Africa developed their own way of preserving meat. They cut it into strips, coated it with salt from the region's inland

▷ **Thinly sliced**
The sale of sliced ham and similar products led to the invention of machines that could cut the meat accurately.

salt lakes, and left it out it dry. This curing method was further developed in the 17th century by Dutch settlers who added vinegar, sugar, and coriander to produce biltong. Egypt, too, enjoyed rich natural salt resources. Ancient Egyptians preserved fish and birds, as well as beef and pork, and even put small "meat mummies" into tombs to feed the dead in the afterlife.

Celtic mastery of cured ham

In the alpine regions of the Pyrenees, the Celts developed their own practice of curing meat. They were considered masters at curing hams. The 1st century BCE Greek historian and geographer Strabo praised the quality of the ham from the Pyrenees, as well as hams from the Iberian side of the mountains, which became renowned throughout the Roman Empire, until they were prohibited in the 8th century by the Moorish invaders.

By the 15th century, Italy had become known for meat curing. In Lombardy, bresaola, salted air-cured beef, had become a speciality, and in the Tyrol region, juniper-infused speck evolved.

Bringing home the bacon

Bacon, made from the belly or the back, is cured for fewer days than speck and similar products, and so is essentially raw. It was in the English county of Wiltshire in 1770 that John Harris first began to cure bacon on an industrial scale, using the wet-cure method of immersing the meat in brine. In North America, bacon consumption has been increasing since the late 1990s.

▽ **Hams hung out**
Iberian hams are cured over many months in vast cellars such as this one in Salamanca, Spain.

◁ **Breakfast treat**
Bacon is famous as the partner to eggs in the traditional British breakfast, which has provided morning sustenance for centuries.

Sausages and offal

meat without waste

△ **Sausage maker**
Machines similar to this 19th-century device are still in use today by small-scale sausage makers.

Offal (organ meat) has been consumed by humans since our prehistoric ancestors first started to hunt animals for food—no part of the kill was allowed to go to waste. Sausages came much later as a way of using leftover meat.

Archaeologists have found evidence of fires used for cooking more than a million years ago, yet the earliest humans may have had to survive for centuries without fire. And with no fire to cook it, muscle meat was tough to swallow. Offal, on the other hand, freshly cut from a slaughtered animal, was warm and soft and unrivalled for its concentration of nutrients.

From pâté to sausage

Some of the earliest records relating to offal come from ancient Egypt, where goose liver was produced from force-fed birds, long before the French did the same and gave it the name foie gras. Liver is still a popular street food in Egyptian cities, particularly calves' liver, which is fried and served in pita bread or baguettes, with fresh chili and lime. Goose liver was also on the menu in ancient Greece, and in ancient Rome geese and sows were fattened with figs to enlarge and improve the flavor of their livers. Apart from liver, many other types of offal are eaten the world over, including brains, kidneys, hearts, and lungs.

Both the Greeks and Romans were known to make sausages from ox blood, although the Babylonians of Mesopotamia had been stuffing animal intestines with spiced meats more than 1,000 years earlier. The first literary mention of blood sausage dates back to around 675–725 BCE in the Greek epic *The Odyssey*, in which Homer describes filling intestines with fat and blood. Around the same time that the Romans were enjoying smoked sausages from Lucania in southern Italy, flavored with pepper, cumin, and pine nuts, their Chinese contemporaries were devouring *lap cheong*, sweet-and-savory air-dried sausages, and *yun chang*, made from duck liver. Thailand developed its own sausages in the form of *naem*, a sour fermented pork sausage, and *sai krok isan*, a fermented and grilled pork and rice sausage.

▷ **Renaissance kitchen**
Sausage-making was a December tradition in Italy to provide meat through the winter months. Strings of sausages are being cooked in a huge vat in this 16th-century tapestry.

The word "offal" is derived from "off fall," referring to the meat that falls away during butchering.

As spices from Asia began to arrive in Europe in the Middle Ages, sausage making underwent a revival. In the warmer climate of southern Europe, dry sausages such as the many forms of Italian salami, were preferred because they lasted better in the heat; fresh sausages were made in northern Europe where they were less likely to spoil in cooler weather. By the 19th century, many regions in Europe had their own speciality sausages. Germany developed a huge variety of regional sausages, or *wurst*, such as the marjoram-dominant *Nürnberger Rostbratwurst*, recorded since the 14th century, and the *Weisswurst* of Bavaria, created by a Munich butcher in 1857.

ITALIAN-STYLE SALAMI

Origins
Italy

Major producer
Italy

Main food component
37 percent fat

Source of
Iron, sodium, vitamin B2, vitamin B3, vitamin B12

◁ **Hooked up**
Traditionally cured dried sausages are made in a huge variety of forms from many different meats, including pork, beef, and venison.

Chicken
a worldwide source of mass-produced meat

Outnumbering any other bird on the planet, chickens have provided a convenient high-protein food source, both meat and eggs, since wild junglefowl were first domesticated in South Asia around 8,000 years ago.

Which came first, the chicken or the egg? It food terms, it was the egg—the egg-providing chicken being too valuable to eat. Quite where the chicken originated is debatable. It was probably first bred about 6000 BCE from its wild relative the red junglefowl, but for cockfighting rather than as a food source. Domestication may then have occurred independently across a number of distinct areas in South and Southeast Asia, and southern China.

A luxury meat

Around 2000 BCE, chickens spread westward to the Middle East, Africa, and Europe from the Indus Valley, in what is now Pakistan and northwest India. They also moved eastward to the Polynesian islands and may have even reached South America 200 years before the arrival of European settlers. Although chickens were selectively bred to produce "layers" for eggs and plump "broilers" for meat, it was as a layer that they dominated, with the obvious logic that layers provided a long-term and ongoing source of food. Ancient Egyptians were the frontrunners in the art of egg incubation, creating complexes of chamberlike ovens to keep eggs at the optimum hatching temperature. In most cases, only old male birds and hens

△ **Help with hatching**
As long ago as the 16th century, people were devising ways of ensuring the production of as many chickens as possible. This hatching "machine" dates from 1570.

⊲ **Clay chicken**
Chickens were valuable animals in ancient Rome. This rooster-shaped jug from the 1st century CE is a sign of the importance of these birds.

that were no longer laying viable eggs were killed and eaten. That made chicken meat a rarity, generally only eaten on special occasions or by the rich. In ancient Rome, chickens were bred both for egg laying and for meat. They were the most expensive type of livestock, priced at around nine times the amount paid for beef or mutton. Demand was such that in the 2nd century BCE, laws designed to clamp down on decadence decreed that chickens be limited to one per meal.

The Romans worked out that castrating roosters would encourage them to fatten of their own accord—a type of chicken that became known as a capon. Roman cooks also pioneered new cooking methods that were designed to keep the meat moist.

> Americans eat about 90lb (41kg) per person a year—more than any other nationality.

As the Roman Empire and its organized farming practices declined, so did the fortunes of the chicken, which became smaller and was replaced as a meat on medieval tables by more resilient birds such as geese and partridge. Europeans brought chickens to North America, but in a land already full of turkeys and ducks there was no particular need to breed chickens for meat. In the mid 19th century, however, England's Queen Victoria, a lover of exotic birds and keeper of poultry, was gifted seven Cochin chickens from China, and the introduction

Vögel XXXI.
Fig. 6.
Fig. 8.
Fig. 4.

of this beautiful fluffy-feathered bird proved a turning point in the popularization of the fowl. "Hen fever" gripped England and the USA in the 1850s, with breeders competing with each other to raise the most striking and elegant birds.

Modern methods

Raising chickens for the table remained a small-scale, local occupation, with the birds living outside and roaming free, until the boosting of feed with antibiotics and nutrients in the mid 20th century allowed chickens to be kept indoors in cages and in ever-increasing numbers. A World War II shortage of beef and pork in the US, where chicken was not rationed, led to a three-fold increase in national consumption. The nation's growing taste for chicken was marked by the 1952 opening of the first Kentucky Fried Chicken restaurant. Today, KFC franchises contribute to more than 121 million tons of chicken meat consumed each year, in excess of one-third of all global meat production.

Origins	Asia
Major producers	US, Brazil, China
Main food component	21 percent protein
Source of	Iron, vitamin B6, vitamin B12
Non-food uses	Animal feed, pillow stuffing and paper (feathers)

"Do not count your chickens before they are hatched."

AESOP, GREEK FABLE WRITER, 6TH CENTURY BCE

◁ **Poultry breeds**
An illustration of different poultry breeds shows the variety of breeds available in Germany in the 18th century.

▷ **Food for the army**
In popular myth, the dish chicken marengo was named after the victory of Napoleon at the Battle of Marengo in Italy in 1800.

△ **The first Thanksgiving**
Now firmly associated with Thanksgiving, turkey may not have been part of the first Thanksgiving meal in 1621.

Turkey   Mexico's gift to the world

When the Spanish conquistadors set foot in Mexico in 1519, they found that the indigenous peoples had domesticated one of the native birds. Commonly known as the turkey, it is now an important food source in many parts of the world.

△ **Spectacular plumage**
A fully grown male turkey is an impressive bird, whose colorful plumage and bright red wattle are unmistakable.

Bone remains found around Tehuacán, Mexico, indicate that the earliest human consumption of turkey took place there around 200 BCE–700 CE. It was an important food source for the Maya, whose homelands extended from northern Honduras to southern Mexico. They not only hunted the bird for food, but they used its feathers and bones for ceremonial dress, medicine, and musical instruments. Even today in Mexico, turkey with chocolate-flavored *mole* sauce is considered the national dish.

By the time the Spanish arrived in the 14th century CE, the turkey had spread from its native habitat in the mountainous central plateau of Mexico to the north. Early reports of this large bird with delicious meat filtered back to Europe, and by the 1530s turkeys were being farmed for the delectation of the Spanish upper classes. They were already known in Rome by 1525, and were so sought after by the Italian aristocracy that in 1561 the church banned them from banquets as they were thought to be too luxurious.

"The turkey is … a much more respectable bird, and withal a true original Native of America."

BENJAMIN FRANKLIN, 1784

In England, turkey farming took off in the late 1500s and, as the birds became more affordable for the general public, the first recipes began to appear in print. Boiling was the most common cooking method and the resulting stock used for gravy or sauce. Roasting was also popular, especially using a spit, with the drippings caught underneath for making gravy.

"Carbonating" the bird

English writer Gervaise Markham helped promote turkey even further in his 17th-century cookbooks. He advised fattening turkeys and suggested a variety of cooking methods such as the French technique of "carbonating" (grilling). By the 18th century commercial enterprises were expanding to supply the growing demand, with the English county of Norfolk emerging as the hub of turkey farming. Writers of the time reported seeing the road to London from Norfolk jammed with tens of thousands of turkeys, their feet wrapped in hessian for protection on the long march. The esteemed black Norfolk turkeys were among the cargo on board English colonists' ships to the east coast of North America. When bred with the native wild turkey, the Norfolk blacks became the ancestor to the oldest American breeds: the Narragansett, Bronze, and Slate. Almost every cookbook of the day included sections on turkey, and colonists took these recipes to North America, establishing their own tradition of turkey cooking. The influential 18th-century *Art of Cookery* contained 19 recipes for preparing and stuffing roast turkey, which in North America had become the traditional dish served for Thanksgiving celebrations. Historians question whether turkey was actually served at the Pilgrim's original Thanksgiving dinner, but by the 19th century the celebration was unthinkable without a stuffed turkey as the centerpiece.

The Christmas turkey arrives

In England, the future King Edward VII is credited with having made roast turkey fashionable at Christmas in the late 1800s, but it had probably begun to feature on Victorian festive family dinner tables well before then. In Charles Dickens' popular ghost story, *A Christmas Carol*, which was first published in 1843, Scrooge sends the Cratchits a turkey for Christmas Day, though the family had been saving up for the traditional goose.

More recently, the leanness of turkey meat helped to earn it legions of health-conscious fans in the late 20th century. Turkey bacon became a popular substitute for its high-fat pork counterpart, and turkey salads, stir-fries, and cold turkey for sandwiches brought it into the mainstream for everyday consumption.

△ **Shepherding their flock**
Turkeys were widely farmed in Europe in the 19th century as illustrated in this painting by Italian painter Francesco Paolo Michetti of two children tending their flock.

◁ **To market**
Turkeys were driven down the road to market even in 1930s Britain. The same journey had been made by turkey farmers with their flocks since the 18th century.

Origins
Mexico and Central America

Major producers
US, Brazil, Germany

Main food component
23 percent protein

Source of
Phosphorus, potassium, vitamin B3, vitamin B6

Duck Asia's favorite poultry

From Peking duck in Nanjing to duck *à l'orange* in Paris, the domesticated descendant of the mallard has inspired some of the most exotic dishes to emerge from the kitchens of creative chefs.

The story of duck cuisine essentially belongs to China and its neighbors in Southeast Asia. Some 4,000 years after they first domesticated the wild duck, or mallard, the Chinese still consume more duck than any other nationality, and Peking roast duck is considered their quintessential dish. Although Peking, or Pekin, duck is named after the city that became Beijing, it actually originated in Nanjing, a former imperial capital on the banks of the Yangtze River.

◁ **Wild mallard**
The species from which domestic ducks originate, the mallard can be found in the wild in many regions.

Fit for an emperor
In the imperial capital, the finest chefs in the kingdom devised special dishes to tantalize the palates of the nobility. During the Yuan dynasty (1271–1368), the royal physician to the imperial court, Hu Sihui, wrote a cookbook in 1330 detailing what is thought to be the first recipe for Peking duck. The most important step was fattening the bird over a six-week period. Serving the crispy skin was, and still is, an important part of the dish. Chinese scholars and poets have waxed lyrical over the taste of Peking duck in centuries past, and its legendary status lives on in modern China. When US Secretary of State Henry Kissinger met the Communist leaders in Beijing in 1971 at the height of the Cold War, a stalemate in their talks was broken with a seven-course Peking duck lunch, a move that later became known as "duck diplomacy" and set the scene for détente between the two superpowers.

The Chinese diplomats may not have been aware that the US enclave of Long Island boasted its own celebrated duck breed, the Long Island Duck, descended from nine ducks imported from China in 1873. Roast duckling is famously part of the region's cuisine—so much so that the local professional baseball team is called the Long Island Ducks.

Worldwide appeal
Duck is also popular in many other parts of Asia. In Korea, the duck-based *oritang* soup is a speciality of the city of Gwangju, while in Indonesia a traditional method of preparation is to rub the whole bird in spices and cook it slowly in a terra-cotta pot.

In Europe, French cooks embraced the duck, making foie gras, cassoulet, the Gascon preserved duck speciality confit, and most famously *canard* (duck) *à l'orange*. In fact its origins go back many centuries to the Middle Eastern tradition of balancing the rich fatty flesh of duck with tart fruit, a practice adopted in many countries.

▽ **Increased firepower**
In the early 20th century, punt guns were developed to enable hunters to kill large numbers of waterfowl with a single shot.

MALLARD

Origins
Worldwide

Major producers
China, France, Malaysia

Main food component
18 percent protein

Source of
Zinc, B vitamins

Non-food uses
Cushions, bed coverings (feathers)

Scientific name
Anas platyrhynchos

△ **Calling all ducks**
The enthusiasm for hunting and eating ducks has led to the development of many aids to help the hunter, such as this wooden duck caller.

▷ **Snared in Sicily**
In ancient Rome, ducks may have been caught mainly by snaring as depicted in this 4th-century CE mosaic from Sicily, Italy.

In parts of Asia, stir-fried duck's head is believed to promote brain power.

Banquets and feasting

Luxurious feasts and banquets were common in ancient Egypt, as tomb paintings from Thebes and elsewhere demonstrate. The Greeks, too, were fond of a feast; Homer describes them vividly several times in both *The Iliad* and *The Odyssey*. But the most lavish of all ancient world feasts were those held in Rome.

A typical Roman feast consisted of three courses: the *gestatio* (hors d'oeuvres), the *mensa prima* (main course), and the *mensa secunda* (dessert). Starters included cheeses, olives, eggs, and mushrooms, followed by selections of legumes, boiled or pickled vegetables, steamed greens, and salad. Favored main courses were pheasant, thrush or other songbirds, lobster, shellfish, venison, wild boar, and peacock, while stuffed sow's uterus, rabbit fetuses, peacock tongues, milk-fed snails, pickled sea urchins, boiled parrot, and roasted dormice were common delicacies.

Renaissance feasts were even more elaborate. The food was served in stages, called "removes." Each consisted of several individual dishes, served one after another. The practice continued over subsequent centuries. At a banquet hosted by England's Charles II in 1671, for example, guests were served 145 different dishes during the first course alone. Each course was heralded by the appearance of what in Tudor times were called "subtleties," carried in procession. Some were edible, others were not, but all were awe-inspiring in their complexity. At a 1527 feast held by Cardinal Wolsey for French ambassadors, one of the most spectacular subtleties was a giant chessboard made of sugar paste and complete with all its pieces. It so captivated his guests that the cardinal had it packed up and sent back to France with them.

◁ **Riches on display**
Feasts have been held throughout history to mark occasions such as marriages—and as good opportunities to display one's wealth.

Venison a meat of royal sport

Prehistoric cave drawings of deer, together with antlers found at ancient archaeological sites across the world, reveal that venison has sustained humans for thousands of years.

A meat that has for hundreds of years been associated with the sport of hunting, venison gets its very name from the Latin word for hunting, *venatio*. The native red deer was evidently an important source of food for Neolithic people in Europe, as were fallow deer in the Middle East and western Asia. In North America, for thousands of years before the arrival of Europeans, early indigenous tribes hunted whitetail deer, while sika deer were pursued in eastern Asia.

Meat and mythology
The world's oldest written recipe for venison—stewed in broth with garlic—is inscribed on Babylonian clay tablets dating from around 1750 BCE. Venison was among the meats eaten by the ancient Greeks, perhaps all the more valued because hunting was a rite of passage for aristocratic young men. Wealthy Romans similarly hunted deer for sport. They introduced fallow deer to Britain and created deer parks on their estates. While deer were sacred to both the Greek

▷ **Hunting in disguise**
Deer in North America were hunted by the native tribes wearing deer skins.

hunting goddess Artemis and her Roman counterpart Diana, their meat could be freely enjoyed. However, in Japan, deer were protected as messengers of the gods in the ancient Shinto religion. Elsewhere in Asia, where Buddhism was the main religion, the beliefs of that faith precluded both hunting and consumption of meat.

A noble dish
In Europe, deer hunting again became the preserve of the elite in medieval times. Venison—valued for its rich flavor and served roasted, boiled, baked, and in soups and stews—featured on the menus of royalty and nobility throughout the ensuing centuries. The tasty meat still retains a somewhat aristocratic image in Europe but, mainly because of an increase in deer farming, is now readily available and considered an especially good source of lean protein.

SIKA DEER

Origins
Asia

Main food component
22 percent protein

Good source of
Iron, vitamins B1, B3

Scientific name
Cervus nippon

▽ **Chinese chase**
The Chinese nobility—whose religion, Confucianism, did not prohibit hunting—enjoyed the pursuit of deer.

Rabbit and hare
food source and agricultural pest

Unlike most other livestock, which has been bred for food for thousands of years, the rabbit was not domesticated until the 5th century. A staple food for all classes in medieval Europe, it has since infiltrated most other parts of the globe.

EUROPEAN RABBIT

Origins
Europe

Main food component
19 percent protein

Source of
Iron, vitamin B3

Scientific name
Oryctolagus cuniculus

When Phoenician seafarers from the eastern Mediterranean landed on the shores of the Iberian peninsula around 3,000 years ago, they were struck by the population of wild rabbits they encountered. According to one theory, they named the land Hispania, meaning "island of the rabbit," incorporating the Phoenician word for rabbit, *span*. Hispania became

> Baby rabbits cut from the womb were deemed by the pope to be "aquatic" and so approved as Lenten fare in the Middle Ages.

España in Spanish and Spain in English, both names honoring the native wild rabbit. After Spain became part of the Roman Empire around 200 BCE, some coins depicted rabbits as symbolic of Spain. Coinage from the reign of the Emperor Hadrian, whose ancestors were Spanish, depicted the ruler on one side and a rabbit on the other, sitting at the foot of a female figure who represented Spain.

Food for the monastery table
The Romans began to farm wild rabbits for their fur and meat, eventually introducing them to other parts of Europe. In 5th-century France, monks started to breed rabbits selectively, and during the Middle Ages rabbit breeding for food

▷ **Fast mover**
Hares are fast runners, making them a special challenge for hunters who often use dogs to flush them out of their hiding places.

△ **Ready for the pot**
This scene of a 16th-century Flemish kitchen interior includes a rabbit hanging on a wall ready to be skinned and cooked. At this time, rabbit was widely eaten throughout Europe in stews and pies.

and fur expanded across Europe. Hare, a slightly larger member of the rabbit family, was also widely hunted and consumed, and dishes such as jugged hare and lièvre à la royale were created for the aristocracy.

Colonial expansion by European countries introduced the rabbit to many parts of the world, causing devastation to native habitats, notoriously in Australia. In China, rabbit became a popular meat in the southern province of Sichuan, where spicy rabbit head is still considered a delicacy. In Europe, eating rabbit meat declined among the middle classes in the 20th century, but it remained an important source of food for poorer folk.

Quail, partridge, and pheasant ground-feeding game birds

These three game birds, as the name implies, are hunted for sport, but quail, partridge, and pheasants have also provided food from the wild long before domesticated fowl such as chicken reached most parts of the globe.

COMMON PHEASANT

Origins
Asia

Main food component
24 percent protein

Source of
Iron, vitamin B3

Scientific name
Phasianus colchicus

The quail, partridge, and pheasant are three of the most popular game birds in culinary history. Of the trio, the quail is the most widespread because, unlike the other two, it is a migratory bird. Quail bone remains have been found in rock shelters used by early human hunter-gatherers in Europe thousands of years ago, although how the birds were caught is not known. Around 3000 BCE, the ancient Egyptians caught wild quail in large numbers using nets. The 5th-century BCE Greek historian Herodotus noted that they air-dried and salted birds were eaten raw. The Greeks themselves, and the Romans, used quail for cock fighting rather than food. This was probably due to the risk of poisoning—if a quail eats seeds from a poisonous plant, the toxins build up in its fat reserves.

Records of breeding quail date to about 770 BCE in China. By the 11th century CE, the domesticated quail was being raised in Korea and Japan, where this bird also found an appreciative audience for its singing skills. The Japanese spent several centuries selectively breeding quail for their voices, and by the mid 18th century, the quail craze was in full swing, with enthusiasts competing fiercely to produce the bird with the most tuneful trill.

▷ **The artful pheasant**
Pheasant was a favorite of Victorian dining tables. The cock was admired for its looks and was showcased in a variety of presentation dishes.

In Europe, wild quail were netted on a seasonal basis, caught as they flew low over coastal areas on their migration path. Eventually, with the development of more sophisticated rifles, shooting replaced netting in the 18th and 19th centuries. Quail were typically eaten whole and cooked quickly, roasted or grilled, with plenty of fat to stop them drying out. The same principle applied to other game birds, because their meat tends to be lean.

Ottoman favorite

Unlike most quails, partridges live on the ground and do not migrate, making them easier to catch. The dominant European species is the gray partridge, but Turkey is home to three species and has held partridge in high esteem for many centuries. Hunting and eating partridge was a favored pursuit of sultans of the Ottoman Empire (1299–1922), and the bird appears as a motif in traditional folk art, poetry, and song. The local word for partridge, *keklik*, is reflected in the name of many Turkish villages, where partridges have traditionally been reared and released for hunting.

One of the largest of the game birds, the pheasant has also been hunted since the Stone Age. A short-distance flyer offering more meat than its smaller counterparts, the pheasant was introduced to Europe from Asia, probably before 1000 BCE. The Romans bred them for food, spreading a taste for them to France and Britain as their empire expanded. In England, pheasant were held in high esteem and featured on medieval banquet tables. Their striking appearance later made them a favorite of shooting parties, especially in England and North America.

△ **Journey's end**
The tradition of catching migrating quail has persisted for some 5,000 years, as this sketch of quail being rounded up in Syria in 1862 illustrates.

▽ **Flight of fancy**
The Minoan palace of Knossos on Crete was decorated with beautiful frescoes. This 20th-century reproduction of one depicting partridges also features some fancifully colored eggs.

> "On the First day of Christmas my true love sent to me: a Partridge in a Pear Tree."

"THE TWELVE DAYS OF CHRISTMAS," TRADITIONAL ENGLISH CAROL (1780)

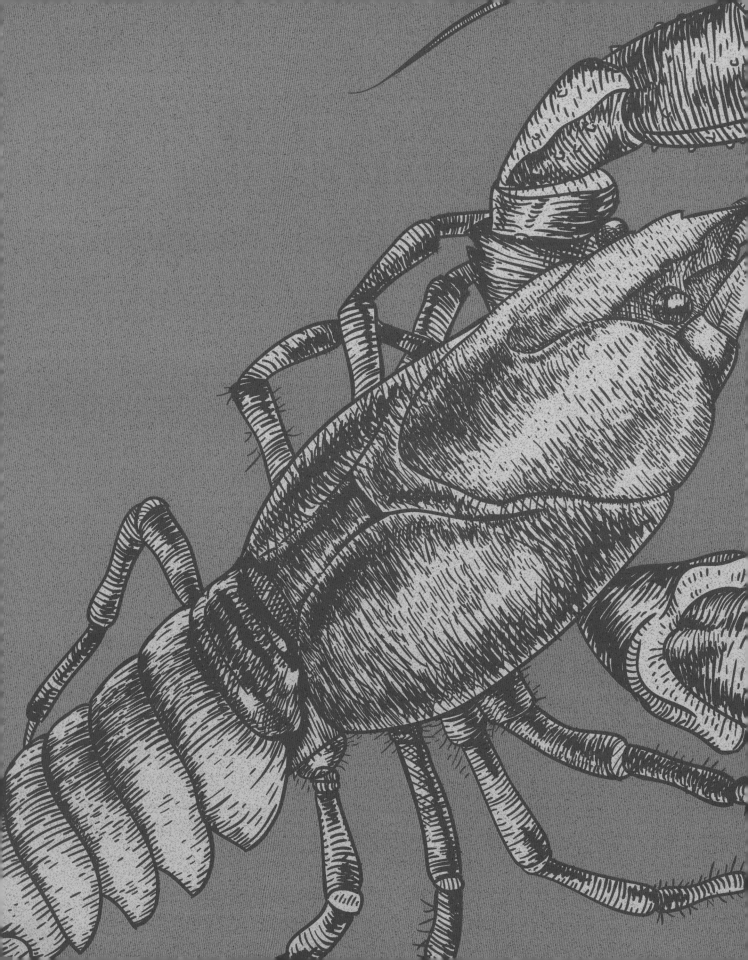

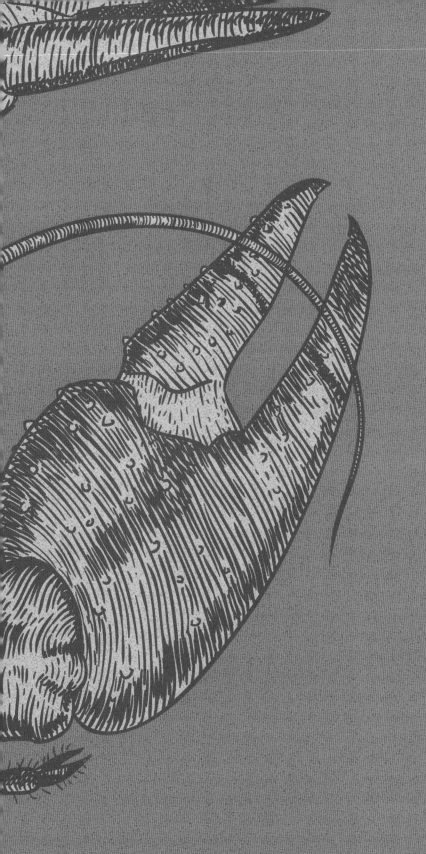

Fish and Shellfish

Fish and shellfish

Long before our ancestors had mastered the techniques required to catch fish, they had developed a distinct taste for them. From the earliest stages of their development, ancient humans picked seafood from rocks, gathered fish washed up in storms, snatched shallow swimmers from the shoreline, or grabbed salmon as they leapt from the water on their way to spawn. But in order to extend their fishing skills, humans required equipment: they had to learn how to fashion boats and to craft nets, baskets, harpoons, hooks, and lines. Fish have the advantage in their aquatic home territory since humans are out of their comfort zone. Fish can move faster, know where to hide, and can travel vast distances. Humans had to learn how to outwit them, and that took time.

The beginnings of angling

Caves in South Africa attest to consumption of shellfish and shallow-water fish 140,000 years ago, but the earliest proof of fishing with hooks has been found in East Timor, in Southeast Asia. Here archaeologists unearthed more than 38,000 fish bones, along with fish hooks made from shells that are estimated to be between 16,000 and 20,000 years old. In North America, evidence reveals that people fished for salmon at least 11,500 years ago, with some cultures relying almost entirely on fish for survival. The Inuit people of the Arctic Circle, for example, developed skills for preserving fish to ensure a year-round supply of food, even in the harshest conditions.

Gradually, over hundreds of years, our ancestral anglers learned to adapt their technical skills in order to lure in different types of fish, tailoring both tackle and bait to suit the habits and preferences of a wide variety of prey species. They quickly learned that salmon could be netted, caught by hand, or speared in the shallows in which they spawned. Tilapia could easily be netted from the shore, and could also be encouraged to reproduce in confined, man-made pools. In lagoons and clear, calm waters, spearfishing was one of the most physically as well as technically demanding skills, requiring both keen eyesight and lightning reflexes. In some parts of the world, more unusual methods of

△ **Captured in art**
Fish have been revered and consumed by people for millennia. Cave carvings of salmon were made as early as 25,000 years ago.

▷ **Recreational fishing**
By the 19th century, fishing for sport had become popular in Europe and North America. Species such as trout became trophies as well as food.

fishing developed. One of these is *ukai*, the Japanese practice of fishing with trained cormorants, which was developed around 1,300 years ago and is still being used today.

Roman fishing techniques

The scholars of ancient Rome have provided historians with a rich source of information about early fishing methods. Writing in the 1st and 2nd centuries CE, Pliny the Elder, Ovid, and Oppian devoted entire works to fishing. Both Pliny and Oppian refer to "fish-aggregation devices": floating objects—usually placed in the sea—which were designed to attract fish. When the fish gathered around these objects, they became easy targets for anglers. A more unusual tactic involved wading out into the sea armed with nets or spears, then shouting to lure dolphins in from the sea. The dolphins inadvertently drove schools of fish toward shore, where they were easily caught. The dolphins were rewarded with food—including bread dipped in wine, according to Pliny.

Ancient civilizations also farmed fish. The earliest proof of this dates to 3500 BCE in China, where carp were bred in freshwater ponds and waterlogged rice paddies. A millennium later, ancient Egyptians were farming tilapia in purpose-built pools along the shores of the Nile. Indonesians adopted a similar technique during the 11th century by trapping young milkfish in coastal ponds when the tide came in, then transferring them to prepared seawater pools: one of the first examples of marine aquaculture.

Modern fish farming began in the mid-1700s, when German farmer Stephan Ludwig Jacobi manually fertilized trout from the river on his land and successfully hatched the eggs. Despite advances in aquaculture since then, however, trawling has become the modern method of choice for harvesting fish.

> Between 1980 and 2010, more fish were harvested from fish farms than were caught in the wild.

The problem of overfishing

The Dutch pioneered the fishing trawler in the 15th century, followed by additional developments by the British in the 17th century. Yet it was the advent of large-scale commercial fleets with industrial methods from the 1960s onward that drastically depleted the fish stocks of the world's oceans in the late 20th century. Consumer demand for a variety of fish at cheap prices, coupled with the phenomenal popularity of sushi, has only increased the problem. Restricting fleet fishing and investing in aquaculture seem the only viable options if the sea is to regenerate its supplies of fish.

△ **Trawling for food**
Dragging nets behind boats to catch hundreds of fish at once has been done for centuries—even in freezing, rough conditions such as the North Sea.

▷ **Ancient tradition**
Divers hunt for fish with traditional spears in the coral reefs of Melanesia, as humans have done around the world since Paleolithic times.

▽ **Farming in the snow**
As wild fish stocks have plummeted, more fish farms have been created around the world to meet demand, including salmon farms in Iceland.

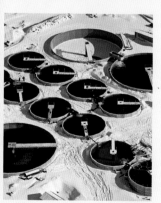

◁ **A fine fish**
Salmon can weigh up
to 104lb (47kg) and
are prized by anglers.

ATLANTIC SALMON
Origins North Atlantic
Main food component 20 percent protein
Source of Omega-3 and omega-6 fatty acids
Non-food uses Medicinal (oil)
Scientific name *Salmo salar*

Salmon the amazing freshwater–saltwater fish

Prized for thousands of years for its distinctive hot-pink color, delicate flavor, and culinary versatility, the salmon has been elevated to superfood status in modern times thanks to its omega-3 fatty acid content.

English writer and experienced rodman Izaac Walton described the salmon as "the King of freshwater fish" in his 1653 book *The Compleat Angler*. He may have been thinking of the dense pink flesh or the ease with which salmon could be caught during the spawning season, when they swim upriver from the sea to lay their eggs. What he may not have known is just how clever the salmon is. Using skills honed over millions of years, the fish is able to assess water speed and water and gravel depth to decide the optimum place to lay its eggs. Different species have even adapted to different parts of the same river, so they do not infringe on one another's breeding territory.

The English cooks of Walton's day would certainly have been well aware of the versatility of salmon as a food. The *Gentyll manly Cokere* (c.1500) book of recipes included "samon rostyd in sause," in which salmon is roasted on a griddle, then served with a sauce of wine, cinnamon, onions, vinegar, and ginger. In 1585, English cook Thomas Dawson championed the unusual "salmon and onion salad with violets" in his book *The Good Huswifes Jewell*, while French-trained chef to the aristocracy Robert May advocated poaching salmon whole in orange juice, wine, and nutmeg, as detailed in his book *The Accomplisht Cook* (1660).

A tale of two oceans
The salmon used in these recipes was the Atlantic salmon. A single species (*Salmo salar*—*salmo*, meaning "to leap" and *salar*, meaning "salt"), the fish is native to European waters and the eastern seaboard of North America, from western Greenland to Quebec in Canada and Connecticut in the US. Ancient evidence of Atlantic salmon consumption appears in a 25,000-year-old cave painting at the Abri du Poisson rock shelter, along the Vézère River in the Dordogne region of France, which depicts a salmon 3⅓ft (1m) long in great detail. On the same river, evidence has been found that humans modified the waterway with pools for catching salmon 12,000 years ago.

△ **Skilled fishermen**
The Columbia River in Washington state was teeming with Pacific salmon in the 19th century, providing a source of sustenance for the American Indian tribes.

▷ **Salmon spear**
This barbed three-pronged copper leister was used by Inuit of the central and eastern Arctic to spear migrating salmon they had trapped with stone weirs.

> After it spawns once, a Pacific salmon dies, whereas the Atlantic salmon can spawn again and again.

◁ **Basket traps**
On the Severn River in England, traditional salmon-fishing methods using conical willow "putcher" baskets survived well into the 20th century.

The world's largest ocean is the breeding ground for the Pacific salmon, of which there are several species, all of which occur naturally in parts of the North Pacific. American Indians fished this salmon 9,000 years ago, and archaeological finds at Prince Rupert harbor in British Columbia, Canada, reveal that from 500 BCE to 1000 CE the local inhabitants almost exclusively ate Pacific mammals and salmon. When European settlers arrived they found the fish so plentiful that they apparently soon tired of eating it.

In Japan, salmon were symbolic, as well as a staple food, for the indigenous Ainu people of the island of Hokkaido. They regarded the first salmon of the year as divine messengers and sited their villages along rivers known to have good salmon runs. Each household preserved as many as 2,000 fish to store for lean times. The Ainu also had at least 10 words for salmon, depending on different features of the fish, such as sex, developmental stage, and size.

human body can absorb more of the protein. In 1995, the *Journal of the American Medical Association* published research indicating that one weekly serving of salmon, or any other oily fish, could reduce the risk of heart disease and some cancers in humans. This study provided early evidence of a new role for salmon as a health-boosting food. The fish contains high levels of omega-3 fatty acids, which have been shown to lower blood pressure, reduce fat in the blood, and reduce the risk of blood clots.

The benefits of smoking

The discovery of the high omega-3 levels in salmon helped to explain why the Inuit people of North America and Greenland have long enjoyed such good health, despite a diet that lacks fruit and vegetables and the nutrients they contain. The Inuit's salmon-rich diet is an important factor in a low incidence of autoimmune and inflammatory disorders, such as the skin disorder psoriasis, thanks to the anti-inflammatory effects of the omega-3 fatty acids in the fish. Since wild salmon are a seasonal catch, mainly in spring and summer, the Inuit developed smoking

Acid partnership

Centuries of culinary history reveal a common thread, not just in how salmon is prepared but what it is served with. Whether baked, grilled, poached, or smoked, the mild-flavored, oily fish has long been paired with acidic partners such as fresh lemon and white wine in Northern Europe; vodka in Russia; preserved lemon in the spicy herb paste chermoula in North Africa; or fresh tomato in Hawaii's *lomi lomi* dish, introduced to the island by early western sailors. These acidic partners not only provide flavor and counterbalance to the oil in the fish, they also help to break down the extracellular protein in salmon's connective tissue, which means the

> ## "Cider and tinned salmon are the staple diet of the agricultural classes."
>
> EVELYN WAUGH, *SCOOP* (1938)

◁ **Canned delicacy**
A Spanish advertisement featuring a "fish waiter" celebrates the quality of canned salmon.

techniques to preserve the fish and ensure a year-round supply. During the long winters, they were almost completely dependent on smoked fish.

With no trees to provide fuel for their fires, the Inuit of Greenland used heather for smoking the fish. This was traditionally carried out in a smokehouse—a small shack that protected the fish from scavenging seabirds. Burning at low temperatures, the smoking process was slow, keeping the fish soft. The fish was dried out as much as possible prior to smoking, and then salted—a crucial step in the process because without it the fish would sour or spoil. Some North American tribes would dry out the fish in the sun and wind instead of smoking it, or sometimes use a combination of both methods.

In Scandinavia, a different method of preservation resulted in the salmon dish gravlax, from the Norse words *grav*, meaning "coffin" or "hole in the ground," and *lax*, meaning "salmon." In the Middle Ages, fishermen would cure the salmon by burying it in sand along the shoreline and allowing the salty water to wash over it. Today, the fish is marinated in salt, sugar, and dill, and served with a mustard sauce that no medieval Norseman would have recognized.

When refrigerated transport was developed in the 1840s, the demand for heavily salted and smoked salmon declined. Instead, more tender types of soft-smoked salmon became a delicacy, with different flavors achieved depending on the location, curing ingredients, and the fuel used for smoking. Russians cured theirs with sugar and vodka; the Scots smoked salmon over fires of oak and beech; while in England, smokehouses in the capital developed the "London Cure," a lightly smoked salmon that was soft and mild.

In the late 19th century, Jewish immigrants from Poland brought smoked salmon New York, where Jewish communities then devised their own preserving technique, using a cure of salt and sugar to create lox, most famously paired with cream cheese on a bagel.

▷ **French innovation**
In the 1840s French fisherman Joseph Remy joined forces with cabinet-maker Antoine Géhin to devise these boxes for rearing young salmon—a milestone in fish farming.

△ **Cured by smoke**
Salmon are traditionally smoked suspended on rails over slow-burning wood.

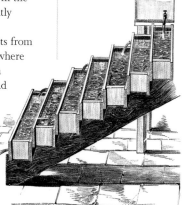

Catfish firm-fleshed fish of coasts and rivers

Named for its whiskered face and the purring sound it makes when caught, the catfish is the key ingredient in a variety of local fish dishes from West Africa to Southeast Asia and in the American South.

Fish from the vast Siluriformes order, to which the many species of catfish belong, are eaten more often than any other fish on the planet, in part because the group is so diverse and widespread. Catfish live in rivers and coastal areas of every continent except Antarctica, and range from the tiny members of the Aspredinidae family, which only grow to a fraction of an inch in length, to the European Wels catfish, which can reach 15ft (4.5m).

Global phenomenon

Catfish have been fished and eaten on almost every continent for millennia. Archaeologists have found catfish mummies in ancient Egyptian tombs, indicating that they were a valued food source. This fish remains a popular food in West Africa, where it is used for stews such as Nigeria's catfish pepper soup.

Southeast Asia has also embraced the catfish—as a favorite street food as well as in more formal dishes. In Myanmar (formerly Burma), the traditional soup *mohinga* includes catfish.

In the US, angling for catfish for the table has long been a tradition in the South, and in the 20th century catfish farming was developed as a major industry, with Mississippi being the most important producer of farm-raised catfish. The fish is so valued in the US that June 25 was declared National Catfish Day by President Ronald Reagan in 1987. Critics of this meaty fish say it has a muddy taste because it is a bottom feeder, but the taste can also be sweet and depends entirely on the feeding habitat.

CHANNEL CATFISH
Origins North America
Main food component 16 percent protein
Source of Vitamin B3, vitamin D
Scientific name *Ictalurus punctatus*

△ **The cat's whiskers**
All catfish have pairs of sensitive whiskerlike feelers, called barbels, around their mouth. The fish use them to search for food.

◁ **Lucky god**
Ebisu, one of the seven lucky gods of Japan, cuts up a catfish, while the woman next to him fans the coals of a hibachi in readiness to grill the meat.

△ **Bringer of good fortune**
In Japan, the koi is a symbol of luck, good fortune, and prosperity, so this 19th-century porcelain plate would have been a welcome gift.

Carp
the lucky fish

Native to freshwater lakes and rivers in Europe and Asia, the carp has been introduced to waterways all over the globe. Today, it is the world's most widely farmed fish, although it is now considered an invasive species in some countries.

BLACK CARP

Origins
Eastern Asia

Main food component
18 percent protein

Good source of
Vitamin D

Scientific name
Mylopharyngodon piceus

The carp was well known to the fishermen of the Roman Empire, who farmed this fish in specially built pools in the Danube river delta in south-central Europe. Long after the Romans had departed, the locals continued to value carp as a food source.

From the medieval period onward, the tradition of farming carp for the table was continued by monks throughout Europe. In southern Alsace in France, fried carp became a speciality. Carp was introduced to England in the 1400s, and is thought to have been served at the coronation banquet of Richard III in 1483. Today, this fish is eaten in Eastern Europe as a delicacy on religious feast days. The Polish Christmas menu typically includes carp, as the bones are said to symbolize the crucifixion.

Fortunate fish

Carp were introduced to Japan from China in the 1st century as a food source, but were bred in both countries in a variety of colors to decorate garden ponds. This practice continues today, especially in Japan, where carp, or koi, are the national fish, and are considered a symbol of good luck.

Asian carp were imported to the US in 1872. Because they bred quickly, were hardy, and grew to a generous size, the fish were seen as a commercially viable and valuable source of food.

◁ **Dragon-headed carp**
Carp must be strong to battle up a waterfall to reach their spawning ponds. In Chinese mythology, the carp that succeeds turns into a dragon.

Tilapia

farmed by the ancients

Adaptable, hardy, and prolific breeders, tilapia have been exploited as a food since the Egyptians discovered how easy they were to catch more than 6,000 years ago. The fish is, after the carp, the world's most popular farmed species.

NILE TILAPIA

Origins
Africa, Middle East

Main food component
26 percent protein

Source of
Selenium, vitamins B3, B12, D

Scientific name
Oreochromis niloticus

The tilapia's prolific reproductive capabilities earned it a sacred role in ancient Egypt as a symbol of fertility and rebirth. Tilapia amulets were worn by women hoping to become pregnant and were sewn into funerary shrouds to promote rebirth in the afterlife. The fish was also associated with the creator god Atum, who spat semen from his mouth to produce new gods, an act that paralleled the tilapia's habit of brooding its eggs in its mouth before letting the hatchlings swim free. Tilapia swim close to the water's surface and prefer the shallows, so it was simple for the Egyptians to secure a permanent supply of the fish by creating closed pools along the shores of the River Nile. The ancient Greeks and Romans followed suit and farmed tilapia, with nobles keeping fish farms on their estates to ensure a constant stock.

◁ Out of Africa
The Nile tilapia, common to many of Africa's rivers and lakes, is now farmed on every continent except for Antarctica.

Ghana, grilled tilapia is a popular street food, typically accompanied by fermented cassava or corn paste, chilli, and onions. Tilapia is also the main ingredient in fermented fish pastes, such as *terkin* in Sudan and *jaadi* in Sri Lanka. However, few places value tilapia

A female tilapia holds up to 200 eggs in her mouth, incubating them for around five days.

Crossing continents

In sub-Saharan Africa, tilapia is a staple food and still mostly fished from the wild, along the shores of the Senegal River, which winds through Senegal, Mali, Mauritania, Gambia, Guinea, and Guinea-Bissau. The traditional Senegalese dish *thieboudienne* often consists of a whole tilapia, served with rice and heavily spiced with *nététou*, made from the African locust bean. In

more than Taiwan, where the fish played a crucial role after World War II. In an act of daring at the close of the war, two Taiwanese soldiers interned in Singapore stole hundreds of tilapia fry from a Japanese fishery, and smuggled them back to Taiwan. The few fish that survived formed the basis for a fish-breeding program that has expanded to make Taiwan one of the world's largest producers. Today, tilapia are still commonly referred to as *wuguoyu*, a word that combines the surnames of the two enterprising Taiwanese soldiers.

◁ Home-grown fish
In ancient Egypt, tilapia were commonly kept in pools, some of which may have been in the homes of the nobility, as suggested by this tomb fresco from around 1350 BCE.

Traditional methods
Tilapia fishermen cast fishing baskets into the shallow waters of Lake Turkana in Kenya, as they have done for thousands of years.

Mackerel oily delicacy

With its characteristic markings, mackerel is easy to spot and is one of the tastiest, cheapest, and most nutritious fish. A valued source of protein and healthy essential oils, mackerel has been a mainstay of coastal communities for millennia.

Its greenish blue body, black and green striped back, and silver underside make mackerel one of the most distinctive saltwater fish. It swims in large shoals, its tapering, streamlined body; retractable fins; and broad, deeply forked tail making it especially efficient at carving a fast path through the water.

Most mackerel belong to same family as tuna but have a shorter life span than their larger relative. Two species of Atlantic mackerel live in the North Atlantic and Mediterranean. The Pacific short mackerel is most abundant from the Indian Ocean to the South Pacific. The Indian rake-gilled mackerel lives in waters from the Red Sea to the western Pacific.

Viking food

Mackerel remains have been found in settlements in the Aegean dating from at least 7,000 years ago. Further north, excavations in Norway from the first millennium suggest that the Vikings ate the fish,

and their descendants continued to do so. In the 19th century, salted, smoked, and preserved mackerel were a mainstay of the Norwegian diet. At this time, salted mackerel were also included in the rations of African slaves in the Caribbean.

A modern delicacy

With its dark, oily flesh and strong flavor, mackerel remains popular in Northern Europe. Young mackerel known as tinkers are a favorite delicacy in New England. The Pacific short mackerel features in Thai cuisine as *pla thu*. Its innards are not wasted and are a key ingredient of *tai pla* sauce, used to make a fish curry. Dried mackerel is also enjoyed from the shores of the Caribbean to Southeast Asia.

◁ **Swift swimmer**
The narrow body and retractable fins of the mackerel aid this fish in its fast-swimming lifestyle.

ATLANTIC MACKEREL

Origins
North Atlantic

Main food component
19 percent protein

Source of
Iron, magnesium, vitamin A, vitamin B12, omega-3 fatty acids

Scientific name
Scomber scombrus

△ **Minoan catch**
The Minoans were avid fishermen. This fresco from c.1600 BCE appears to show a good catch of mackerel.

▽ **Beach treat**
Mackerel, freshly roasted over coals on the shore, are a local delicacy at Puerto Vallarta, Mexico.

Eel snake of the sea

One of the most mysterious fish and a favorite food of the Japanese, this snakelike inhabitant of both fresh and salt water has an ancient heritage.

The freshwater eel is a strange creature, which started evolving more than 50 million years ago. It mainly lives in fresh water but is born at sea and returns to die at sea. There are many different species of eel, including the European (common) eel, the American eel, the Japanese eel, the Moray eel, and conger eels.

Food for kings and paupers

Eels have long been valued as a food source. Gaius Hirrius, a prominent Roman of the 1st century BCE, was famous for being the first person to have ponds solely for raising eels (some sources claim these were lampreys), which he is reputed to have supplied for the lavish banquets of Julius Caesar.

European peasants in later centuries often relied on eels as a protein source because they were relatively easy to catch with nets. In 730 BCE, the English Bishop Winfrid of Colchester noted "the people had no idea about fishing, and caught only eels." In the 18th and 19th centuries, jellied eels became a favorite dish in the East End of London. Today, Scandinavians love smoked eel, which is often served on rye bread. Eels also commonly feature in various Asian cuisines. Japan is famous for grilled eels dipped in a spicy soy sauce (*kabayaki*).

▽ **Endangered eel**
The European eel is now a critically endangered species, mainly as a result of habitat loss and degradation.

△ **Japanese favorite**
Whole restaurants are devoted to eels in Japan where, unlike other fish, they are not eaten raw in sushi because eel blood contains a poisonous substance that must be rendered harmless by cooking or hot smoking.

EUROPEAN EEL
Origins
Europe
Main food component
18 per cent protein
Source of
Vitamins A, B3, B12
Scientific name
Anguilla anguilla

"The first eel of the season must be eaten by the fisherman to ensure good fishing for the year."

DANISH SAYING

Trout feisty pink-fleshed fish

The trout is member of the same 100-million-year-old family as its larger cousin, the salmon. This hard-to-catch fish is no longer a rare delicacy at the dinner table, thanks to mass fish farming.

Nibblers rather than biters, trout are a challenging catch for any angler. This feeding habit is reflected in the fish's name, derived from the Greek *troktes*, meaning "one who gnaws." Their natural habitat is the northern hemisphere, but over the past 150 years trout have been introduced widely to lakes, rivers, and streams on all continents except Antarctica. Like salmon, trout return to the same spawning grounds each year. Unlike salmon—all of which migrate between sea and inland waters—many trout inhabit only fresh water.

True to form

There are three groups of "true" trout: brown trout, rainbow trout, and cutthroat trout. The brown trout, is native to Europe, where it was much prized in the Middle Ages. It is also known as the sea trout in its sea-dwelling form. In the second half of the 19th century, brown trout were introduced to North America from Britain and Germany and then to many other countries in Africa, Asia, and Australasia.

The rainbow trout, named for its colorful blue and green spotting and purplish lateral stripe, is native to the rivers and lakes along the Pacific coasts in northwest North America and northeast Asia. In its larger, sea-going form, the fish takes on a silvery blue color,

which has given it the name steelhead trout. On the Japanese island of Hokkaido, the Ainu people fished the rainbow trout as a summer staple from its lakes and rivers, even according the fish legendary status as a creature that carried the whole world on its back. Another North American fish, the cutthroat trout, was the first trout

△ **Vintage tackle**
Over the years, the sport of fly-fishing for trout has spawned a wealth of specialist equipment.

"For trouts are tickled best in muddy water."

SAMUEL BUTLER, 17TH-CENTURY ENGLISH WRITER

Europeans encountered in the Americas. The Spanish explorer Francisco Vásquez de Coronado described it as present in the Pecos River in New Mexico in 1541.

Bringing in the fish

A 15th-century French monk, Dom Pinchon, is credited with the discovery of a method for the artificial propagation of trout. Two centuries later a German landowner, Stephan Ludwig Jacobi, using the same principles as Dom Pinchon, built the first trout hatchery. His methods were largely forgotten until, in the late 19th century, the practice of raising, or "farming," rainbow trout spread throughout the US and later to other parts of the world.

The trout has pale, often pinkish flesh and delicate flavor. The wild variety is more highly prized than the earthier-tasting farmed fish, especially if the former has fed on shellfish. *Truite à la meunière* and *truite aux amandes* are among classic French trout dishes. In Scandinavia, trout is often used instead of salmon in gravlax, while fermented trout is the basis of the traditional Norwegian dish, *rakfisk*.

RAINBOW TROUT

Origins
Northeast and northwest Pacific coasts

Main food component
20 percent protein

Source of
Magnesium, zinc, phosphorus, vitamin B3, vitamin B12, omega-3 fatty acids

Non-food use
Medicinal (oil)

Scientific name
Oncorhynchus mykiss

◁ **A string of success**
Catching wild trout presents a challenge to any angler, so a large catch such as this landed by an American fishing party in California, was undoubtedly a cause for celebration.

▷ **Variations on a theme**
There are dozens of trout species from all over the world. They differ in size and coloration, but all display spots on their sides.

John Dory   strange-looking but tasty

The John Dory is one of the ocean's oddest, most unpalatable-looking fish, with a name shrouded in mystery, and yet it has long been prized for its delicate and versatile white flesh and mild, sweetish taste.

Origins
Worldwide

Main food component
21 per cent protein

Source of
Calcium, iron, vitamin A, vitamin C

Scientific name
Zeus faber

If a book should not be judged by its cover, then the long, spiky fins; huge, ugly head; big eyes; and large, protruding jaw of the John Dory should not write it off as a potential food. A loner in its habits, the fish lives close to the sandy bottom or weed-covered rocks of the sea bed, relatively close to shore, in water around 16–1,300ft (5–200m) deep. The highly mobile jaw and a habit of sneaking up on prey help to compensate for the John Dory's poor swimming ability, making it a fearsome enemy for the likes of the herrings, sand eels, anchovies, pilchards, and shellfish on which it feeds. Although mostly a warm-water fish, the John Dory has a wide distribution, from Scandinavia and the North Sea, across the

Mediterranean, around the whole coast of Africa, throughout the Red Sea, Arabian Sea, and Indian Ocean, and into the Pacific.

Behind the name

A common fish with such a bizarre appearance was bound to generate myth and legend, not least around the names it attracted. In 1758, the Swedish botanist Carl Linnaeus, who devised the system for naming organisms, was impressed enough by the John Dory to give it the genus name *Zeus* after the father of all Greek gods.

The origins of the common name are less clear. It is the title of an English folk song from the early 17th century about a sailor who meets King Jean (John) of France, but any link to the fish is lost in time. Another theory states that the name John Dory is related to the French words *jaune*, meaning "yellow," and *dorée*, meaning "gilded," both referring to the golden-bronze color of the fish.

An alternative name, St. Peter's fish, relates to the large, round, dark blotch surrounded by a lighter halo on the middle of each side of the John Dory. Legend has it that this is the thumbprint of St. Peter, who was asked by Jesus to pick the fish out of the Sea of Galilee. The saint did so but was so surprised by the fish's unprepossessing appearance that he threw it back, leaving behind an impression of his thumb. Despite the fact that the John Dory could never have lived in the Sea of Galilee, which is a freshwater lake, the saintly legend traveled far enough to give rise to

◁ **Stamp of approval**
The John Dory has twice appeared on the postage stamps of Burundi, a landlocked Central African country. The pictured example is from 1974.

the names *Saint-Pierre* in French and *pez de San Pedro* in Spanish. The "thumbprints" are, in fact, an evolutionary adaptation designed to divert predators, who see the blotches as eyes and attack these rather than the John Dory's real eyes, giving the fish an opportunity to get away.

The beauty inside

John Dory comes from an ancient order of ray-finned fish, called the Zeiformes, which date back to the Cretaceous period around 145 million years ago. The flat, bony, spike-covered body it has evolved, offering a relatively limited amount of edible flesh, has not always made the John Dory a popular catch. However, it was known and eaten by the Romans, and

> ## "The first man that John Dory did meet was good king John of France."
>
> TRADITIONAL ENGLISH BALLAD

recommended by the English cook Eliza Acton, who, in her 1845 cookbook *Modern Cookery for Private Families*, said, "The John Dory, though of uninviting appearance, is considered by some persons as the most delicious fish that appears at table."

Modern delicacy

Relatively unknown in North America, the John Dory has acquired a favorable reputation among British gourmets and in Australia and New Zealand, where the fish is also found. The fish's firm, white flesh can be steamed, fried, grilled, poached, or baked, and it serves as an alternative to other white-fleshed fish such as sole or turbot. Its bone-packed carcass makes an excellent stock.

△ **Bizarre appearance**
The John Dory is one of the most strange-looking of edible fish with its "wrinkly" head, gaping mouth, and numerous spikes on its back and underside.

▷ **Biblical association**
The alternative name for the John Dory is St. Peter's fish, referring to the association with St. Peter. The black mark on its side is said to be the saint's thumbprint.

EUROPEAN PILCHARD

Origins
Mediterranean, Atlantic, Black Sea

Main food component
24 percent protein

Source of
Vitamin B12, vitamin D, omega-3 fatty acids

Scientific name
Sardina pilchardus

Sardines the classic canned fish

This nutritious oily fish, packed with health-giving fatty acids, has long been fished and eaten by Europeans of countries on the eastern shores of the Atlantic Ocean. It became one of the first fish to be canned on a large scale.

The term sardine—apart from meaning fish from the island of Sardinia—is imprecise, but many authorities use it to refer to the young of the European pilchard (*Sardina pilchardus*), which is common in the northeast Atlantic and Mediterranean. In the Indo-Pacific region, sardine is another name for a different species, the South American pilchard (*Sardinops sagax*).

Sardines have been salted and pressed since antiquity, although the Romans considered them "coarse and second-rate." In the 18th century, they began to be preserved in vinegar, oil, or melted butter. They were first canned by Joseph Colin, a French confectioner from Nantes. He opened France's first fish cannery in 1824 and soon sardines were at the heart of a canned fish industry stretching from Southern Europe to the west coast of America. Even today, most sardines are eaten canned rather than fresh, although fresh sardines are especially popular in Mediterranean cuisine where, for example, grilled sardines appear as Spanish tapas.

Collapse and revival

Pacific sardines once supported the Californian fisheries immortalized in US author John Steinbeck's novel *Cannery Row*, a reference to a Monterey street once lined with sardine canning factories. The industry collapsed in the 1950s, although it has since seen a revival. Today, some 85 percent of Californian Pacific sardines are processed and exported to China, Japan, and South Korea.

▷ **Preserved in oil**
Sardines, like all oily fish, are high in omega-3 fatty acids. These American-caught sardines were preserved in cottonseed oil and canned for sale in the 1920s.

◁ **Packing their catch**
The European pilchard is so abundant that it is heavily exploited by commercial fishing fleets, with around 1 million tons being caught every year. These fishermen are loading their catch into crates off the Dalmatian Coast.

Anchovies
silver miniatures

These small silvery fish have a long food history, dating back to ancient times. Today, they are eaten fresh and also salted and preserved in oil in jars or cans.

△ **European fish**
The Turks are the greatest commercial fishers of European anchovies, catching most of them in the Black Sea in winter.

Looking like a tiny version of its relative the herring, the anchovy's habit of swimming in large schools and preference for living not too far from shore has, over the ages, made it one of the most popular fish for food and as a bait for catching larger fish. Six of the 144 species around the world are fished commercially.

Fermented anchovies were a key ingredient in the favorite condiment of the classical period and the early Middle Ages, garum, which is known as *colatura di alici* in contemporary Italian cuisine. Garum was a kind of fermented fish sauce, produced in large quantities along the Italian, Spanish, and French coasts as well as the northern shores of the Black Sea at the time of the Roman Empire.

Ode to an anchovy

In 14th-century England, according to food historian Dorothy Hartley, anchovy sauce was what kept the pork in Melton Mowbray pork pies pink inside and gave them their unique savory taste. The fish are also a key ingredient in Worcestershire sauce. Fish sauce using fermented or dried anchovies as a base has been a staple of Southeast Asian cuisine for hundreds of years. The greatest anchovy aficionados, however, are without doubt the Turks. *Hamsi*, as they call anchovies, feature in myriad Turkish dishes and are the subject of poems and songs.

◁ **Cured by salt**
In 19th-century Sicily, fresh anchovies were traditionally cured in barrels of salt, a method still practiced today.

PERUVIAN ANCHOVETA

Origins
Southeast Pacific

Main food component
21 percent protein

Source of
Omega-3 fatty acids, calcium, iron

Scientific name
Engraulis ringens

Herring treasure from the sea

For centuries, herrings were a staple food for the poor as the fish were plentiful and cheap. In Scotland, herrings were known as "silver darlings," while in Norway, they were given the even more romantic description of "the gold of the sea."

Early people living on the Atlantic coast were catching and eating herring some 3,000 years ago, but it was not until the Middle Ages that their potential as a source of nourishing, affordable food was realized. It was probably the Scots who first began fishing for herring on a noteworthy scale—as early as 836 CE, there is a record of Dutch traders coming to buy salt herring from them.

Where the Scots led, others were quick to follow. In France, the first mention of fishing for herring is in a charter granted to the Abbey of St. Catherine-du-Mont, near Rouen, in 1030, which stated that a saltworks near Dieppe was allowed to pay its taxes in salted herring rather than cash. Royal intervention helped to encourage the herring trade's growth. In 1155, Louis VII forbade the buying and selling of any fish other than mackerel and salted herring at the market at Étampes, an important royal town near Paris.

Vying for supremacy

From early in the 11th century, the Swedes were the first to fish for the vast shoals of herring to be found in the Baltic. The Germans soon joined them, as the

◁ **Canned for flavor**
The refinement of canning techniques enabled herrings, often with additional flavorings, to reach a wider market in inland areas.

canny merchants of Bremen and Lübeck were quick to realize how they could benefit by gaining control of this lucrative trade.

Religion was an important stimulus. During the Middle Ages, Catholic Europe's demand for herring during Lent and on other fasting days spawned the further growth of what was already a substantial industry. The Dutch, in particular, prospered—it was said by some that Amsterdam was founded on herring bones. By 1476, herring fishing was one of Holland's most important industries. Its growth owed much to the ingenuity of Willem Beukels, who, in 1338, found a new and better way of curing herring and preserving the catch in barrels. The fish were gutted as soon as possible after they had been netted and were then immersed in brine, rather than being sprinkled with salt as had been the previous practice. The Dutch also devised the drift net, dramatically increasing the size of the catch. Wars with Britain and France impacted the Dutch herring industry in the 17th century and it went into a long decline.

In the early 19th century, the Scots became ascendant. Aided by government subsidy, the Scottish fishing industry became the largest in Europe. At its peak in 1907, it was curing and exporting 2.5 million barrels of fish a year, mainly to

◁ **Easy catch**
If this woodcut from Olaus Magnus' *Historia de Gentibus Septentrionalibus* of 1555 is to be believed, Baltic herring were lining up to be caught in Scandinavian waters.

Origins
North Atlantic Ocean

Main food component
18 percent protein

Source of
Vitamin B1, vitamin D, iron

Scientific name
Clupea harengus

Germany, Russia, and other Eastern European countries. In 1913, it was estimated that more than 10,000 boats were engaged in the herring fishing industry. By the end of the 20th century, overfishing had caused a serious decline in herring stocks.

Kippers and rollmops

Over the centuries herrings had been found to be highly versatile. By the 19th century they were being eaten raw, fresh, salted, cured, pickled, and fermented, while tarragon, cherries, sherry, and even curry powder were combined with the fish to create tasty dishes. Kippers became a staple of the British breakfast table thanks to the introduction of a new curing process,

devised by John Woodger of Northumbria, UK, in the 1840s. The herring was split, gutted, and hung up to smoke and dry. The Germans created the soused rollmop, while the Swedes devised *surströmming*. This is Baltic herring caught just before spawning and treated with just enough salt to prevent rotting before being canned and allowed to ferment for at least six months.

△ **Herring lassies**
As the men unload their catch, teams of women—dubbed "herring lassies"—line the dock at Scarborough, UK, gutting the fish before they are packed into barrels.

"The herring … is, of all Neptune's gifts, The sweetest by far to me."

ALEXANDER NECKHAM, ENGLISH THEOLOGIAN (1157–1217)

Barbecues

No one is certain when early humans began using fire to cook meat. What is clear, however, is that barbecue as understood today—meat coated in spices, a marinade and/or sauce, and slow-cooked over a grill or pit—first emerged in the Caribbean. The origins of the name "barbecue," however, remain something of a mystery. Conventional wisdom says that it was invented by the Spanish, who coined the word *barbacoa* to describe the method of slow-cooking meat over a wooden platform that was practiced by Caribbean tribespeople. Others maintain that the Spanish got their word from a similar one used by the Taíno people of the Antilles, which best translates as "meat-smoking apparatus." The Spanish took their newfound culinary knowledge to the North American continent, where, according to some authorities, they also found American Indians cooking their meat in much the same way.

In the US, the barbecue is believed to have begun in colonial Virginia. Even the first president, George Washington, was a great enthusiast. His diaries are filled with references to barbecues, one of which lasted for three days. Barbecuing is now an intrinsic part of US culture, so much so that three national holidays—Memorial Day, Independence Day, and Labor Day—are heavily associated with it.

Yet by no means does the US have a monopoly on barbecue culture. The Australians have their "barbies," while the South African *braai*—Afrikaans for "roast" or "barbecue"—is so thoroughly ingrained in the country's culture that it crosses all its ethnic groups. Similarly, the Argentine *asado* involves at least half a day of barbecuing with the whole family.

◁ **From smoke to sauce**
Some historians believe barbecuing began with the early meat-smoking techniques used by indigenous tribes in the Caribbean.

Cod the fish that started a war

One of the most commercially important foods in history, the cod—with its white, firm flesh—helped to forge trading links across Europe and push the Old World into exploration of the New World.

▽ **Fish of the cold deep**
The Atlantic cod has three dorsal fins, two anal fins, and a distinctive chin barbel.

The almost unbroken popularity of cod has also nearly been its downfall. For more than 1,000 years, the big, meaty creature has been the victim of a fishing frenzy, as countries have vied with each other to haul vast catches out of the sea. This fuelled first European, then international trading rivalries, all to satisfy an insatiable appetite for cod's versatile flesh, whether fresh, wind-dried, or preserved in salt.

The lure of the Atlantic

Cod belongs to a large and ancient group of ray-finned fish that started to evolve during the Cretaceous period 145 million years ago. The most widely consumed

important source of food for the Vikings. They preserved the fish by hanging it out in the open air to dry until hardened to create stockfish, a traditional method of preserving cod still used in Norway. In 2017, Norwegian scientists published the results of a DNA study of cod bones dating from between 800 CE and 1066 CE retrieved from ancient wharves in the southern Jutland town of Haithabu (also called Hedeby, in present-day Germany), an early medieval Baltic trading port. They found that 1,000 years ago, traders were carrying stockfish more than 1,000 miles (1,600km) from northern Norway into the ports and markets of Northern Europe. This exchange was one

> "I have always been fond of … the glutinous codfish from Newfoundland."

GIACOMO CASANOVA (1725–1798), *THE STORY OF MY LIFE* (1828)

species, the Atlantic cod, can reach a length of up to 71in (180cm) and weigh more than 110lb (50kg). It lives in the North Atlantic and also close to the coasts of Greenland and Iceland, extending as far south as the Bay of Biscay. Young cod do not venture far from the shore, but seek out deeper, cooler parts of the sea as they grow. The other heavily fished cod is the smaller and darker-skinned Pacific cod, which inhabits northeastern Pacific Ocean waters, particularly around Alaska.

Cod, caught in the Arctic waters beyond northern Scandinavia, was an

◁ **Sturdy vessel**
The dogger was a fishing boat used in the late Middle Ages by Dutch and English fishermen to fish for cod in the North Sea.

of the first major commercial activities that began to link European ports and create economic ties across the continent.

Salt and the new found land

The ancient Egyptians and Romans used salt to preserve fish, but it was the medieval Basques of northwest Spain who perfected the salting of cod, which is called *bacalao*, employing a method they already used on whale meat. As whalers, the Basques were used to sailing far into the North Atlantic to hunt their prey and also found cod abundant in the same waters. In the early 14th century, they were well placed to take commercial advantage of the spike in demand for cod that followed a string of bad harvests. Salt cod became increasingly popular throughout Europe, especially on Fridays, when meat-eating was forbidden.

Portuguese, French, and English fishermen soon followed the Basque lead and began to look further afield than their immediate coastal waters to find cod. American Indians had been fishing for cod long

before Europeans began to venture across the Atlantic, and it was the abundance of cod in the seas off Newfoundland, in particular, that helped draw explorers to this far-flung New World in the 15th and

▽ **Cod in the New World**
In an engraving from a book of the 1830s, a team of fishermen land, gut, fillet, and dry the day's catch at a cod fishery on the Atlantic coast of North America.

16th centuries. In 1497, Raimondo di Soncino—Milan's ambassador to London—reporting on the voyage of Genoese navigator and explorer Giovanni Caboto (John Cabot) on behalf of Henry VII of England, observed that the sea off the Labrador coast of northeast Canada was "covered with fish which are caught not merely with nets but with baskets." Other imperial nations, including France, Spain, and Portugal, were also drawn to Newfoundland by the

Origins
North Atlantic, Pacific, and Arctic oceans

Main food component
18 percent protein

Source of
Vitamins A, B3, B12, D

Scientific name
Gadus morhua

Catch of the day
A Norwegian fisherman holds up two cod caught in Arctic waters. Norway remains one of the top cod-fishing nations.

plentiful supplies of cod around its coasts. By 1550, 60 percent of all fish eaten in Europe was cod, much of it Newfoundland salt cod. But while the English focused their fishing efforts close to shore using small boats and lightly salting, washing, and drying the cod on land, the French, Spanish, and Portuguese struck out further from shore, salting the fish on board ship before transporting it back to Europe to be dried. Cod salted this latter way formed the basis for the many *bacalao* and *bacalhau* dishes that became popular in Spain and Portugal, respectively, and then in their South American colonies. Lightly salted British cod was favored in the Mediterranean and Norway, where it was called *terranova fisk* (Newfoundland fish), although this was later replaced by the name *klipfisk*, meaning rock- or cliff-fish.

Changing fortunes

With the catastrophic defeat of their Armada in 1588, and the subsequent gradual decline of their empire, the Spanish stopped fishing deep into the North Atlantic, leaving the way clear for French and English fishing boats. La Rochelle on France's Atlantic coast was already Europe's most important Newfoundland fishing port, sending out half of all expeditions to Newfoundland in the first half of the 16th century. It also had the advantage of being able to fill the holds of its boats with salt from the works on the nearby Île de Ré. Fishing ports in northern Brittany also prospered, benefitting from an historical exemption from the French salt tax and the short distance from coastal salt works at nearby Guérande and Noirmoutier.

In England, by the end of the 16th century, around 200 new fishing boats were being outfitted each year, although the French still outnumbered the English fishing fleet by two to one. The English industry was centred in the West Country, particularly in Cornwall, Devon, and Dorset, which supplied around 70 percent of the vessels that fished off Newfoundland between 1615 and 1640.

In the 17th century, a drop in temperatures in Icelandic waters—a "little ice age" that lasted until the mid 19th century—led to the collapse of commercial

▷ **Cod catcher**
In the mid 19th century, simple tackle—a hook and lead weight combination—was used for cod fishing in French coastal waters.

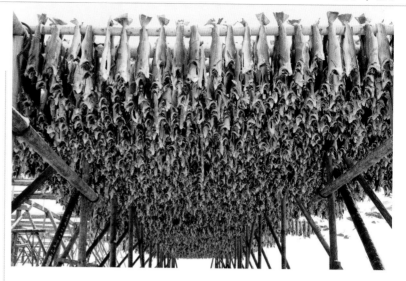

△ **Stockfish ready to go**
Hundreds of cod dry in the open air on the Lofoten islands in Norway—a method of preservation the Vikings would have recognized.

cod fishing in that area of the Atlantic. The focus switched to the North Atlantic and the new American colonies, especially those of the northeast coast, close to rich cod hunting grounds. American Indians taught the newly arrived settlers from Europe how to catch

---

A cod war in 1532 between England and the Hanseatic League, a German trading guild, ended with the murder of the Englishman John the Broad.

---

cod, and many towns in New England, such as Gloucester, Salem, and Dorchester in Massachusetts, grew and prospered over the next 200 years thanks to the fishing industry. Cod proved useful as a food for plantation slaves and for Union soldiers during the Civil War of 1861–1865.

New rivalries

In the first half of the 20th century, Iceland established itself again as a cod fishing power, and in 1958 the country announced the extension of its rights to fish exclusively in its coastal waters from 4 miles (6.5km) to 12 miles (19km). This led to the dispatch of UK warships to protect British trawlers in what became known as the Cod War. In the latter part of the 20th century, the industrialization of cod fishing, including larger boats, bigger nets, and sonar technology, led to heavy overfishing and a steep fall in cod numbers, especially in the North Atlantic. Some stocks have since recovered, but many areas of the sea remain depleted of cod.

▽ **Cod by-product**
The dietary supplement cod liver oil, advertised here in 1900, became popular in the 19th century. It is rich in omega-3 fatty acids, vitamin D, and vitamin A.

▽ **Distinguishing mark**
The haddock has a distinctive vertical black mark on its flank. The largest haddock on record weighed 24lb (11kg).

Haddock enjoyed fresh or smoked

This fish of the cool waters of the northern oceans is perhaps best known for its use in smoked form as the key ingredient in several Scottish fish specialities, as well as in kedgeree, a dish arising from Britain's imperial connection with India.

Although reputedly caught and cooked by the Romans in Britain from the 1st century CE, haddock is first recorded in medieval English—as *hadduc*, a name also given to fishermen or fishmongers. Some of the earliest recorded haddock specialities are Scottish. Finnan haddie—haddock cold-smoked over green wood and peat— dates from at least the early 1600s and is used in the traditional Scottish soup, Cullen skink. The hot-smoked Arbroath smokie is said to have evolved when some haddock that had been left to dry in barrels were retrieved from the ashes of a burning cottage in the village of Auchmithie, Angus, Scotland. In the 19th century, local women smoked the fish on sticks over fires in halved whisky barrels covered with coarse jute sacking; a similar method is still used today. Simply known as *le haddock*, the smoked fish is also a favorite in France.

◁ **Smoked haddock**
In the 18th century, a number of Scottish settlers moved to coastal towns in Maine, taking the secret of making Finnan haddie with them.

Kedgeree, a British breakfast dish of rice, smoked haddock, and hard-boiled eggs— an 18th-century import from British colonial India—was created when the fish was added to a South Asian dish of rice and vegetables, called *khichri* in India. In Norway, where it is called *hyse* or *kolje*, haddock is used in fish cakes and *fiskeboller* (fish balls).

△ **Arbroath smokehouse**
A man hangs rows of haddock by their tails over a wood-chip fire in a smokehouse in Arbroath on Scotland's east coast to produce the traditional Arbroath smokie.

A large female haddock can lay as many as 3 million eggs a year, in several spawnings.

Hake sweet and mild

Like its relatives cod and haddock, hake is an important food fish in several countries. With its firm, medium-flake white flesh and subtle, sweetish flavor, the European hake is particularly popular in Spain.

EUROPEAN HAKE

Origins
Northeast Atlantic, Mediterranean Sea

Main food component
17.5 percent protein

Source of
Calcium, iron

Scientific name
Merluccius merluccius

There are several species of hake living in the Atlantic and Pacific oceans and the Mediterranean Sea. The genus name, *Merluccius*, is from the Latin *mar* or *maris*, meaning "sea," and *lucius*, meaning "pike," perhaps a reference to the fact that the fish are long and slender like their freshwater namesake. In Britain, hake used to be known as whiting. In Spain, it is called *merluza*, and in the south of France, *merlu*. Hake is also called *colin* in France. One American species of fish is commonly called white hake. It is also fished and eaten, but belongs to the genus *Urophycis*.

△ **Predatory fish**
The European hake has a streamlined body and several large, sharp teeth, enabling it to swiftly pursue and grab hold of its smaller prey.

Mystery solved

Adult hake are deep-sea fish, preferring a depth of around 650ft (200m), but have been found as deep as 3,280ft (1,000m). They spend the daylight hours on the seabed then move closer to the surface to feed at night. They are carnivorous, catching smaller fish such as anchovies, pilchards, herring, mackerel, and sand eels. They are also known to catch smaller hake as well as squid. Their lifestyle was only discovered when an analysis of commercial fishing techniques conducted in the 1970s revealed that bottom-trawling would produce good catches of hake during the day but not at night, whereas midwater trawling produced the opposite result.

Best cooked fresh

Hake is a prized food fish and is a common sight on wet fish counters in France, Portugal, and Spain. *Merluza a la Gallega*—hake cooked the Galician way, baked with olive oil, garlic, and paprika and served with boiled potatoes—is found on restaurant menus all over Spain. In Portugal, fillets of hake baked in mayonnaise with slices of sautéed potatoes is a tasty speciality from the Algarve region. It is less popular in the UK and a large portion of the hake fished in the UK is exported to Spain. In the UK and Ireland, hake is most often eaten as frozen fillets or processed as "fish fingers" (fish portions coated in breadcrumbs) or fish cakes.

▽ **Processed onshore**
Nowadays, huge factory ships process their catches at sea, but in 18th-century North America, fish such as hake would be processed where they were brought ashore, often by women.

Origins
North Atlantic and adjacent Arctic waters

Main food component
16 percent protein

Source of
Vitamin B2, vitamin B6, vitamin B12

Scientific name
Melanogrammus aeglefinus

Barramundi
hermaphrodite fish of Antipodean myth

Fished by Aboriginal peoples for thousands of years, the sweet-tasting barramundi has become part of mainstream cuisine in Australia and beyond only in the past 60 years.

The barramundi is a fishy incarnation of an Aboriginal legend, according to which two star-crossed lovers, Boodi and Yalima, ran away from home to escape Yalima's arranged marriage to an elder of the tribe. Hunted down by the tribal elders, the lovers jumped from a cliff into the sea and turned into barramundi, their spiny fins said to be the spears thrown at them as they fled. As a result of the legend, the barramundi is sometimes called the "passion fish" and credited with aphrodisiac properties.

A curious creature

Barramundi live in coastal waters, estuaries, and lagoons from the eastern edge of the Persian Gulf to China, southern Japan, and southward to Papua New Guinea and northern Australia. The young are gray-brown with three white stripes on their heads and white patches on their sides. In adulthood, they are a silvery, olive-gray or gray-blue, their golden-brown eyes acquiring a bright red, reflective glow. Most barramundi are around 31½in (80cm) in length, but they can grow up to 71in (180cm). With its long body, large, comblike scales, pointed head, and wide mouth, the barramundi is a curious sight. It also displays some unusual behaviors. Unlike some migratory fish, such as

◁ **Big catch**
An Australian boy stands proudly next to an 26lb (11.8kg) barramundi he hooked in the waters off Darwin in 1983.

△ **Taking the bait**
For centuries, Polynesian fishermen have used hooks made from shells and bones to catch barramundi and other fish in the tropical waters surrounding the islands of the South Pacific.

salmon or trout, it has a catadromous life cycle, meaning the barramundi is born at sea, migrates to freshwater as a young fish, and when full-grown migrates back to salt water to spawn in estuaries and coastal shallows. It eats just about anything, including other barramundi, and also changes sex—beginning life as a male and reaching sexual maturity at three to four years before turning into a female three or four years later. That female can then produce more than 32 million eggs in one season.

Slow road to wider acceptance

In one of the Aboriginal languages of Queensland, barramundi means "large-scaled silver fish," and indigenous Australians have long hunted the aptly named creature for food. Rock paintings in the Kakadu National Park in the Northern Territory of Australia, dating back more than 50,000 years, show the barramundi along with other fish and animals that Aboriginal families hunted.

The European colonists of Australia 200 years ago had little interest in the country's indigenous foods, and so barramundi was relatively unknown outside traditional Aboriginal cuisine until the mid 20th century, when two siblings, the Haritos brothers, introduced the fish to the wider population. They were members of a Greek family who had migrated to Australia's Northern Territory during World War I, where they had taken an interest in hunting local animals and fishing for indigenous species, learning tracking and fishing techniques from Aboriginal Australians. In 1956, the brothers took barramundi to the Melbourne Olympics and served it to participants in the games, marking the fish's first successful commercial introduction to a wider, non-indigenous

Origins
Indian Ocean, southern Pacific Ocean

Main food component
20 percent protein

Source of
Calcium, sodium, potassium, vitamin A, vitamin D, omega-3 fatty acids

Scientific name
Lates calcarifer

△ **Fish of legend**
An ancient rock painting in Australia shows a barramundi fish swimming above the heads of two figures from the Aboriginal spirit world, known as the Dreamtime.

palate. At this time, the fish was more commonly known as the Asian sea bass, with the name barramundi only being used in Australia, for marketing purposes, from the 1980s.

Many names, many uses

The barramundi's presence in a variety of coastal waters around the Indian and Pacific oceans has earned it more than 70 local names, including *pla kapong* in Thailand; *ikan siakap* in Malaysia; and *bhetki* in Bangladesh, where *bhetki macher paturi*, a popular Bengali dish, sees the fish marinated in mustard paste, wrapped in a

△ **Silver battler**
The barramundi is admired and respected by game fishermen for its strength and fighting qualities.

banana leaf, and slow cooked. In Australia, the barramundi is prized both as a game fish and a versatile food that can be steamed, pan-fried, roasted, grilled, stewed, or baked. With a mild flavor and white, meaty flesh, it is lean and protein-rich.

It also has the highest content of healthy omega-3 fatty acids of any white fish. The barramundi has become an increasingly popular choice for fish farmers across the world, from Vietnam to the US, where fish farms in land-locked Iowa and Nebraska are able to raise barramundi 1,000 miles (1,600km) from the sea.

Mullet red and gray cousins

The ancient Romans were obsessed with the rosy colored mullet—still a favorite on Mediterranean menus—while its stronger-tasting gray namesake appears in more far-flung cuisines, revered especially for its much-prized roe.

GRAY MULLET

Origins
Warm coastal waters worldwide

Main food component
19 percent protein

Source of
Iron, vitamin B1, vitamin B2

Scientific name
Mugil cephalus

Many fish have the common name of mullet, but not all are "true" mullet, that is, from the same family as the gray mullet. In particular, the red mullet is only distantly related. Red mullet is a name used mainly in the UK, the American name is goatfish—a reference to the fish's beardlike pair of barbels protruding from underneath its head.

◁ **Prized specimen**
Such was the Roman craze for red mullet that in the 1st century Emperor Tiberius auctioned one weighing 4.5lb (2kg) for 5,000 sestertii (equivalent to more than $5,300 today).

A Roman passion

The ancient Greeks believed the red mullet was sacred to Hecate, the goddess of magic and the night, and for the Romans the fish became something of an infatuation, both as a food and a prized pet. Around 60 BCE, the Roman lawyer and politician Cicero spoke of "our chief men [who] think that they are in the seventh heaven if they have bearded [red] mullets in their fish-ponds who will come to feed out of their hands." Roman gourmets would "treat" their guests to the sight of a red mullet being poached alive in a crystal vessel, enabling them to witness the unfortunate fish changing color to intense shades of red and blue as it died. A good source of lean protein and with a delicate, almost sweet, taste, red mullet remains popular across the Mediterranean, including Greece, where it appears on menus as *barbounia*, grilled or fried and served simply with an oil and lemon dressing.

Different color, shared versatility

The flathead gray mullet, also known as striped or black mullet in the US, is found in coastal waters of tropical, subtropical, and temperate zones of all seas. It is more akin to sea bass or sea bream than red mullet, with a stronger, sometimes muddy taste. This mullet is widely farmed and is used in many of the world's cuisines. It is eaten raw in Japanese sashimi and salted, dried, and pickled in Egypt as *feseekh*. Salted, dried gray mullet roe is much appreciated as *myeongran jeot* in Korea, *karasumi* in Japan, *haviar* in Turkey, and *bottarga* in Italy.

> Farmed production worldwide now exceeds conventional fishing catches of gray mullet.

◁ **African delicacy**
Bokkom—salted gray mullet dried whole in the sun and wind—is a popular delicacy in South Africa's West Coast region. The skin is peeled away before the fish is eaten.

Safety in numbers
During daylight hours, gray mullet swim together in large groups for protection against predators such as water snakes, turtles, and larger fish.

Plaice and sole
food for the rich and poor

Although closely related and offering similar culinary attributes, plaice and sole have enjoyed different food fortunes thanks to catch sizes and subtleties of flavor.

▷ **Fish for sale**
In *The Fish Seller* by the Dutch painter Willem van Mieris (1662–1747), flatfish are laid out to tempt customers.

With their lopsided appearance, these flatfish look like unlikely dinner table favorites. However, their tasty white flesh has meant that plaice and sole have each found a key role in cuisines of different social groups in many parts of the world. Like all flatfish, plaice and sole have both their eyes on one side of the head. This an adaptation that enables them to look upward while lying flat and concealed on the seabed. Both species are inactive for long periods during the day, coming out at night to feed mainly on worms and molluscs.

Popular among the poor
The plaice lives in the western Mediterranean and off European coasts, reaching as far north as Greenland and Iceland. It is easily identifiable by the bright red or orange spots on its brown or greenish brown upper side. The brighter the spots, the fresher the fish.

Plaice was a cheap and plentiful food in the Middle Ages throughout northern Europe, especially in Britain and Scandinavia, and maintained its name as a food for the masses. Along with herring, plaice was a key part of the diet for poor residents of London, where up to 30 million of the fish were sold annually at Billingsgate Market. The fish was equally popular in Germany, Sweden, and Denmark, where it remains the most common fried fish, served with remoulade (a mayonnaise-like sauce) and fried potatoes. Huge demand for plaice led to a serious depletion in its numbers due to overfishing in the 20th century, particularly in the 1970s and 1980s. Limits

◁ **Sole traders**
19th-century French fishermen bring in a rich catch of sole to satisfy the appetites of fashionable Parisians.

placed on plaice catches since then have seen a recovery in its numbers, and today it remains among the most popular of flatfish.

French favorite
The sepia-colored "true" sole (*Solea solea*) is often known as the Dover sole after the coastal area in Kent, England, where it was fished in great numbers in the 19th century. Its home is the east Atlantic, from Norway to the Mediterranean and the coasts of the West African countries of Senegal and Cape Verde. A related species, the American sole (*Achirus lineatus*), is found in western Atlantic waters. The species of fish known as the Pacific sole (*Microstomus pacificus*), a flatfish from the northwest Pacific, is in fact a type of flounder.

▷ **Japanese catch**
Fishermen from Wakasa province on the north coast of Japan haul in nets full of "sole," which are probably a type of flounder native to those waters.

> "It [plaice] is a low-priced fish, generally bought by the poor."
>
> MRS. BEETON, *THE BOOK OF HOUSEHOLD MANAGEMENT* (1861)

With its mild, sweet taste; relative lack of bones; and scarcity value, Dover sole has a long history as a delicacy mainly for the rich. It was enjoyed by the ancient Romans, who called it *solea Jovi* (Jupiter's sandal), a reference to the fish's flat shape.

Sole was a popular fish at the 17th-century court of the French king Louis XIV, and it features in classic French dishes, such as *sole Véronique* (with champagne, cream, and grapes), *sole Mornay* (with a cheese sauce), *sole meunière* (dredged in flour and fried in butter with lemon juice and parsley), and *sole à la Dugléré* (poached in fish stock and white wine on a bed of tomatoes), invented by Adolphe Dugléré, chef of the Café Anglais, a top Parisian restaurant of the 19th century.

PLAICE

Origins
Northeast Atlantic, North Sea, Mediterranean

Main food component
18 percent protein

Source of
Vitamins B3, vitamin D, selenium, phosphorus

Scientific name
Pleuronectes platessa

Monkfish an ugly treat

Monkfish is unquestionably among the most unattractive of sea creatures, but the firm, tasty flesh of its tail has made this fish highly rated among chefs and fish eaters all over the world.

For years, many people would not countenance eating monkfish because of its unprepossessing appearance. Elizabeth David, a British food writer, described it as a "brute," while Isaac Cronin, author of *The California Seafood Cookbook*, wrote of it being "extremely ugly."

Monkfish certainly look ferocious. They can grow to a length of over 4ft (1.2m) and weigh up to 51lb (23kg). Their huge, flat head and gaping mouth lined with two rows of long needlelike teeth are instantly off-putting. In France, in the past, the fish were deemed so unsightly that fishmongers were not allowed to sell them with their heads on for fear they would scare customers.

▷ **Friendly face**
Contrary to the impression given by this illustration, monkfish are not "friendly" and can give a painful bite.

Monkfish spend much of their time half-buried in the sand of the ocean floor, attracting prey by means of a lure that stretches out above their head. There are three main monkfish species: *Lophius americanus* lives off the eastern coast of the US; *L. caulinaris*, which is

△ **Massive head**
The huge head of the monkfish, with its mouth packed with menacing teeth, dwarfs the rest of its body.

Each female monkfish produces a million eggs from February to October.

found in the eastern Pacific; and L. *piscatorius*, which lives in the northeast Atlantic and the North Sea. What all three have common is their voracity—monkfish have enormous appetites.

What's in a name?
Over the centuries, the fish has been given various vernacular names. In Britain, the name monkfish itself dates back to medieval times, when it was thought the shape of the fish's head resembled that of a monk's cowl. Later, in the US, New Englanders christened it "the lawyer" because of its rapaciousness. In France, it is *lotte* or *baudroie*, while the Italians call it *rane* or *coda di rospo* (toad's tail). In Germany, it is *Seeteufel*, meaning sea-devil.

A culinary delicacy
Today, monkfish is regarded as a delicacy, although only its tail, central body section, and cheeks are eaten. The flesh, which is firm and white, resembles that of lobster— indeed, it is sometimes called "poor man's lobster" because of its similarity to that shellfish in both texture and flavor.

EUROPEAN MONKFISH

Origins
Northeastern Atlantic Ocean, North Sea

Main food component
16 percent protein

Source of
Phosphorus, potassium, vitamins B3, B6, B12

Scientific name
Lophius piscatorius

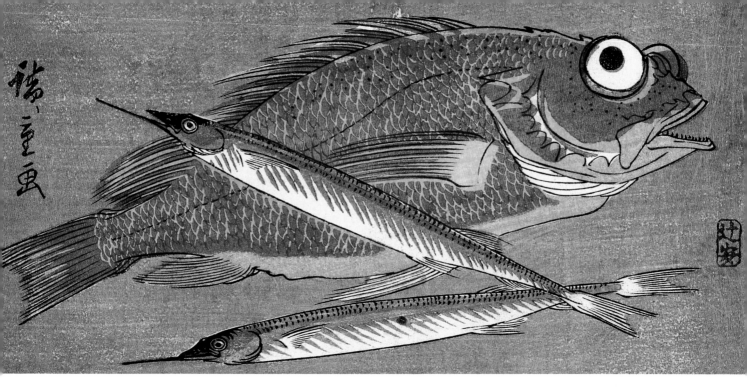

Snapper worldwide fishy favorite

With its firmly textured, mild, moist white flesh, snapper—notably the red variety—is a much sought-after culinary delicacy around the world from the southern states of the US to Southeast Asia.

There are more than 100 species of snapper found in tropical waters around the world. Most of them are good to eat, especially the northern red snapper. This is one of the favorite fish foods of the US—particularly in the South, where fishing for it started in the Gulf of Mexico in the 1840s. Pensacola, Florida, was one of the ports that boomed thanks to the growth of snapper fishing. The city prospered to such an extent that, by the end of the 19th century, it had become known as the red snapper capital of the world. Freight cars loaded with snapper shipped the fish further and further afield. French inventor Ferdinand Carrie's development of an effective refrigeration system meant that the snapper would arrive fresh at their destinations.

Snapper varieties
The northern red snapper's cousin is the yellowtail snapper. It gets its name from the prominent yellow streak running down its body from snout to tail. It is found from Massachusetts to the Caribbean and along the northeastern coast of South America. There are numerous other western Atlantic snappers.

Indo-Pacific snappers are just as varied. Most have a range which includes Southeast Asia extending west to the Red Sea and East Africa. However, what Australians call pink snapper is not a true snapper but belongs to the sea bream family. Although snapper is not categorized as endangered, years of overfishing, particularly in the Gulf of Mexico for red snapper, has led to the imposition of fishing quotas.

RED SNAPPER

Origins
Western North Atlantic

Main food component
21 percent protein

Source of
Potassium, magnesium, vitamin A, vitamin B12

Scientific name
Lutjanus campechanus

▷ **Traditional craft**
Several varieties of snapper are found in the waters of the western Atlantic. Here, a Bahamian fisherman weaves a traditional trap in which to catch snapper.

Tuna fish of the ocean deeps

This fast-swimming fish was valued as a food source by the civilizations of the ancient world, but despised in later centuries. However, in recent decades it has found new popularity on the dining tables of Japan and the West.

In a cave at Jerimalai in East Timor, off the northern tip of Australia, archaeologists have found remains of tuna once fished and eaten by Southeast Asian islanders 42,000 years ago. This masterful fishing community had apparently developed the skills they needed to venture into deep waters where tuna thrive.

Fish of the open oceans

Tuna live in open waters in oceans around the world, often migrating huge distances. The Atlantic bluefin is the most prized of the tuna species, followed by the southern bluefin. Bigeye tuna can grow as long as 8ft (2.5m) and is one of the rarest in the tuna family. Yellowfin, which live in tropical and subtropical waters, have been a popular substitute for the endangered

bluefin for years, but they, too, are now under threat. Albacore, also known as white tuna, is widely fished in temperate and tropical waters worldwide.

Bluefin tuna was caught in the Mediterranean at least 2,000 years ago, where the sheltered waters offered slightly easier hunting grounds than the open ocean. Bluefin tuna from the Atlantic swim in through the strait of Gibraltar to spawn, making them more accessible to fishing boats and early fishing methods. The Phoenicians, a seafaring people of the eastern Mediterranean, used hand lines and nets to catch them. Tuna was also a favorite of the ancient Romans, who preferred it to the oilier fish such as mackerel and sardines that were common in the Mediterranean.

△ **Ancient methods**
The *mattanza*, a traditional Sicilian method of tuna fishing, is depicted in this 18th-century paving.

▽ **Spectacular catch**
Fishermen off the coast of southern France net bluefin tuna in their Mediterranean spawning grounds.

▷ **Getting a bite**
Fishermen off the Mexican coast land tuna using fishing rods. This method of fishing avoids the risk of inadvertently catching other species such as turtles and marine mammals.

Today, the Mediterranean bluefin is the most commercially valuable fish, with around 80 percent of the world catch going to Japan. Tokyo restaurant owners can pay in excess of $1 million for the biggest specimens, which can weigh in at more than 440lb (200kg).

A modern phenomenon

Historically tuna was considered a low-grade fish. The change in attitudes began with the launch of canned tuna in the US in the early 1900s, which unlocked new markets. It was quickly adopted as a convenience food, particularly in North America and Australia. During World War I, it was a staple ration for troops. Later, the advent of refrigeration brought about further increase in tuna's popularity, especially after World War II, when the Japanese developed a taste for tuna sashimi (fresh raw tuna). It is now widely eaten in high-end restaurants worldwide. However, the popularity of the fish has threatened some species with extinction.

ATLANTIC BLUEFIN

Origins
Atlantic Ocean, Mediterranean Sea

Main food component
23 percent protein

Source of
Selenium, vitamin B3, vitamin B12

Scientific name
Thunnus thynnus

"It's better to be the head of an anchovy than the tail of a tuna."

ITALIAN SAYING

The perils of fishing

Ocean fishing has always been a particularly risky business, especially in colder, northerly seas where it can involve battling fierce storms, blizzards, and deadly ice. Fishermen frequently face heavy waves that can sweep them overboard or capsize their vessels entirely.

Historically, fatalities have been high. Between 1866 and 1890, for example, more than 380 fishing schooners and 2,450 fishermen from the US port of Gloucester, Massachusetts, were lost as they braved the perils of fishing for cod off George's Bank, situated about 100 miles (160 km) east of Cape Cod, and the Grand Bank, 1,000 miles (1,609 km) beyond it. In August 1873, just a single storm destroyed nine vessels from Gloucester and caused the deaths of 128 fishermen in the process. It was little wonder that an anonymous reporter, writing three years later, stated that "the history of the Gloucester fisheries has been written in tears."

British fishermen faced similar challenges. The Eyemouth disaster of October 1881, in which 189 fishermen perished, is believed to the single greatest fishing tragedy in the nation's history. Of the 45 vessels that set out to sea from this small Scottish port, only 26 made it back home safely; the rest fell victim to a ferocious storm, and were either capsized or dashed to pieces on the Hurkar Rocks at the entrance to Eyemouth Harbor.

Despite these dangers, fishing is big business and thousands of people depend on it for their livelihoods. Gloucester, which is the oldest fishing port in the US, remains active to this day. In 2013 alone, more than 62 million pounds of fish— worth $42 million— were processed through the port.

◁ **Dangerous tradition**
At the turn of the 20th century, fishermen across the world braved the wildest of seas in tiny wooden boats to bring home their catch.

Octopus, squid, and cuttlefish

many-tentacled delicacies

With a habitat that spans all the seas of the globe except the Black Sea, the octopus, along with its cephalopod relatives, was known to many ancient civilizations both as a source of food and an object of fascination.

With a prominent head, bulbous eyes, and eight waving tentacles, the octopus captured the imagination of ancient cultures like few other creatures. Adding to its mystique was the ink sac from which it spurts black liquid when alarmed, a trait it shares with its relatives the squid and cuttlefish.

Soft-bodied wonders

Octopus, squid, and cuttlefish have no bones or shells, which means that most of their body is edible. Their scientific name, cephalopod, means "head-armed," an apt term given that structurally they comprise just a head and arms. The octopus has eight arms, while the squid and cuttlefish each have ten. Because of their soft structure there are few fossils leaving clues about the evolution of these sea creatures. However, scientists have traced their DNA to a common ancestor that existed 100 million years ago.

Some of the earliest human records of the octopus family come from the art and literature of ancient Greece. The Greeks gave the octopus its name, oktōpous, meaning eight footed, and it appears frequently as a motif on pottery with one example dating to 1500 BCE. The Greek playwright Aristophanes referred to eating fried squid in the 5th century BCE. The Greek word for squid, kalamos, became calamaros in ancient Rome.

Monstrous legends

The octopus and the squid have both inspired legend. In Greek mythology, the Hydra is a monster with seven or eight heads at the end of long tentacles—when they are severed they regenerate, just as the octopus grows back its tentacles if they are damaged. In the Aztec culture of Peru and Mexico, the octopus, along with other sea creatures, was revered. In Japan's ancient Ainu culture, dating from the first millennium CE, the octopus-like Akkorokamui was worshipped. It was thought to have the power to grant health and knowledge but could also wreak havoc.

Local knowledge on how to tenderize octopus, squid, and cuttlefish is common to all cultures where they are eaten. In ancient Rome, octopus was often cooked in wine, vinegar, or other acidic liquid with the aim of breaking down the tough connective tissue. The Greeks traditionally thrashed octopus on rocks to tenderize it, while the Japanese approach was to rub it with salt. Along with Korea, modern Japan is one of the biggest consumers of octopus and squid today.

△ **Decorative motif**
The Minoans of the second millennium BCE were keen fishermen and would have been well acquainted with the octopus both as food and as decorative inspiration for their pottery.

▷ **Tentacles and suckers**
Members of the cephalopod family are depicted in this German publication of the early 1900s.

COMMON OCTOPUS

Origins
Tropical and semitropical waters worldwide

Main food component
15 percent protein

Source of
Iron, phosphorus, vitamin B3, vitamin B12

Scientific name
Octopus vulgaris

△ **Ready meal**
Squid prepared in a variety of ways are popular street snacks in Korea and Japan. Here, dried squid are displayed on a Korean street stall.

"[I'd] like to see him ravenous for squid … And have it come … sizzling to his plate …"

ARISTOPHANES, GREEK PLAYWRIGHT, c.425 BCE

Gamochonia. — Trichterkraken.

Shrimp, prawns, and lobsters

appetizers or the main event

Equipped with five pairs of legs, these walking delicacies were an easily obtainable source of food for early civilizations, from plentiful prawns that could be swept up in nets to lobsters caught in traps.

Lobsters, crayfish, prawns, and shrimp are among the oldest animal foods eaten by humans. All four types of creature are classified as decapods because they have ten legs. The front pair of legs is typically clawed for feeding and defense; the other pairs are for walking—these animals all live on the sea- or riverbed and walking is their main method of transport. Lobsters are the largest with strong walking legs, followed by crayfish, then prawns and shrimp.

Dried, minced, and fried

Although the terms prawns and shrimp are often used interchangeably, they have different gill structures, and shrimp are generally smaller. Prawns and shrimp are the most numerous of the decapods, with around 2,000 species spread through the world's oceans and waterways. They are also the easiest to eat since their shells are soft.

Mediterranean shrimp and prawns were popular in ancient Greece and Rome, where they were often roasted and fried in a honey glaze or minced, formed into patties, and fried.

Shrimp has been a feature of Chinese cuisine from at least the 7th century. After his travels in Asia, the 13th-century Venetian explorer Marco Polo reported that crustaceans were a major part of the diet in China, eaten fresh but also dried and used to make sauces. Freshwater shrimp were caught in baited baskets along the Pearl River and sold by the banks, some still alive. Dishes such as dried shrimp stir-fried with spinach, or the Sichuan dish of green beans deep-fried with shrimp, have changed little since Polo visited.

Instant classic

In the US, shrimp were fished from the Louisiana bayou in the 17th century using massive dragnets, and were incorporated into the regional Creole and Cajun cuisine. In 1917, mechanical harvesting of shrimp was introduced, providing a plentiful supply of fresh shrimp to other parts of the country. The early 1920s saw the introduction of the shrimp cocktail. This popular party food of the Prohibition era was served

△ **A raft of knowledge**
This fisherman of the Kanak people of New Caledonia in the South Pacific is taking his traps out to catch lobster in the tidal lagoons of the archipelago in which they congregate.

△ **Banquet centerpiece**
Lobsters were a luxury food in 17th-century Europe. A huge cooked lobster is the main attraction in this still life painted by Flemish artist Adriaen van Utrecht in 1644.

" … we had asparagus and a lobster, which made me wish for you."

JANE AUSTEN, ENGLISH WRITER, LETTER TO HER SISTER (1799)

in cocktail glasses usually reserved for alcohol. The prawn cocktail later became a classic first course at American and British dinner parties of the 1960s.

Luxurious lobster

While shrimp and prawns were widely available and relatively cheap in the late 20th century, lobster had gained a reputation as exclusive and expensive. This was not always the case. In previous centuries, people living on coasts caught and ate lobsters as a staple part of

◁ **Prize catch**
A New England fisherman marvels at the size of the American lobster caught in his traditional trap.

their diet, but by the 17th century, lobster had achieved fashionable status. English diarist and socialite Samuel Pepys recorded that he served lobster at an elegant dinner in 1663, and the The Art of Cookery by 18th-century English cookbook writer Hannah Glasse contains several lobster recipes suitable for fine dining.

In colonial New England, lobsters were so plentiful they were considered commonplace. They were used as bait and for fertilizer, and they were also fed to prisoners and slaves as a cheap source of protein. The introduction of canning and rail transportation in the mid 1800s brought lobster to a much wider market. Not only were city dwellers developing a taste for the delicate lobster meat sold in cans, but the burgeoning New England tourist trade made a feature of the local fresh lobster, which was served in fancy restaurants. Due to high demand, prices began to rise in the 1880s, and by the first few decades of the 20th century, lobster had become a delicacy that only the rich could afford.

AMERICAN LOBSTER

Origins
Atlantic coast of North America

Main food component
16.5 percent protein

Source of
Vitamin B12, vitamin E

Scientific name
Homarus americanus

Crab food in a shell

Prized by gourmets for their delicate flesh, crabs have often presented a challenge to diners because of their hard shell, claws, and long, fiddly legs.

△ **Fresh crab**
An average-size blue crab will yield about 2oz (60g) of cooked meat to a persistent picker. This crab has yet to be shown the cooking pot.

Considered an expensive speciality in the modern food market, crabs were part of the hunter-gatherer diet for prehistoric coastal dwellers the world over. Crabs live in all the world's oceans, and in freshwater in tropical and subtropical parts of the globe. They form the most diverse group of crustaceans (animals with a hard shell and multiple legs), with thousands of species. However, while many other types of seafood are mentioned in ancient texts, crabs are little documented. The 4th- or 5th-century CE text attributed to the 1st-century Roman gourmet, Apicius, mentions only one recipe for crab, describing croquettes, similar in style to contemporary crab cakes.

years to the Babylonians, who originally named it "the crayfish." According to ancient Greek mythology, Hercules was bitten by a crab sent by his stepmother Hera to distract him from

> "Take the meat out of the … great claws … flour and fry them."

THE ACCOMPLISHT COOK, ROBERT MAY (1685)

Preserved in the night sky

Although it may not have formed a large part of the ancient diet, the crab was significant nonetheless, lending its Latin name, *cancer*, to one of the constellations of the zodiac, visible in both northern and southern hemispheres. Knowledge of this constellation, the faintest of the 12, stretches back 3,000

killing the serpent Hydra. Although Hercules crushed the crab underfoot, Hera honored the animal by placing it in the sky.

Getting under the shell

As a food source, crab has always been problematic for humans because of its hard outer shell, nipping pincers, and the relatively small amount of meat it yields. There is evidence crabs were collected in plaited baskets from the waters around Scotland in prehistoric times, and they seem to have been popular in Britain

▷ **Ancient deity**
From 100–700 CE, the Moche culture ruled the coastal areas of northern Peru. They left behind a wealth of ceramics, including this bottle bearing the image of a crab god.

BLUE CRAB

Origins
Western Atlantic Ocean,
Gulf of Mexico

Main food component
18 percent protein

Source of
Calcium

Scientific name
Callinectes sapidus

during the Roman occupation. Historical records reveal that crabs were sold at fish markets in Britain from medieval times onward. They were typically boiled and served cold with a dressing of vinegar. Although they were appreciated for their sweet, delicate meat, crabs had a reputation for being awkward to eat at formal dinners.

The exceptions are soft-shell crabs. These are crabs that are caught within 12 hours of molting their firm shell, allowing almost all of the animal to be eaten without additional processing apart from cooking. In the US, the best-known soft-shell crab is the blue crab, which is abundant along the Atlantic coast. Eating boiled or steamed blue crab in the summer months has become an institution around the Chesapeake Bay estuary that borders Maryland; Delaware; Virginia; and Washington, D.C.

In Japan, the Japanese blue crab, or shore-swimming crab, is another species valued for its soft shell. It is served in sushi or deep fried in tempura. The Mediterranean blue crab, a species native to the lagoons of Venice, Italy, is the inspiration for a speciality of the region—a dish called *molecchie fritte* (or *moleche fritte*), in which crabs are soaked in beaten egg and fried.

Turning red

The largest and most expensive of all are the king crabs, renowned for their tender white meat edged with a red border. In the Bering Sea, the red, or Alaskan, king crab can reach a leg span of 6ft (1.8m), although only roughly a quarter of the animal can be eaten. Snow crabs from the North Pacific also have a reputation for especially sweet flesh, as does the Pacific-dwelling Dungeness crab and the pink-colored spider crab, which lives in Japanese waters.

All crabs, no matter what color they are when they are living, turn red when they are plunged into boiling water. The phenomenon is explained by a red pigment called astaxanthin, which is part of the shell but is hidden under a protein coating while the crab is alive. When the shell is heated, the protein coating dissolves to reveal the astaxanthin, which remains stable under high temperatures, giving the cooked crab its red color.

▽ **No way out**
Crab fishermen using traditional methods leave baited baskets on the sea floor then return later to pull them up into their boat and see if any crabs are trapped inside.

Clams, mussels, and oysters bite-size delicacies

Whether prized open with a sharp tool or coaxed ajar with heat, these self-contained packets of protein include a range of shellfish, some of which are cheap and plentiful, while others are viewed as the height of luxury.

△ **Hinged shell**
Like all bivalves, the oyster has a two-part hinged shell, which it can shut tight. A special knife is needed to get at the plump flesh within.

Since ancient times, oysters have been considered the most prestigious of molluscs. Their large size made them an obvious choice for harvesting, and the possibility of finding a pearl inside was an added attraction. Above all, their taste when eaten raw made them highly desirable, and early connoisseurs appreciated the subtle variation in flavor among oysters from different locations. The Romans cultivated them in the Mediterranean from the 1st century BCE. Oysters continued to be cultivated until the fall of the empire. Scallops (a type of clam) were also considered worthy of fine dining in the classical world, and the distinctive fan-shaped scallop shell was used repeatedly as a decorative motif in artworks.

From plenty to scarcity
In areas where they were plentiful, such as the coasts of Britain and France, scallops and oysters provided food for the poor. In *The Pickwick Papers*, Charles Dickens' 1837 novel of London life, Sam Weller says, "Poverty and oysters always seem to go together." On the other side of the Atlantic,

century, farming them had become common practice in Europe. The first mussel farm was founded in L'Aiguillon sur Mer on the Atlantic coast of France in 1235, with ropes strung from wooden poles driven into the seabed. Farming of mussels, which mature more quickly than oysters, soon spread around the North Atlantic and Mediterranean. Popular dishes include the French bistro classic *moules marinières* (mussels cooked in a creamy white wine sauce) and *moules frites* (mussels served with French fries).

Clam cuisine
By the 19th century, shellfish were becoming increasingly popular in North America. Clams, with their small amount of meat, seemed like hard work to harvest, but on the US east coast, they became part of the local cuisine, notably clam chowder, and of its culture, with the tradition of clam bakes. Clams also feature in the *pasta alla vongole* of Italy, in the curries of Kerala in southern India, and the hot-pot dishes and soups of Japan—all meals that have a long tradition based on local harvesting of these bivalves.

△ **Closed shells**
Healthy mussels, like these live blue mussels, keep their shell closed when out of water, so open ones must be discarded before cooking. Heat kills them and so the shells open.

"Oysters are more beautiful than any religion … They forgive our unkindness to them."

SAKI, BRITISH WRITER (1870–1916)

oysters were eaten regularly by coastal American Indians, and early European explorers reported seeing specimens up to a foot (0.3m) in length. It was not until the late 19th century that oysters became a luxury. The turning point was the Industrial Revolution, when pollution killed many natural oyster beds along Atlantic coasts. Combined with over-harvesting in previous centuries, it was enough to severely shrink supply, causing prices to rise.

In contrast, mussels and clams remained relatively cheap, although they, too, suffered from over-harvesting and pollution in some areas. One reason for the steady supply of mussels is that, since the 13th

▽ **Digging for clams**
Clams live buried deep in the sandy, silty, or muddy bottom of the intertidal zone. At low tide, they can be dug out by hand as these South Korean women are doing.

◁ **Diving in**
Free diving for oysters was a centuries-old fishing tradition in small coastal villages in Japan. The women held their breath while searching the seabed, sometimes returning to the surface victorious, their prize held aloft for collection.

BLUE MUSSEL

Origins
North Atlantic coasts

Main food component
12 percent protein

Source of
Iron, phosphorus, vitamins B1, B3, B12

Scientific name
Mytilis edulis

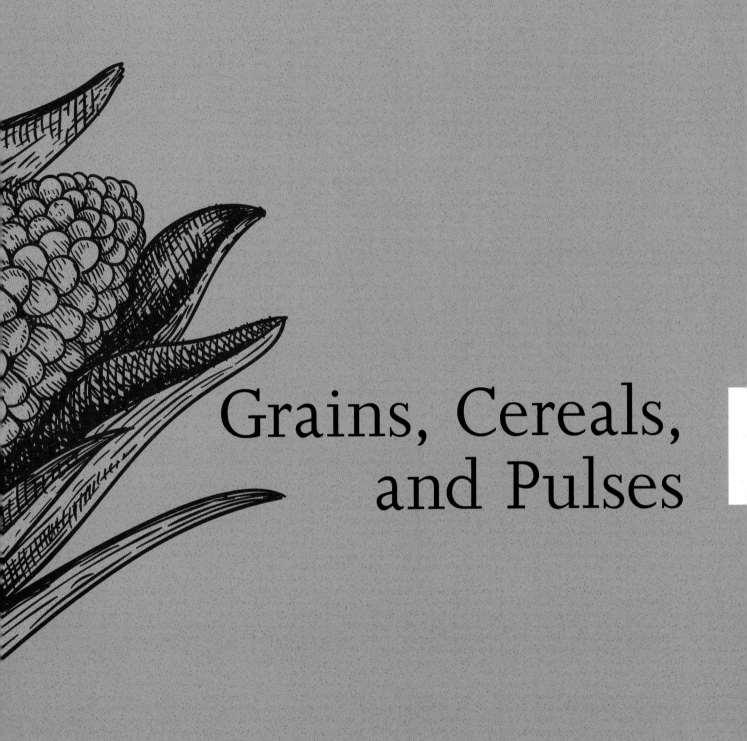

Grains, Cereals, and Pulses

Grains, cereals, and pulses

The world as we know it has to some extent been built upon grains. They have been a vitally important food for humans ancient and modern, and many populations all around the globe would have been unable to survive without them. These tiny grass seeds don't look very promising, although some come from much larger plants such as maize. But they are all hugely rich in carbohydrates: a source of calories and energy. They are, in effect, the foundation of civilizations.

The seeds of agriculture

Maize, rice, wheat, barley, sorghum, millet, oats, and many other types of grain have been cultivated for thousands of years in different parts of the globe. At first, primitive peoples simply picked all the seeds from various wild crops wherever they found them growing—eating some, then storing the rest in pits or earthen vessels for use over the winter months. Eventually, when our ancestors began to stay in one place rather than following a nomadic lifestyle, they realized that harvesting all wild grains in an area resulted in a poorer crop the following year. As a result, they began to scatter grain seeds to grow for the next harvest. Seeds were selected from the strongest plants for this purpose, and very gradually the strains of these plants evolved. It was during this long transition period that people turned from hunter-gatherers into farmers and began sowing in drills, rather than simply scattering, their precious seeds.

Parching for extraction

Wheat, which has often been called the king of grains, was one of the first grasses to be domesticated and cultivated. In early varieties it was difficult to extract the grain from its coating or bract, so the grains had to be parched first. This slight burning freed the grain from most of the chaff so that it could be ground between two stones to be made into gruel or flat, unleavened hearth cakes. Gradually wheat plants with seeds that were more readily hulled were selected and grown, as this made harvesting and storing easier to achieve.

△ **Early accounts**
Some of the earliest human records are concerned with the distribution of grain. In Mesopotamia, examples of this type of accounting were written in cuneiform between 3100 and 2900 BCE.

◁ **A rich harvest**
Emmer—a type of wheat—and barley were grown and harvested with serrated hand scythes in ancient Egypt. As grain meant wealth, it was often the subject of tomb paintings.

△ **The staff of life**
Bread was vital in imperial Rome, and loaves were baked in dome-shaped ovens. By the middle of the 2nd century BCE, the first *Collegium Pistorium*, or Bakers' Guild, had been formed.

In China by 2700 BCE, early farmers concentrated their efforts on growing "five sacred grains" as main crops: barley, soybeans, rice, wheat, and millet. All were considered to be the grains that were most vital to life. It is usual to associate China with rice-growing, but in northern China millet actually remained the main crop for thousands of years. Rice, which dominated grain-growing in southern China, was traditionally sown in paddy fields and planted by hand in slow-moving water. The development of many new varieties allowed it to be grown in more than a hundred countries in a wide range of conditions, and today thousands of varieties, stretching from brown to wild to white, exist.

In contrast, it was maize that provided the basis on which the great Aztec and Incan empires were founded in what is now Mexico and Central and South America. In the 16th century, when Spanish explorer Hernán Cortés and his men tried to ride their horses through Aztec maize fields, the plants grew so thick that they found them to be almost as impenetrable as a wall. Kernels dating back to 6700 BCE have been discovered in Peru.

From bread to porridge

Barley, once a staple grain used for making beer and bread, was nonetheless low in the gluten needed to make a lighter loaf, so it gradually fell out of favor as wheat became more widely used. Oats, although very nourishing, were regarded as food for barbarians by the ancient Greeks, and were famously described by English lexicographer Dr. Johnson in his 18th-century dictionary as "a grain which in England is generally given to horses."

Cereals were often ground into flour, but were also cooked whole in oatmeal-like dishes in the same manner as pulses and legumes. The latter included peas, beans, and lentils of many kinds. They are a very ancient food; the word "pulse" derives from Latin *puls*, meaning a thick bean or lentil porridge. Pulses were particularly useful to early humans as they could be eaten fresh or dried and stored for use when other crops had finished or failed. Beans and lentils have been found in many Egyptian tombs, and chickpeas were reputedly grown in the Hanging Gardens of Babylon.

> ## Ancient Egyptians added yeast to barley flour to bake bread, then crumbled that into water to make beer.

The ancient Greeks dedicated a temple to Kyanites, god of beans, while the Romans held a festival called Fabaria in honor of Carna, goddess of death. Roman priests, however, believed beans were impure and refused to eat them. Peas and beans of all kinds have been found at archaeological sites in many countries.

△ **The cost of progress**
The advent of steam-powered threshers during the 19th century meant vast amounts of grain were harvested—but the machines put hundreds of laborers out of work.

▷ **Not just birdseed**
Harvested for thousands of years, millet remains a vital crop in developing countries. In Niger, it accounts for 65 percent of cereals consumed, and is ground into flour to make bread.

△ **Milling mules**
In China, rice was milled in several different ways. One of the most common used mules, oxen, or horses harnessed to a wheel that crushed or ground the grains to make a fine flour.

Winnowing
In Asia, traditional methods of winnowing rice to separate the chaff from the grain are still practiced.

Rice food for billions

Rice has been cultivated for around 10,000 years and today it is Asia's most important food crop. The delicately flavored grains are the dietary mainstay for over 3.5 billion people— around half the world's population.

WHITE RICE   BLACK RICE   BROWN RICE

△ **Rice varieties**
The nutritional value of each type of rice is determined by the degree of refinement and by the species. White rice is highly refined and less nutritious than the black and brown varieties.

Rice as a food and a crop is embedded in the culture of Asian countries. It is a ritual food in the Japanese Shinto religion and it is also important in Hinduism, where *akshata* (uncooked pieces of rice mixed with turmeric) symbolizes prosperity, fertility, and bounty. It is usually thrown over the head of the devotees during *pujas* (prayers) at weddings, a tradition that has been adopted and adapted in the West. In Thailand, rice is revered as "Mother Rice."

The great debate

The question of where rice, which belongs to a family of grasses that includes wheat and corn, was first domesticated has been debated for years. Archaeologists have discovered fossilized traces of Asian rice (*Oryza sativa*) in the Yangtze Valley dated to 12000–11000 BCE. They have also uncovered agricultural tools made from animal shoulder bones dating back to 5000–4000 BCE, which they believe were used in rice cultivation by the Neolithic Hemudu culture, which inhabited southern China around 5500–3300 BCE. Archaeologists working in India, however, argue that rice cultivation may have begun in the Ganges river valley, and rice grains and early pottery have been uncovered at Lahuradewa in Uttar Pradesh, dating back to around 6500 BCE.

△ **Rice at the center**
In Japan, as in numerous other Asian countries, many meals are based around rice.

African evidence

Impressions of grains of African rice (*O. glaberrima*) in ceramics dated 1800–800 BCE have been discovered in Ganjigana in northeast Nigeria, and 3,000-year-old charred grains have been found in nearby Kursakata. Although it is not known if these are cultivated or wild rice grains, in the 1990s archaeologists uncovered evidence of domesticated African rice dated 300– 200 BCE at the ancient African city of Jenne-Jeno on the Niger Delta.

Slow to spread

Rice cultivation spread across the world relatively slowly, perhaps because it is labour intensive and requires a workforce living in settled communities that is readily available to build and maintain paddy fields. It is thought that soldiers of Alexander the Great's army may have taken the grain to Greece after his India campaign of 327–326 BCE and from there it spread to southern Europe and parts of North Africa.

In Italy, where risotto is a traditional dish, the earliest documentation of rice cultivation dates to 1475 BCE, when Galeazzo Maria Sforza, Duke of Milan, sent a sack to the Duke d'Este in Ferrara with a letter saying it would yield 12 sacks of edible grains. Rice

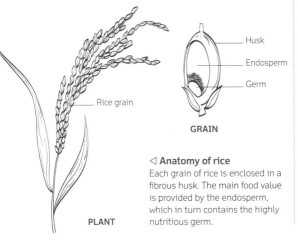

Husk
Endosperm
Germ

Rice grain

GRAIN

PLANT

◁ **Anatomy of rice**
Each grain of rice is enclosed in a fibrous husk. The main food value is provided by the endosperm, which in turn contains the highly nutritious germ.

ASIAN RICE

Origins
Asia

Major producers
China, India, Indonesia

Main food component
76 percent carbohydrate

Source of
Iron, vitamin B3, vitamin B9

Non-food uses
Fuel, fiber, insulation (husks)

Scientific name
Oryza sativa

△ Pounding the grains
In Japan and many other parts of Asia, rice grains were pounded by hand to free the grain from the husks.

▽ Cultivation in China
Rice-growing in China and elsewhere, as shown in this 18th-century painting, was a labor-intensive business, usually involving the entire village in planting the crop.

quickly became a key crop in the Po Valley—its fertile, swampy plains provide the ideal conditions in which rice still thrives today.

Rice is thought to have reached the Caribbean by the late 15th or early 16th centuries, and to have been introduced to Mexico by the Spanish in the 1520s and to Brazil by Portuguese colonizers and their African slaves around the same time. Rice arrived in South Carolina around 1685, when a ship sailing from Madagascar put in to Charleston Harbor for repairs following a storm. The ship's captain, John Thurber, is said to have met Henry Woodward, the first English settler in the area, and given him a bag of rice, setting the region on the path to being a major rice producer. The original Carolina rice was a variety of *Oryza glaberrima*. Slaves with rice-growing skills were needed to cultivate this labour-intensive type, but when the slave economy collapsed after the Civil War it was replaced by *O. sativa*, which can be grown with a smaller labour force.

> In India, rice used to be called *dhanya*, meaning "the sustainer of the human race."

The long, the short, and the medium
Today, rice is a major food crop, with over 441 million tons of milled rice produced every year. More than 40,000 varieties of rice are cultivated. The three main types are short-grain, such as the Italian Arborio used in risottos, soups, and puddings; medium-grain, which is used mainly in savory dishes; and long-grain, such as the much-prized Basmati, which contain a type of starch that enables the grains to remain separate when cooked.

Around 90 percent of all the rice produced is consumed in Asia. It is especially important as a dietary

staple for the most poor people in lower-income countries, who spend half their earnings on rice, but it is valued by all levels of society. Rice is eaten all over India and is particularly important in the south, where rice with dhal is on the daily menu of everyone from laborers to the wealthy. It is also eaten ground and parboiled with split peas to form a batter to make the spongy *idlis* popular in south Indian cuisine or the crispy pancakes called *dosa*. Rice remains a key part of southern Chinese cuisine, too, usually steamed but sometimes fried. In Laos and northeast Thailand sticky (glutinous) rice is a favorite.

Rice is also enjoyed in a multitude of sweet dishes, from Japanese *mochi*—a rice cake made of short-grain Japonica sticky rice pounded, molded, and stuffed with sweet soya bean curd, which is found on most Japanese restaurant menus—to the traditional English nursery favorite rice pudding. In West Africa, rice bread, cake, and porridge are served at weddings and funerals, while jollof rice is a popular one-pot dish.

◁ **Terraced landscape**
The construction of terraces to create rice paddies is common in China and in other rice-growing countries. These rice terraces in Yuanyang County, Yunnan, China, are typical.

"Without rice, even the cleverest housewife cannot cook."

CHINESE PROVERB

Barley rugged survivor

One of the first grain crops to be domesticated in the Fertile Crescent of the Middle East, barley has been a food staple for up to 10,000 years. Today, it is perhaps better known in the West for its role in alcoholic drinks such as malt whiskey.

Barley was central to the development of farming in the Fertile Crescent, the region in the Middle East where humans, who had previously led a nomadic hunter-gatherer lifestyle, first settled in agricultural communities around 8,000–10,000 years ago. A member of the grass family, barley's ability to thrive in conditions too cold or salty for its more fussy relative wheat, was part of its unstoppable success as it spread out across temperate parts of the world over the ensuing millennia. Barley reached Spain between 5000 and 4000 BCE and extended into northern Europe, reaching Britain by around 500 BCE. The cultivation of barley also spread via Egypt into other parts of North Africa and eastwards into Asia, arriving in China, India, Tibet, and Japan between 2000 and 3000 BCE.

Ancient uses for an ancient grain

Thousands of years ago barley was used to make porridge and a flatbread, and even brewed into beer—things that still occur in parts of the world today. In ancient Egypt, it was consumed both as a food and a beverage, a favorite drink being *haq*, a low-alcohol beer. In addition, the ancient Greeks used barley to make *paximadi*, a twice-baked rusk. Today in Crete, *paximadi* (or *dakos*) is still served, sprinkled with water, spread with diced tomatoes, and drizzled with olive oil. Until the fall of the Roman Empire, barley was a staple food for some Romans, too. Gladiators were called *hordierii*, literally "barley men," because they were fed a high-carbohydrate diet of barley and beans plus an ash-based drink.

By the Middle Ages and until the 16th century, people throughout Europe made their bread using barley. As well as being used to make porridge, barley is added to soups and stews, and made into barley water, a fortifying drink. Barley was introduced to North America in 1493 by the explorer Christopher Columbus on his second voyage.

Food and drink

Today, barley is the fourth most important cereal crop (after wheat, rice, and maize). More than half of the world's total crop is grown in developing countries, for example Ethiopia, where it is one of the grains used to make *ingera*, a flat pancake. In other parts of the world, including the US, barley is mainly grown for animal feed, but it remains popular in Middle Eastern cuisine, where it is an ingredient in salads, and on the Tibetan Plateau, where toasted barley flour is a staple. Barley tea featured in Asian cuisine for centuries and is still enjoyed in India, Japan, and Korea. Barley has also made its mark in the world of whiskey—it is the only ingredient other than water used to make the renowned single malt whiskeys of Scotland, Ireland, the US, and, more recently, Japan. It is now also widely used in the brewing of craft beer.

△ **Barley varieties**
The choice of barley variety depends on its intended use. Varieties for food use have a high grain yield, while for brewing a high starch content is desirable.

Origins
Middle East

Major producers
Russia, France, Germany

Main food component
78 percent carbohydrate

Source of
Iron, vitamin B3

Non-food use
Animal feed

Scientific name
Hordeum vulgare

△ **Woman's work**
In ancient Egypt, beer was brewed by women. Baked barley bread was crumbled, sieved into water, then fermented.

▷ **Drilling barley**
By the 19th century, wheat had long overtaken barley as the favored grain for making bread in Europe, but barley was still grown for other uses.

"Only reapers, reaping early in among the bearded barley, hear a song that echoes cheerly ..."

ALFRED, LORD TENNYSON, "THE LADY OF SHALOTT" (1842)

Traditional harvest
One hundred years ago in a field near Jerusalem, harvesting barley with only a short-handled scythe at hand was a back-breaking but vital task.

Oats a northern staple

A key cereal crop and animal food since ancient times, oats today provide a popular and sustaining base for breakfast cereals, oatmeal, cookies, and breads.

Husk

Bran

Endosperm

Germ

▷ **Anatomy of oats**
Oat grains have a fibrous outer husk that covers another fibrous layer called bran, which encloses the nutritious oat endosperm and germ.

Origins	Western Asia
Major producers	Russia, Canada, Poland
Main food component	66 percent carbohydrate
Source of	Magnesium, potassium, phosphorus, vitamin B9
Non-food use	Animal feed
Scientific name	*Avena sativa*

Cultivated oats derive from wild oats, a weedy grass, the remains of which archaeologists have found in Greece, Israel, Jordan, Syria, Turkey, and Iran dating from about 12,000 years ago.

The ancient Romans grew oats but thought them fit only for animals, although according to the 1st century Roman writer Pliny the Elder, "the races of Germany … live entirely on oatmeal porridge." In the Middle Ages in Europe, oats were grown as part of a three-year crop rotation that also included wheat and barley. During the same period, oatmeal was used to make pottage, a kind of vegetable stew, and also added to black pudding, a type of sausage made from the blood of slaughtered animals.

Breakfast breakthrough

By 1600 oats had become an important crop in northern Europe and a staple food of the Scots. Oats were introduced to North America by European colonists, where their first recorded planting was in Cuttyhunk, an island off the Massachusetts coast, in 1602. The Quaker Mill Company, founded in Ohio in 1877, first packaged oats as a breakfast cereal and in 1882, after the company was sold, Quaker Oats became the subject of the first US national magazine advertisement campaign for a breakfast cereal.

Today, oats rank fifth in terms of economic importance in world cereal production (after wheat, rice, corn, and barley). The cereal forms the basis not only of oatmeal, but also of the modern breakfast favorites muesli and granola, as well as being used in bakery foods such as oatcakes, oatmeal cookies, and oat bread. Oats are a key ingredient of the famous traditional Scottish specialty, haggis.

> " …in England [oats are] given to horses, but in Scotland support the people."
>
> DR. SAMUEL JOHNSON, ENGLISH WRITER, 1755

▷ **Bringing in the rye**
Rye threshing was beginning to be mechanized in early 20th-century Germany, but it was nevertheless a labor-intensive task.

◁ **Packing oats**
Oats entered the modern age when the American Quaker Mill Company started marketing oats as a breakfast food. This drawing from the 1890s shows women workers in the company's factory.

Rye a sturdy grain

Native to western Asia, this hardy annual cereal is widely cultivated, above all, for use in bread and in the brewing of whiskey.

◁ **Grains of rye**
Rye grains have bristly husks that contain the narrow gray-green seeds pictured here.

The Roman chronicler Pliny the Elder was perhaps the first to mention rye specifically when he observed the grain growing in the Alps during his army service there in the 1st century CE. Modern cultivated rye is the descendant of a perennial grass, mountain rye—a grain thought to have originated in the inhospitable highlands of western Asia around 3000 BCE. This annual grass, which is tolerant of cool conditions, spread to Europe around 2000 BCE and then eastward toward the Himalayas. It reached Scandinavia between 1700 and 500 BCE.

The Germanic tribes including the Anglo-Saxons, who brought the grain to the British Isles, and the Franks, who took it to France, valued rye as a dependable source of food. In France, a dense, gray rye bread was still a staple in rural areas up to the early 20th century. The Vikings used rye in flatbreads and circular unleavened loaves. They also made sourdough rye loaves. Today, bread made from rye remains popular throughout Scandinavia, Germany, and the countries of the Baltic region.

Introduced by the French

The grain traveled with early settlers to North America. French explorer Marc L'Escarbot planted rye in Nova Scotia in 1606, and rye is still cultivated in the northern states of the US as well as in Canada. Today, rye is best known as an ingredient in crackers and a variety of breads and crispbreads, as well as breakfast cereals. It is the basis for alcoholic drinks such as rye whiskey and rye vodka in several countries.

Origins
Western Asia

Major producers
Germany, Poland, Russia

Main food component
76 percent carbohydrate

Source of
Magnesium, potassium, phosphorus, vitamin B9

Non-food uses
Animal feed, thatching, paper-making

Scientific name
Secale cereale

Wheat source of our daily bread

Cultivated since the birth of agriculture in the Middle East more than 10,000 years ago, wheat has spread around the world to become the key ingredient in many staple foods.

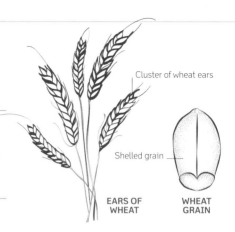

Cluster of wheat ears

Shelled grain

EARS OF WHEAT   **WHEAT GRAIN**

Wheat, which is a type of grass belonging to the genus *Triticum* is, together with barley, the oldest cultivated cereal. Today, wheat takes up 16 percent of the land devoted to crops worldwide. Wheat's success as a food crop owes much to its versatility. It can grow in most climates and from sea level to elevations of more than 4,000ft (1,220m). The grain can be stored for long periods of time and it is easily ground into flour, which can be used to make food staples such as bread, pasta, and noodles. Wheat is the most important source of carbohydrate in the majority of countries and is also an important provider of protein.

The grain that fed the world
The wild ancestor of wheat has been traced back to Karacadag mountain, a volcano in southeast Turkey. Here, and in other areas of the Fertile Crescent, such as Syria, Iraq, and the Nile Valley, the first wheat was cultivated around 9500 BCE. It differed from

wild wheat in having larger seeds and stronger stems that would break and allow the seeds to disperse only when harvested. The cultivation of wheat played a major role in the agricultural revolution that saw the transition of humans from hunter-gatherers to farmers. It reached Cyprus as early as 9000 BCE, and within another 3,000 years had spread to Greece, Egypt, and India, and then to China, Korea, and Japan between 2500 and 800 BCE.

Wheat, ancient and modern
In Western Europe, some of the earliest wheat remains were found in the Swiss Alps in a well-preserved 4,000-year-old wooden "lunch box," which contained two ancient varieties, spelt (*Triticum spelta*) and emmer (*T. dicoccon*). Best known in western countries as farro, emmer was the most popular wheat in the ancient world, and is the variety from which durum wheat (*T. durum*) derives. The ancient Egyptians grew wheat and were skilled bakers, turning wheat flour into the first leavened breads, while the ancient Greeks also cultivated wheat, especially emmer and durum. The Roman Empire's

△ **Anatomy of wheat**
The "ears" of wheat grow in long clusters. Each ear consists of a grain enclosed in a fibrous husk.

▷ **Harvest by hand**
Until the advent of mechanized methods, wheat was harvested with hand tools such as this sickle.

▽ **Massive machines**
A "battalion" of combine harvesters tackle the harvest in 1950s Nebraska, one of the major wheat-growing Midwestern states.

▷ **Working the fields**
This Italian painting from the 15th century depicts a harvest scene that would have been familiar throughout Europe.

rapid expansion was fed by wheat, brought by ship from Sardinia, Sicily, and Africa, and then from conquests further afield, such as Britain, where, by 360 CE, its wheat was feeding the Roman army on the Rhine in Germany. The Romans were the first to distinguish "hard" or "strong" wheat, with high gluten content suitable for bread making, from "soft" wheat, with a low gluten content, which is better for making cakes, cookies, pies, and pastries.

Spanish explorers took wheat to the Americas in the 16th century. Today, the Wheat Belt runs more than 1,500 miles (2,400km) from central Alberta in Canada to central Texas. It is one of the world's largest wheat-growing areas, part of a US national wheat total of 46 million acres (18.6 million hectares). More than 90 percent of grain comes from the hardy common, or bread, wheat (T. *aestivum*), which adapts to most terrains and climates, and is highly productive.

However, some of the more ancient varieties have been revived in the 21st century for their distinctive taste and their potentially greater health benefits. Spelt is valued for the dense, nutty-tasting bread it makes and its low gluten level. Einkorn had been pushed aside by the rise of industrial farming, although it survived in drier areas such as Morocco and Turkey, where it is boiled to make bulgar. It is high in fiber and, like spelt, is valued for the nuttier flavors of its bread.

Origins	Western Asia, Egypt
Major producers	China, India, Russia
Main food component	72 percent carbohydrate
Source of	Magnesium, phosphorus, folate
Non-food use	Animal feed
Scientific name	*Triticum aestivum* *T. dicoccon* *T. spelta* *T. durum*

▷ **Traditionally trussed**
Wheat was traditionally secured after harvesting into sheaves. These were later stacked and brought back to the farm for threshing.

Each year, more than 772 million tons of wheat are produced around the world.

Pasta Italy's famous food

Although its exact origins are lost to the mists of time, today pasta is widely recognized as one of the first convenience foods—thanks to its cheapness, ease of storage, and affinity for a wide variety of accompanying sauces and fillings.

Although virtually a byword for Italian cuisine, pasta probably originally hails from Asia, where its close relatives, noodles (*see* pp.234–235), are a dietary staple. One of the differences between the two is that pasta is made from hard durum wheat, while noodles use "soft" wheat and/or other grains such as buckwheat or rice. Pasta dough is also kneaded then extruded through a machine—forced through a perforated end piece to create different shapes, while noodles are flattened by rolling and then cut into strands.

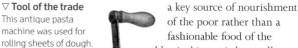

▽ **Tool of the trade**
This antique pasta machine was used for rolling sheets of dough.

An uncertain ancestry

The origins of pasta, which simply means "paste" or "dough," are vague, partly because its ingredients, basically just flour and water, make it hard to trace its ancestry or distinguish it from other ancient foods made from similar ingredients, such as flatbreads. As a key source of nourishment of the poor rather than a fashionable food of the wealthy, its history is less well documented than more luxurious food items.

According to some food historians, a type of pasta was known to the ancient Greeks and Romans, but it was probably a kind of thin flatbread rather than pasta as we know it today. The Roman poet Horace refers to *laganum* in the 1st century BCE, a word similar to the modern Italian lasagna, and some recipes from ancient Rome mention layers of *lagana* in dishes. However, a recipe by the early Greek food writer Athenaeus of Naucratis for *lagana*—fine sheets of dough mixed with lettuce juice and spices and then deep fried—is clearly not the meat, pasta, and sauce layered dish known as lasagna today.

"The best maccaroni [sic] in Italy is made in Naples."

THOMAS JEFFERSON

△ **Hung out to dry**
A young man hangs lengths of fresh pasta on drying rails in Naples in 1900. The Neapolitan way of drying pasta naturally was said to give their products a special quality.

Two things are known: by the Middle Ages, the Italians had adopted pasta as a food staple and the Venetian explorer Marco Polo did not introduce it to Italy from China. While it is not known how pasta first reached Europe, although Arab traders may well have played a part, there was already a thriving trade in *obra de pasta* (dried pasta products) in the Mediterranean by the time Marco Polo returned from his voyages eastward in 1295.

The main centers for dried pasta production in the medieval period were Sicily followed by Sardinia and Genoa. Ravioli (stuffed pasta) boiled in meat broth appears in cookbooks such as the *Libro de Arte Coquinaria* by Maestro Martino, chef to Rome's Patriarch of

Origins
Asia

Major producers
Italy, US, Turkey

Main food component
75 percent carbohydrate

Source of
Calcium, magnesium, phosphate, vitamin B3

Aquileia around 1450, while a recipe for "rauioles" appears in the 14th-century English recipe collection, the *Forme of Cury*.

Across the Atlantic

Pasta continued to be a favorite food of Italians as well as making an appearance in the cuisines of other European countries throughout the following centuries. Thomas Jefferson loved the pasta he was introduced to during his time in Italy so much—particularly the macaroni made from semolina flour—that he bought a pasta-making machine and shipped it back home in 1793.

One of the key factors in popularizing pasta was the widespread mechanization of pasta production in the 19th and early 20th centuries—first in Naples and then elsewhere in Italy and beyond. Another factor was the large number of Italian immigrants crossing the Atlantic and taking their taste for pasta to America with them and transforming this starchy staple into the ubiquitous foodstuff it is has become.

Today, pasta comes in myriad sizes and shapes. There are more than 300 types in Italy alone, ranging from the thick, wormlike *bigoli* and twisted *strozzapreti* (priest stranglers) of northern Italy to the quill-shaped penne and petal-like orecchiette (little ears) of the south. Other versions include Germany's spaetzle, Poland's *pierogi*, the Ukraine's ravioli-like stuffed *vareniki*, and Greece's rice-like orzo. In the US, thanks to the Italian influence, pasta is made and served in much the same way as it is in Europe, although the famous spaghetti with meatballs is probably an American invention.

▷ **Shaping up**
Pasta comes in a huge range of shapes, sizes, and colors. Today Italy boasts several hundred shapes of pasta products.

Street food

Where, when, and how street food originated is unclear, but as early as the 6th century BCE, fried fish and lentil soup were popular street foods in classical Greece. In imperial Rome, eating food in this way was a part of daily life, whether quickly snatched up at *thermopolia,* the forerunners of today's fast-food restaurants; *popinae,* wine bars frequented by the lower classes; or open-air bars known as *camponae* that were popular during long, hot Roman summers. Roasted chickpeas seasoned with cumin and salt and sausages spiced with pepper and pine nuts were particular favorites. The Byzantines also loved street food. Under Ottoman rule, lamb kebabs; stuffed mussels; *kokova,* a sandwich of grilled sheep's intestines; and *macuri,* a vibrantly colored soft toffee paste from central Anatolia (modern-day western Turkey) were all everyday street fare.

Across the Atlantic, Aztec street traders sold *atote,* a kind of maize gruel. But the most popular street fare were tortillas—dipped in a sauce of ground chilis and water—and steamed maize tamales. In the early 1500s, Spanish missionary Father Bernardino de Sahagún saw tamales filled with meat, fish, mushrooms, rabbit, and even frogs on sale in Mexico.

It was in the 19th century that street food became a truly global phenomenon. German emigrants brought hamburgers and hot dogs to the US, while Victorian Britain added fish and chips to its menu. Chinese street food also spread from its homeland in the form of pork or chicken blood soup, fish balls, noodle dishes, steamed buns with various fillings, and dumplings in all shapes and sizes. Indian street food is just as diverse; Mumbai, the country's street-food capital, has an estimated 250,000 active vendors.

◁ **Taking it to the streets**
Squares the world over are a prime location for street-food vendors. In Marrakesh, some stallholders even provide seating.

WHEAT AND EGG NOODLES

BEAN-THREAD NOODLES

RICE NOODLES

△ **The fat and the thin**
Noodles of varying thicknesses made from different ingredients are used for a range of dishes, from soups to stir-fries.

Noodles

Asia's versatile foodstuff

Pasta's eastern relative, noodles have been a staple food across Asia for at least two millennia and remain key ingredients in present-day kitchens from China and Japan to Southeast Asia and the Philippines.

In 2005, Chinese archaeologists reported uncovering prehistoric remains of millet noodles in a sealed earthenware bowl at the Late Neolithic site of Lajia, in northwest China. This proved, they claimed, that boiled noodles were prepared in the area some 4,000 years ago. Whether or not this is true, noodles seem to have been eaten in China by the 2nd century BCE.

The Tang dynasty poet Du Fu in the 1st century CE extolled *leng tao*, cold green noodles eaten in summer, which he described as "cold as snow when gliding through the teeth." A noodle called *shui yin*, made by pulling dough into strips the thickness of chopsticks, features in the 6th-century CE Chinese text *Qi Min Yao Shu*.

China's modern essential
Noodle production became mechanized in the 19th century, with the first machine-made noodles appearing in the 1850s. Today, China is the world's largest consumer of noodles. Made from a variety of starches including wheat, rice, mung beans, and tapioca, they often have added ingredients such as egg, shrimp, or spinach.

Noodles also come in a variety of shapes and sizes and are served in many ways—added to soup with vegetables, meat, or seafood, for example; or stir-fried with spring onions, oil, and soy sauce. They are often eaten at celebrations in China—"longevity" noodles are traditionally eaten on birthdays, while noodles with gravy are served with the first meal following a move into a new house.

Japan and beyond
Japan also has a rich history and variety of noodles, or *menrui*, which extends back to the 8th century CE, when they are thought to have been introduced from China. Ropelike twisted *somochi* rice noodles were apparently a favorite on special occasions at this time

RICE NOODLES

Origins
China

Major producers
China, Japan, Indonesia

Main food component
80 percent carbohydrate

Source of
Sodium, phosphorus

and during the Heian (794–1185 CE) period, while thin wheat noodles, or *somon*, appeared later during the Kamakura period (1185–1333 CE).

The two most common types of noodle in Japan today are the thick, soft udon (wheat) noodles and the chewy, pale, slightly bitter tasting, soba (buckwheat) noodles. Noodle-making in Japan is an art and masters of the craft can often be seen at work in the windows of specialist noodle restaurants as a strategy to encourage new customers to enter.

Instant success

No history of noodles is complete without mention of Chinese–Japanese Momofuku Ando's invention of instant noodles in 1958, which caused a global revolution in eating. Noodles—*pancit* or *pansit*—are also a staple in the Philippines, where they were originally introduced by the Chinese, and are served in many forms in supermarkets and specialist restaurants called *panciterias*.

◁ **Team work**
Traditionally, sheets of fine noodles were hung out on rails to dry. This Japanese print shows a young girl and a servant drying out freshly prepared noodles in a garden.

"The longer the noodles you eat, the longer your life."

CHINESE SAYING

▽ **Friendly fare**
In China, informal meals of noodles, usually eaten with chopsticks, are occasions for celebration of family and friendship.

Couscous granules of sustenance

The time-consuming process of turning cereals into the soft granules of couscous has occupied the womenfolk of North Africa for millennia. This simple food is now eaten in many parts of the world.

It is not known where couscous, North Africa's answer to pasta, first originated. However, vessels that may have been used for making it have been found in tombs in North Africa dating back to the 2nd century BCE during the reign of the Berber king Massinissa.

Couscous consists of crushed granules of durum (hard) wheat. However, in sub-Saharan Africa it is still made with crushed millet as it was in ancient times. The name derives from the Berber *seksu* or *kesksu*, meaning well-rolled, well-formed, or rounded, referring to how it is prepared.

> ### The world's first couscous factory started production in Algeria in 1907.

Making couscous involves sprinkling ground cereal grains with water before hand rolling them to create small granules. Sprinkling the granules with dry flour keeps them separate while they are sieved until they form a mass of similar-size granules. Traditionally, the prepared granules are steamed in a two-part steamer, known by its French name of *couscoussier*, consisting of a large pan (in which the broth is boiled) with an interlocking pan set on top of it. The upper pan, where the couscous is placed, has a perforated base that allows steam rising from the boiling liquid in the lower pan to cook the couscous in the pan above. Once cooked, the steamed couscous is topped with vegetables, a spicy or mild broth, and served with meat, such as chicken, lamb, or mutton.

Arguments over origin

As well as the vessels dating from Massinissa's time, others resembling modern *couscoussiers* have been identified in the Tiaret region of Algeria dating from the 9th century. Some authorities argue that couscous originated in the medieval Sudanic kingdom in what are now Niger, Mali, Mauritania, Ghana, and Burkina Faso from where it spread throughout North Africa and the sub-Saharan region, reaching Turkey in the 16th century where it remains popular to this day.

Couscous appears in an anonymous 13th-century Spanish–Moorish cookbook, which features a recipe for *alcuzcuz fitīyānī*. A 13th-century Syrian historian from Aleppo also refers to couscous. The grain was known in Italy, too—Bartolomeo Scappi's cookbook of 1570 features a Moorish dish called *succussu*. In the 17th century, the French writer Rabelais refers to *coscoton á la Moresque* (Moorish couscous). Today, couscous is a staple throughout North Africa and in many parts of the Middle East. It is also popular in France, Spain, Portugal, Italy, and Greece.

Versatile accompaniment

During the 20th century, wheat replaced millet as the most popular grain for making couscous. In North Africa, it is still most often eaten in the traditional fashion with meat and vegetables, but it can also be served sweet. Algeria and Morocco have a dessert called *seffa* consisting of couscous sprinkled with almonds, cinnamon, and sugar. In Tunisia, sweet milk, dried fruits, and nuts are used to make a similar dish.

Labor-intensive couscous preparation is today giving way to quick-cooking, pre-steamed, and dried couscous. This is especially true in the West where it is sold in boxes or pouches pre-seasoned with added chickpeas or vegetables.

△ **Served in style**
In North Africa, couscous is traditionally served in highly decorated ceramic dishes.

Origins
North Africa

Main food component
23 percent carbohydrate

Source of
Selenium

▷ **Pounding the grain**
Grinding grains using traditional tools in sub-Saharan West Africa took time and effort for villagers.

BROOMCORN MILLET

Origins
Asia, Africa

Major producers
India, Nigeria, Niger

Main food component
73 percent carbohydrate

Source of
Iron, magnesium, zinc, B vitamins

Non-food uses
Bird and animal feed, fuel

Scientific name
Panicum miliaceum

Millet   ancient grain of arid regions

A staple food for our ancestors, millet was grown in the famous Hanging Gardens of Babylon. The grains of this ancient cereal are still widely consumed especially in hot, arid parts of the world.

Millet's short growing season—it is ready to harvest just 45 days after planting—was one of the factors that made this grain valuable to our prehistoric ancestors, allowing it to be grown in temporary or seasonal settlements to supplement what they caught or foraged. This type of grain includes members of a huge grass family comprising more than 6,000 species. Proso, also called broomcorn millet (*Panicum miliaceum*), and foxtail millet (*Setaria* sp.) were among the most important cultivated crops in ancient times. The remains of charred millet grains suggest millet was cultivated along China's Yellow River as long ago as 6000 BCE. Foxtail millet—with wheat, sorghum, rice, and soya beans—was one of five sacred grains in ancient China. Another species, pearl millet (*Pennisetum glaucum*), was cultivated in northern Mali between 2500 and 2000 BCE from where it spread to India by 1500 BCE.

Bread and porridge
Known as *kenkhros* to the ancient Greeks and *milium* to the ancient Romans, millet was used to make porridge and a coarse, unleavened bread. It was also an important crop in the Middle Ages in Europe—for example, in Poland, where it was widely used to make porridge and flatbreads. Today, millet remains one of the world's most important cereal grains, often used in breakfast cereals and bread.

▷ **Foxtail millet**
The brushlike appearance of the flower clusters of this common species of millet have given rise to its common name.

Buckwheat

a modest grain that is key to many dishes

This grain, with its origins in China, is a key ingredient of Japan's signature soba noodles. Over the centuries it has found a place in the culinary traditions of Europe and America in breakfast cereals, pancakes, and dumplings.

Despite its common European name, buckwheat is not related to wheat nor is it technically a cereal. Instead it is a "pseudocereal," a non-starchy food grain. In fact, it is more closely related to sorrel and rhubarb than to wheat. The name buckwheat probably derives from the Dutch, *boechweit*, meaning beech wheat, possibly because its triangular seeds look similar to the larger but also triangular beechnuts.

The original birthplace of buckwheat has long been debated. Archaeologists have found remnants of cultivated grains in China dating back to 2600 BCE, and of buckwheat pollen in Japan dating back to between 3500 and 500 BCE. Recently, plant geneticists have traced back the wild ancestor of common buckwheat to the Sanjiang region of China.

Famine relief

The earliest written mention of buckwheat appears in Chinese writings of the 5th and 6th centuries CE. In Japan, buckwheat, or soba, was the subject of an imperial edict issued in 722 CE recorded in the famous historical text, *Shoku-Nihongi*, in which farmers were urged to plant the crop as a buffer against famine that could result from a poor rice harvest. It thus became an important food in Japan, where the hulled seeds were originally simply cooked. In later centuries they were ground and used to make porridge, soba cake, and soba dumplings. Today, in the form of soba noodles, buckwheat remains one of Japan's most popular and best-known foods.

▷ **Bringing in the harvest**
Whole communities frequently work together to bring in the harvest. In this painting by French artist Jean-François Millet, women gather the sheaves, while men thresh the crop.

Kasha and crêpes

Buckwheat reached Europe via Turkey and Russia in the 14th and 15th centuries, where its hardiness and ability to grow in areas inhospitable to other grains made it a popular peasant staple. The Dutch introduced it to North America in the 17th century.

In Europe, buckwheat production reached its height in the 19th century but it remains popular in a variety of dishes, from Eastern Europe's kasha (buckwheat porridge) and Polish *pierogi* (stuffed dumplings) to the traditional crêpes (pancakes) and galettes (flat cakes) of Brittany, France.

> "Buckwheat porridge is our mother ... "
>
> TRADITIONAL RUSSIAN SAYING

△ **Early mechanization**
The buckwheat harvest was made less labor-intensive by the introduction of machinery.

Origins
China

Major producers
Russia, China, Ukraine

Main food component
72 percent carbohydrate

Source of
Iron, potassium, B vitamins

Scientific name
Fagopyrum esculentum

WHITE WHEAT BREAD

Origins
Central Asia

Main food component
44 percent carbohydrate

Source of
Iron, calcium, vitamin B3, vitamin B9

Bread the global sustainer

The most universal of all dietary staples, bread—white or brown, leavened or unleavened—is so central to many civilizations and cultures that the very word has become synonymous with food.

Almost from the moment the first humans realized that plants could be torn, crushed, mixed, and transformed by heat, bread was born. The discovery of worn-down areas on unwashed grindstones together with traces of starch grains from cattail plants (bulrushes) and ferns in Italy, the Czech Republic, and Russia dating back some 30,000 years suggest that Stone Age hunter-gatherers were grinding flour—and using it to make bread—well before the dawn of agriculture, around 12,000 years ago.

Ancient flatbreads
These early breads would have been flatbreads cooked on flat "bakestones" heated over a fire, a method widely used in Scotland to cook flat unleavened oaten "bannock cakes" well into the 19th century, and still a culinary feature of many regions, including Mexico (tortillas), India (chapatis, naan),

and the Middle East (*taboon*, matzo). The earliest flour was hand-ground to form a coarse, whole grain distantly related to that used to make dark breads, such as pumpernickel, still popular in Germany and Central Europe. As agricultural techniques, such as the cultivation of stronger-stemmed, more productive wheats, spread from areas of the Fertile Crescent including present-day Iraq and Turkey, so did bread-making. By 3000 BCE, flatbreads were being baked in tandoor ovens in India and even

▽ **Timeless task**
This street vendor in Jaipur, India, prepares chapati (flatbread) in the same way it has been prepared in that region for millennia.

as far north as Britain, where two 5,500-year-old lumps of bread were found in 1999.

Early ceramic loaf pans discovered near the ancient Mesopotamian city of Uruk, now in Iraq, point to bread-making around 4000 BCE to 3100 BCE. Bread is noted repeatedly in the *Epic of Gilgamesh*, dating from around 2000 BCE, for example, where Gilgamesh offers the goddess Ishtar "bread and all sorts of food fit for a god."

Rising with the Egyptians

Bread was vital to the diet of ancient Egyptians. Hundreds of bread loaves, some more than 5,000 years old, left as offerings in tombs and graves, have

◁ **Ancient bakery**
In ancient Egypt, bread- and beer-making may have been linked as indicated by this wooden model of a bakery and brewery from ancient Egypt (2010–1961 BCE)

comedy *Omphale*, described Thearion's baking as "… a magic show made in Athens." The Greeks were also the inventors of the front-loading oven, which made baking quicker and more efficient and helped to take it out of the home and turn it into a commercial trade.

The ancient Romans were enthusiastic bakers, too, using Egypt as their main supplier of wheat. According to the Roman chronicler Pliny the Elder, professional

"Do not eat bread while another stands by without extending your hand to him."

EGYPTIAN NEW KINGDOM PROVERB

▽ **Feeding the troops**
A regular supply of bread was essential to any military campaign. British troops are pictured here baking bread for soldiers at the front line during World War I.

survived. The early Egyptians were skilled at baking both unleavened bread—made with barley; spelt; and durah, a kind of millet—and leavened (risen) bread made with emmer, an ancient type of wheat known today as farro and still used to make bread in Italy. Wealthy Egyptians preferred white bread, made with finely sifted flour, while commoners were expected to eat coarse, dark varieties. Bread in Egypt was a currency as well as a food, with pyramid builders—such as those who worked on the Great Pyramid of the pharaoh Khufu around 2600 BCE—paid in loaves and beer. Egyptian bakers also managed to isolate the yeast that made bread rise and manufacture this for widespread use from around 300 BCE.

Shared knowledge

Bread-making skills spread from Egypt to Europe, where cities in ancient Greece vied with each other to produce the best loaves. In the 4th century BCE, the Athenian baker Thearion was picked out for particular praise, including by the writer Antiphanes, who, in his

bakers were established in Rome in the 2nd century BCE and formed a craft guild. Outside the Porta Maggiore, bas-relief carvings on the tomb of the baker Marcus Vergilius Eurysaces, dating back to between 50 BCE and 20 BCE, document the process of bread-baking in the city. More than 30 bakeries have also been uncovered at the ancient Roman site of Pompeii, including whole loaves carbonized after the eruption of Vesuvius in 79 CE.

Milling and baking revolution

By the Middle Ages, bread was a staple throughout Europe, with a thick slice of stale bread often serving as an edible plate called a trencher, a practice that

△ **Bringing home the bread**
Many households in the past did not have an oven in which they could make bread and bought their loaves from a bakery, such as this 17th-century Italian example.

persisted until the 16th century, when pewter plates came into extensive use. The rivalry between white and brown bread that had begun in ancient times continued. In London, for example, the "brown-bakers" and "white-bakers" trade guilds did not unite as one company of bakers until 1645. In the late 18th century, England emerged as the hub of the Industrial Revolution, powered by steam engines such as those installed to power 20 pairs of flour-producing millstones in London's first great factory, the Albion Mills. Built in 1786, it processed 10 bushels (363 liters) of wheat an hour, giving its owners a monopoly over the price of flour and driving many traditional millers out of business. The mill mysteriously burned down in 1791, allegedly to great rejoicing from flour sellers

who danced on London's Blackfriars Bridge in celebration.

The Albion Mills factory was ahead of its time, however, and wind and water remained the main sources of power for mills until the 19th century, when they were gradually replaced throughout Europe by the Swiss-invented steel rollermill, which made it easier to manufacture white flour—and bread.

In Paris, an Austrian army officer, August Zang, introduced a new steam oven. The French breakfast table staple, the baguette, did not appear until 1920, when a new law prevented French bakers from working between 10pm and 4am. The traditional longer loaves could not be produced in time for breakfast, so a shorter version—the baguette—was the answer. The mechanization of bread production continued in the 20th century as gas ovens replaced wood- and coal-burning brick ovens.

The modern loaf

One of the most significant turning points in the consumption of bread came in July 1928 when a machine invented by the US engineer Otto Rohwedder turned out the first sliced and wrapped loaves at the Chillicothe Baking Company in Missouri. By the 1930s, around 80 percent of bread sold in the USA was presliced and wrapped. Americans took to the sliced loaves so wholeheartedly that the phrase "the best thing since sliced bread" became a universal term of approval.

In the 1960s, the demise of small-scale traditional bakeries was hastened by the development in the United Kingdom of the Chorleywood production method, which cut the long period of fermentation needed for dough to rise. This significantly reduced the time it took to produce bread, but also reduced the quality of the bread.

Despite the mass production of bread around the world, many regional varieties have survived. Black and brown rye breads, with origins in the Middle Ages, are popular in Scandinavia and Central and

> Sliced bread was banned in the US in January 1943 to help the war effort. The ban was rescinded in March 1943.

△ **Making more dough**
For centuries people have sought to reduce the labor of bread making. This antique dough-maker might have provided a solution for some.

Eastern Europe. In the Middle East, flatbreads, such as Iran's *sanguake* and Armenia's *lavash*, are still as popular they were in ancient times, while India, especially, has a wide array of flatbreads or roti, including *puris* (fried small puffed breads), *parathas* (a flaky, often stuffed, flatbread), and *puran poli* (a sweet flatbread).

Far Eastern countries such as China and Japan, however, have been slow to adopt bread as a staple food and have not developed any significant bread-baking traditions. In China, bread-making has traditionally been confined to the north of the country, where steamed breads, such as *mantou*, possibly introduced by the invading Mongols in the 13th century CE, are popular. Japan embraced bread products only after World War II.

Old skills revived

In the West, the 21st century has seen a revival of bread making employing centuries-old methods in small-scale bakeries, and using specialty flours and traditional techniques of leavening. Some breads produced in this way, such as sourdough, would be familiar even to ancient Egyptian bakers.

◁ **Bread as propaganda**
In many countries and at many times bread has been used as a byword for prosperity. This 1947 Russian poster uses bread as a symbol of well-being.

▽ **Food for the masses**
As early as the 18th century, bread making in France was a large-scale activity, requiring many people to make and knead the dough.

Maize the world's most versatile grass

From its early cultivation by ancient civilizations in a Mexican valley, maize has evolved into a global super crop, grown in more than 160 countries, with thousands of varieties providing a staple food for billions of people.

Also known as corn, maize was so important to ancient Mesoamerican peoples that corn deities were worshipped. It is a member of the huge family of grasses, or cereals, that includes wheat, barley, and rice. The precise origins of domesticated maize were debated for much of the 19th and 20th centuries. However, plant geneticists have now traced its ancestry to teosinte, a wild grass from Mexico and Central America that shares much of the genetic material of maize. What long baffled experts was the vast difference between this weedy grass with only 6–12 meager kernels in a hard outer shell, and the familiar green giant with its plump cobs packed with glistening kernels.

Maize is thought to have first been cultivated around 9000 BCE in what is now south-central Mexico. Farmers chose which kernels to plant according to characteristics

◁ **Maize mythology**
This Mayan amulet from Mexico depicts a headdress containing maize cobs. According to a Mayan creation myth, humans sprang from corn.

such as size, taste, and ease of grinding. Over millennia, the cobs became larger and the rows of kernels increased, eventually reaching the size found on the modern plant.

The three sisters

Maize, along with beans and squashes, formed "the three sisters," the staple crops of the indigenous peoples of Mexico and Central America. In this system of cultivation, which began around 5000 BCE, maize was planted first and provided support for the bean plants. Once harvested, it was easy to store and then eaten whole or ground into flour. The plants also

Origins
Mexico

Major producers
US, China, Brazil

Main food component
19 percent carbohydrate

Source of
Vitamin B1, vitamin B3, vitamin C

Non-food uses
Animal feed, ethanol (fuel alcohol), biodegradable cups, paper coatings, fabrics, carpeting

Scientific name
Zea mays

△ **Colorful corn**
In addition to the familiar cobs of golden maize, many colored variants of corn are grown for both human and animal consumption.

△ **Corn in a can**
This label for an American brand of tinned corn dates from around 1890. Canning advances in the 19th century increased the availability of maize to urban populations.

> "What more can a reasonable man desire … than … ears of green sweet-corn boiled?"

HENRY DAVID THOREAU, *WALDEN* (1854)

provided materials for basket-making and fuel for fires. After Europeans arrived in the Americas in 1492, Spanish settlers began to cultivate maize and traders transported it back to Spain, from where it soon spread to Italy. By the 18th century, maize had reached China, Korea, and Japan. After World War II, traditional varieties were bred to form hybrids that could adapt to colder and wetter northern European conditions.

Hardy and adaptable

Today, maize is the main food crop of South America, Central America, Mexico, the Caribbean, and sub-Saharan Africa, where it is the staple food for half the population. It is one of the most adaptable cereal crops,

growing in a wide range of conditions. It is as versatile a food as it is a crop. It is eaten whole as "corn on the cob," added to casseroles such as *ajiaco* (a Colombian potato, chicken, and corn stew), and milled to produce cornmeal, which is used in a variety of breads, from the traditional southern US corn bread to tortillas (Mexico) and *arepas* (Venezuela), and as the basis of Italy's polenta. Maize is also widely used in the food industry to make corn oil, cornflakes, cornflour, and the sweetener corn syrup.

▽ **Popcorn vendor**
An early 20th-century popcorn vendor stands next to his specially adapted vehicle. Popcorn became a hugely popular snack in the US in this period.

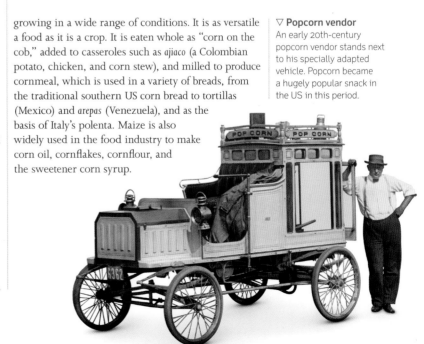

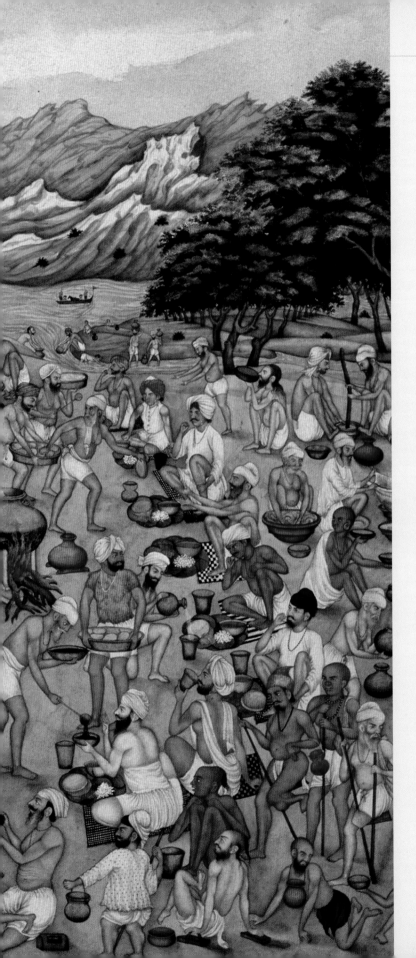

Food and religion

Religion and food have been linked inextricably in different cultures and throughout history all over the world. For many, food is an integral part of a religious experience, as in the case of Rosh Hashanah, the celebration marking the start of the Jewish New Year. During the festivities, symbolic foods known collectively as *simanim* are prepared, including slices of apple dipped in honey to symbolize a sweet year ahead.

Many people choose to eat or avoid certain foods because of religious beliefs. In Islam, foods are categorized as *halal*—those that may be eaten—and *haram*—those that must be avoided. Similarly, Jews divide foods into kosher (allowed) or *treif* (forbidden).

In Hinduism, cows are sacred animals but, while the eating of beef is forbidden, the consumption of dairy products, such as milk, butter, cheese, and yogurt, is allowed. Some Buddhists refuse to eat onions, scallions, garlic, chives, and leeks, while Jains avoid eating root vegetables as well as meat and fish.

Eating food communally is an important part of Sikhism. Each *gurdwara*—literally "the door that leads to the Guru," the name Sikhs give to a place of worship—contains a *langar* or kitchen, where, regardless of creed, sex, or color, all people are welcome to a free meal. The idea came from Guru Nanak Dev Ji, the first guru of Sikhism. The guru rejected the Hindu caste system, whereby people of different castes shun eating together, in favor of equality. Everyone shares the tasks of food preparation, cooking, serving the food, and cleaning up afterward. It is a demonstration of *sewa*, selfless service to others in the *sadhsangat* (community).

◁ **Caste-less camp**
Sikh sacred spaces, such as the 19th-century camp of holy man Baba Bir Singh, fed thousands of people a day from all walks of life.

Lentils the pulse of many cultures

One of the first crops ever to be cultivated and once considered food for the poor, protein-rich lentils are now an essential element of human diets the world over, and have discovered a new role as a staple for vegetarians in the West.

Origins
Middle East, Central Asia

Major producers
Canada, India, Turkey

Main food component
63 percent carbohydrate

Source of
Iron, zinc, vitamins B2, B3, B9, vitamin K

Scientific name
Lens culinaris

Lentil plants originated in the Middle East and Central Asia some 9,000 years ago. They can grow up to 1¾in (45mm) in height and have pale blue flowers. The oblong pods of this pulse are about ½in (15mm) long, inside which lie one or two small round or oval seeds. Most are green or brown but they may also be black, red, yellow, or orange.

The common name for the plant and its seeds derived from the Latin *lens*. This word was later adopted to describe the double convex-shaped glass (lens) used in ophthalmology.

Ancient origins

The earliest charred remains of lentils were found in the Franchethi Cave in Greece and date back to around 11000 BCE. Similar remains dated between 9000 and 8000 BCE were unearthed in Tell Mureybit, an ancient Syrian site. Along with other grains, lentil cultivation is thought to have started in the Neolithic era around 7000 BCE in the Fertile Crescent (which covers present-day eastern Turkey, northern Iraq, and Syria). Lentil remains were also found in the ruins of a Bronze Age lakeside village at the Swiss Lake Biel.

RED SPLIT LENTILS

BROWN LENTILS

Food for the poor

In ancient Greece, lentils were seen as a food for the lower classes. They were used to make soups and bread as well as a porridge or *phake*, which comes from the Greek word *phokos* for lentil. They are mentioned in the writings of the Greek playwright Aristophanes and in Rome the poet Juvenal describes a lentil dish eaten by the poor called *conchis*, in which lentils were cooked together with their pods.

Lentils may have been popular in ancient Greece but the same cannot be said for medieval Europe. Although they were available, very few lentil recipes appear in medieval cookbooks until the 16th century. In England they were looked upon with disdain and viewed by the wealthy as food only fit for animals.

While lentils were long despised in Europe, they remained an important part of the diet in many parts of Africa and Asia. In India the split seeds are used to make dhal, which accompanies nearly every meal, and is an important source of protein for vegetarians.

Food for the modern world

With changing views on health and nutrition in the West, which often advocate reduced consumption of meat, lentils are now gaining in popularity the world over and have become a fashionable food. For example, in France, Puy lentils have achieved a similar status to some of the most expensive French wines, while the taste and feel of small, black beluga lentils on the palate has been compared to that of caviar.

GREEN LENTILS

◁ **From orange to green**
There are numerous varieties of lentils with different colors and cooking properties. Lentils are not eaten raw and must be boiled first.

△ **A hasty deal**
In a story from the Bible, Esau returns so hungry from the fields that he exchanges his birthright with his brother Jacob for a bowl of lentil stew.

▷ **Vast vat**
The head cook at the Golden Temple, Amritsar, India, prepares a huge cauldron of lentil soup to share with the community as part of the tradition of Guru ka Langar.

Towering success
The sales of navy beans, used in canned baked beans, reached new heights in the West in the 20th century.

Navy and kidney beans nuggets of goodness

Since the 15th century, these varieties of the common bean have spread from their origins in the Americas to become a popular source of protein-rich calories in many countries around the world.

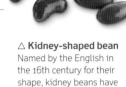

△ **Kidney-shaped bean**
Named by the English in the 16th century for their shape, kidney beans have a dark red outer skin.

The story of this pair of related beans starts in Central and South America, where the wild ancestors of the common bean originated. Archaeological evidence suggests that both types were first domesticated in the Andes mountains in Peru and in Mexico, probably between 9,600 and 7,000 years ago.

The beans, being easy to grow and store, soon became an important crop. By the early 1500s, both varieties of bean were being cultivated in the Americas. The Incas ate navy beans roasted, the Mayans boiled their beans with chilis, while the Aztecs mixed navy beans with boiled corn pulp and lime to create a dish called *atolli*.

△ **Pods of plenty**
All varieties of the common bean produce edible seeds in elongated pods that are also often eaten.

Crossing the Atlantic

It may have been Columbus who brought the first navy bean seeds back to Spain in the early 16th century, although this is uncertain. What is known

> Navy beans, known in the UK as haricot beans, were part of sailors' rations in the 1800s.

is that in 1528, Pope Clement VII presented some large kidney-shaped beans to Pierio Valeriano, an Italian scholarly writer. Valeriano sowed the beans in pots and ate the subsequent harvest, noting that the dish he ordered to be prepared with the beans tasted delicious. The beans, which the Italians named *fagioli*, were soon being grown throughout northern Italy. They were so highly esteemed that, legend has it, when Clement VII's

niece Catherine de' Medici married the future French King Henri II in 1533, she brought these beans with her. She is also said to have brought a team of chefs from her homeland, who would have known how to prepare them. These white beans soon became popular in France, especially in Provence, where they were called *fayoun*. In southwestern France, they became an essential ingredient in the hearty, rich stew known as cassoulet.

Exactly when the beans were renamed is uncertain. The earliest reference to the change is in a dictionary published in 1640.

Spanish settlers brought kidney beans into Louisiana in the late 1700s. At about the same time, Haitians fleeing to New Orleans following a slave rebellion in their homeland brought spicy Caribbean recipes for beans and rice with them. In New Orleans itself, red beans and rice became a favorite Creole dish. The city's love for kidney beans continued into the 20th century. According to reporters for the Federal Writing Project in 1936, "red beans are to New Orleans what the white bean is to Boston and the cow pea is to South Carolina." Most versions of chili con carne—the spicy Texan speciality—contain red kidney beans.

Enjoyed worldwide

Today, kidney beans are eaten all over the world. In northern India, they are the essential constituent of *rajma*, a spicy, thick curry. In La Rioja, a region of Spain, *caparisones*, a stew prepared using a local variety of red kidney beans and chorizo sausage, is a traditional dish.

NAVY BEANS (DRIED)

Origins
Central and South America

Major producers
Brazil, India

Main food component
33 percent protein

Scientific name
Phaseolus vulgaris

△ **Bean feast**
Many varieties of common bean are called haricots in France. The color of the seeds is highly variable.

Adzuki and mung beans

small beans of well-being

Members of the same family, these beans have become significant sources of nutrition in the Asian countries in which they are cultivated.

▷ **Field of beans**
Adzuki beans are stacked and dried in the fields after the autumn harvest in Hokkaido, Japan.

Native to Asia, both these members of the *Vigna* genus have a history of cultivation dating back many centuries. Adzuki beans (*Vigna angularis*) may have originated in China and Korea and were probably introduced to Japan some time between the 3rd and 8th centuries CE. Mung beans (*V. radiata*) seem to have originated further west. Carbonized mung beans have been found in sites in India dating back more than 4,000 years. Mung bean cultivation later spread to China, Southeast Asia, and Africa.

Lucky red bean

Adzuki beans can be popped like corn or dried and ground to produce adzuki bean meal. With a nutty taste and higher sugar content than most other beans, they are a popular ingredient in desserts and candy. In fact, most of the adzuki beans grown in Japan are used to make a sweet bean paste known as *an*, or *anko*. The adzuki's lovely red hue also makes it a favorite ingredient in festive dishes in Japan to celebrate happy family occasions.

In China, red is considered not only lucky but is the color of celebration, so it is not surprising that sweetened red adzuki bean paste is a popular filling for mooncakes, typically eaten for good luck during their mid-autumn festival.

In Japan, it is traditional to cook adzuki beans with rice for girls when they reach puberty as a gesture of blessing.

Mung beans are mentioned in early Sanskrit literature, the *Yajur Veda* (c.1000 BCE), where they are called *masura*. The Buddha considered mung beans to be "full of soul qualities" and "devoid of faults." Today, mung beans are important in Asian diets and are ever more popular in the West, particularly among vegans. Cooked, they are included in salads, soups, baked goods, and ice cream, or ground into flour. They are also used for making the transparent "cellophane" noodles, also called Chinese vermicelli.

In India and Pakistan, mung beans are often used to make a spicy dhal in the same way as lentils, and the sprouted beans are popular in salads and stir-fries in both East and West.

MUNG BEAN

Origins
India

Major producer
India

Main food component
63 percent carbohydrate

Source of
Calcium

Scientific name
Vigna radiata

◁ **Green shoots**
Mung beans are wonderfully versatile. They are widely eaten cooked in various ways, and the sprouts are popular in salads.

▽ **Bursting out**
In the right conditions, adzuki beans, like mung beans, sprout. They first develop tiny roots and then send out a leaf stem.

Soy beans

the world's most nutritious vegetable plant

A versatile and nutritious protein-rich food source, soy beans are one of the great global staples. Initially despised in the West as indigestible and fit only for cattle fodder, they are now widely eaten as a healthy alternative to meat.

There is a degree of controversy surrounding the early history of soy beans. The *Great Soviet Encyclopedia* (1926–1990) cites them as having their origins in China around 5,000 years ago. However, the oldest preserved soy beans, discovered in archaeological sites in Korea, have been dated to around 10,000 BCE. This suggests they were growing in the wild even earlier. What is known is that soy beans were being domesticated in the eastern part of northern China at least 3,000 years ago.

The modern soy plant grows to 3ft (1m) in height. It bears red, purple, or white flowers, which develop into hairy pods up to 2in (5cm) in length, each containing two to three pea-size seeds. Depending on the variety, these beans can be round or oval and range in color from yellow or green to brown or black.

△ **Japanese cruet**
This simple jug holds soy sauce, which has an intense flavor.

In the 6th century CE, Chinese Buddhist monks took soy beans to Korea and Japan where they quickly became a staple dietary ingredient, much valued as a protein source in a country where meat was scarce. Silk Road traders carried them throughout Southeast Asia.

Struggle for acceptance

German botanist Engelbert Kaenfer took the first soy beans to Europe in the late 17th century, but early attempts to grow them as a crop there largely failed. They were described as being tough to eat, their flavor too "beany," and they were deemed indigestible. Attempts to establish cultivation in North America were similarly unsuccessful for many of the same reasons—until World War II, that is, when soy bean oil replaced imported fats and oils that had become scarce, and farmers began to feed soy bean meal as fodder to cattle. Soy bean consumption in the West really took off after 1945, when the beans were used to sustain war survivors in Europe. Americans also started to recognize the soil-regenerating potential of the crop when grown in rotation with maize. Soy beans continued to provide animal feed and were used in the oil-manufacturing industry.

◁ **Expelling demons**
In Japan, the ancient custom of Mamemaki involved throwing roasted soy beans out of a door or at a person dressed as a demon to represent the expulsion of evil spirits from the home.

△ **Vast-scale farming**
Modern soy bean cultivation now occurs on a massive scale in the main areas of production such as Brazil.

Origins
China or Korea

Major producers
US, Brazil, Argentina

Main food component
18 percent protein

Source of
Calcium, iron

Non-food uses
Animal feed, fiber

Scientific name
Glycine max

Meanwhile, Ford car factories started to make car accessories from the oil-cake residue after the oil had been pressed out.

Embraced by America

Suddenly soy was big news. Cultivation spread from the American Midwest, and soon soy bean fields were seen in about 20 states, in particular on the banks of the Mississippi, from where the beans were shipped to the Gulf of Mexico.

▷ **Young and green**
Edamame is a Japanese name that means "beans on a branch." The soy beans are picked when immature and cooked in the pod.

"[the soy bean] has a sweet and warm nature ..."

LE HUU TRAC, VIETNAMESE WRITER (1720–1791)

The US quickly became the largest exporter of two-thirds of the world's soy beans, and still is today. The remaining one-third of exports come from Brazil, Argentina, and China.

As one of the richest, least expensive protein sources, the soy bean is now a mainstay of the human diet throughout the world. It is consumed as soy milk and tofu (soy bean curd), and the sprouted beans are added to salads and stir-fries. Edamame beans (young soy beans) are often steamed or boiled and eaten as a healthy snack. Other traditional Asian soy foods including *tempeh*, *miso*, and fermented bean paste are now commonplace in the West.

Lima beans
potential poison and life-saver

These highly nutritious beans save millions of impoverished people in Africa, Southeast Asia, and South America from starvation.

Origins
Peru
Main food component
63 percent carbohydrate
Source of
Phosphorous, potassium, magnesium, vitamin B3, vitamin K
Scientific name
Phaseolus lunatus

This member of the legume family is both life-saving and a real threat to health. Eaten raw, the beans contain significant qualities of the poison cyanide and, because heat eliminates the toxin, must always be cooked. Lima beans (also called butter beans) emerge from flat, 3in (7.5cm) oblong pods.

▷ **Decorative beans**
Lima beans were a vital food for the Moche civilization of Peru. This Moche stirrup pot from the 3rd–5th century CE is decorated with a bean design.

The common name of this bean, "lima," refers to the capital of the country—Peru—from which the bean originates. Their alternative name, "butter bean," refers to their creamy texture. There is some debate as to whether there is any difference between lima and butter beans, but they both belong to the same species *Phaseolus lunatus*. It may be that both lima and butter beans originated from the same plant but were domesticated in different areas—South America and Central America—resulting in two different forms.

Peruvian migrant
Archaeological findings suggest that lima beans originated in Peru c.7000 BCE, and evidence of the important part they played in Peruvian life can be seen on the pottery of the Moche people of northern Peru. Cultivation eventually moved northward to Mexico and the Caribbean. In the late 15th century, Spanish explorers brought the beans to Europe and Asia, while Portuguese traders took them to Africa, where they thrived. Over the succeeding centuries, the lima bean was adopted in many regions as a carbohydrate staple with a high (21 percent) protein content.

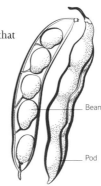
Bean

Pod

△ **Inside the pod**
Each green pod contains 2–4 beans. These are usually cream or green in color, but some varieties are mottled brown or purple.

△ **Bowl of plenty**
In her *Still Life with Broad Bean Pods*, 17th-century artist Giovanna Garzoni faithfully captures what must have been a common sight in Italian kitchens of the period.

Origins
North Africa, Middle East
Major producers
China, Australia, France
Main food component
58 percent carbohydrate
Source of
Vitamin B1, vitamin B2
Scientific name
Vicia faba

The beans get their scientific name *lunatus*, meaning moon-shaped in Latin, from their half-moon shape.

Fava beans ancient source of nutrition

Mystery and superstition surround the history of the fava bean. Ancient Egyptians regarded them as unclean and objects of danger—so much so that priests were forbidden to look at them, let alone eat them.

Legend has it that, despite their dietary importance, some ancient Egyptians and Greeks avoided fava beans, possibly because they were thought to house the souls of the dead. Stories suggest that 1st-century BCE Greek mathematician Pythagoras met his demise when marauders chased him into a bean field. He didn't want to risk trampling on any souls, which hampered his attempts to flee and, unable to escape, he was murdered.

It is thought that fava beans (also known as broad beans) are one of the most ancient cultivated crops, together with chickpeas, lentils, and peas. The earliest known traces of fava beans were found in Israel and date back to 6800–6500 BCE. Archaeological remains dating back to 3,000 BCE have also been found in the Mediterranean region and Central Europe. Fava beans are thought to have played a significant part in the daily diets of many Mediterranean peoples and those of Near East civilizations.

Today the fava bean is popular all over the globe. Its ease of cultivation and hardiness has helped it to travel far beyond its native Middle East and Asia, to northern Europe, the Americas, Africa, and much of Asia, forming a key ingredient in many traditional stews and vegetable accompaniments.

△ **Bean pod**
Modern varieties of fava bean can be 1in (3cm) thick and up to 4in (25cm) long. Each pod can hold up to eight oval fava bean seeds.

Chickpeas food for the poor

Familiar in the West as the main ingredient of Middle-Eastern dishes such as the popular dip hummus, chickpeas provided the civilizations of the ancient world with a ready source of protein-rich calories for thousands of years.

The story of chickpeas goes back 11,000 years to the time that wild chickpeas were first domesticated in present-day southeastern Turkey and Syria. The oldest known variety of chickpea is the desi bean, which reached India in around 2000 BCE. It was there that kabuli, the most common form of chickpea today, originated. Desi are relatively small, dark beans with a yellow interior. Kabuli chickpeas are larger and beige-colored throughout with a thin skin.

Chickpeas were a favorite food in ancient Egypt, Greece, and Rome. The Greeks ate them boiled or mashed. The Greek philosophers Socrates and Plato

In 18th-century Europe, roasted chickpeas were ground and used as a coffee substitute.

both referred to the nutritional benefits of chickpeas. The family of Cicero, the celebrated Roman orator of the 1st century BCE, are thought to have grown chickpeas, while Pliny the Elder recommended them as a health food in the 1st century CE. Recipes for chickpeas appeared in the 4th–5th century book of recipes attributed to the 1st-century Roman gourmet Marcus Gavius Apicius. Galen, physician to the 2nd-century Emperor Marcus Aurelius, thought that chickpeas were not only more nutritious than beans—the other Roman dietary staple—but also caused less flatulence. They were, he said, an ideal food for the poor, who often could not afford meat or fish.

Spreading west

In the first millennium CE knowledge of chickpeas spread throughout Europe. The 8th century Holy Roman Emperor Charlemagne ordered chickpeas to be grown in his northern European gardens. Arabs brought the legumes to Spain and Sicily, and during the Middle Ages Sephardic Jews in Spain and Portugal habitually pre-prepared a chickpea stew to eat on the Sabbath, when cooking was forbidden. In medieval Egypt, dried raw chickpeas were ground and mixed with water and spices to form a batter. Balls of this were fried to make falafel. Hummus, a chickpea dip, also originated in the Middle East.

In the 1500s, Spanish and Portuguese explorers brought chickpeas to the Americas. Today, the US grows and exports a large quantity of chickpeas, mainly to Europe. In India, they are by far the most popular legume—used in curries and ground into flour used for rotis and chapatis.

△ **Pods and leaves**
The chickpea plant has small, oval leaves and blue-veined white flowers. The pods each contain up to three seeds, or peas.

▷ **Scale of popularity**
An early 20th-century Turkish chickpea trader weighs his wares. For centuries Turkey has been a major consumer of chickpeas and remains so today, although it is no longer a top producer.

△ **Medieval health food**
In the Middle Ages—as their inclusion in the 13th-century health treatise *Tacuinum Sanitatis* implies—chickpeas were viewed as being of value for health rather than a gourmet treat.

Origins
Western Asia

Major producers
India, Australia, Pakistan

Main food component
63 percent carbohydrate

Source of
Iron, magnesium, zinc, vitamin B2, vitamin B3

Scientific name
Cicer arietinum

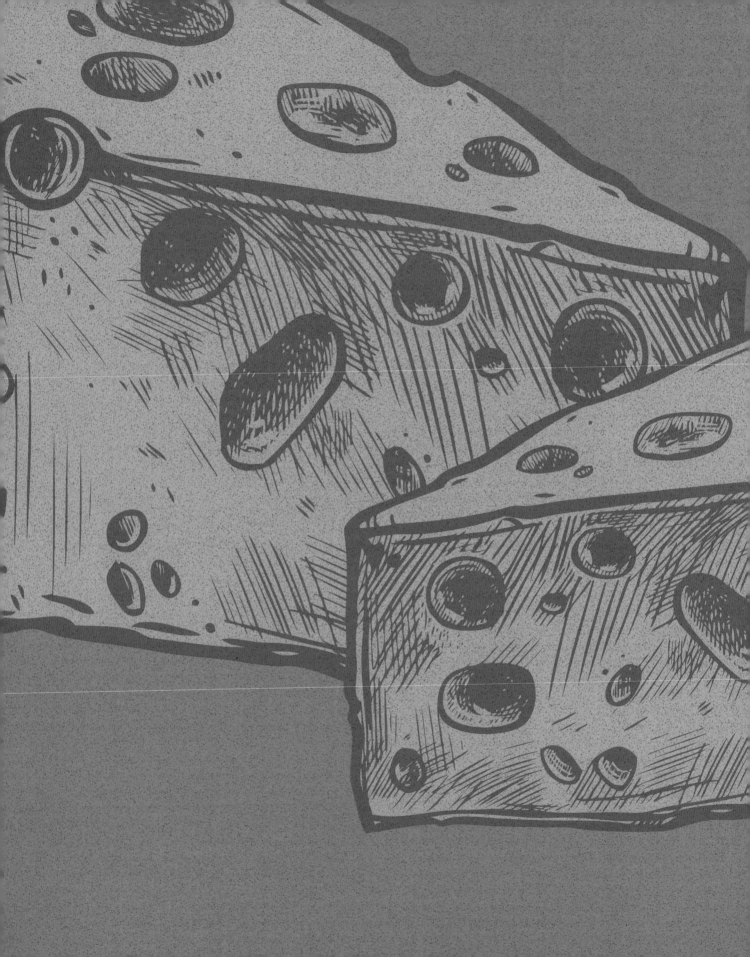

Dairy
and Eggs

Dairy and eggs

Given that many prehistoric peoples were unable to digest lactose in milk, it seems extraordinary that dairy foods became such a central part of the human diet in many parts of the world. Certainly milk and its by-products have never featured significantly in the cuisine of the Far East, Southeast Asia, or the Americas, but in Europe, Central Asia, and the Middle East life often depended on dairy consumption.

Tough to swallow

Around 9,000 years ago, when communities in the Middle East began domesticating sheep, goats, and cattle, they started milking them. But it was not a ready-made source of food. It was virtually indigestible to all adults. They were missing the lactase enzyme needed to break down the lactose sugars in milk. Neolithic humans were born with the ability to produce the lactase enzyme so that they could digest their mother's milk, but in early childhood the enzyme was switched off, leaving whole populations lactose-intolerant, unable to digest milk properly.

As the years progressed, two things happened that made dairy foods the catalyst for change. The first was that dairy communities discovered how to make fermented milk products such as yogurt, kefir, sour cream, and cultured cheese. Lactic acid, present in the stomach of milk-producing mammals, was the secret ingredient, breaking down the lactose in the milk to make it more digestible. Fermented dairy products also lasted longer than fresh milk, offering the possibility of a long-term food supply, especially for times of the year when livestock were not lactating. This gave dairy-farming communities an edge when it came to survival.

The second change was that dairy-farming communities developed a tolerance for lactose, the probable result of interbreeding between individuals who carried a genetic mutation that allowed lactose digestion, combined with higher fertility among those with the mutant gene. Scientists estimate this process took close to 7,000 years. During this same period, a dairy-rich diet is thought to have altered human physiology. Rich in calcium for bone growth and the amino acids required for

△ **Ancient dairy farming**
Milking cows was already common in ancient times as this wall painting from a tomb in Saqqara, Egypt, shows. It dates from around 2400 BCE.

▷ **The devil's milkmaid**
Images of devils aiding dairymaids flourished in medieval Europe. They reveal how dairy work, managed by women, was little understood by men.

▽ **Feeding the troops**
Officers of the 2nd Italian Army man a cheese factory in 1916. Nutritious and easily portable, cheese was a regular part of Italian army rations.

muscle-building, dairy foods are also one of the richest dietary sources of iodine, another mineral that is essential for growth.

Eggs were the other major source of iodine that helped to sustain the healthy growth of early civilizations. Unlike dairy, which was geographically limited, eggs were universal, found in almost all human cultures around the world. In regions such as Japan and southern China, where herding was rarely practised, eggs provided an easily obtainable supply of calories and essential fats with none of the labor-intensive work of milking, straining, or churning.

> Butter and "good cheese" are two of the foodstuffs included on a provision list for the *Mayflower* pilgrims.

More dairy means taller people
Numerous studies have shown the correlation between a society that is nutritionally rich and the height of its people; some research has even suggested that there is a direct correlation between dairy intake and height, which may be one explanation for why the Dutch, with a high per-capita dairy intake, are among the world's tallest people. Thus, in places where milk products formed a staple part of the diet, as in northern Europe, humans developed a larger physique than in regions with little or no dairy. Fermented dairy foods—kefir and yogurt in particular—had the added advantage of containing probiotics: the good bacteria that help the gut digest and maintain a healthy balance, fending off gastric illness and creating a healthier population.

The ultimate aged cheese
Of all the dairy products, butter and cheese offered the greatest longevity as, preserved with salt, they could last for months and sometimes years. Hard cheese was the ultimate long-storage solution for milk. In drier, cooler climates, it was possible to age cheese for longer periods, because it contained less moisture. Parmesan, Gouda, and Cheddar are examples of aged cheese, although few can compare with Nepal's yak cheese, which can keep for up to 20 years. Cheese became a local speciality right across Europe, the Middle East, central Asia, Pakistan, and India, with its great variation in taste and consistency reflecting the diet of the region's herds and environmental conditions.

The invention of pasteurization in the 19th century changed the way people consumed dairy products. Removing the bacteria from milk made larger-scale production of milk, butter, yogurt, and cheese commercially viable, and factories soon began to process these products, transporting them in refrigerated containers to a hungry marketplace.

▽ **Dutch staple**
Dairy products have been staple foods of the Dutch for centuries. This photo from 1900 shows Dutch dairymaids carrying milk buckets.

△ **Milk for the masses**
Developed in the 1930s, automated pasteurization and homogenization machines allowed milk to be produced and sold on an industrial scale.

▷ **More to milk than cows**
Yak milk, butter, yogurt, and cheese are a vital part of the diets of nomadic Tibetans. Women still use traditional methods to make yak milk cheese.

Milk a drink that is also a food

For early humans milk was a toxic substance that only children could digest, but it became a powerful source of nutrition for all, helping communities survive when harvests failed and evolving into one of the world's most versatile foods.

Few foods have required such a major leap in human adaptation to become consumable. Milk from animals was toxic to Stone Age adults. Although their children were born with the lactase enzyme that enabled them to break down lactose, the main sugar in milk, and digest their mother's milk, by the time they reached adulthood the enzyme switched off, causing illness if they consumed animal milk.

Adapting to nature

Around 10,500 years ago, the earliest farmers in the Middle East began to domesticate animals, such as cattle, sheep, and goats. These early cattle herders found a way to make milk digestible by fermentation processes that converted milk to foods such as cheese and yogurt, which we now know have reduced lactose levels. Archaeologists have found milk traces in pottery in Britain and Eastern Europe dating from

◁ **Traditional milk carrier**
The Rendille people of East Africa are nomadic herders by tradition. This decorated milk gourd was woven by a bride before her marriage.

7000 BCE, along with vessels for straining that would have been used for making curd and other dairy products.

By this time, farming and herding had spread beyond the Middle East as far as Central Europe. Around 5000 BCE, a genetic mutation occurred that allowed the lactase enzyme to emerge, and it eventually dispersed among the populations of Europe where dairy farming had become entrenched, and in pockets of the Middle East where cow's milk was part of the diet. A Sumerian carving inside the Temple of Ninhursag, at Tell al-'Ubaid in Iraq, depicts cattle-milking and cheese- and butter-making from around 2500–2000 BCE. By 3000 BCE, the domesticated dairy cow had reached North Africa,

COW'S MILK

Origins
Middle East

Major producers
US, India, China

Main food component
5 percent carbohydrate

Source of
Calcium, vitamin D

Non-food uses
Casein paint, casein-based glue, protein supplements

▽ **Milk for sale**
Traditionally, milk was stored in metal churns to keep it cool. This German family living in Cologne in the 1890s are preparing take their milk to market.

CUBA.- Le laitier.

VÉRITABLE EXTRAIT DE VIANDE LIEBIG.

◁ **Daily milking**
Domesticated cows must be milked twice a day. This 19th-century French recipe card, from the meat extract company Liebig, depicts a Cuban milkman.

permitted huge increases in milk production to serve the growing urban populations. The invention of the glass milk bottle around the same time facilitated milk distribution in convenient quantities for consumers.

Many milk-makers

Cows are the dominant milk producers across the world, but significant amounts are also produced by sheep, goats, camels, and buffalo, which can survive in far less fertile conditions. These animals have been the main source of milk in the hotter regions of the world for millennia, often providing nutrients and hydration when water was scarce.

△ **Manual separator**
The application of centrifugal force separates milk into skim milk and cream, which is used to make butter.

playing a central role in ancient Egyptian agriculture, and within a thousand years had arrived in northern India with Aryan nomads.

Into the modern world

By the Middle Ages, milk and its by-products had become basic elements in the European diet. Early in the 16th century, the Spanish took cattle to the New World. In 1624, the first cows arrived in New England, and by the end of the century, cattle had arrived in the western states. Industrialization in 18th- and 19th-century Europe and North America drove people into cities, away from sources of safe, fresh milk. The discovery of pasteurization at the end of the 19th century, which made milk safer and fresher for longer through rapid heating and cooling,

In China and Southeast Asia, 90 percent of people are believed to lack the enzyme for digesting milk.

Yogurt and kefir

deliciously digestible milk products

△ **Milk strainer**
The survival of vessels for yogurt-making, such as this 6th-century BCE bowl from Lydia in modern-day western Turkey, is evidence of yogurt's long history.

COW'S MILK YOGURT
Origins Middle East
Major producers Germany, France, Greece
Main food component 12 percent carbohydrate
Source of Calcium, potassium, vitamin D

Discovered by chance thousands of years ago, the process of fermenting animal milk created thickened, longer-lasting by-products such as yogurt and kefir.

▽ **Yogurt shop**
Yogurt is still made the traditional way for small-scale production in the ancient Indian city of Varanasi. It is used in drinks (lassi) and to make different curry sauces.

The word yogurt is derived from the Turkish *yoğurt*, hinting at its origins in western Asia where, 8,000 years ago, herding communities discovered how to make fermented milk products. It is thought that the milk was stored in bags made from animal stomachs, which contained natural enzymes. These enzymes acted as a starter culture when the temperature was warm enough for incubation, thickening the milk and giving it the characteristic sour taste of yogurt. Not only did yogurt taste good, it kept longer than fresh milk. It was also easier to digest, since the active cultures in yogurt break down the milk sugar called lactose. This was an important discovery for early civilizations since most people were lactose intolerant.

The culture of eating yogurt spread eastward, and ancient Indian Ayurvedic texts refer to the health benefits of consuming fermented milk products. In India, *dahi* is a type of yogurt made from cow's milk. In Nepal, Bhutan, and Tibet, a variety of yogurtlike products are made from yak's milk. In the West, the reputation of fermented milk's restorative effects caused the ancient Greeks to embrace it, although they had previously deemed milk "barbaric." They developed their own type of yogurt, called *oxygala*— "acid milk"—which was often mixed with honey.

Kefir's magical grains

Techniques for making fermented milk were brought to Russia by the Tatars, semi-nomadic people originally from Mongolia. In the Caucasus Mountains on the southern border of present-day Russia, shepherds are thought to have created a unique type of fermented milk product called kefir. Made from cow's, goat's, or sheep's milk, it required the addition of a starter culture of kefir grains, containing a mix of bacteria and yeast. The technique reached other parts of Europe in the 19th century, where it was hailed for its value in the treatment of tuberculosis and digestive problems.

Mongolian mare's milk

On the steppes of Central Asia, where horses were the dominant livestock, the Mongols, Kazakhs, and other tribes created another variation of yogurt, *kumiss*, made from mare's milk. Accounts from the Venetian and Flemish explorers Marco Polo and William of Rubruck, who visited the Mongols in the 13th century, describe the khan's personal supply of *kumiss* made from his herd of 10,000 white horses. According to Rubruck, the 300 warriors at the khan's army camp drank *kumiss* daily, made from milk supplied by 3,000 mares and fermented in horse-hide containers. Their great thirst for *kumiss* may have been fuelled in part by its mild alcohol content, a result of the high sugar content of mare's milk.

△ **Hard sell**
"Thousands enjoy daily" boasts the headline of this Swiss advertisement promoting the benefits of drinking or eating yogurt regularly.

> "If you want yogurt in winter, carry a cow in your pocket."
>
> TURKISH PROVERB

Turkish remedy

In Turkey, medieval books describe how yogurt was used by the region's nomads, recommending it to soothe sunburned skin and as a remedy for diarrhea. Allegedly, it was a bad case of diarrhea, suffered by Francis I of France in 1542, that compelled his Ottoman allies to offer yogurt as a remedy, triggering a French vogue for yogurt.

It wasn't until the early 20th century that medical researchers were able to isolate and identify the lactic acid bacteria in yogurt and establish the science behind the health benefits of eating it in its natural form. For many people around the world, this is the main reason to eat or drink it, but many millions more simply enjoy sweetened yogurt with fruit as a dessert or use it as an added ingredient in myriad savory dishes and sauces.

△ **Starter kit**
Kefir grains are a culture of lactic acid bacteria and yeasts mixed with protein, fat, and sugar. They are added to milk to make the drink that is also called kefir.

Cream and butter
milk by-products that enrich and sustain

From ghee to buttermilk to the cream poured over fruit and desserts, the versatile and comforting spin-offs from milk have earned a valued place in many cultures for their taste and nutritional benefits.

BUTTER (FULL MILK)

Origins
Middle East

Major producers
India, US, New Zealand

Main food component
80 percent fat

Source of
Vitamin A, vitamin D, vitamin E

When humans first began to keep livestock, around 10,000 years ago, they also discovered that if they left milk to sit for a day a thick, fat-rich layer formed on the top—cream. And if they skimmed off that cream and stirred it continuously, it turned into butter. The earliest written evidence for this appears on a 4,000-year-old limestone tablet uncovered in the Sumerian city of Uruk, now Warka in Iraq. The tablet itemizes dairy products made from the milk of cows and sheep, including cream and butter.

◁ **Titanic churning**
A carving at the 12th-century Angkor Wat temple complex in Cambodia shows demons shaking huge beams to turn a sea of milk into butter.

became an important ritual of the Vedic religion that became established in India around 1500 BCE. The reverence for butter lives on in modern India. In the Hindu hierarchy of foods, an inferior food cooked in ghee can become superior, lamps in sacred places are fuelled by ghee, and at Hindu weddings male guests compete to see who can eat the most ghee.

Sacred ghee
The butter made by the Sumerians was probably clarified, a process that removes the milk proteins and water to leave pure butter fat, known as ghee in India. Clarified butter can be stored for longer periods in hot weather and can reach higher temperatures in cooking. In the Hindu mythology of ancient India, the god Prajápati was believed to have created the world when he churned ghee by rubbing his hands together then poured it into a fire. The pouring of ghee into fire

Life-preserving butter
In more temperate regions, full-milk, unclarified butter was preferred since it provided more nutrition. Himalayan peoples mixed tea, introduced to them during the Chinese Tang dynasty (618–907 CE), with yak butter to make a beverage that provided warmth and important fats. To the ancient Greeks and Romans, butter was fit as food only for the barbarian tribes of northern Europe, where it was a readily available and important source of nourishment. In Ireland, butter up to 5,000 years old has been found buried in peat bogs—

▽ **Butter maker**
The role of the dairywoman, seen here turning a butter churn, was vital in the dairy-farming communities of many parts of Northern Europe in the 19th century.

▷ **Working together**
These women in Ceylon (now Sri Lanka) churn milk, either from cows or buffalo, into ghee, using no more than an earthenware bowl and a churning stick.

probably an early form of food preservation. Use of the butter churn, which existed in Scotland from at least the 6th century CE, became widespread by the 13th century, with the making of butter the responsibility of the dairywoman, typically the farmer's wife or a dairymaid employed by the local landowner.

Changing fortunes

The demand for butter reached such a peak in 19th-century France that Napoleon III called for the creation of a viable substitute. In 1869, the chemist Hippolyte Mège-Mouriès invented "oleomargarine," a butterlike substance made from rendered beef fat and milk. The name was later shortened to "margarine." Shortages of butter during World War II increased the popularity of margarine which by the 1980s was touted as the healthier option. The tables were turned, however, in the early years of the 21st century, when the fats in margarine were found to be far less healthy than butter's natural fats.

Cream remained a culinary luxury until, in the late 19th century, Gustaf de Laval, a Swedish engineer, invented a centrifugal milk-cream separator. This ushered in mass production of cream, sparking a boom in desserts topped or filled with easily made whipped cream.

> "May you be the butter in the cattle-pen, may you be the cream in the sheepfold."
>
> ANCIENT SUMERIAN SONG TO THE GODDESS NISABA

△ **Ice cream for all**
A trade card from 1885 advertises a new ice cream maker in the US, where large-scale ice cream manufacturing had begun in 1851. The launch of the American soda fountain in 1874, offering ice cream sundaes and floats, marked the start of ice cream's rapid rise in popularity.

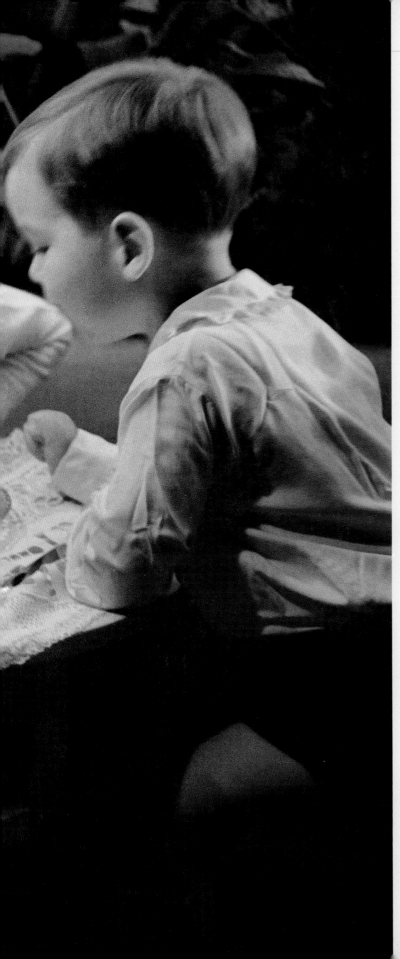

Celebrations and special events

Regardless of culture or religion, food and celebration go hand in hand all over the world. China, for example, marks the start of its New Year with a 15-day festival in which the entire country practically comes to a halt. Traditional fare includes noodles, dumplings, fish, spring rolls, *tangyuan* (sweet rice balls), and glutinous rice cakes called *nian gao*. Noodles symbolize happiness and longevity, while dumplings and spring rolls mean wealth. *Tangyuan* stands for family togetherness, while fish, served at the end of the meal and to the eldest first, signifies increased prosperity.

Golden pastries called moon cakes, filled with lotus seed and red bean or black bean paste, are central to China's mid-autumn festival and are thought to portend good fortune. Chinese wedding guests feast on roast suckling pig, fish, pigeon, chicken, lobster, and buns stuffed with lotus seeds. The lobster (representing a dragon) and chicken (a phoenix) are served together as they signify the *yin* and *yang* of the joined families.

Besan ki burfi—fudgelike cookies made of chickpea flour, ghee, sugar, and cardamom and topped with nuts—are what Hindus, Jains, and Sikhs feast on during Diwali, the five-day festival of lights honoring Lakshmi, goddess of prosperity. *Gulab jamun*, fried dough balls bathed in syrup, is another Diwali treat, as are *mithai (*sweets), *jalebi* (a deep-fried saffron-flavored dessert), and *kulfi* (Indian ice cream).

Food also plays a leading part in Jewish festivals. Purim, for example, celebrates the deliverance of the Jews from slaughter in Persia in the 4th century BCE. Triangular *hamantaschen* pastries are sweet cookies filled with poppy seeds, fruit preserves, prunes, nuts, dates, apricots, chocolate, and other sweet surprises. *Kreplach*, meat-filled dumplings that are often served in soup, also feature on the Purim menu.

◁ **Birthday wishes**
Whether it's a personal milestone such as a birthday or a religious holiday celebrated by millions, particular dishes form an inextricable part of cultural occasions.

Cheese milk for keeping and flavor

Discovering the chemical process that separates milk into curds and whey gave ancient dairy communities a rich source of storable protein and laid the foundation for a variety of cheese-making traditions.

△ **Cottage industry**
Cheese-making was an important activity in medieval Europe. In this 15th-century German illustration, a dog drinks the whey from freshly made cheese.

Anthropologists cannot say when humans first began making cheese, but the oldest known evidence for it is a collection of 34 pottery cheese strainers estimated to be at least 7,500 years old. Found in the Kuyavia region of Poland, the perforated vessels contained traces of milk residues, creating a clear link to cheese-making. This early cheese was probably similar to the French goat's milk cheese picodon, which is made in the mountains of Ardèche and Drôme using an almost identical type of strainer.

For ancient dairy communities, cheese was a way of storing the nutritional benefits of milk. Whereas milk would spoil within a day or two, cheese would stay fresh for weeks, months, or years in the case of some hard cheeses. Because cheese was in a solid form, it was also easier to transport than liquid milk, cream, or yogurt. Another benefit for these early human populations, many of whom lacked the enzyme to digest the sugar in milk (lactose), was that the process of turning milk into cheese dramatically reduced the level of lactose, making it easier to digest.

Transformed by enzymes
The key to this chemical reaction is the presence of rennet, a group of enzymes made in the stomachs of young grazing mammals to help them digest their mother's milk. In cheese-making, rennet is added to milk to help separate it into liquid whey and solid curds. Although today vegetarian rennet can be made from fungus or genetically modified microorganisms, animal rennet was the original catalyst and remains so for many cheeses, including some such as Parmesan and Gorgonzola, which the regulations decree must be made with calf rennet.

Throughout history, cheese has been made from almost any animal that could produce milk. Yak milk provides the basis for several traditional cheeses in Tibet, Bhutan, Nepal, and Mongolia. One of the best known is chhurpi, a cheese prepared from yak buttermilk, which can be either soft or hard. The buttermilk is boiled and the resulting solid yet soft cheese is wrapped in soft cloth and hung up to drain. To make hard chhurpi, the soft cheese is pressed to remove even more water, then it is sliced and left to dry in the sun or smoked over a fire. Small sticks of

> ## "How can you govern a country which has 246 varieties of cheese?"
>
> CHARLES DE GAULLE, FRENCH GENERAL AND STATESMAN (1958)

chhurpi have been a traditional snack in the Himalayan region for centuries, and the cheese can stay edible for up to 20 years if stored properly in a wrapping of yak skin.

Cheeses from other animals
Both India and Italy have a history of making cheese from water buffalo milk. In the state of Jammu and Kashmir in the north of India, a soft stretchy cheese called kalari is made from buffalo milk, and throughout India chenna is made from buffalo or cow's milk. Buffalo may have been introduced to Italy via the Middle East around 600 CE. By the 12th century, buffalo herds were well established on the temperate fertile plains south of Rome, providing milk for yogurt and mozzarella cheese. In the Middle East, cheese was typically made from goat's and sheep's milk, sometimes from a mix of both. Many of these cheeses are still a staple part of the Middle Eastern diet, including semi-hard nabulsi made

▷ **Grate work**
The ancient Greeks were great cheese lovers. This 6th-century BCE terra-cotta figurine from a village north of Athens, Greece, shows a man grating a block of hard cheese.

▷ **Wooden mold**
Oscypek is a Polish smoked cheese made from salted ewe's milk, which is pressed into a distinctive spindle-shaped mould.

from unboiled goat's milk; soft, unripened ackawi from cow's milk, often studded with sesame seeds; and the ball-shaped Egyptian testouri from sheep's milk. Although camels provide milk to the Arab world, camel cheese is virtually unknown because the milk is extremely difficult to separate.

Preserved in brine

Halloumi has become a popular cheese throughout the Middle East, but it originated on the island of Cyprus in the medieval era. The cheese has an exceptionally high melting point, a result of heating the fresh curds to a high temperature, which cooks them slightly before they are pressed and immersed in brine. Because of its high melting point and very firm texture, Halloumi is usually fried or grilled.

Many cheeses like halloumi use brining to preserve them and to help them develop flavor. During the brining process, the cheese is immersed in salt water for several weeks or months.

Feta cheese, one of the world's oldest cheese varieties and a staple of the Greek diet, is aged in brine for up to six months, and if kept submerged in the liquid can keep for around the same length of time without spoiling. When Greek settlers arrived in Sudan in the early 20th century, their technique for making Feta was adapted by the Sudanese nomadic dairy herders. They used any surplus milk from their cows, sheep, and goats to make gibna bayda, a pickled cheese that is similar in style to feta.

△ **Mass production**
Cheese was first produced on a commercial scale in the 19th century although, as this illustration from a German agricultural book shows, it was still a hands-on process.

CHEDDAR

Origins
Cheddar, Somerset, UK

Major producers
UK, New Zealand, Canada

Main food component
32 percent fat

Good source of
Calcium, vitamin A

LE VÉRITABLE ROQUEFORT DOIT MURIR DANS LES CAVES
SPÉCIALES NATURELLES DE ROQUEFORT
ROQUEFORT
PRODUCT OF FRANCE
SOCIÉTÉ FONDÉE EN 1842
SOCIÉTÉ
SOCIÉTÉ
SURCHOIX
SOCIÉTÉ FONDÉE EN 1842
LA
SOCIÉTÉ
LA PLUS GROSSE PRODUCTION
DU VÉRITABLE ROQUEFORT

Creamy cool-climate varieties

Brining was essential in warmer climates to prevent cheese spoiling too quickly, but in the cooler climates of Northern Europe less salt was needed to ensure preservation. As a result creamier, milder varieties of cheese developed, along with aged, ripened, and blue cheeses. The Middle Ages and Renaissance proved a creative time for cheese. Italy led the way in the variety and types of cheese available, a legacy of the ancient Roman devotion to cheese. Gorgonzola, made in the

---

The world's most expensive cheese is Pule, made in Serbia from donkey milk and sold for 1,000 euros a kilo in 2012.

Po Valley since 879 CE, was just one of hundreds of varieties available. The Romans had introduced cheese-making to Britain, and from the 11th and 12th centuries onward, local experimentation yielded some of today's best-known cow's milk cheeses, such as Cheshire, Stilton, and Cheddar. The British also developed a taste for Parmesan cheese, especially after Pope Julius II gave Henry VIII a hundred wheels of Parmesan as a diplomatic gift in 1511.

Soft and tasty

In France, cheese-making was a central feature of monastery life. Brie, a soft cow's milk cheese, is thought to have been made at the monastery in Reuil-en-Brie since the 8th century, when the Holy Roman Emperor Charlemagne apparently acquired a taste for it. It became a favorite of royalty, and an essential feature of aristocratic banquets. In the late 18th century,

Napoleon Bonaparte helped to popularize Camembert after being presented with the cheese in the town of Surdon, Normandy. Also a soft cow's milk cheese, Camembert was said to be made from a secret recipe handed down by a monk from Reuil-en-Brie. In the Netherlands, a hard, yellow cheese called Gouda was being made from cow's milk by 1697.

Europe's regional cheeses were homemade until 1815, when the first cheese factory opened in Switzerland. After rennet became mass-produced in the 1860s, cheese production on a commercial scale began in earnest. Local tradition was not forgotten, however, and handmade cheese remains one of Europe's most diverse and fiercely protected artisan foods.

Turning blue

Usually, the presence of mold on food indicates it is no longer fresh and may not be safe to eat. Blue cheeses are different. The *Penicillium roqueforti* and *P. glaucum* molds that create blue cheeses and give them their characteristic strong, sharp, tangy flavor are not toxic. The penicillin molds occur naturally and the first blue cheeses are thought to have been discovered by accident when cheese was stored in a cool place such as a cave. Legend has it that the French blue cheese Roquefort was created when a young shepherd saw a beautiful girl and abandoned his lunch of bread and ewe's milk cheese in a cave while he went to flirt with her. When he came across the remains of his lunch a few months later, the cheese was streaked with veins of blue mold and proved to be very tasty.

Today, the creation of well-known blue cheeses such as Italy's Gorgonzola and England's Stilton leaves nothing to chance. Penicillin mold is added when the curds have been drained and pressed to form a cheese wheel. This is then pierced to allow air into the cheese, which enables the mold to grow in the characteristic blue "veins."

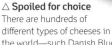

△ Spoiled for choice
There are hundreds of different types of cheeses in the world—such Danish Blue, Camembert, Emmenthal, and Edam—all with distinctive flavors and textures.

◁ True blue
To be labeled "Roquefort," the cheese must be aged in the natural Combalou caves of Roquefort-sur-Soulzon in southern France.

▷ Cheese press
In 19th-century Britain, every dairy farm would make its own cheese. This press enabled several wheels of cheese to be pressed at once.

QUAIL EGG

GOOSE EGG

OSTRICH EGG

▷ **Eggs of many sizes**
Over the centuries, humans have eaten
eggs of a wide variety of birds, many
of which are still eaten today.

DUCK EGG

BANTAM EGG

HEN EGG

Eggs concentrated nutrition in a shell

High in protein, versatile, and with a special ability to bind with other
ingredients, eggs have been a mainstay of human nutrition since our Neolithic
ancestors began to steal them from bird's nests.

Thieved from the nests of wild birds, eggs provided an
easily obtainable source of calories and protein for
Neolithic peoples. At some point, they fathomed that
taking the eggs from the nest encouraged the bird to
lay more and to continue to produce them, extending
the natural egg-laying season. Thousands of years later,
when birds had become domesticated, humans were
faced with a choice—killing the birds for meat, or
keeping birds alive for a long-term supply of eggs.
More often than not, they chose the latter, and the
egg-producing industry was born.

The eggs of jungle fowl, the forerunner of the modern
domestic chicken, were probably being eaten as long
ago as 7500 BCE in South and Southeast Asia. The bird
and the eggs it produced are likely to have reached
Egypt by around 1500 BCE. Archaeologists have
discovered early examples of egg consumption in the
tombs of the ancient Phoenicians, whose city-states,
such as Tyre and Sidon, flourished around 1000 BCE
along the Mediterranean coasts of what are now Syria,
Lebanon, and Israel. Phoenicians ate ostrich eggs, and
the shells were intricately decorated then typically

△ **Chicken and egg**
The ancient Greeks are known
to have enjoyed eating eggs.
This terra-cotta bust is of a
Greek deity holding an egg
and a fowl very similar to a
modern cockerel.

placed in tombs as grave goods. Other ancient cultures also ate and decorated ostrich eggs, including the Persians, Romans, and Greeks. The Chinese were known to eat pigeon eggs, while the ancient Egyptians ate the eggs of many different birds, including ducks, geese, quail, and even the pelican.

How do you like your eggs?

It was in the second millennium BCE that eggs were first documented for their usefulness in binding and thickening flour for baking. Accounts of food in ancient Egypt refer to around 40 different breads and pastries, some made with eggs. Later, the Romans found a use for eggs in a wide range of recipes. They seemed to prefer peafowl eggs to chicken eggs and used them in all kinds of baked goods, including the cake *libum*, which was made with flour, eggs, ricotta cheese, bay leaves, and honey.

Many of the egg dishes eaten today originated in ancient Rome, including omelettes, egg tarts, and poached eggs. A collection of recipes published in the 4th–5th century CE, attributed to Marcus Gavius Apicius, a 1st-century CE Roman gourmet, contained the first known recipe for baked custard, instructing cooks to beat milk, honey, and eggs, and cook the mixture in an earthenware dish over a gentle heat. Eggs were used as a thickening agent to bind sauces and ragouts, and featured in savory dishes such as soft-boiled eggs in pine nut sauce and boiled eggs served with rue and anchovies.

A recipe for health and rebirth

In the 6th century CE, Byzantine physician Anthimus wrote extensively on eggs, evaluating the dietary benefits of eggs from chickens, ducks, geese, quail, pigeons, partridges, peafowls, cranes, thrushes, and other small birds. He promoted hard-boiled eggs as good for the digestion, and advised placing the eggs in cold water and boiling them over a low flame for best results. His recipe for *afrutum* —soufflé with chicken or scallops— demanded ample egg whites to create a generous foam.

△ **Food for the journey**
Ancient Egyptians greatly valued eggs as a food source and included them in the provisions placed in tombs to sustain the departed in the afterlife.

In the Byzantine empire of the eastern Mediterranean, as in other Christian cultures, eggs were a symbol of Christ's resurrection. Eggs had represented rebirth since pagan times, when they were painted in bright colors to celebrate the coming of spring. They were hung in the temples of ancient Egypt in the belief that this would encourage fertility.

For Jewish people it was traditional to eat eggs at Passover, and eventually they were adopted as a Christian symbol at Easter. The British tradition of

> ## "An egg is always an adventure; the next one may be different."
>
> OSCAR WILDE, IRISH PLAYWRIGHT (1854–1900)

▷ **Farm fresh**
In 18th-century Europe, eggs were often sold by individual traders who brought their produce into city-center markets. Here a French egg-seller plies her trade.

selling eggs by the dozen is thought to have originated in Elizabethan times, drawing on the Christian symbolism of the 12 disciples.

In and out of fashion

In recent decades, especially in the West, the egg fell out of fashion in the late 20th century owing to its high cholesterol content, which was thought to increase the risk of heart disease. By the early 2000s these concerns had largely been dispelled, and eggs are now once again viewed as a healthy high-protein food. However, concerns about methods of mass-producing eggs in vast battery farms have led to increased interest in eggs produced by birds raised in more natural conditions.

Main food component
13 percent protein

Source of
Iron, calcium, zinc, vitamin A, vitamin D

Non-food uses
Animal feed, pharmaceuticals

Sugars
and Syrups

Sugars and syrups

According to evolutionary biologists, humans have had cravings for sweet-tasting foods for millennia—and there is good evidence of sugar consumption at least 10,000 years ago. One explanation for this is that a sweet taste in foods typically indicates a large number of calories and a high-energy kick, which would have helped greatly in terms of survival. Humans, therefore, became hard-wired to crave sweet things. Another contributing factor is that early humans gradually evolved an aversion to bitter-tasting substances—a trait that helped them to avoid potentially toxic plants when foraging for food. By extension, the sweeter a food tasted, the safer it was likely to be.

The sweetest food available to many prehistoric peoples was, of course, honey, and evidence indicates that it was being gathered by primitive peoples as early as the Mesolithic Period, up to 10,000 years ago. In the Cuevas de la Araña (Caves of the Spider) in Valencia, eastern Spain, for example, one cave painting clearly shows a human figure climbing vines or ropes and raiding a bees' nest for honey. The figure, known as the "Man/Woman of Bicorp," carries a gourd for taking the stolen honeycomb away and is surrounded by some remarkably angry- and agitated-looking bees.

The beginnings of the sugar industry

While honey and sweet saps occur naturally in the environment, the granular substance we know as sugar began with the advent of cultivation and processing by humans. In the tropics of New Guinea, native canes—tall, tropical grasses with thick, jointed stems—began to be cultivated around 6000 BCE. One type of cane was grown for construction, while another softer, sweeter variety was grown for chewing. The latter was sugar cane which—even in its raw state—provided a refreshing hit of calorie-laden energy via its juice. Through trade with Polynesia, sugar cane reached India, and it was here that a crude form of sugar was extracted from the cane around 400 BCE.

Over the next thousand years, sugar spread slowly around the world, seducing those who could afford it, and edging out honey

△ **Sweet temptation**
Our Neolithic ancestors were drawn to sweet foods just as we are today, as cave paintings at the Cuevas de la Araña show. Honey was prized for its taste and for the energy it provided.

◁ **Keeping bees**
This image from a 15th-century manuscript shows a woman harvesting honey. In the Middle Ages, beehives were kept not only for the honey, but also for beeswax.

△ **New World order**
Sugar processing by slaves in the Americas had its roots in the 15th century when sugar cane was brought from Asia to the Dominican Republic by Christopher Columbus.

and other plant-based syrups and fruits as sources of sweeteners. In its wake, it left behind the brutal legacy of slavery in Caribbean sugar-cane plantations.

Paying for tooth decay

In Renaissance Europe, it was common for the richest people in society to suffer from blackened, rotten teeth due to their excessive consumption of sugar. The expensive import could only be afforded by the wealthy, and Elizabeth I of England provides a royal example. Known for her love of sugary foods, she is thought to have endured severe dental decay. By comparison, the poor, who relied on fruit or wild honey for sweet-tasting foods, suffered considerably less decay. Historians charting dentistry records over hundreds of years have noticed that there was a dramatic spike in decay among the richest classes of early 19th-century England. It was not uncommon for many people to have lost some or even all of their teeth to decay and gum disease by the age of 30. At the same time, sugar imports were increasing at a dramatic rate, and

> Besides adding a sweet flavor, sugar acts as a preservative in foods such as jellies and jams.

between 1704 and 1901, Britain's sugar intake rose by more than 20 times that of previous generations. All across Europe, North America, Asia, and in European colonies around the world, it seemed that people had developed a craving for refined sugar products in the space of a few hundred years.

From sugar beets to diabetes

From the late 19th century onward, once sugar had become a cheap commodity, humans added even more to their diets. This was thanks largely to the launch of sugar-beet processing, which offered a much cheaper alternative to cane sugar. As early as 1826, French lawyer and gourmand Jean Anthelme Brillat-Savarin noted that sugar intake in Europe was "becoming more frequent each day." In his ground breaking book, *The Physiology of Taste* (1825), he cited sugar as one of the main causes of obesity in early 19th-century society.

Today, sugar is blamed for a raft of health problems especially in the West, including obesity and diabetes. Nutritionists estimate that only 20 percent of sugar consumption is direct, in the form of granulated sugar or honey and syrup; 80 percent comes from foods and drinks to which sugar has been added. These hidden sources of sugar—often low-cost alternatives such as corn syrup—are linked to rising rates of obesity. Health-conscious consumers have turned to natural, antioxidant-rich alternatives such as honey and syrups like maple and agave.

△ **A grim alliance**
In the 19th century, slavery and sugar production were inextricably linked. Despite innovations such as windmills, sugar in the West Indies came from slave labor.

▷ **The price of sweet treats**
During the Renaissance, the increase in sugar consumption among the nobility of Europe meant more tooth decay—and more work for local barber-surgeons, who extracted teeth.

△ **Piling it high**
During the 1950s, the government invested heavily in sugar production in India. Today, the country is the world's second-largest producer of cane sugar; only Brazil makes more.

Honey the first sweetener

With its ability to keep indefinitely, its enticing sweet taste, and its numerous health benefits, honey has earned its place as one of the most prized foods in human history.

An 8,000-year-old cave painting in Bicorp, Spain, provides compelling evidence that prehistoric humans were well aware that honey bee nests contained honey, and that it was worth having. It shows a man with a basket on his back clinging to a trailing stem and taking honey from a nest. One tactic was to smoke out the bees, and when they had fled, take the honey without risk of stings. Humans may have followed the clues given by animal honey seekers, such as honey badgers.

A matter of life and death?

Raw honey was not only a sweet relief from a diet of meat and bitter-tasting vegetables and fruit, it was also an invaluable nutritional source. Scientific studies have found that honey plays a role in naturally controlling the body's blood-sugar levels. Its combination of oligosaccharides, glucose, and fructose slows the rate of digestion and delays absorption of nutrients in the intestine, allowing for a slow, controlled release of sugars into the bloodstream. Honey has been shown to help prevent stomach ulcers and create an environment in which "good" bacteria thrive. It also has an antibacterial action that may boost wound healing. These properties may have made the difference between life and death in ancient societies.

◁ **Bee folly**
The Victorians had a romantic view of beekeeping. This sketch of an ornate beehive on a table is from a book about honey bees published in 1827.

Origins of beekeeping

At some point humans switched from robbing nests to cultivating bees in man-made hives. This is thought to have happened in Lower Egypt, which in 3000 BCE was known as "Bee Land" for the abundance of bees in the fertile Nile Delta. Evidence of beekeeping was found in the ruins of Shesepibre, the solar temple of the Fifth dynasty pharaoh Newoserre Any, who lived around 2474–2444 BCE. One hall is decorated with reliefs of seasonal activities, including beekeeping, or apiculture. By ancient Egypt's Sixth dynasty honey was a valuable commodity for trade.

Honey's significance in medieval times is clear in the tax laws of Germany, which stipulated that peasants pay their taxes to feudal lords in the form of honey

▷ **Mythic beekeepers**
This detail from a painting by 15th-century Italian artist Piero di Cosimo depicts fauns and satyrs encouraging a swarm of bees to settle in a hollow tree—an allegory for a successful quest for fertility represented by honey.

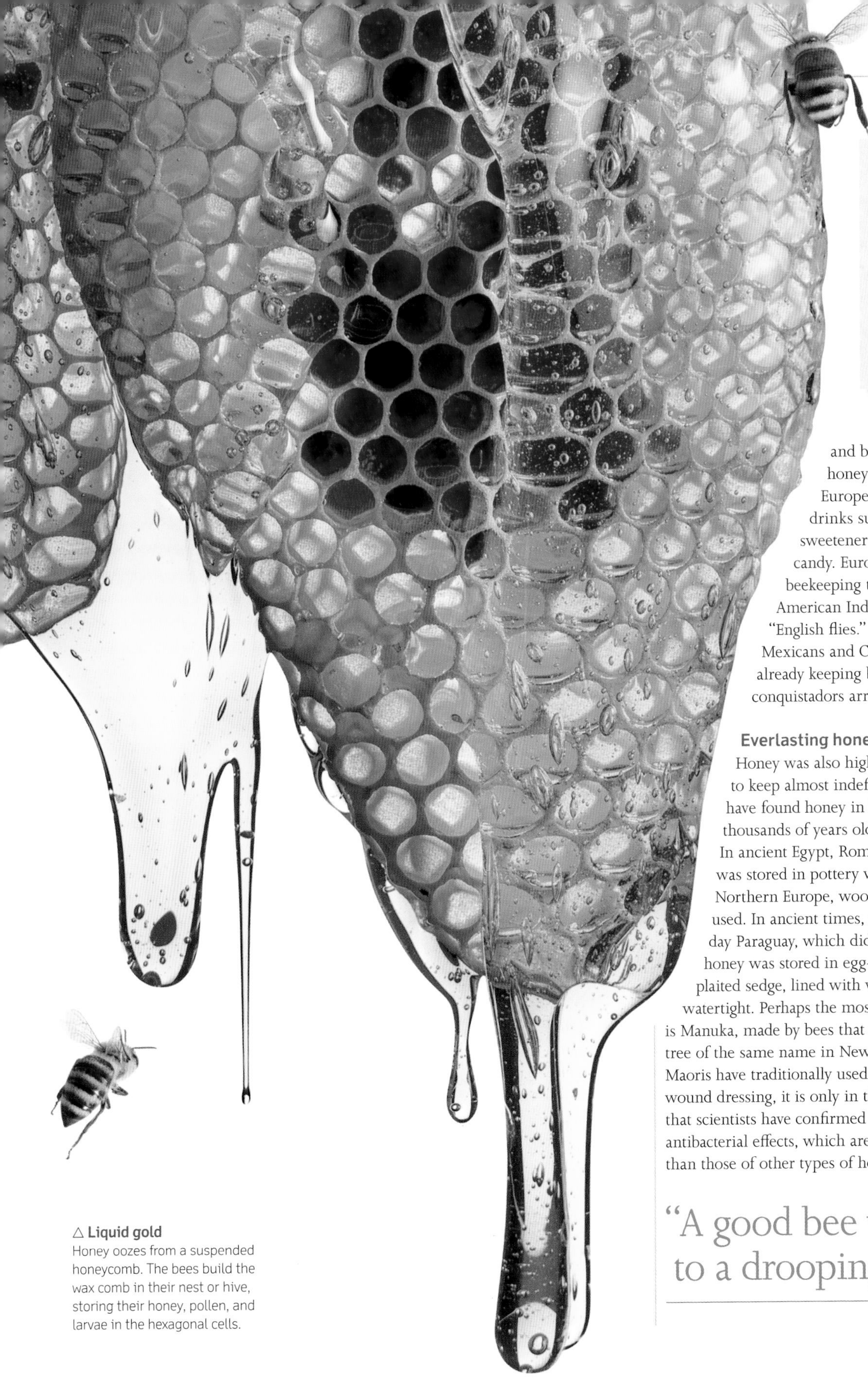

RAW MANUKA HONEY

Origins
New Zealand

Major producers
New Zealand, Australia

Main food component
81 percent carbohydrate

Non-food use
Medicinal (antibacterial)

and beeswax. The use of honey was widespread in Europe—it was the basis for drinks such as mead and a sweetener for bread, cakes, and candy. European settlers introduced beekeeping to North America, where American Indians called honey bees "English flies." Further south, however, Mexicans and Central Americans were already keeping bees when Spanish conquistadors arrived in the 16th century.

Everlasting honey

Honey was also highly valued for its ability to keep almost indefinitely—archaeologists have found honey in Egyptian tombs thousands of years old that is still good to eat. In ancient Egypt, Rome, and Greece, honey was stored in pottery vessels, while in Northern Europe, wooden barrels were often used. In ancient times, in the region of present-day Paraguay, which did not have fired pottery, honey was stored in egg-shaped baskets of plaited sedge, lined with wax to keep them watertight. Perhaps the most precious honey of all is Manuka, made by bees that feed on the nectar of the tree of the same name in New Zealand. Although the Maoris have traditionally used Manuka honey as a wound dressing, it is only in the past few decades that scientists have confirmed the full extent of its antibacterial effects, which are significantly greater than those of other types of honey.

"A good bee will not go to a drooping flower."

ROMANIAN PROVERB

△ **Liquid gold**
Honey oozes from a suspended honeycomb. The bees build the wax comb in their nest or hive, storing their honey, pollen, and larvae in the hexagonal cells.

Maple syrup

the sweet taste of spring

The classic American accompaniment to breakfast pancakes and bacon, maple syrup is the condensed, unrefined liquid sugar from the maple tree. Its uncloying sweetness is unmatched by its more highly manufactured imitators.

Origins
North America

Major producers
Canada, US

Main food component
67 percent carbohydrate

Source of
Zinc, vitamin B2

Maple syrup is produced only in Canada and the northeast of the US. American Indians—mainly in southeastern Canada, New England, and the Appalachian Mountains, where maple species flourished—had been making it from the sap of maple trees long before Europeans arrived. These regions also provided ideal conditions for the trees to generate their sweet sap—cold nights and warm days. Although there are 128 species of maple, only a few are well suited to making maple syrup with an unusually high sugar content of between 2 and 5 percent. The sweetest of all is the aptly named sugar maple (*Acer saccharum*), but

the black maple (*A. nigrum*) and red maple (*A. rubrum*) also produce sweet sap. Sugar is produced in the leaves during the summer, then transported to the wood, where it is stored during winter as carbohydrate. When the weather begins to warm, the carbohydrates in the wood are converted into sucrose, which dissolves in the sap.

Sweet stories
In the indigenous folklore of North America, one Iroquois legend relates how an Indian chief, Wokis, pulled his tomahawk from a maple tree to go hunting

△ **Syrup spoon**
This carved wooden ladle was used by the Menominee Indians of the Great Lakes region of North America for maple syrup production.

on a warm summer's day. Later in the day, his squaw went to collect water for cooking, but passed by the tree and saw liquid oozing from the gash made by the tomahawk. She collected it to save a trip to the spring and prepared the evening's meal with it. The chief thought it delicious and from then on, the community began tapping maple trees for the sweet sap.

Legend aside, it is clear that at some point American Indians realized that the sap from the maple trees was sweet and good to eat. Boiled over a fire it reduced to a brown syrup, and cooked further formed crystals. Maple syrup became an important source of nutrition and energy, and was celebrated at the first full moon of the spring, referred to as the Sugar Moon. The Anishinaabe people named the month from late March to April *Izhkigamisegi Geezis*, the month of boiling, after the sugar boiling that took place at the start of spring. Early settlers quickly learned the technique for tapping maples from the local people, providing sweetness when sugar or molasses was in short supply. Colonial tappers called maples "sugar bushes," drilling holes in the trunks and using buckets to collect the sap.

Making the grade

Today, around 80 percent of the world's maple syrup comes from the Canadian province of Quebec. It is graded according to density and color—the darker the syrup, the stronger the flavor. Most of the syrup produced is sold in its natural form for pouring over fruit and desserts. Canada also produces a variety of maple syrup-based candies.

△ **Winter collection**
Men use traditional buckets to gather the sap from maple trees in the northern US in the early 20th century.

▽ **Reducing the sap**
In the 19th century and earlier, the syrup was boiled in the woods near where it was collected.

Maple sap is typically 98 percent water and yields just 2 percent of its volume as syrup.

Sugar crystals of sweetness

RAW CANE SUGAR

Origins
New Guinea

Major producers
Brazil, India, China

Main food component
100 percent
carbohydrate

Non-food use
Fuel (ethanol)

For over 2,000 years, solidified sugar syrup produced from sugar cane remained a luxury for the few until the discovery of beet sugar made it affordable to all.

On the tropical island of New Guinea in the South Pacific 8,000 years ago, sugar cane grew wild. This tall, strong-growing species of grass has sugary sap, and the native New Guineans would chew pieces of stem until they could suck out the sweet juice. Around this time, they began to cultivate the plant so that they had a guaranteed source of sweetness. Over the centuries, trade took sugar cane east to Polynesia, and it eventually took root in Hawaii in the 1st century CE. Sugar cane also traveled westward to Indonesia and the Philippines, and reached India by around 3000 BCE. It was here that sugar cane began its transformation into one of the world's most precious commodities.

Making "stone honey"

From India, sugar cane was introduced to China around 800 BCE, and Chinese texts from this time referred to India's sugar cane fields. In 510 BCE, when the Persian emperor Darius invaded India, he noted the existence of "a reed which makes honey without bees." By 400 BCE, the Indians had developed a crude technique for making a type of powdered sugar by evaporating sugar syrup. Eventually, it would harden into a solid form that became known as "stone honey." In China, cakes of white stone honey, or shi-mi, imported from India were among the country's costliest commodities.

> Around 70 percent of the world's supply of sugar is derived from sugar cane.

When Alexander the Great returned to Greece from his campaign in India in 325 BCE he brought some of the country's sweet "honey powder" with him.

White crystals

During the 1st century CE, Greek physician Dioscorides described sugar as "… a kind of concentrated honey, called saccharon, found in canes in India and Arabia, like in consistence to salt, and brittle to be broken between the teeth." Yet two centuries later, around 350 CE, India developed a method for turning sugar cane into granulated crystals, the next evolution in sugar's rising popularity. It became one of India's main exports, traded westward to Persia and Egypt, where from 700 CE techniques for sugar processing were honed further, especially those for purifying and refining. The Arab world had begun to produce its

△ **Cane crusher**
This 19th-century Peruvian wooden mill was operated manually, so crushing the sugar cane to extract the sweet sap was hard work.

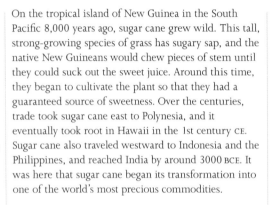

△ **Sugar stick**
These Egyptian boys are getting some sugar the original way, by chewing on a piece of sugar cane.

◁ **Sugar refinery**
The old process of refining sugar is depicted in this Dutch engraving from *c*.1600. The workers cut the canes into small pieces to be crushed in a mill to extract the sugary liquid. This is then poured into molds to form conical loaves.

Sweets for sale
This fancifully costumed confectioner of the 1730s is depicted displaying all the wares of her trade, including candied fruit and paper cones filled with candy.

△ **Tool for the job**
Today, sugar cane can be harvested by self-propelled machines, but it used to have to be cut with a knife or machete.

own sugar. After the Crusaders had acquired a taste for sugar during their travels to the Holy Land in the Middle Ages, the Arabs started to trade it with Europe. With production limited to India and the Middle East, coupled with growing European demand, sugar commanded a high price.

Medieval health food

In Europe, wealthy medieval households treated sugar as a rare spice, using it in meat dishes and soups, as well as in cakes and pastries. According to the dietary approach at the time, which classified foods as either warm or cold, dry or moist, sugar was classed as a warm, moist food. It was considered to have a beneficial effect on the constitutions of the sick and healthy alike. According to the 11th-century health treatise *Tacuinum sanitatis*, "refined sugar … has a cleansing effect on the body and benefits the chest, kidneys, and bladder … It is good for the blood and therefore suitable for every temperament, age, season, and place." Guillaume Tirel, chef to the royal courts of France in the 14th century, advised adding sugar to most savory dishes, especially those for the sick. In his manuscript *Le Viandier*, he advises that any dish

"If you can't give any sugar then speak sweetly."

INDIAN PROVERB

prepared for an ill person "must have sugar in it." The sweet taste of sugar also made it an essential in medicines of the time, counteracting the bitterness of the active plant ingredients.

Trading in sweetness

Venetian traders of the Middle Ages were quick to find a place in the sugar trade, establishing their own plantations on the island of Cyprus, and inventing water-powered crushing mills. The mills produced sugar syrup from harvested cane, which was then solidified into small blocks, or loaves, for ease of transport. The 14th-century handbook of Italian sugar merchant Francesco Pegolotti lists over a dozen forms of sugar on the European market, including powdered sugar, lozenges, lumps, and loaves, as well as sugars scented with violets and roses. By this time, candy stores had sprung up in the major Italian cities, selling paper cones of candies made from cane sugar.

Worth their weight in sugar

Despite the busy trade, sugar was still a rarity, nicknamed "white gold" because of its cost. In 16th-century Europe, a small bag cost the equivalent of a day's wages. Even in the Middle East, which produced some of the finest sugar, it was expensive. When Sultan Ahmad al-Mansur began construction of the Badi Palace in Marrakech, Morocco, in the late 1500s, the cost of the luxury building materials—gold, Italian marble, and onyx—was calculated according to their weight in sugar.

Earlier in the same century, the first sugar cane plantations were established in the Caribbean after the explorer Christopher Columbus had brought sugar cane cuttings from the Spanish-controlled Canary Islands on his second voyage to the Americas. Sugar production in this

△ **Powered by steam**
The invention of the steam engine transformed sugar production. This massive sugar mill was operating in a Cuban refinery in the 1880s.

part of the world would profoundly shape history over the next few hundred years, not only in its use of slave labor, but as the primary supplier of sugar to Europe.

While the Spanish were busy establishing sugar production in the Caribbean, the Portuguese focused their efforts on plantations in Brazil. The growing and processing efforts by these two European naval powers would have amounted to nothing without a well-developed market for making sales. The Dutch were instrumental in expanding the commercial network for sugar in Europe. They also helped to boost the production of sugar in the West Indies, so that by the latter part of the 17th century, the price of sugar had dropped by half. Even so, it was still not affordable for most people.

A new source

Two centuries later, a discovery by a German chemist would trigger a dramatic change in the fortunes of sugar. Through his experiments with beets, Andreas Margraff discovered that these root vegetables contained sucrose, which was indistinguishable from cane sugar. Europe's first beet sugar factory first opened in modern-day Poland in 1801 and more soon opened in northern France, Germany, Austria, Russia, and Denmark as cultivation of sugar beets spread. Sugar became far cheaper and more plentiful. From being a luxury item for the rich, sugar became a staple for ordinary people during the 19th and 20th centuries, when sweet tea, jams, candy, cakes, and cookies became everyday fare. Today, sugar is widely used in the food and drinks industry.

△ **Sweet and pure**
Philadelphia was the center of the American sugar refining industry in the 19th century. Franklin Sugar was one of the largest refineries in the city.

◁ **A good harvest**
When it is ready to be harvested, sugar cane can be twice as tall as a fully grown man. A skilled harvester, like these in the West Indies, can cut 1,100lb (500kg) of canes an hour.

Oils and Condiments

Oils and condiments

Oils have been produced all over the globe from a vast array of fruits, vegetables, flowers, seeds, and nuts for millennia. In the ancient world, oils were used not only for cooking, but for lighting lamps (including for rituals as well as everyday use) as well as for use in ointments and balms, medicines, and even preserving bodies such as of pharaohs in ancient Egypt. Oils were also used as a method of preserving foods in Egypt, as well as in Rome and Greece. Vegetables survived reasonably well when stored in oil, and small round cheeses were preserved in the same way.

The ubiquitous olive

Neolithic people were probably collecting olives as early as 10,000 years ago in what is now the Middle East, in order to press them for oil. Certainly remains of olive oil dated to 8,000 years ago have been found in pot shards at a huge archaeological site called Ein Zippori in northern Israel. In fact, once written records developed, the olive is mentioned so frequently in the history of oils that it is easy to forget how many other plants provided people with this important and useful substance. Even the English word oil is from *elaia*, the Greek for olive. In the Middle Ages, oil was used for cooking in Europe but animal fats or greases made from them (such as goose fat) were often preferred by those living in the more northerly countries, probably due to their easier availability.

Other types of oil

Various types of oils began to be used on different continents as plants were taken across the world by travelers and explorers. Avocado and almond, sunflower and sesame, coconut, corn, and many more have all spread from country to country in this way. South American groundnut or peanut oil is now used on every continent; it is particularly useful as it has no flavor and can be heated to a high temperature without burning. In India, sesame, rape, and mustard seeds were all crushed for their oils, either by hand in a mortar or on a flat stone with a stone rolling pin. Eventually, however, a kind of grindstone used since around 1500 BCE developed into the *ghani*, a much larger version that was

△ **Pressing for health**
Olive oil has been part of the human diet for thousands of years. In the late 20th century, scientists discovered that it also contains health benefits, such as anti-inflammatory compounds.

◁ **Mechanizing production**
Many methods were used in the ancient world to extract olive oil. including treading on olives. By the 3rd century, mechanized presses were widely used in the Roman Empire.

△ **Cool comfort**
Large pottery vessels such as amphorae were the most common containers used to store olive oil. Many were placed underground, where cool temperatures prevented spoilage.

operated by an animal such as an ox or bull to produce oil. It resembled a giant pestle and mortar, but was adapted so that the central vertical pestle was linked to a yoked bull. This method is still in use now for a variety of seeds, but on a very small scale. The same kind of equipment was used in Sri Lanka and Afghanistan. There is a brief reference to an oil press in Sanskrit literature of 500 BCE but the equipment is not described. Methods of pressing seeds have since been modernized, speeded up, and temperature-controlled, but it is interesting to think that many oils that were first used in ancient times are still being used today.

Condiments: the flavor enhancers

The history of condiments follows a similar pattern to that of oils. The word itself comes from the Latin *condire*, to pickle or to preserve—something that was used to enhance the flavor of food, and especially a pungent seasoning. A large number of condiments have been used for millennia and many of them can be traced back to their ancient roots.

Garum was a pastelike sauce made from fermented fish by the Romans. Its influence was widespread and the Romans put it on almost everything they ate. Archaeologists found a pottery jar of garum at a Roman site in northern England labeled "best quality." In the East, pickles were used more subtly, with emphasis placed on balancing the flavors of salty, bitter, sweet, and sour. Ketchup, now familiar everywhere, began as *kecap* in the Far East, but it changed dramatically as it traveled west. The first ketchup recipe that used tomatoes was not published in the US until 1812. Many condiments evolved through people using native ingredients, but all have traveled and adapted to suit the tastes of the people who have

> The earliest known olive presses date from the 6th century BCE in Turkey and used a beam and stone weight.

adopted them. One such example is Worcestershire sauce, named for the town in England where it was created. In the early 19th century, an aristocrat who had spent time in India asked two chemists, John Wheeley Lea and William Perrins, to make a concoction from an old recipe he brought home with him. The chemists disliked the taste and stored the portion they had kept for themselves. Retasting it some time later, however, they found the sauce's taste more to their liking and began to make and sell it.

Perhaps the most important condiment of all is salt, although it is much too important to be thought of, like many condiments, as an optional extra in our diets. Too little is just as bad for both humans and animals as is too much.

△ **To market by boat**
In the Philippines, vinegar, or *suka*, has featured in cuisine for generations and was often moved by boat. It is made from sugar cane, coconut palms, or nipa palms.

▷ **Fish factory**
The fermented fish sauce known as garum was so popular in ancient Rome that special "factories" were established to process the salted fish that formed its main ingredient.

△ **Black economy**
The Solovetsky monastery, founded in the 15th century on an island in the White Sea, owed its astonishing wealth to salt. Salt produced here was black, due to being mixed with seaweed.

Olive oil the oil of the classical world

A staple of Mediterranean cuisine from ancient times to the present day, olive oil is now renowned across the world, both for its taste and health-giving properties. The ancient Greek poet Homer called it liquid gold.

A species of wild olive tree grew millions of years ago in present-day Italy, but the tree was first cultivated in the eastern Mediterranean. Remnants of crushed olive pits and olive pulp found at Kfar Samir, a sunken settlement off Israel's Haifa Coast, show that olive oil was made there as early as 4500 BCE. Throughout the Mediterranean region, archaeological finds including olive presses and amphorae reveal the oil's economic importance in ancient times. Written in the script of

the Mycenaean Greeks, the words for olive trees and olive oil appear on clay tablets found at Knossos, Crete, dating from around 1450 BCE.

Ancient oil boom

Ranging in color from yellow to a rich deep green, the oil pressed from the fruit of the olive tree was—together with grapes and grain—one of the three staple foods of the ancient Western world. From early

△ **Old-style oil storage**
Olive oil used to be stored and transported in pithos, large earthenware jars like this one found at the Minoan Palace of Malia on Crete.

in the 1st millennium BCE, it was traded across the Mediterranean by the Phoenicians, who lived in present-day Lebanon, Syria, and northern Israel. It was important not just as a source of nourishment, but was also used in lamps, cosmetics, perfumes, and to embalm the dead. In ancient Greece, athletes rubbed the oil on their skin before contests to reduce muscle fatigue and to ease sprains—in Homer's *Odyssey*, Odysseus was massaged with the "golden oil" after his epic voyage.

In Roman times, olive oil was produced at hundreds of sites in Spain, Portugal, and North Africa and transported to Britain, Germany, France, and other parts of the empire. In the 1st and 2nd centuries CE, annual olive oil production in Andalusia, Spain, is estimated to have reached 26.4 million gallons (100 million liters).

From tree to table
After picking the fruit from the tree, the olives were washed and pitted, then the pulp was pressed in baskets and rinsed through with water. The oil was then left to

△ **New invention**
An olive press that could extract more oil is shown in this Dutch engraving from "New Inventions for Modern Times" (*c*.1600).

Origins
Eastern Mediterranean

Major producers
Spain, Italy, Greece

Main food component
93 percent fat

Source of
Vitamin E, vitamin K

Non-food uses
Soap, cosmetics

△ **Proof of land**
In the Biblical story of Noah and the Flood, a dove returns to the ark with an olive branch, reflecting the importance of this plant to ancient societies.

cultivation to the disposal of the waste products. When Spanish and Portuguese colonists took young olive trees to South America in the 16th and 17th centuries, they quickly became established in the valleys of Peru and Chile, where the climate was similar to that of the Mediterranean. In the 18th century, Franciscan missionaries planted olive trees in southern California and by 1870 small orchards along the Californian coast grew different varieties of olive. Within 15 years, however, the industrial advances that facilitated oil extraction from maize and seeds meant that olive oil production was no longer viable for Californian growers, who began instead to cultivate olives for eating.

In Europe, olive oil production had increased to meet the needs of growing city populations in the 18th and 19th centuries. However, here, too, in the late 19th and early 20th centuries, sales declined as a result of

"The wise store up choice food and olive oil, but fools gulp theirs down."

THE BIBLE, PROVERBS 21:20

separate, before being skimmed at least twice, and finally stored in large vats. In his *Natural History* (79 CE), the Roman scholar Pliny the Elder rated olive oil from Central Italy as the very best. He recommended the first pressed oil for optimum flavor and warned that, unlike wine, olive oil did not age well.

The Romans used olive oil in just about everything: dressings, sauces, soups, fried meat and fish, stews, pies, and savory and sweet puddings. The fall of the western Roman Empire temporarily stalled olive oil production in Italy, but it continued in the eastern Byzantine Empire and in Spain, North Africa, and the Middle East after the Islamic conquests that began in the 7th century CE. Olive oil was fundamental to Arab cuisine and used in myriad savory and sweet dishes.

The olive goes west
In the Middle Ages, the production of olive oil flourished in Spain, Italy, and Greece, where it remained part of the everyday diet. In Italy, village rules regulated every part of the process from

△ **Olive harvest**
This 2nd-century CE mosaic in the North African city of Chebba, Tunisia, shows a Roman laborer gathering olives, having first beaten the tree to make the ripe fruit fall to the ground.

△ **Wooden press**
Olive presses remained unchanged for centuries—this one is being operated by Berber people in Algeria. It takes 11lb (5kg) of olives to produce 2 pints (1 liter) of oil.

competition from newer oils and fuels. Demand continued to fall until the mid 20th century, and manufacturers had to compete on price. As a result of these commercial pressures, widespread adulteration of olive oil with cheap cotton and seed oils occurred.

Raising standards

The International Olive Oil Council (now the International Olive Council) was established in 1955 to help regulate standards, production, and international trading agreements. Today, its members account for 98 percent of the world's olive production. The IOC stipulates that virgin olive oil must be produced in a way that does not alter its chemical structure.

The council has also defined the differences between extra virgin olive oil, virgin olive oil, and ordinary virgin olive oil in terms of their percentage of oleic acid—the highest-quality extra virgin olive oil has the lowest percentage of oleic acid (less than 0.8 percent). Ordinary virgin oil that has more than 3.3 percent of oleic acid is not considered fit for consumption. Although not affiliated to the IOC, the North American Olive Oil Association tests olive oils produced and sold in the US against IOC standards.

Twenty-first-century gold

Americans now celebrate September 30 as National Extra Virgin Olive Oil Day. This top-quality virgin olive oil has become highly sought after for its taste and the

"The Mediterranean ends where the olive ceases to grow."

GEORGES DUHAMEL, FRENCH WRITER (1884–1966)

health benefits that nutritional science has revealed. As a major component of the increasingly popular and reputedly healthy Mediterranean diet, a high intake of olive oil is considered a key contributor to longevity and low rates of heart disease among some communities in Italy.

Cooks around the world—including countries in the Far East that have no traditions of olive growing or the culinary use of olive oil—increasingly employ this versatile product. Global consumption has risen by more than 70 percent since 1990–1991, reaching close to 900 million gallons (3,400 million liters) a year. The trend marks major changes in the diets of countries such as the UK and Germany, and in Japan, where sales of olive oil have increased by an astonishing 1,400 percent since the early 1990s.

Italy, which boasts an estimated 250 million olive trees and more than 500 varieties of olive, still consumes the most olive oil, with Spain in second place, and in third place the US, where sales have risen by 250 percent in 27 years. Such figures are a powerful testimony to the resurgent popularity of this delicious "liquid gold."

▷ **Superior quality**
Olive oil produced from groves on the French Mediterranean coast was advertised as superior by Parisian grocery stores in the early 1900s.

▽ **As far as the eye can see**
Covering more than 3.7 million acres (1.5 million hectares), the olive groves of Andalusia in southern Spain produce more olive oil than anywhere else in the world.

Sunflower oil liquid sunshine

Valued as an alternative to dairy fats, the pale yellow oil from the seeds of the sunflower is widely used in home kitchens and in the food-processing industry throughout the world.

The story of sunflower oil begins in the Americas, where in prehistoric times American Indians collected wild sunflower seeds for food. Following the arrival of the Spanish in the New World during the 16th century, the cultivated sunflower arrived in Europe, and was probably first planted for its ornamental value. The sunflower was only commercially exploited when it was introduced to Russia by Tsar Peter the Great in the early 18th century. The Russians not only ate them with gusto, but also extracted their oil. By the early 19th century, some 2 million acres (800,000 hectares) of Russian land was devoted to sunflowers. By 1830, sunflower oil was being manufactured commercially. Over the following decades, Russian plant breeders increased the oil content of the sunflower varieties grown from 20 percent to more than 50 percent as well improving their resistance to disease.

△ **Industrial scale**
Wherever sunflowers are grown commercially, modern harvesting methods are used as here in Dugald, Canada.

The 1716 patent for sunflower oil extraction was for use in treating wool and leather.

Spreading softly

When saturated animal fats such as butter became linked with heart disease in the mid-20th century, food manufacturers seized on sunflower oil for the new soft spreads. Today, it is widely used in the food industry in spreads, baking, and snacks as well as in domestic kitchens as an ingredient in dressings and as a cooking oil. In recent years, new sunflower oils higher in oleic acid, a healthy monounsaturated fat, have been developed.

OF SWEET GUM AND MULLEIN.

▽ **Field of plenty**
At the peak of the flowering
season in mid summer,
sunflowers provide a dazzling
display of color.

◁ **Healthy association**
In this advertisement for an
herbal cough remedy, the
image of a maize plant clearly
conveyed a healthy message.

Corn oil golden extract

Initially underestimated as a by-product, the oil derived from
maize has become one of the staples of the domestic pantry
and of the manufacture of a huge variety of foods.

The first step in the history of corn oil was the
development in 1842 of a new industrial process that
freed the protein, starch, fiber, and all-important germ
from corn kernels. Although at first manufacturers
were interested in only two maize products—
cornstarch and corn sugar—Thomas Hudnut, a mill
owner from Indiana, began to look for ways to use the
discarded germ. In the early 1880s, he invented a
mechanical means of extracting oil from the germ.
After his death, Hudnut's son, Benjamin, perfected the
method, coining the name mazoil for the resulting
golden oil. By 1902, the Hudnut mills were selling
100,000 gallons (380,000 liters) a day.

The distinctive flavor of corn oil—as well as its
stability, ease of storage, and its high smoke point—
made the product highly marketable. Corn oil sales
received an additional boost in the mid-20th century,

▷ **Oil source**
Corn oil is extracted from the
germ inside each kernel of the
cob once the starchy outer parts
have been processed.

when oils derived from plant sources became seen as
healthier than animal fats. By the 1960s, few Western
kitchens were without a bottle of corn oil or a tub of
corn oil-based margarine.

Multiple uses

While its health benefits have been questioned by
some, corn oil remains one of the most widely used
oils across the world for cooking and in the
manufacture of products such as potato chips,
mayonnaise, salad dressings, and crumb coatings.

Food on the move

On October 4, 1883, the *Express d'Orient* left Paris's Gare de Strasbourg on its inaugural journey. The train was the brainchild of Belgian entrepreneur Georges Nagelmackers, who had founded the Compagnie Internationale des Wagons-Lits (International Sleeping-Car Company) the previous year. It was the last word in luxury, with an elegant dining car and excellent food. As the train steamed toward Strasbourg, passengers feasted on a ten-course dinner which included oysters, turbot, chicken chausseur, *chaud-froid* of game, and chocolate pudding.

Nagelmackers, however, got the idea from the US, where, in 1867, George Pullman, who had previously won fame as a builder of sleeping cars, introduced the first dining car to the traveling world. Named *Delmonico,* after New York's celebrated restaurant, it ran between Chicago and Springfield. The idea caught on and was adopted by railroads such as the Michigan Central, Baltimore & Ohio, Northern Pacific, and Santa Fe. In 1879, Pullman also supplied Britain's Great Northern Railway with its first dining car, which ran between London's King's Cross Station and Leeds.

In the first US dining cars, a typical meal consisted of broiled mutton chops, breaded veal cutlets, and buffalo, all washed down with a glass of Champagne. By the 1920s and '30s, dishes like braised lobster à l'américaine, mountain trout au bleu, and curry of lamb madras had appeared on the menu. In the kitchen, three cooks and a chef made as many as 300 meals in a three- to four-hour period three times a day, while waiters prepared salads, breads, and beverages—all relatively inexpensively, even by the standards of the day. In 1940 a three-course meal with soup, prime beef rib, potatoes, vegetables, and ice cream cost just $1.50 on the Pennsylvania Railroad.

◁ **First-class dining**
In the late 1930s, first-class passengers on the UK's Great Western Railway enjoyed three-course meals for around 18½ pence.

Si Vous Voulé de la Moutarde, J'en fais

Moutarde

boête
à la
Moutarde

Vinegar

acidic condiment and preservative

Origins Worldwide	
Major producers US	
Main food component None	
Non-food uses Cleaning agent, disinfectant, traditional medicine	

Ever since it was discovered several thousand years ago that wine turned to vinegar when it was exposed to the air, this acidic liquid has been used as a condiment, food preservative, and pickling agent.

△ **Extra aeration**
The Schützenbach barrel, invented in 1823, let more air reach the wine, increasing the conversion to acetic acid.

The exact history of vinegar is unknown, but it was certainly ubiquitous in ancient Rome, where it was used as a food dressing and in pickles with brine. It was also used for *posca*, a refreshing drink originally from ancient Greece made by diluting wine vinegar with water flavored with herbs, which was drunk by soldiers and members of the lower classes.

The word vinegar comes from the 13th-century French description, *vinaigre*, which means sour wine. Vinegar is essentially acetic acid and water. It can be made from a wide range of cereals, fruits, vegetables,

"The sweetest wine turneth to the sharpest vinegar."

JOHN LYLY, ENGLISH WRITER (*c*.1600)

herbs, and flowers that have been fermented to produce alcohol. Malt vinegar, popular in modern-day Britain for sprinkling on fish and chips, is made from an ale brewed from malted barley. Also called alegar, it has a coarser taste than the best wine vinegars. Rice vinegar, commonly used in East and Southeast Asian cuisine, has been made in China since around 1200 BCE. In 15th-century Korea, vinegar was made from rice, barley, and even iris flowers.

Technology advances
In the Middle Ages, the vinegar producers of Orléans, France, developed an improved method of making vinegar. Wine was poured into a large oak barrel until it was not quite full and a small amount of "mother of vinegar"—a naturally occurring substance formed of cellulose and *Acetobacter* bacteria—was added to start the process of converting the alcohol to acetic acid. The barrel was then sealed and a few small holes were

◁ **Ingenious contraption**
This strange-looking apparatus, worn by a French traveling salesman in the 17th century, was used to dispense both mustard and red wine vinegar.

drilled in the lid to expose the liquid to air. Once the vinegar was ready, about 85 percent was drawn off, leaving a mass of the vinegar bacteria at the bottom of the barrel. This would start the next ferment when more wine was added, creating a continuous process.

Concentrated and mature
Today, most vinegars are made on an industrial scale, but artisan producers in some parts of the world continue to make special ones. Balsamic vinegar from Italy is dark, rich, and syrupy. It is made from the

△ **Traditional technique**
Unlike many Chinese vinegars, Shanxi vinegar is made from sorghum, wheat, barley, and peas. Here, the hot mash is being cooled before the next stage of the manufacturing process.

concentrated juice of Trebbiano and Prosecco grapes aged for a minimum of 12 years in a series of progressively smaller casks made of different woods. Shanxi extra-aged vinegar is an expensive strong, dark vinegar from China. The demand for this product is so great that fake versions are common.

Salt earliest food preservative

Today, salt is a widely available, inexpensive mineral that is taken for granted, but for thousands of years it was highly prized. Salt is essential for life—the ancient Greek poet Homer called it a "divine substance."

Common salt, or sodium chloride, is found all over the world in one form or another, and almost 70 percent of the Earth's surface is covered in salt water. For thousands of years, humans have obtained salt by evaporation from the sea or salt springs, or from salt mines. Salt is the only mineral that can be eaten without being processed in any way. As well as adding flavor to food, salt has been used since the earliest times in many other different ways—for preserving, healing, rituals, and for barter.

According to some traditions, salt had sacred or magical properties. In medieval times in parts of Northern Europe, salt was sprinkled around butter churns to stop witches from souring the butter, and it was also used to protect people and animals from the bad intentions of witches and fairies. Salt has been the cause of wars and played an important part in folk tales and legends all over the world. One such story concerns an Indian princess, who said that she loved her father "as much as salt." He was angry until he realized what a compliment she was paying him.

Salt collection in ancient times

Known as China's Dead Sea, the ancient Yuncheng salt lake in Shanxi province has been used for salt collection since around 6000 BCE. Every summer, as the lake's waters receded in the sun's heat, salt could be scraped

▷ **Primitive tools**
This wooden pickaxe and shovel were used to mine salt in the 5th century BCE from the Hallstatt salt mine in the Austrian Alps.

up from the exposed shore. Salt production in China was very advanced. The first written record dates to 800 BCE, and by then salt taxes made up more than half of the government's revenues. The world's first brine wells were drilled in Sichuan province in 252 BCE to exploit saltwater pools underground.

The two oldest known rock salt works both date back to the 5th millennium BCE. The Duzdagi salt deposits in the Araxes Valley, Azerbaijan, were being exploited by 4500 BCE and by 3500 BCE were mined intensively. The prehistoric settlement of Solnitsata—Bulgarian for "salt pit"—near present-day Provadia, Bulgaria, also dates to around 4500 BCE. The residents boiled salt water from a nearby spring and made salt bricks, which were used to preserve meat and were also traded.

Powers of preservation

The ancient Egyptians used salt for mummifying their dead. Called natron, this preservative was a naturally occurring mixture of different forms of sodium and common salt. The preservation process worked very well—many mummies more than 4,000 years old have been found still in good condition. The Egyptians also used sea salt, harvested from salt pans at Alexandria on the Mediterranean coast, to cure and preserve meat and fish both for home consumption and for export. For many early communities, when animals had to be slaughtered in late

◁ **Salting factory**
In the 2nd century BCE, the Roman city of Baelo Claudia in Andalusia, Spain, produced salted fish and garum, the much-loved fish sauce.

△ **Pure salt**
Dried white salt is transferred into wooden containers at this Austrian salt refinery in the early 20th century.

Origins	
Worldwide	
Major producers	
US, India, China	
Source of	
Sodium	
Non-food uses	
Preservative, gritting, cleaning products	
Scientific name	
Sodium choloride	

autumn because there was insufficient fodder to keep them through the winter, salt played a vital role in preserving the meat. Dry salting was the simplest method, whereby the meat was rubbed with salt and put in a tub with more salt. Meat that was wet salted was put into a barrel filled with a strong salt solution or brine—"strong enough to float an egg"—together with spices that had antibacterial properties. Meat preserved this way kept for years—as sailors over the centuries could attest—but it became less palatable over time until eventually it was too hard to eat.

Salting fish also allowed them to be kept almost indefinitely, but they, too, became very hard after long keeping. A 14th-century domestic manual written in Paris, France, tells how this problem should be dealt with after salted fish had been kept for 10 or 12 years: "And when it hath been kept a long time and it is desired to eat it, it behoves to beat it with a wooden hammer for a full hour."

"Salt is born of the purest of parents: the sun and the sea."

PYTHAGORAS, GREEK PHILOSOPHER AND MATHEMATICIAN (c.570–490 BCE)

The salting of vegetables was a traditional way to preserve summer's plenty for the long winter months. In Eastern Europe, especially, this was done on a large scale. Layers of vegetables covered with layers of salt were packed into stone jars, kept closed until the food was needed. An alternative method was to salt the produce then keep it in vinegar.

▷ **Salt of the earth**
This illustration from 1885 shows the simple but effective device used to produce salt from saline soil in Urua (present-day Democratic Republic of Congo) in Central Africa.

△ 17th-century saltcellar
The high value of salt was reflected in the rich design of the containers in which it was served in previous centuries.

▽ Evaporation pools
Salt has been extracted from pools in Peru's Sacred Valley since they were created by the Incas in the 15th century.

For centuries, salt produced by solar evaporation from the area around Bourgneuf Bay, western France, was considered to be the best for preserving meat. Its large crystals penetrated the flesh slowly and no salt "skin" formed as it would if finer salt were used. Known as "bay salt" it was, however, gray and full of impurities. The Dutch found a way around this by redissolving the bay salt in seawater then heating it in open pans until all that was left was white salt. By the 17th century, this "salt on salt" refining method was also being used in English coastal saltworks. In the 16th century, blood, eggs, and ale had all been used for refining salt.

Symbol of status and trust
The importance of salt throughout history is illustrated by the numerous words and sayings that are derived from it. The *salinator* was the official responsible for fixing salt prices in ancient Rome, and "salary" comes from *salarium*, the salt allowance given to Roman

Made from Korean gray sea salt, Amethyst Bamboo 9x is the world's most expensive salt.

soldiers. The Romans sprinkled salt on green leaves to "allay their bitterness," leading to the word "salad" from the Latin *salata*, meaning salty. In medieval times, "above the salt" and "below the salt" were the places people were seated at a lord's table according to their place in society.

Once so valuable that it was known as "white gold" in several cultures, the preservative power of salt gave it an almost mystical quality. Salt became a symbol of purity and loyalty in different religions and of trust and friendship in the secular world. The Russian word for hospitality translates as salt-bread, and when Arabs offer bread and salt to their guests acceptance creates trust between them.

The universal need for salt made it a valuable commodity, so communities lucky enough to have a good supply were able to prosper through trade with less fortunate places. And salt, being so necessary, made an obvious target for taxation, which often raised its cost to several times its market value. First used in ancient China, this form of taxation has been used over the centuries by many rulers all over the world, but perhaps the most notable example is the *gabelle*, or salt tax, in France. Imposed in the 13th century, and seen as a good way to raise money by successive monarchs, the tax eventually became one of the causes of the French Revolution in 1789.

Today, salt is so commonplace and readily obtainable thanks to cheaper and improved methods of production and transport, that it is easy to forget the high esteem in which it used to be held.

◁ **Curing pork**
Pork haunches are rubbed with rock salt at this Parma ham business in northern Italy. They will be stored for 9 to 18 months until they are cured.

"Trust no one unless you have eaten much salt with him."

CICERO, ROMAN POLITICIAN AND LAWYER (106–43 BCE)

Soy sauce Asia's classic condiment

First made in China around 2,000 years ago, soy sauce was originally a way of making precious salt go further. Today, this strongly flavored condiment made from fermented soy beans adds flavor to Asian cuisine around the world.

The earliest written evidence of soy sauce was found on a bamboo strip in a 1st-century BCE Han dynasty tomb in China. However, it is thought that at first soy beans were consumed as a fermented paste rather than the now familiar thin sauce. By the 3rd century it was recorded that fermented soy beans were being successfully brewed in Korea. When Buddhism was introduced to Japan in the 6th century, the monks also brought with them a number of foods and condiments based on soy beans. Japan's fish-based sauce was replaced by *shoyu*, or soy, and by 1558, a clear soy sauce was being made near Edo.

Four ingredients are used to make a classic soy sauce— soy beans, which have a high protein content; wheat, whose slight sweetness balances the strong flavor; salt, which also acts as a preservative against unwanted bacteria; and spring water. The addition of a mold called *Aspergillus oryzae* causes the mixture to ferment. It takes two years of fermentation to produce the highest-quality soy sauce. Dark soy sauce is used for dipping and is aged for longer than light soy sauce. Soy sauce was first brought by Dutch traders to Europe from Japan in the late 17th century, although Europeans were unable to master the art of its production.

△ **Pride of place**
A small bottle or jug of soy sauce is an essential presence on most Japanese and Chinese dining tables. A narrow spout allows just the right amount to be dispensed.

△ **Fermentation factory**
In 17th-century Japan, naturally brewed soy sauce had to be made by hand and producing it in large quantities was a lengthy, laborious process.

Origins
China

Major producer
Japan

Main food component
12 percent protein

Source of
Sodium

Fish sauce
pungent yet popular

A smelly sauce made from fermented salted fish might not sound appealing, but this condiment had a major role in ancient Roman cuisine, and today it is a staple ingredient in the cuisines of East and Southeast Asia.

Origins
Mediterranean, Asia

Major producer
Thailand

Main food component
5 percent protein

Source of
Sodium, potassium, magnesium, vitamin B6

Fish sauce was an essential element of classical Greek and Roman diets. Known as *garum* or *liquamen*, it served both as a condiment and a cooking ingredient. As popular as ketchup is today, garum was produced by the Romans in factories on the Mediterranean coasts of Italy, Spain, and Egypt and on the shores of the Black Sea, where there was plentiful salt.

Sun, salt, and fish
Various methods were used in its manufacture. Small fish, usually anchovies, or large fish—or the entrails of even larger ones—were salted and left to ferment (not to rot as is often thought) in large stone vats left open to the heat of the sun for two to three months. The very bad smell produced while the garum was maturing meant that, by law, the factories had to be sited away from villages and towns. The resulting intensely flavored, clear, golden liquid was drained off and stored in terra-cotta jars. The residue was called *allec*, and this, too, was used in cooking. Rich in protein and minerals, it was said to be good for teeth and even to counteract the bite of a "sea dragon."

Ancient and modern variants
Different quality levels of garum were produced, and one of the most sought-after was made exclusively from mackerel. Described by the Roman author Pliny the Elder as "that exquisite liquor," its high quality was reflected in its price, which was as expensive as perfume. Not everyone was a fan, however. Seneca, the Roman

◁ **Distinctive shape**
Terra-cotta amphorae with elongated bases were used by Roman merchants to transport liquids such as garum, oil, and wine.

philosopher, said of garum: "The costly extract of poisonous fish, burns up the stomach with its salted putrefaction."

The origins of fish sauce in Asia are uncertain, but today no kitchen in East or Southeast Asia, where it is used during cooking and added at the table, is complete without it. In Vietnam, it is known as *nuoc mam*, and is made from anchovies and salt, often with chillies added. In Japan, the sauce is made from locally available fish or squid, and there are many regional variations. Thai *nam pla* sometimes has chilis added.

In ancient Rome, the best garum was given to the elites, the lowest-quality to slaves.

▷ **Piled high**
As recently as the 1960s, clay jars were still being used as containers for fish sauce in Vietnam.

Herbs and Spices

Herbs and spices

A herb is defined as a plant whose leaves are used for food, medicine, scent, and/or flavor. A spice, in contrast, is considered an aromatic or pungent vegetable substance, mainly derived from tropical plants, and used to flavor food and drink. Ancient peoples were surrounded by all kinds of plants and, like so many other animal species, their instincts guided them to herbs that were useful and safe to eat. It is possible that they may have wrapped meat in leaves to store or transport it, and in this way they would have gradually discovered the flavors and preservative qualities of many herbs and plants.

Ancient medicines, ancient flavors

There are numerous references to herbs in the writings of many ancient civilizations, such as China and Egypt, but their applications were mainly medical. The Greeks and Romans, on the other hand, developed an early appreciation of herbs, using them not only in cooking, but in cosmetics and perfumes as well, and attaching all kinds of superstitions to them along the way. The expanding Roman Empire introduced many unfamiliar plants, including herbs common in the Roman world, to the countries and cultures it conquered. As a result, these peoples modified and adapted the use of these plants to their own tastes, customs, and cuisines.

Herbs and religion

Because of the seasonal nature of cultivation, the growing, gathering, and storing of herbs became bound up with early peoples' observance of, and reverence for, the elements of nature, so it was a natural step to associate them with gods and goddesses linked to the sun, moon, and seasons. As Christianity gradually displaced earlier pagan religions in the West, its priests, nuns, and monks developed their knowledge of herbs, mainly in a medicinal context. By the Middle Ages, European monasteries had become well established as authorities on herbs, they planted herb gardens and kept written records about their uses and properties. Today, these properties are fully understood and their continued cultivation seems assured.

△ **Herb collecting**
During the Middle Ages in Europe, herbs were used not only in cooking, but also around the home as natural insect repellents, deodorants, and even as protection from evil spirits.

◁ **Releasing the flavor**
Grinding spices using mortars and pestles has proved a practical method of extracting flavor for centuries, particularly in countries like India, where cuisine is heavily spice-based.

△ **Rich rewards**
Following the Crusades, trade in spices from East to West increased rapidly. Spice traders could grow very wealthy indeed—provided they survived the perils of the maritime spice routes.

The lure of the exotic

Every country has its herbs, but spices, grown mainly in Asia, the Middle East, and the Mediterranean, were exotic, and their rarity made them even more desirable. Strange tales were told about the dangers of collecting spices guarded by flying snakes or ferocious giant birds—and of course there was a risk of a ship sailing off the edge of the world if it strayed too far from land. Such legends provided a way of keeping prices high as well as deterring others from trying to find the sources of such valuable commodities.

Spices had been bought and sold for millennia, but trade reached its peak in the 1st century CE when Roman appetites for them seemed insatiable. Exotic meats were cooked with all kinds of spices, and nothing was eaten without a sauce of some kind. They were shipped from India to Rome and used in wine, perfumes, and bath oils as well as food. One popular ancient spice plant was silphium from Cyrenaica (modern Libya). Romans used it in food, as medicine, and even as a form of birth control. In fact, they enjoyed it so much that they drove it to probable extinction, for scientists have yet to find any surviving examples.

Spices such as silphium were good to trade because they kept well over time and distance. The Silk Road, a network of land and sea routes connecting the Far East to the West, brought luxury goods, including spices, to Europe and beyond. It is even thought by some scholars that the amount of gold Rome sent in exchange for spices actually hastened the fall of the Roman Empire. Whatever the case, the spice trade certainly brought untold riches to other places. Venice, for one, prospered by being the control center of the import and export of spices for centuries.

> The first known herbal is believed to have been written by Chinese emperor Shen Nung *c.* 5,000 years ago.

From the Crusades to kitchen cupboards

In the 12th and 13th centuries, Roman Catholic Crusaders brought many spices back across Europe, creating a new demand for these exotic substances. The high prices that these goods incurred meant that they were only seen on the tables of the rich, but this mainly served to fuel demand. In 1602, the Dutch East India Company was established, and it held an almost unbreakable monopoly on the spice trade that lasted nearly 200 years. Eventually spices spread even further, especially when they were taken to America by early settlers. With the rise of communication and transcontinental modes of transportation, herbs and spices are now found in kitchens around the world.

△ **The other East India Company**
In 1600 England's Queen Elizabeth I chartered the East India Company to challenge Dutch dominance of the spice trade in Asia. The British company soon focused on India.

▷ **Weighing up the cost**
As early as 2000 BCE, spices were brought from the Far East to Middle Eastern countries. Previously only available to the rich, by the 19th century they were more affordable.

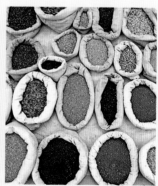

△ **The spices of life**
Today, bagfuls of different spices are a common feature of the markets of Asia, particularly in countries like India, where it would be unthinkable to prepare food without them.

FLAT-LEAF PARSLEY

Origins
Mediterranean

Major producers
The Netherlands, Italy, France

Source of
Calcium, iron, vitamin B9

Scientific name
Petroselinum crispum

◁ **Underworld herb**
The ancient Greeks associated parsley with Persephone, Queen of the Underworld, portrayed in this 5th-century BCE relief with her husband, Hades.

Parsley breath sweetener

Parsley is much more than just a garnish. Packed with vitamins and minerals, the fresh-tasting leaves of this herb have been used to flavor food since ancient times.

△ **Darkly green**
The vivid green of curly leaf parsley provides added visual impact to otherwise dull-looking dishes.

Native to the Mediterranean, parsley has been cultivated for more than 2,000 years and was used medicinally before it entered the kitchen. There are more than 30 varieties of parsley (*Petroselinum crispum*), the most popular being curly leaf parsley and its stronger-tasting Italian cousin, flat-leaf parsley. The curly leaf variety has dark green leaves with curly divided tips, while the flat-leaved version is paler, more deeply divided, and feathery.

The devil's herb
The ancient Greeks associated parsley with death. Rather than eating it, they planted it in their burial sites and adorned their tombstones with handfuls of leaves. The Romans used parsley to flavor sauces and salads and often chewed it to sweeten their breath after eating garlic or onions. Both the Greeks and the Romans are said to have fed their chariot horses parsley leaves to give them strength.

During the Middle Ages, parsley became known as the devil's herb, and the fact it took so long to germinate was thought to be because its seeds had to go to the devil nine times and back before sprouting, unless planted on Good Friday. In the 8th century, the Holy Roman Emperor Charlemagne is believed to have cultivated parsley in his gardens, possibly for culinary use.

Parsley has a sharp, peppery flavor and is used in soups, sauces, salads, stuffings, and marinades. The finely chopped leaves are also often sprinkled over dishes just prior to serving to add color and a fresh taste. The Middle Eastern dish tabbouleh, a salad made with tomatoes, bulgur wheat, mint, and vegetables, features generous amounts of chopped parsley.

Mint refreshing appetite stimulant

Renowned in myth and with a long history as a flavoring and a medicine, mint is also commonly used today in sweet and savory foods, candy, and infused as a thirst-quenching tea.

PEPPERMINT

Origins
Asia

Major producers
Morocco, Argentina, Spain

Source of
Calcium, iron, vitamin B3, vitamin C

Non-food uses
Medicinal, fragrance

Scientific name
Mentha x piperita

Originating in Asia from where it spread to Europe via North Africa, mint is now grown the world over. It is named after the river nymph, Menthe (or Minthe). According to Greek legend, Menthe was turned into a plant by Persephone, Queen of the Underworld, to be squashed and trodden upon, after she discovered her husband Hades' infidelity with the unfortunate nymph. Unable to break the spell, Hades instilled the plant with a wonderful aroma to ensure that he would never forget her.

There are thought to be around 25 different species of mint. Spearmint (*Mentha spicata*), often known as common or garden mint, is the most used in the kitchen, while its stronger-tasting cousin peppermint (*Mentha x piperita*) has been more valued medicinally.

> According to European folklore, rubbing mint leaves into a purse brings good luck and prosperity.

▷ **Leaf shape**
The leaf shape of mint varies according to the type. Common mint (pictured) has serrated oval leaves.

Traces of mint have been found in an Egyptian tomb dating from between 1035 and 332 BCE. Records also show that it was popular with the ancient Greeks, who used it as a cleanser to scour their dining tables. In later centuries, the Romans used it to flavor food and stimulate the appetite.

Firm flavor

Today, fresh or dried mint is widely used to flavor a wide variety of dishes. Mint sauce or jelly is a favorite accompaniment to roast lamb in the UK, it is added to yogurt-based side dishes such as tzatziki in Greece or raita in India, and the chopped leaves are added to salads such as tabbouleh in the Middle East. Mint tea is drunk throughout the Middle East. The herb has also become the most common flavoring for chewing gum, and is used in many forms of candy.

▽ **Fragrant harvest**
Mint was once commonly grown in southern England. Cultivation all but ceased during World War II, but was revived in the early years of the 21st century.

Sage the guardian of herbs

First valued in ancient times for its reputed health-giving properties, this classic staple of European herb gardens has been used for ceremonial rites as well as food flavoring for millennia.

△ **Artist's view**
Painted by one of France's most eminent botanical artists, Pierre Jean François Turpin, this engraving accurately depicts the sage leaves and flowers.

There are more than 900 species of sage, the most widely used being common sage (*Salvia officinalis*). Its Latin name is derived from *salvere*, which means to be well. Native to the northern coastal regions of the Mediterranean, sage also grows wild in northern and central Spain and the western part of the Balkan peninsula. It is now found growing throughout most of the world. The plant bears pairs of lance-shaped, gray-green velvety leaves that extend from a wiry stem.

Sage has mauve-blue flowers and a musky, earthy aroma. It is an evergreen that grows to 32in (80cm) in height, though cultivars vary in size. Traditionally associated with longevity, legends abound about long-lived princes who regularly downed cups of sage tea, while an old country rhyme says: "He who drinks sage in May shall live for aye."

Highly valued

The ancient Greek "father of botany" Theophrastus noted that sage was a useful herb in his *Historia Plantarum* (c.350–287 BCE). Historical records show that sage was originally used in ancient Greece and Rome to preserve meat and as a memory enhancer. The Romans considered sage to be so sacred that they held ceremonies for its planting and harvesting.

Sage was recorded growing in Britain by the 1500s by the London-based herbalist John Gerard, who mentioned it in his *Herball* of 1597. He wrote that sage was "singular good for the head and braine," and also helpful for a whole list of ailments.

As a culinary herb, sage found favor in many European cuisines. Today, it is widely used throughout the Western world to add flavor to a variety of savory dishes, especially pork, veal (notably in the Italian dish saltimbocca), poultry, and even cheese. It is also popular as a refreshing infusion.

◁ **Flavorful and decorative**
The softly hairy leaves of the sage bush not only transform many savory dishes, but also provide a popular garden foliage plant.

Origins
Northern Mediterranean

Major producers
Albania, Morocco, Turkey

Source of
Calcium, iron, vitamin A

Non-food uses
Herbal medicine, essential oil

Scientific name
Salvia officinalis

Rosemary
an herb to remember

This slightly woody and astringent-tasting herb is deeply rooted in myth and legend, as well as having an established place in modern kitchens.

△ **Heavenly reward**
According to legend, during her flight to Egypt, the Virgin Mary spread the baby Jesus's clothes to dry on a rosemary bush. As thanks for its service, God turned the plant's flowers from white to the same blue as Mary's cloak.

Native to North Africa and the Mediterranean, rosemary's Latin name *ros maris* (dew of the sea) is a reference to its origins in coastal areas. Growing up to 7ft (2m) high, rosemary has thin, dark, evergreen, needlelike leaves and blue flowers in summer. Vast, spreading clumps still grow wild on southern European hillsides.

Diverse uses

Early civilizations in areas near coasts where rosemary grew put it to various uses, both ceremonial and domestic. During the mummification process, ancient Egyptians inserted sprigs of rosemary in the linen wrappings of mummies. Rosemary was among the 600 plants mentioned by 1st-century Greek physician Dioscorides in his encyclopedia of herbal medicine *De Materia Medica*, and in ancient Greece, rosemary twigs were woven into the hair of scholars to boost memory and help them focus during exams. The belief in the memory-boosting properties of the herb persisted through succeeding centuries and was referred to by the English playwright William Shakespeare in his 1601 play Hamlet: "There's rosemary. That's for remembrance: pray, love, remember."

Rosemary is included in the *Capitulare de villis* of the 8th-century Holy Roman Emperor Charlemagne, advising that it should be grown on his estates. In the 1st century, Roman armies had brought plants with them to Britain, where it was valued for its assumed medicinal properties, and it was cultivated in southern regions. During the Black Death (1346–1353), people in Britain and throughout Europe burned rosemary in their homes in hope of warding off the plague. Three hundred years later, the early settlers took rosemary with them to the New World.

Today, rosemary is highly valued in many countries in cooking, medicine, cosmetics, and as an ornamental shrub (not least because its natural oils repel mosquitoes and other insects that harm vegetable crops). In Europe and America, it is used to flavor meat and poultry, and is sometimes added to breads, cakes, and cookies.

▷ **Linear leaves**
The narrow and pointed leaves of the rosemary bush grow densely on newly sprouted stems.

Origins
North Africa and Mediterranean coast

Major producers
France, Italy, Spain, Tunisia

Source of
Calcium, iron, vitamin B6

Non-food uses
Herbal medicine, cosmetics, essential oil

Scientific name
Rosmarinus officinalis

> "[Rosemary] comforteth the harte and maketh it merrie."

JOHN GERARD, ENGLISH HERBALIST (1545–1612)

<table>
<tr><td>**Origins**
Asia</td></tr>
<tr><td>**Major producers**
Israel, Spain, Turkey</td></tr>
<tr><td>**Scientific name**
Artemisia dracunculus</td></tr>
</table>

Tarragon the little dragon

Native to Mongolia and Siberia, since medieval times tarragon has been a popular flavoring in European cuisine, especially that of France.

◁ **Flavored vinegar**
Over time, tarragon leaves can impart their aniselike flavor to vinegar for use in salad dressing.

▽ **Healing leaves**
Tarragon was included in *A Curious Herbal* (1739), a book describing the medicinal value of selected herbs, by Scottish illustrator and author Elizabeth Blackwell.

Plate 116.

Tarragon.
Eliz. Blackwell delin. sculp. et Pinx.

1. Flower
2. Fruit
3. Seed

Dracunculus hortensis.

Belonging to the sunflower family, tarragon is known in French as *estragon*. The botanical name may mean "little dragon" from the Latin word *dracunculus*. This could be because it was thought to cure poisonous snakebites or it could refer to its serpentine root system. Its genus name *Artemisia* may be an acknowledgment of the Greek goddess Artemis.

With smooth, long, dark green leaves and a mild anise flavor, French tarragon bears tiny green flowers in summer. It is more popular in the kitchen than its less aromatic cousin Russian tarragon, which has brighter green leaves, is less aromatic, and has a slightly bitter taste.

Sweet touch

Tarragon is thought to have been introduced to Europe by the invading Mongols in the 13th century. It is thought they used it as a sleep aid, breath freshener, and food flavoring. Over the ensuing centuries, it became a popular culinary herb across Europe, much valued by cooks and herbalists alike for its distinctive flavor. The 17th-century English herbalist and diarist John Evelyn is recorded as saying: "… the tops and shoots like those of rocket must never be excluded from salads. Tis highly cordial to the head, heart and liver."

A long-time favorite in the French kitchen, tarragon is one of the four herbs in the classic French *fines herbes* mix as well as a major seasoning in *Béarnaise* sauce, remoulade, vinaigrette, and Dijon mustard. It is also used to flavor vinegar, pickles, relishes, and sauces. In Georgia, it is a popular ingredient in a spicy, syrupy cordial known as *tarhun*.

"There is no good vinegar without tarragon."

ALEXANDRE DUMAS, FRENCH NOVELIST (1802–1870)

Origins
Middle East and India

Major producers
France, Israel, US

Source of
Iron, calcium, vitamin C

Scientific name
Ocimum basilicum

◁ **Pots of goodness**
Commonly grown in medieval herb gardens of the Mediterranean region, basil was reputed to relieve stomach pains, appetite loss, and flatulence.

Basil an herb of love and hate

This plant, regarded as a symbol of hatred and fear in the classical world, became a token of love in the Middle Ages. Its aromatic leaves are now widely used as a flavoring in a variety of Asian and Italian dishes.

Often referred to as the "king of the herbs" or "the royal herb," the name basil is derived from the Greek word *basileus*, meaning kingly, and reflects its importance during the Middle Ages. It is native to India and the Middle East, where it is thought to have been cultivated for at least 5,000 years before arriving in the Mediterranean via spice routes from Asia.

There are around 160 varieties grown around the world, with sweet basil being the most widely grown. With light green silky leaves and small white flowers, it thrives best in a warm, temperate climate.

Token of love

Many superstitions surround this highly aromatic herb. The ancient Greeks thought scorpions bred under basil pots, while the Romans regarded it as a symbol of hatred, although in later centuries it became a token of love in Italy—young men would present their loved one with a pot of basil along with a poem and a pompom on the feast days of St. John and St. Anthony. This sentiment was reflected in the poem "Isabella: or The Pot of Basil" by the 19th-century English Romantic poet John Keats. The ancient Greeks and Romans also thought that the more they swore as they planted their basil seeds, the stronger the plants; that carrying basil was meant to bring wealth; and that receiving a pot of basil as a house-warming present would bring good luck.

In modern times, basil is best known for its pungent, aromatic flavor. Fresh basil has become an essential ingredient in pesto sauce and other pasta sauces, as well as in tomato and mozzarella salads. Asian varieties of basil are now also widely used in stir-fried dishes, salads, and curries.

▽ **Flavor of Italy**
Bunches of bright green basil leaves are a common sight in Italian kitchens, bringing their distinctive flavor to many traditional dishes.

Thyme

herb of courage and cleansing

There are around 60 varieties of thyme, including lemon, orange, woolly, and broad-leaved. Most are native to western Asia and the Mediterranean, where they have been cultivated for thousands of years—for magical powers as much as taste.

Origins	Mediterranean
Major producers	Morocco, Poland, Turkey
Source of	Vitamin K, iron
Non-food uses	Medicinal, cosmetics (oil)
Scientific name	*Thymus vulgaris*

△ **Sprig of health**
Thyme, a member of the mint family, contains thymol, a compound used as an antiseptic in mouthwash.

▽ **Herbal remedy**
Prepared and sold by apothecaries, in medieval Europe thyme had several medicinal uses. It was said to promote sleep and prevent nightmares.

Few herbs can lay claim to as many uses beyond the cooking pot as *Thymus vulgaris*, otherwise known as common, garden, or French thyme. The ancient Egyptians employed its preservative qualities as part of the mummification process. The ancient Greeks and Romans also used its fragrance and antiseptic qualities in massage and bath oils.

The name "thyme" is thought to have originated either from the Latin word *fumus*, meaning "smoke," or the Greek word *thumos*, meaning "soul" (believed by the ancient Greeks to take a smokelike form). This association could refer to the frequent practice of burning thyme for purification and consecration purposes at religious ceremonies in the temples of ancient Greece where the herb was also held sacred to Adephagia, goddess of bountiful harvest and gluttony.

Protector and enhancer

The popularity of the herb spread throughout the Roman Empire as far as Britain, where in the 14th century it was used in posies and strewn on the ground to protect against plague. In Dutch and German folklore of the same period, any place where thyme grew wild was thought to be blessed by the fairies.

During the Middle Ages, thyme was also seen as a symbol of courage. The wives of knights going on crusade would embroider thyme leaves and bees onto their husbands' clothing to give them strength as they went into battle. Bees, attracted to the plant's whorls of white-to-pale-blue flowers, had long been associated with the herb in the creation of an amber-colored honey highly prized by ancient Athenians, who used thyme grown on nearby Mount Hymettus.

Alongside the reputed medicinal uses and the magic properties that have accompanied thyme, the herb has enduring popularity, fresh or dried, as a flavoring for soups, salads, and sauces that complement meat, fish, and poultry dishes. Thyme is included in the classic French herb mixes of bouquet garni and *herbes de Provence*. Introduced from Europe, thyme also features in many dishes from the Caribbean, and is a key ingredient in the Middle Eastern seasoning *za'atar*.

The ancient Greeks believed that eating thyme could counteract poisoning.

Oregano

the taste of comfort and joy

Best known today as the herb sprinkled on top of a classic Italian pizza, in ancient times oregano was valued not only for its flavor but also as a medicine and bringer of good luck and peace in the afterlife.

Oregano is particularly linked with Italy and tomato sauces, and it was in the late 18th century that the two came together as a topping on the pizza of Naples. Until then, oregano had been used only to flavor meat or vegetable dishes. It was the pizza connection, though, that popularized the herb in the US, as servicemen returning home from Italy after World War II brought with them a taste for oregano. The herb is closely related to majoram, which has a more muted flavor.

Valued by the Greeks

Oregano is native to the Mediterranean and was first widely used in Greece. The origins of its name are uncertain, but it may be linked to two Greek words, *oras* ("mountain") and *ganos* ("joy"), which possibly refers to the ancient Greek belief that the herb was the creation of Aphrodite, the goddess of love. The Greeks held the herb in high esteem—chewing oregano leaves

Origins
Mediterranean, western Asia
Major producers
Turkey, Greece
Source of
Iron, calcium, manganese, vitamin K
Non-food use
Herbal medicine
Scientific name
Origanum vulgare

"There is scarcely a better herb … for relieving a sour stomach."

NICHOLAS CULPEPER, *COMPLETE HERBAL* (1653)

was considered one of the best antidotes to seasickness; newly wed couples often adorned themselves with oregano crowns, hoping for the happiness they might bring; and the leaves were laid on graves to help the dead rest in peace. The flavor of oregano was also appreciated: the meat of goats and sheep that had grazed on the herb was especially prized.

Oregano was adopted by the Romans, from where it became a signature flavoring of Italian cuisine and spread into North African cooking. It has remained a common ingredient in Greek dishes, used often in salads and to enhance the flavor of grilled meats.

▷ **Fresh leaves**
Oregano is a low-growing plant with slightly woody, red-tinged, mid-green oval leaves and purple, pink, or white flowers.

◁ **Healing powers**
The high oil content in oregano means it dries well. In traditional Chinese medicine, oregano is used to treat digestive problems and boost the immune system.

Bay leaf the savor of victory

◁ **Grinding tool**
Pestles and mortars for grinding herbs and spices have changed little over the 6,000 years or more that they have been used.

Used to make crowns for victors in battle in ancient times, bay leaves are now primarily valued in the kitchen for their flavor and pungent aroma.

According to Greek mythology, when the God Apollo tried to seduce the nymph Daphne, her father turned her into a bay tree to protect her. To this day, the bay tree is often called the Daphne tree in Greece.

Native to Anatolia and the Mediterranean, the bay laurel tree, with its pointed, glossy green leaves and clusters of small, star-shaped, pale yellow flowers, is now grown the world over for its aromatic properties.

Wreathed in legend

For the ancient Greeks and Romans, bay was a symbol of peace and victory, which is reflected in its Latin name *Laurus nobilis*, meaning noble laurel.

To show that they were special in the eyes of the gods, emperors, soldiers, athletes, and even poets in the classical world were crowned with wreaths of bay leaves. Traditionally, bay trees were planted outside front doors to bring good luck and keep evil spirits away.

Bay was also regarded as a purification herb and was used as a "burning" herb by pagans and Christians during Europe's Dark Ages to drive away evil spirits. In 16th-century England it was recorded as a popular herb to strew on floors to disguise bad smells.

Versatile aromatic herb

Today, bay is an essential ingredient of the French herb blend, bouquet garni, to which it adds a sharp, slightly bitter but delicate floral flavor. It is a widely used seasoning across Europe for stews, soups, sauces, casseroles, and marinades. It is often also used to flavor and decorate pâtés and terrines.

Origins
Anatolia (part of modern Turkey), Mediterranean

Major producer
Turkey

Non-food uses
Perfumes, hair care

Scientific name
Laurus nobilis

△ **A garden in Pompeii**
A painting of a garden from Pompeii, the Roman city destroyed in the 1st century CE, indicates the importance of bay in Roman times.

▷ **Roman laureate**
The wreath of laurel—or bay—leaves denoted victory and heroism in ancient Rome. Roman emperors, such as Julius Caesar, are often depicted wearing laurel wreaths.

Curry leaf a taste of Asia

The shiny, aromatic leaves of the small evergreen curry leaf tree are the source of one of the key flavors of South Asian cuisine.

Not to be confused with curry powder, curry leaves, known variously in India as *kadi patta*, *kari-patta*, or *meethi neem* (sweet neem) provide a distinctive flavor to curries and vegetable dishes.

Native to southern India, Pakistan, and Sri Lanka, the evergreen curry leaf tree belongs to the citrus fruit family and bears clusters of small fragrant white flowers in summer. The leaves release a delicate nutty, lemony aroma when bruised. The botanical name for the plant—*Murraya koenigii*—refers to the 18th-century German botanist Johann König, who worked as a naturalist in southern India and recorded descriptions of plants used in traditional Indian medicine.

Accounts of curry leaves being used to flavor vegetables appear in early Tamil literature dating back to the 1st century CE, and references appear again a few centuries later in the Kannada literature of southern India. The leaves are still closely linked with these regions; the word "curry" originates from the Tamil word *kari* for spiced sauces.

Origins
South Asia

Major producer
India

Non-food uses
Traditional medicine

Scientific name
Murraya koenigii

Spicy addition

Traveling Indians brought curry leaves to many cuisines around the world. For example, they are often included with other spices in fish curries prepared in Malaysia, Singapore, and the Thai islands. Today, curry leaves are cultivated and used to season foood in Sri Lanka, Southeast Asia, Australia, the Pacific Islands, and Africa, as well as in India.

The leaves are often fried in hot oil or ghee with onions and other spices, and used as a base for curries or poured over an already-made dish. Curry leaves are also used in a thick chickpea soup popular in the north Indian states of Punjab and Rajasthan, known variously as *kadhi* or *karhi*, and in yogurt or buttermilk.

The application of oil infused with curry leaves is reputed to disguise gray hair.

△ **Green flavors**
Curry leaves are common in markets in South Asia. This woman is selling a variety of fresh herbs, including curry leaves in the foreground, in a market in Andhra Pradesh, India.

◁ **Symmetrical sprig**
Bright green curry leaves grow in symmetrical rows along the stems of the plant.

Coriander
a seed for immortality

With its flavor-packed leaves, tiny seeds, and distinctive aroma, coriander is famously not to everyone's taste. But over the years this plant has become popular both as a fragrant herb and a spicy flavoring.

Origins
Mediterranean and Anatolia (Asian Turkey)

Source of
Calcium, potassium

Scientific name
Coriandrum sativum

Reputedly used to scent the Hanging Gardens of Babylon in ancient Persia, coriander is native to the Mediterranean region and Anatolia (part of Turkey). It is also known as cilantro and is related to parsley (another name for the herb is Chinese parsley). Its bright green leaves are aromatic and have a slightly citrus flavor and its small white or pinkish flowers give rise to small, spherical seeds.

Seeds of immortality
Mentioned in Sanskrit, ancient Egyptian, Greek, and Latin texts, coriander is said to have been grown in Persia 3,000 years ago. It was cultivated in ancient Egypt for medicinal and culinary purposes where its seeds were dried and used as a spice. Jars of coriander seeds were among the provisions found in the tomb of Tutankhamun, put there possibly to accompany his spirit to the land of the dead.

Coriander seeds were transported 5,000 years ago from the Mediterranean along the Silk Road to China, where the plant became highly revered and was thought to increase the chance of immortality. It was introduced to Mexico and Peru by the Spanish conquistadors in the 16th century, and in the early 17th century it became one of the first herbs to be cultivated by European settlers in Massachusetts.

Flavor and garnish
Although the whole plant is edible, in Europe the culinary focus is mainly on the seeds, which are used to flavor foods ranging from stews to cakes, breads, and pickles. In Central and South America and Southeast Asia, the chopped leaves are used as a garnish or in fresh sauces to accompany fish, meat, and poultry as well as in salads and soups. The leaves are used in similar ways in the Middle East. In parts of Southeast Asia, the root of the plant is also used in cooking. Both seeds and leaves are used in Indian curries and the ground seeds are an ingredient in the aromatic spice mix, garam masala.

△ **Tomb find**
Tutankhamun's tomb contained jars of coriander seeds, a spice highly valued by the ancient Egyptians. This depiction shows British Egyptologists Howard Carter and Lord Carnarvon opening the sarcophagus containing the young pharaoh's mummy.

◁ **Fresh and green**
The small, round leaves of the coriander plant have serrated edges. Their tangy taste adds an extra dimension to food when they are added as a garnish.

Sugar-coated coriander seeds were a delicacy in 16th- and 17th-century Europe.

Dill an aid to over-indulgence

Valued and widely cultivated by the civilizations of the ancient world for its medicinal properties, this herb, with its graceful, feathery leaves, has become a key flavoring in northern European kitchens.

△ **Stomach soothing seeds**
Dill seeds are used to flavor many foods and drinks. They also have a reputation for easing indigestion.

In a reference to its traditional use as a remedy for insomnia, dill gets its name from the Norse word "dilla," meaning to lull. It is a member of the same family as parsley and native to Central Asia and southeast Europe. The plant bears clusters of yellow flowers on fernlike, feathery leaves similar to those of its close relative, fennel.

Dill was certainly known in the ancient world. Twigs of dill have been found in the tomb of the 14th-century BCE pharaoh Amenhotep, suggesting it was used at this time along with other herbs to embalm the dead. It was also valued by the ancient Greeks as a sign of wealth and a cure for hiccups. Both the Greeks and Romans used it as a seasoning in cooking—there are more than 40 mentions of dill in a collection of recipes in the Roman cookbook *Apicius* (published in the 4th century).

Origins
Central Asia, southeastern Europe

Source of
Vitamin C, manganese

Non-food use
Indigestion remedy

Scientific name
Anethum graveolens

Healing brew
In the early Middle Ages when tales of witchcraft abounded, drinking a cup of tea brewed with dill leaves and seeds was thought to help drive away the evil curses of a witch. The 8th-century Holy Roman Emperor Charlemagne had bowls of dill seeds placed on banqueting tables for those who had over indulged to dip into to soothe digestion and ease bloating. With its fragrant, delicate flavor, dill is an important ingredient in German and Scandinavian cuisine, famously in gravlax—salmon marinated with salt, sugar, pepper, and finely chopped dill. It is also often used to flavor pickles as well as potato salad, sauerkraut, stews, and soups.

▷ **Feathery fronds**
With its umbrella-like clusters of yellow flowers and delicate leaf fronds, dill is decorative as well as flavorful.

Pepper

prized spice

One of the oldest spices in the world—and these days one of the most popular—pepper was being used in Indian cuisine more than 4,000 years ago.

Pepper was once so highly prized that in 410 CE Alaric, the first king of the Germanic tribe the Visigoths, demanded 3,000lb (1,360kg) of peppercorns as part of the ransom for the city of Rome. And in the Middle Ages, pepper commanded a price 10 times higher than that of any other spice.

Native to southern India, black pepper (*Piper nigrum*) is the fruit of an evergreen, woody, vinelike plant that grows to a height or length of 33ft (10m) or more. The plant bears clusters of white flowers, which turn into long ribbons of pea-size fruits or "corns." Pepper gets its spicy taste from piperine, a volatile oil found in the outer fruit and seed.

The color of the pepper produced is determined by the way the fruits are harvested and handled. Black peppercorns, for example, are sun-dried ripe berries. Green peppercorns are soft under-ripe berries, usually preserved in brine. White pepper is made from the

> **Spicy strings**
> The berries of the pepper plant, peppercorns dangle from the stems in clusters.

seeds left over after the skin and fleshy parts have been removed from the ripe berries. Pink peppercorns, however, come from a completely different plant, the Brazilian pepper tree (*Schinus terebinthifolius*).

Traveling the ancient world

When pepper was first exported from India—and by which trade route—is not known, but archaeologists found peppercorns in the nostrils of the mummified body of Ramses II, suggesting that the spice was used in ancient Egyptian burial rituals at least as long ago as the 13th century BCE. In India, pepper was used both in traditional medicine and as a condiment.

The famous Hindu epic poem, the *Mahabharata*, written in the 4th century BCE, describes feasts that included meats flavored with black pepper.

Pepper was a favourite flavoring in Roman cuisine, and it was also used as preservative. As trade in pepper thrived under the Roman Empire, it became an expensive and sought-after commodity. The trade was largely under the control of Arab merchants, who supplied the Romans through the port city of Alexandria. After the decline of

△ **Preparing pepper**
This 14th-century Persian illustration shows the harvesting and drying of black peppercorns in India, preparing them for trading.

Origins
Southern India

Major producers
India, Vietnam, Indonesia

Non-food use
Traditional remedies

Scientific name
Piper nigrum

◁ **A big deal**
By the 16th century, the Indonesian island of Java already had a thriving pepper trade. The merchant on the far left is weighing peppercorns for a buyer.

the Roman Empire, the trade remained an Arab monopoly, with traders keeping their sources of pepper secret in order to maintain high prices.

Changing hands

During the Middle Ages, as the trade in pepper and other spices between Asia and Europe grew, pepper was so highly valued for its flavor by Europeans that it became a lucrative commodity. Nearly every city had its spice street, where traders gathered to sell their wares, and which was often named after the prized pepper—for example, Rue de Poivre in Paris, France.

By the 14th century, Genoa and Venice had become centers of the pepper trade from the East. However, in 1498, the Portuguese explorer Vasco da Gama discovered a route to India around the southern tip of Africa, heralding the beginning of Portugal's dominance of the pepper trade. This lasted until the end of the 16th century, when the Dutch became

The term "peppercorn rent" dates back to the Middle Ages, when pepper was accepted instead of money. These days it means a very low rent.

the world's leading power in the spice trade. By the beginning of the 19th century, control of the trade had passed to Britain.

Nowadays, pepper is the most widely used spice in the world. Ground or whole, it adds piquancy and warmth to an endless array of dishes from meats, fish, and pasta to casseroles and soups. It is also used in sauces, dressings, stocks, and pickles.

◁ **Antique grinder**
Portable grinders enabled merchants to sell ground pepper as well as whole black peppercorns to their customers as desired.

Mustard

fiery condiment

Ancient civilizations in Europe and Asia, where mustard plants grew wild, first used the white, brown, or black seeds to make the condiments and sauces that are still popular today.

ASIAN MUSTARD

Origins
South Asia

Major producers
Canada, Nepal

Non-food use
Traditional remedies

Scientific name
Brassica juncea

◁ **Vivid yellow**
Mustard plants have distinctive yellow flowers and delicate leaf fronds.

The name mustard comes from the ancient Romans, who steeped mustard seeds in crushed grapes (must) to make *mustum ardens*, or "burning must." There is archaeological evidence that the southern Asian Indus Valley civilization of 3330–1300 BCE cultivated mustard, and it is also mentioned in ancient Sumerian and Sanskrit texts. According to Greek mythology, mustard was a gift from Asclepius, the god of medicine, and Ceres, the goddess of agriculture.

Related to cabbages

In fact, mustard is the name given to several members of the brassica (cabbage) family, and the color of the seeds depends on the species. *Sinapis alba* (native to Europe and the Middle East), yields white seeds, *Brassica nigra* (from Europe and the Middle East) black seeds, and *B. juncea* (from Asia) brown. A recipe for a mustard sauce appears in a 4th–5th-century CE collection of recipes attributed to the 1st-century Roman gourmand Marcus Gavius Apicius. The Romans took mustard seed with them to Gaul, and by the 13th century, Dijon had become the hub of French mustard production, as it is to this day. The first use of mustard as a condiment in England was in the late 14th century. Today, Canada is the world's largest producer of mustard seed.

Mild, hot, or fierce

Grinding the mustard seeds and mixing them with water and vinegar forms the condiment popular in the West, where it is used mainly to accompany cold and hot meats, such as sausages and hot dogs. Mustards are made with varying degrees of "hotness" from the mild French mustards to the hot English type. In the Netherlands and northern Belgium mustard is used to

▷ **Taking the mustard**
Numerous brands of commercially produced mustard products were marketed in the United States and elsewhere as the condiment gained popularity in the 20th century.

TABLE TALK
CONTENTS 1½ OZ.
MUSTARD
PACKED BY
ST-PARKER COMPANY
DULUTH, MINN.

Mother's Pride BRAND
PURE SPICES
3 OZS. NET
MUSTARD

TREXLER PARK
GROUND
MUSTARD
NET WEIGHT 1 OZ
LEHIGH
WHOLESALE GROCERY Co., Inc.
DISTRIBUTORS
ALLENTOWN, PA.

Heart's Delight
GROUND
MUSTARD
NET WT. 1½ OZ.
SCOVILLE, BROWN & CO.
DISTRIBUTORS
WELLSVILLE, N.Y.

FARGO BRAND
MUSTARD
FOOD PRODUCTS CO. OF AMERICA
DISTRIBUTORS, GENERAL OFFICES, CHICAGO, ILL.

make soup along with cream, parsley, garlic, and salted bacon. The Chinese and Japanese, who use brown mustard seeds, prefer their mustard fiercely hot. Mustard seeds are also widely used in Indian cuisine, where they are often fried before being used to flavor curries, rice, and other dishes.

> ## "When he had meat he had no mustard."
>
> PROVERB INSCRIBED ON SUMERIAN
> CLAY TABLET, 2000 BCE

Caraway Roman savior

Caraway originated in Asia Minor (modern Turkey) around 5,000 years ago and this graceful plant is thought to be the oldest cultivated spice in Europe.

Caraway grows wild in Northern and Central Europe and Central Asia. The remains of caraway have been uncovered in Mesolithic sites in Turkey in food debris left behind by prehistoric humans. Early Arabs are thought to have been the first to use "karawya" (the Arabic name for the seeds) to flavor food, and caraway seeds have also been found in ancient Egyptian tombs. The ancient Greek physician Dioscorides noted in his encyclopedia of herbal medicine, *De Materia Medica* (c.70 CE), that eating the seeds aided digestion.

Caraway roots are said to have saved a Roman army from starvation during the siege of Dyrrachium in 48 BCE, when the legionaries cooked and mixed them with milk to make a molded cake called "chara." The Romans took caraway with them when they invaded Britain, and Shakespeare mentions it in his play *Henry IV, Part II*, when Robert Shallow invites Sir John Falstaff to partake of "a last year's pippin [apple] … with a dish of caraways."

Wide-ranging uses
Caraway seeds enhance the flavor of northern European cheeses, rye bread, and sauerkraut, and they are also added to soup and stews, such as goulash. They are an essential ingredient in the popular liqueur kümmel, and are also found in Middle Eastern dishes as well as in harissa, a hot chili paste from northwest Africa.

Origins
Asia Minor (modern-day Turkey)
Major producers
Netherlands, Germany
Non-food uses
Aid to digestion; flavoring for alcoholic drinks, toothpaste, and mouthwashes
Scientific name
Carum carvi

▷ **Leaves, flowers, and seeds**
This illustration of a caraway plant from Carl Lindman's *Bilder ur Nordens Flora* (1905) shows the white flowers, feathery leaves, and one of its brown seeds.

Portable food

In recent years, online companies that use app-based ordering to deliver specially prepared meals have spawned a revolution in everyday living. Yet Mumbai's system of lunchbox deliveries and returns has them beaten. Transporting lunches may sound simple in theory, but what *dabbawalas*, or lunch delivery men, do six days a week for 51 weeks a year is a remarkable feat—so impressive, in fact, that professors from Harvard Business School visited Mumbai to study the system. What they found was that the *dabbawalas* are so efficient that they make only one mistake out of every six million deliveries.

From their beginnings in 1890, when Mahadeo Havaji Bacche, a wealthy Parsi banker, employed a young man from a nearby village to deliver a daily lunchbox from his home to his Mumbai office, *dabbawalas* have become world-renowned. Initially, Bacche created a team of about 100 of them, but today there are around 5,000 delivering between 175,000 and 200,000 lunchboxes to Mumbai's hordes of office workers every morning, and collecting and returning them home every afternoon.

The lunches come in circular metal tins called tiffins or *dabbas*. Each *dabba* contains two to four sections. The bottom and largest is for rice, while the others hold a curry, a vegetable side dish, chapatis, or a dessert. All the food is home-cooked and freshly made. A *dabbawala*'s day starts around 8am, when he picks up lunchboxes in the Mumbai suburbs for delivery in the city center. The *dabbas* are taken to local rail stations by cart, bicycle, or motorbike, where, having been color-coded according to their destinations, they are loaded onto city-bound trains. At the station, they are passed to more *dabbawalas* for office delivery. After lunch, the process is reversed.

◁ **Carrying the cans**
Lunchbox-laden carts are pushed through the Mumbai streets by teams of *dabbawalas* who have fed the city for more than 125 years.

Cardamom
Viking import

One of the most versatile of the Asian spices, cardamom has long been valued by cultures the world over for its distinctive flavor and fragrance.

Origins
Southern India

Major producers
Guatemala, India, Indonesia

Non-food use
Breath freshener

Scientific name
Elettaria cardamomum

Cardamom was known to the ancient Egyptians, who chewed the seeds to cleanse their teeth and freshen their breath. However, this member of the ginger family has its origins much further east in the forests along the Western Ghats of southern India.

The plant has large lance-shaped leaves with white flowers, which mature into pods with a triangular cross section, each containing three rows of dark brown, sticky, aromatic seeds. There are two main types of cardamom: green and black. Green cardamoms have a delicate, sweet flavor. Black cardamoms have a coarser and stronger flavor.

References to cardamom have been discovered on a clay tablet from the ancient Sumerian city of Nippur dating back to 2000 BCE. Thousands of years later in the 9th century CE, the Vikings, who encountered it on their travels in the eastern Mediterranean, introduced it to Northern Europe.

Modern-day versatility
Cardamom is widely used in rice dishes and is used in Asian cuisine in sweetmeats, desserts, and teas, as well as savory dishes. In Arab countries it is used to add a distinctive taste to coffee. Sweet breads and buns in Scandinavia are often flavored with cardamom.

▷ **Pod preparation**
Cardamom pods ready for packaging and shipping to overseas destinations are carefully cleaned and graded according to size and color by a group of women in India.

△ **Fresh and plump**
The best and freshest cardamom pods are plump and green, and the seeds inside are sticky.

◁ **Rich pickings**
Women pick cardamom pods in Kerala, India. Peak harvest time in this region is from September to November.

Lemongrass

distinctively delicate

Long valued in Thai cuisine for its fragrant, lemony flavor, lemongrass is gaining culinary recognition the world over to flavor Asian-style dishes, and as a tea.

Surprisingly, there are 45 species of this willowy, tall grass, but *Cymbopogon citratus* is the species mainly used in cooking. When crushed or chopped, its leaves release a distinctive, lemony scent. It grows in clumps from a bulbous base and is found throughout the tropics, although the plant is thought to have originated in India and Southeast Asia. The name "Cymbopogon" is believed to come from the Greek *kymbe*, meaning boat, and *pogon*, meaning beard, referring to the shape of its tiny white flowers.

In Asia, lemongrass has been used to flavor foods such as soups and stews for 5,000 years. In eastern India and Sri Lanka, it was combined with other herbs to make a drink locally known as fever tea used to treat fevers, irregular menstruation, diarrhea, and stomach aches. Much secrecy surrounds the history of this herb, but there are unconfirmed stories of lemongrass being distilled for export in the Philippines as early as the 17th century.

Modern popularity

Lemongrass is widely used fresh or freeze dried as an integral ingredient in Southeast Asian cuisine. It is a key flavoring in the well-known Thai soup, *tom yum*. As Thai cuisine has become more popular around the world over recent years, the demand for lemongrass has increased. It pairs particularly well with curries, marinades, stews, and seafood soups. It also makes a refreshing herbal tea.

Origins
India, Southeast Asia

Major producers
Guatemala, China

Source of
Calcium

Non-food uses
Insect repellent

Scientific name
Cymbopogon citratus

▽ **Fragrant stems**
This fast-growing plant can reach a height of 3⅓ft (1m). It has a bulbous base from which the leaf stems grow in concentric rings.

Widely used as an insect repellent, lemongrass is nicknamed "mosquito grass."

FLOWER

SEED POD

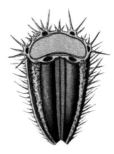

SEED POD INTERIOR

Cumin flavor of the East

Reputedly the second most popular spice after black pepper, cumin has been used as a food flavoring from the Mediterranean to eastern Asia for over 5,000 years.

A member of the parsley family, cumin has threadlike, feathery leaves with tiny white to pale pink flowers. The oval-shaped seeds, which are the part used as a spice, are yellow-brown with pale ridges. Cumin is native to the eastern Mediterranean, and is even mentioned in the Bible, which speaks of harvested plants being threshed with rods, a method still practised in eastern Mediterranean countries.

Favored of the ancient world

Cultivated in ancient Egypt more than 5,000 years ago, cumin was used for flavoring and embalming. The Greeks kept a pot on the table as a condiment and sent soldiers off to war with a loaf of cumin bread. The numerous references to cumin in a collection of recipes attributed to the 1st century Roman gourmet Marcus Gavius Apicius, and published in the 4th or 5th century, suggest that it was a popular flavoring in ancient Rome, too.

Europe and beyond

Roman influence brought cumin to the rest of Europe, where its popularity increased in the Middle Ages. It was often grown in monastery gardens at that time. It was not until

▷ **Mixing it up**
As well as being widely sold as a single spice, cumin is included in many commercial spice mixes.

the early 20th century, however, that cumin was introduced to North America by Spanish and Portuguese immigrants.

With its nutty, peppery taste, cumin is used in many of the world's cuisines. In India it is a staple ingredient of spice mixes used in *kormas*, *masalas*, and soups. In the Netherlands and Switzerland, it is used to add its distinctive flavor to cheeses and, in France and Germany, it is added to cakes and bread. It features throughout Europe in pickling mixtures and in North African meat and vegetable dishes. Black cumin seeds are darker and smaller than ordinary cumin seeds and are widely used, in preference to ordinary cumin, in the cuisines of northern India, Pakistan, and Iran. It is often found in cheeses such as halloumi, sprinkled on bread, and used in pickles.

△ **Seeds to savor**
The pale brown seeds of the cumin plant can be used whole (often roasted) or ground to a fine powder.

Origins
Egypt

Major producers
India, Syria, Turkey

Non-food uses
Medicinal, fragrance

Scientific name
Cuminum cyminum

Star anise

an enticing Asian spice

Although it has a pretty shape, star anise is not just an ornamental spice; its distinctive licorice-like flavor is much prized in Southeast Asian and Indian cuisine.

ANIS ÉTOILE.

◁ **Leaf and flower**
The dark green leaves of the star anise tree are long and pointed, often concealing the pale yellow flowers that grow at their base.

Also known as badian anise and Chinese anise, this star-shaped spice is the fruit of a small evergreen tree that belongs to the magnolia family. Originating in southern China and Vietnam, star anise (*Illicium verum*), is not related to anise (*Pimpinella anisum*), a native of the eastern Mediterranean, although its flavor comes from the same compound, anethol. The botanical name of the plant *Illicium* comes from the Latin word *illico*, meaning enticement, referring to the wonderful fragrance of this spice, which has a mild licorice flavor.

16th century by the English privateer Thomas Cavendish, who believed the fruits originated in the Philippines.

Today, star anise—whole or ground—is an important ingredient in Chinese and Vietnamese cuisine, especially in the Chinese five-spice blend and the Vietnamese *pho boo* soup. It is also used to flavor teas, pickles, and curries in Indian cuisine. Star anise has become increasingly popular in modern Western cuisines as a flavoring for fish dishes and for poaching fruits such as figs and pears.

Origins
East Asia

Major producers
China, Vietnam

Non-food use
Traditional medicine

Scientific name
Illicium verum

A Japanese relative of star anise (*Illicium anisatum*), which is used in incense, is highly toxic.

The yellowish-white flowers, often with a pinkish tinge inside, appear in summer followed by the distinctive star-shaped fruits. Harvested before they are ripe, the fruits are dried and ground to make a red-brown powdery spice or left whole.

Lucky star

According to Chinese folklore, star anise helped protect against the evil eye and finding one with more than eight points was considered lucky. Originally used medicinally by Chinese herbalists, it is only relatively recently that its potential as a spice has started to be more widely recognized in the West. It was introduced to Europe in the

▷ **Stars of the kitchen**
The distinctive brown fruit that forms the spice known as star anise encloses a seed in each of its many segments.

△ **Chilis on sale**
Dried chilis are among the many products for sale in this South American market stall.

Chilis world-conquering hot spice

The fruits of small shrubs native to Mexico, chilis have been cultivated for 7,000 years and are now a crop of all tropical regions, adding heat and spice to many of the world's cuisines.

Christopher Columbus mistook chilis for members of the pepper family when he encountered the plants on his arrival in the New World because of their "hot" taste. Chilis are part of the *Capsicum* genus, which belongs to the Solanaceae plant family, which also includes the tomato and potato. There are around 25 species of chili, but only five are cultivated.

Chilis come in all shapes, sizes, and colors, from red, yellow, bright orange, and green to purple and black. Most are thin and pointed, and they can be as small as a pea—such as the bullet-shaped bird's-eye

chilis popular in Southeast Asian cooking—or as long as the cayenne pepper, which can measure up to 12in (30cm). The spicy taste of chilis ranges from mild and tingling to very hot, depending on the concentration in the fruit of capsaicin, a compound found mostly in the pith that surrounds the seeds.

Fast-spreading spice

Chili seeds have been found at archaeological sites in Tehuacán, in south-central Mexico, dating back to 7000 BCE, with the first cultivation taking place in the

Origins Mexico	
Major producers China, Mexico	
Source of Vitamin C	
Non-food use Medicinal (capsaicin)	
Scientific names *Capsicum annuum* *C. frutescens* *C. chinense* *C. baccatum* *C. pubescens*	

CAYENNE

MORRÓN

same region around 2,000 years later. The Genoese explorer Christopher Columbus is thought to have been the first European to encounter chilis, on his voyages to the Americas, beginning in 1492. He brought the first plants back from the Caribbean to Spain, where they were initially grown in Spanish monasteries and used as a cheaper alternative to pepper to flavor food. From there, chilis soon became established in Italy, especially in the southern region of Calabria.

> Unaffected by the hot taste of capsaicin, birds often eat and spread chili seeds.

Traders from Portugal, introduced to chilis by Spanish merchants passing through Lisbon on their way to the Americas, took them to South Asia. The spice became a staple part of the local cuisine in the Indian coastal settlement of Goa—including the fiery, chili-infused vindaloo (its name derived from the Portuguese *vin d'alho*, meaning a wine and garlic sauce). From India, traders took chilis further east to China and Southeast Asia.

Chilis, thanks in part to their usefulness as a dried commodity, spread quickly along trade routes, and within 50 years of their introduction to Europe they were being used across much of Asia, along the coast of West Africa, through North Africa, and in the

▷ Misleading colors
The appearance of a chili is no guide to its strength. Some red large red chilis are mild, while a small green one can pack a real punch.

Middle East. Arab traders dominated the spice trade to Europe at that time, and chilis found their way to Europe by this route. In southern Europe (such as Hungary and Bulgaria), paprika, a ground spice made from sweet peppers and chilis, became a popular ingredient in dishes such as goulash and *paprikash*. The spicy fruits traveled from India to England (where they were knows as "ginnie" or "guinea" peppers) in the 1540s, but were not quite so popular, northern Europeans preferring to get their heat from mustard and horseradish. The 16th-century English botanist John Gerard claimed the chili: "hath in it a malicious quality, whereby it is an enemy to the liver and other of the entrails … it killeth dogs."

NORA

A global flavoring
Chilis are now the most widely grown spice in the world, with China, especially the provinces of Sichuan and Hunan, producing around 50 percent of global output, followed by the home of the spice—Mexico. Fresh, dried, pickled, or powdered, the fruits are used to add a hot punch to many meat, vegetable, and fish dishes and play an integral role in Mexican, Central American, South American, Asian, Middle Eastern, and North African cuisine. The ají chili, which was first grown in Andean countries such as Peru

AJÍ

and Bolivia around 7,000 years ago, is used as a flavoring in many dishes and also as a condiment—a bowl of salsa is a familiar sight on dining tables. In the US, thanks to the popularity of Mexican food, the market for hot, chili-based sauces has grown more than 165 percent since 2000. So much so that chili condiments are now vying with old favorites such as tomato ketchup for top-seller status.

JALAPEÑO

ANCHO

◁ Weighing in
By the beginning of the 18th century, the Dutch dominated the chili trade and introduced chilis to Japan. Here, Japanese officials and Dutch traders supervise the weighing and packing of red chili peppers at Nagasaki.

FRESNO

BIRD'S EYE

Tea a story of ritual and intrigue

The story of the transformation of the leaves of an evergreen shrub from Asia into a beverage much-loved around the world is a fascinating one, involving industrial espionage and even a revolution.

Tea containers have been found in Han dynasty tombs from 206 BCE–220 CE, which indicates how long tea has been enjoyed in China. The beverage is made from the leaves and buds of a large evergreen plant of which there are two major varieties: C. sinensis var. sinensis (Chinese tea) and C. sinensis var. assamica (Assam or Indian tea). Both varieties have glossy green leaves and white flowers. The type of tea depends on the processing. White tea is made from the buds and the young leaves. Fully fermenting the leaves and roasting them makes black tea, while for oolong tea the leaves are partly fermented then dried. Green tea is made from steamed and dried leaves.

In China, it wasn't until the Tang dynasty (61–907 CE) that tea became a national drink. Around the same time, Japanese Buddhist monks studying in China are thought to have introduced the drink to their country. It soon became an important part of Japanese culture in a ceremony known as "the way of tea," a ritual that is still practised today.

Costly commodity

Tea was largely unheard of in Europe until the 16th century when Portuguese traders living in the East acquired a taste for it. In 1606, Dutch traders using Portuguese trading routes shipped the first consignment of tea from China to Holland, where the drink found instant popularity, and soon spread throughout Europe among the elite. A little later, sailors

△ **Object of beauty**
Tea is drunk several times a day in Chinese households. Some teapots, such as this Sancai porcelain pot, are more decorative than practical.

▽ **Picking tea**
Good-quality tea is harvested by hand from the tops of bushes. Only the top two leaves and bud of new shoots are picked. These women are picking tea in early 20th-century Japan.

CHINESE TEA

Origins
China

Major producer
China

Scientific name
Camellia sinensis var. *sinensis*

◁ **Political protest**
On December 16, 1773, American colonists boarded the East India Company ships moored in Boston Harbor and threw their cargo of 342 chests of tea overboard.

returning home on ships owned by the British East India Company took tea to England, and a 1658 newspaper advertisement announced the sale of "China drink" at a coffee house in London. Drinking tea became so fashionable among the wealthy that by 1664 the company was importing tea from China.

Changing the course of history

By the 18th century, the East India Company was delivering tea to the American colonists. However, the British parliament's 1773 attempt to levy a tea tax on the imports led to widespread protests the same year, including the Boston Tea Party—a landmark event in the American Revolution.

In the following century, the Chinese rejected the British habit of paying for tea with opium. With the end of Britain's monopoly on trade with China, the British turned to India to cultivate tea plants—having stolen some plants and the secrets of how tea is processed—and by 1888 imports of tea from India surpassed those from China. Today, India produces nearly one-third of the world's tea. It remains enjoyed around the world as a hot beverage, sometimes with milk and sugar, with lemon, or with added spices, as in the *masala chai* of India. Iced tea is popular in many countries, particularly in the US, where it is by far the most common way of drinking tea.

◁ **Single serving**
This Victorian metal tea strainer was filled with loose tea leaves and placed in a cup of boiling water until brewed. Tea bags weren't invented until 1908.

> "It is better to be deprived of food for three days, than of tea for one."
>
> ANCIENT CHINESE SAYING

Cloves
aromatic flower buds

Cloves were once exclusive to the Maluku Islands—the former Spice Islands of Indonesia. Today, this aromatic spice is cultivated in tropical regions from Africa to Asia and South America.

Origins
Maluku Islands
(Indonesia)

Major producers
Indonesia, Mauritius,
Tanzania

Non-food use
Traditional remedy for
toothache

Scientific name
Syzygium aromaticum

Looking a bit like small nails when dried, the French name of this spice *clou de girofle* meaning "nail of clove" is a reference to its appearance. The part that is used in cooking is the dried unopened flower bud of a tropical evergreen tree, *Syzygium aromaticum*, which has large glossy leaves and clusters of creamy colored flowers. Cloves are first mentioned in Asian literature in the Han dynasty in China (206 BCE–220 CE), where they are called the "chicken tongue spice." Introduced to the Mediterranean from the Maluku Islands (also known as the Moluccas) by Arab traders in the 4th century CE, by the 8th century cloves had become a major part of the European spice trade. By the 16th and 17th centuries cloves were one of the most precious spices in the world with bitter wars being fought for control of the trade.

The spice wars
During the 16th- and 17th-century Dutch revolt against Spanish rule, the King of Spain and Portugal, Philip II, as retribution against the rebellious state, excluded the Netherlands from Lisbon's spice markets. In 1605, this prompted the newly formed Dutch East India Company to invade the Portuguese-ruled

◁ **A rich harvest**
From the early 19th century to the 1970s, Zanzibar produced most of the world's cloves. This illustration from the 1880s, shows clove harvesting on the archipelago when the trade was at its height.

△ **Nailed down**
Cloves have a hard stem and a fragile center—the flower bud—that crumbles easily. The overall shape is like a nail.

△ **Spicy journey**
Arab traders were responsible for spreading the taste for many exotic spices around the world. Here a group of merchants is pictured heading eastward to India in the 8th century CE.

Allspice unique to the West

The only spice grown exclusively in the western hemisphere, allspice lends its warm, sweet flavor to a range of Caribbean and Middle Eastern dishes, and European pickles and pies.

Maluku Islands. On gaining control of the islands' spice trade, the Dutch pulled up any clove trees growing in areas outside their control. They also established export rules to keep the price high, which affected world trade as well as providing a substantial boost to Dutch coffers for more than a century.

The Dutch East India company was unable to maintain its monopoly, however, and the French managed to smuggle out clove seedlings to the Indian Ocean islands of Mauritius and Réunion in 1772, from where the plants were transported all over the tropics, including Zanzibar in 1818. For a century, Zanzibar was the world's largest producer of cloves.

A spice for today
Today, the sweet earthy taste of cloves lends itself well to classic spice blends such as Chinese five spice, Indian garam masala, Moroccan *ras-el-hanout*, and French *quatre épices*. In India cloves are often chewed to freshen breath, while in the West they are added to apple pies, pickles, and mulled wine, and are pressed whole to flavor onions and hams.

Courtiers in ancient China
chewed cloves before
speaking to the emperor.

Native to the West Indies, southern Mexico, and Central America, allspice is the sun-dried, unripe berry of an evergreen tree belonging to the myrtle family. It has glossy green leaves and small white flowers. These produce reddish-brown berries slightly larger than peppercorns that each contain two seeds.

Records show that more than 2,000 years ago allspice was used by the Mayans as an embalming agent to preserve the bodies of their dead and they also used it to flavor chocolate.

Mistaken identity
Allspice was discovered growing in Jamaica in the 15th century by the explorer Christopher Columbus who, thinking its seeds resembled peppercorns, called it "pimienta," which translates from the Spanish as pepper. Allspice was imported to Europe by the Spanish in the 16th century and was later given the name allspice by the 17th-century English botanist John Ray, who thought its spicy taste combined the flavors of cinnamon, nutmeg, and cloves. It soon became a popular flavoring (whole or ground) in both sweet and savory dishes.

These days, allspice is used in the Middle East to season roast meats, in India in pilafs and some curries, and in Europe it is used whole as a pickling spice or ground to flavor cakes, desserts, and preserves. It is also an important ingredient in Jamaican jerk chicken recipes as well as in *pimento dram*, a Jamaican cocktail of rum and allspice. In the food industry it is used to flavor sauces, sausages, and meat pies as well as Scandinavian pickled herrings and sauerkraut.

Origins
West Indies, southern Mexico, Central America

Major producers
Mexico, Jamaica, Guatemala

Non-food uses
Preservative, perfume, traditional medicine

Scientific name
Pimenta dioica

Cinnamon
a fragrant bark

Origins	Sri Lanka
Major producers	Sri Lanka, Indonesia, China
Non-food uses	Scent for incense, anointing oil, perfume
Scientific name	*Cinnamomum verum*

Once an exotic spice that only the wealthy could afford, cinnamon is now a popular pantry staple used to flavor both sweet and savory dishes.

PLANT

Mace

NUTMEG   MACE

△ **Outer layer and inner seed**
The nutmeg plant has dark green leaves and tiny flowers from which the fruit forms. The covering of the fruit is the spice mace and the seed is nutmeg.

Cinnamon comes from the inner bark of a medium-size evergreen tree whose outer bark has been scraped off at harvesting. The inner bark, beaten out in long lengths, curls as it dries to form the familiar hard brown rolls or quills.

There are several species of cinnamon, which fall into two categories. Ceylon (or Sri Lankan) cinnamon, "true" cinnamon (*Cinnamomum verum*), is light brown and coiled in a single spiral, and has a mild delicate flavor. Southeast Asian or Chinese cinnamon (*C. cassia*), also known as cassia, has a stronger, more bitter taste and woodier texture than the Sri Lankan type.

> Cinnamon was often burned to scent the funeral pyres of the nobility in ancient Rome.

As early as 2000 BCE the ancient Egyptians were using cinnamon as a perfuming agent for embalming bodies. It is referred to several times in the Old Testament as an ingredient in anointing oil. Cinnamon was well known to the ancient Greeks and Romans, who used it to preserve foods and as a seasoning, although their Arab suppliers kept its source a secret. This remained a mystery to Europeans until the early 16th century. But after

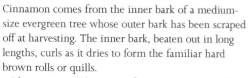

▷ **Cinnamon seller**
Evidence of cinnamon being imported into France is apparent from this 15th-century illustration.

△ **Bringing in the bark**
Under the direction of Portuguese traders, workers in the Maluku Islands stripped the fragrant bark from cassia trees ready for export. In the 16th century, most was shipped to Europe via East Africa.

discovering cinnamon growing wild in Ceylon (present-day Sri Lanka) in 1505, the Portuguese controlled the cinnamon trade until 1636, when the Dutch took over the island. In the 18th century, Britain gained control of the trade and passed it to the East India Company, who retained it until 1833.

In Western cuisine, cinnamon is mainly used in cakes, cookies, and desserts as well as savory dishes. In India, it is an ingredient of the garam masala spice mix. It also adds its sweet warmth to savory dishes such as Moroccan tagines and Iranian *khoresh*.

Nutmeg and mace
the spice twins

Much prized in Medieval Europe for its culinary and medicinal uses, the seed that produces the delicately flavored spice nutmeg is wrapped in another spice, mace.

Origins
Indonesia

Major producers
Grenada, Indonesia, India

Non-food uses
Perfume, pharmaceuticals

Scientific name
Myristica fragrans

△ **Nutmeg grater**
Invented in the 1800s, the Edgar nutmeg grater was aimed at making grating easier. The nut is clamped in position on one side and the grater moved using the handle opposite.

▽ **Business in Batavia**
Spice traders conduct their business in Batavia (modern-day Jakarta, Indonesia), from where the Dutch controlled the nutmeg trade in the 17th century.

First described by the Roman chronicler Pliny the Elder, who wrote of a tree bearing nuts with two flavors, these spices come from an evergreen tree and waxy, pale yellow, bell-shaped flowers. The crimson-red, lacy covering of the fruit is removed and dried to form the brownish orange spice mace. The kernel of the seed, which is dried, is known as nutmeg. The tree is believed to have originated in Indonesia's Maluku Islands (also known as the Moluccas).

Nutmeg was known in ancient Rome—possibly used to flavor alcoholic drinks—although it is thought to have been a rare delicacy. Arab traders probably carried nutmeg and mace to Constantinople (present-day Istanbul), around the 8th century, and by the 12th century the twin spices had been brought to western Europe by the Crusaders.

Vying for control

By the mid 16th century, Portuguese traders had taken control of the valuable nutmeg trade, which they held until the beginning of the 17th century, when the Dutch became the predominant traders of this precious spice. In 1770, however, a French expedition managed to smuggle out nutmeg seedlings, which they then planted in their Indian Ocean colony of Mauritius. During the early 19th century the British established their own nutmeg plantations in the Caribbean, Malay peninsula, and other tropical colonies. Today, Grenada supplies almost 40 percent of the world's nutmeg. Nutmeg and mace continue to be valued for the warm, sweet, musky flavor they add to savory and sweet dishes in cuisines around the world.

Ginger an underground spice

Origins
Unknown, possibly India

Major producers
India, China, Nepal

Source of
Vitamin B6, vitamin C

Non-food use
Medicinal (remedy
for nausea)

Scientific name
Zingiber officinale

Used in both fresh and dried form, ginger adds a hot and citrusy flavor to Asian-style savory dishes such as curries. It is also a popular flavoring for cakes, biscuits, and fruit-based desserts.

The name ginger comes from a Sanskrit word *srngaveram*, which means horn or antler. This refers to the shape of its creeping underground stem, or rhizome (sometimes called root), from which the spice is produced. Ginger is a perennial plant with short, reedlike stems and green, lance-shaped leaves that shoot up from buds on the rhizome every year. Used for culinary and medicinal purposes since ancient times, the rhizome can be white, yellow, or red.

Early records

The exact origins of ginger are uncertain. It may be from India, although the first formal records of this pungent spice are found in medical literature of China's Han dynasty (206 BCE–220 CE). By around 300 CE, ginger had become a popular spice in the Roman Empire, where it was recorded as a taxable commodity. It was used medicinally and to flavor tea and wine as well as meats, and young rhizomes were preserved in a honey syrup. After the fall of the Roman Empire, ginger remained an important commodity in the European spice trade, controlled by Arab merchants.

By the 13th and 14th centuries, dried and ground ginger was being used to flavor practically every type of food. It was also shipped to Europe from the East in a preserved form to be used in confectionery. England's 16th-century Queen Elizabeth I was particularly fond of ginger.

Cultivated today in many tropical countries, including some parts of Australia, China, India, Indonesia, Jamaica, Nepal, Nigeria, and Thailand, the strength and flavor of ginger is determined by compounds called gingerols, which vary according to where the plant comes

▷ **Ginger store**
Chinese potters have created jars for storing spices such as ginger since the 2nd century BCE. This example of a ginger jar is from the Kangxi period (1661–1722) of the Qing dynasty.

> " … eat a ginger after waking up and forget about doctors."

CHINESE SAYING

from, the climate of the area, and the time of harvesting. Chinese ginger has a pungent flavor, South Indian and Australian a more lemony flavor, while Jamaican is more delicate, and African ginger has a hotter taste. One of the main spices in Asian cuisine, ginger features widely in Indian and Arabic dishes. Pickled ginger is popular in Japan, especially to flavor sushi, and is used in Korea to flavor kimchi, the fermented cabbage-based accompaniment. Ginger is used mostly in the West in baked foods such as cakes and cookies, but as Asian cuisine has become more popular it is also used in savory dishes. The grated root is often infused as a refreshing tea.

▷ **Root and leaf**
The edible portion of the plant is the knobbly rhizome from which long stems and narrow pointed leaves grow.

▷ **Ginger preparation**
A woman works in a ginger-drying shed in Kerala, India. The world's major producer of ginger, India exports much of its crop in dried form.

Saffron the world's most expensive spice

Origins
Greece, Asia Minor (modern-day Turkey)

Major producers
Iran, Spain, Greece

Non-food uses
Dye

Scientific name
Crocus sativus

Made from the flowers of a member of the crocus family, saffron is thought to have been first cultivated in or near Greece in the Bronze Age, where it was used to flavor food and wine as well as providing a rich yellow dye.

▷ **The saffron gatherers**
A female worker gathers saffron in this famous Minoan fresco of the second millennium BCE from Akrotiri, Santorini (ancient Thera).

The name saffron, which is derived from the Arabic word *zafarin* meaning yellow, refers to the hand-picked stigmas of the flowers of the saffron crocus. Dried, these form tiny red threads which, when soaked or added to food, produce the familiar yellow coloring.

Saffron has been widely cultivated in the southern Mediterranean since ancient times. Egyptian texts from 1500 BCE describe crocuses growing in the gardens at Luxor. And a mural found in the ruins of the Palace of Knossos in Crete dating back to the same era depicts what is now believed to be a monkey picking saffron flowers.

Early cultivation

By the 3rd century CE saffron was also cultivated in Kashmir in northern India, where some of the finest crops are still grown. Records show that the Moors were cultivating saffron in Spain as early as 960. It was not until the 13th century, however, when crusaders returned with saffron crocus corms (bulbs), that cultivation began in Italy, France,

Egyptian queen Cleopatra is said to have bathed in saffron for its supposed aphrodisiac effects.

▷ **Spicy strands**
Only tiny quantities of dried saffron strands are needed to produce a noticeable impact on the dishes they are used to flavor and color.

Turmeric the golden spice

Perhaps best known as the spice that gives some curry dishes their yellow color, turmeric is also thought to have healing properties due to its active ingredient curcumin.

and Germany. A pilgrim with a saffron corm hidden in his staff is said to have introduced the plant to England in the 14th century, and two centuries later one Essex town had been renamed Saffron Walden in its honor.

Flavor of flowers

Today, saffron is mainly produced in Iran and Spain and is the most expensive spice in the world because it is still harvested and processed by hand, just as it was in ancient times. It takes 70,000 flowers to produce just 5lb (2.25kg) of raw stigmas, which when dried amount to 1lb (450g) of saffronthreads.

The aromatic saffron threads are usually ground before being soaked and added to savory dishes such as Middle Eastern and Asian rice dishes, paellas in Spain, and bouillabaisse (fish stew) in France. They are also used in sweet dishes and drinks in the Middle East and India. Some traditional northern European buns and cakes such as the Swedish *lussebulle* and the celebratory revel bun from Cornwall, UK also use saffron.

Known as *haridra* in Sanskrit, *haldi* in Hindi, and *jiang huang* in Chinese, turmeric is one of the most characteristic spices of many Asian cuisines. It is also known as Indian saffron because of its bright yellow hue. Turmeric is a member of the ginger family. The spice is derived from the plant's fleshy rhizomes (underground stems), which are harvested in winter, boiled or steamed, and then dried and ground.

◁ **Fresh and dried**
The flesh of fresh turmeric is pale yellow, but when dried and ground becomes a deep orange-yellow that stains.

Out of Asia

Tumeric's exact origin is unknown, but it is thought to have first been cultivated thousands of years ago in India, probably initially for its dye. Alexander the Great, King of Macedonia, probably brought it to Asia Minor (modern-day Turkey) and the Mediterranean in around 330 BCE. Turmeric reached China in around 700 CE, East Africa a century later, and West Africa by 1200. It is now cultivated throughout the tropics.

Sometimes used as a cheaper option to saffron, turmeric is a key ingredient in curry powder and curries the world over. It is also used in the Middle East and North Africa to flavor and color sauces, syrups, rice dishes, meat, and vegetables. Research is continuing into the possible pharmacological uses of curcumin, a chemical in which turmeric is rich.

Origins
Unknown, but probably South or Southeast Asia

Major producers
India, Pakistan, China

Source of
Iron, vitamin C

Non-food uses
Traditional medicine, dye

Scientific name
Curcuma longa

▷ **Field of flavor**
Turmeric plants have long, pointed leaves that grow from the base of the plant at ground level. The crop is usually ripe for harvesting within 10 months.

△ **Delicate-flavored flower parts**
The saffron crocus has pale purple petals that surround the yellow, pollen-encrusted stamens. The dark orange threadlike stigmas are the part harvested as saffron.

Vanilla fragrant pods from Mexico

With its unique taste and aroma, vanilla has become almost the standard flavoring for ice cream, custards, and many other sweet dishes. Originally from Mexico and Central America its popularity spread worldwide.

Vanilla seems to have been first grown by the Totonac people of east-central Mexico around one thousand years ago. When the Aztecs from the north conquered the Totonacs in the 15th century, they developed a taste for vanilla in their chocolate drinks, as did the Spanish a few years later when they conquered the Aztecs in 1521. Cocoa flavored with vanilla soon became popular across Western Europe.

Curing and drying

The vanilla plant is one of around 100 species of vanilla orchid. This climbing orchid has pale yellow-green flowers, which mature into long green pods. In commercial

◁ **Prince of pollination**
Edmond Albius found fame for his discovery, at the age of 12, of a method to pollinate vanilla plants by hand, stimulating commercial production.

production, the harvested pods are cured and dried in a lengthy process. In the early 17th century, Hugh Morgan, an apothecary to Queen Elizabeth I of England, suggested the use of vanilla as a flavoring for sweetmeats (desserts). By the following century, the French were using vanilla to flavor ice cream—a taste discovered in the 1780s

△ **Black and dry**
The parts of the vanilla plant that are used to provide flavor are the pods and the seeds they contain. These are green in their fresh form but turn black when dried.

> "The centuries last passed have given the taste [an] important extension … vanilla."

JEAN ANTHELME BRILLAT-SAVARIN (1725–1826), FRENCH EPICURE

△ **Ice cream seller**
A street-trader in Germany in the early 20th century does good business selling ice creams in the favorite flavors of the time—vanilla and raspberry.

by the American ambassador in Paris, Thomas Jefferson. He liked it so much that he copied down a recipe, which is preserved in the Library of Congress.

Vanilla production was revolutionized by Edmond Albius, a 12-year-old slave from Réunion, an island in the Indian Ocean known then as Ile de Bourbon (hence Bourbon vanilla). In the mid 1800s, he learned how to pollinate vanilla flowers—using a stick and flick of the thumb. French colonist adopted the technique and vanilla plantations began to spring up across the globe. About 75 percent of the world's vanilla now comes from Madagascar and Réunion.

Inferior quality

Much of the vanilla produced today is used to make vanilla extract. Good quality pure vanilla extract is expensive and must contain at least 35 percent alcohol and have low sugar levels. Synthetic vanilla can be made from petrochemicals but the flavor is inferior.

▷ **Fragrant orchid**
The vanilla plant is a member of the orchid family with pointed leaves and greenish yellow flowers. This illustration is from an 1887 German botanical treatise.

Origins
Mexico and Central America

Major producers
Mexico, Madagascar

Non-food uses
Perfumes, incense, room fragrances

Scientific name
Vanilla planifolia

Orchideae.

Vanilla planifolia Andr.

INDEX

Page numbers in **bold** refer to the main pages for the topic.

Acknowledgments

Dorling Kindersley would like to thank Elizabeth Wise for the index; Jamie Ambrose, Peter Frances, and Miezan van Zyl for additional editing; Polly Boyd for proofreading; Steve Woosnam-Savage and Francis Wong for additional design work; Duncan Turner for design research and development; Sarah Smithies for additional picture research; Steve Crozier for hi-res retouching.

DK India would like to thank Hansa Babra, Nidhi Rastogi, and Anjali Sachar for design assistance; Nand Kishore Acharya, Neeraj Bhatia, Mohd Rizwan, Rajesh Singh, Vikram Singh, and Anita Yadav for DTP assistance.

Hugh Schermuly and Cathy Meeus would like to thank the following for editing the text: John Andrews, Connie Novis, Gill Pitts and Rachel Warren Chad.

The publisher would like to thank the following for their kind permission to reproduce their photographs:
(Key: a-above; b-below/bottom; c-center; f-far; l-left; r-right; t-top)

1 AF Fotografie. **2 Alamy Stock Photo:** Frank Carter / Age Fotostock. **4 123RF.com:** Andreyoleynik (ca, cra, cla, fcra). **Alamy Stock Photo:** Juliane Berger / Ingram Publishing (fcla). **5 123RF.com:** Andreyoleynik (fcla); Zenina (cra); Sergey Pykhonin (ca); Marina99 (fcra); Macrovector (cla, ca/ Honeycomb). **6-7 Getty Images:** Fine Art Photographic / Corbis Historical. **8 Getty Images:** Gavin Hellier / Photographer's Choice. **9 Getty Images:** Pierre Briolle / Gamma-Rapho (clb). **10 Getty Images:** PHAS / Universal Images Group (bl). **10-11 Getty Images:** Print Collector / Hulton Archive. **12 Getty Images:** VCG / Visual China Group. **13 Getty Images:** Thomas Barwick / Stone (br); Culture Club / Hulton Archive (tc). **14-15 Alamy Stock Photo:** Juliane Berger / Ingram Publishing. **16 Alamy Stock Photo:** David Hiser / National Geographic Creative (bl). **Getty Images:** Shem Compion / Gallo Images (br); Universal Images Group / Hulton Fine Art Collection (bc). **17 Alamy Stock Photo:** Photo Researchers / Science History Images (bl). **Getty Images:** Ullstein Bild (bc); Boyer / Roger Viollet (br). **18 Rex Shutterstock:** British Library / Robana. **19 Alamy Stock Photo:** John Crowe (br). **Dreamstime.com:** Anatoly Zavodskov (tr). **Getty Images:** Florilegius / SSPL (ca). **20 Getty Images:** Leemage / Universal Images Group. **21 Dover Publications, Inc. New York:** (tr). **Getty Images:** Universal Images Group / Hulton Fine Art / Hulton Fine Art Collection (br); Heritage Images / Hulton Archive (bl); Owen Franken / Corbis Documentary (tl). **22-23 Getty Images:** Dmitri Kessel / The LIFE Picture Collection. **22 Depositphotos Inc:** Nafanya1710 (ca). **Harryandrowenaphotos:** (bl). **23 Getty Images:** Stock Montage / Archive Photos (br). **24 Alamy Stock Photo:** Thestudio (tr). **Getty Images:** Hulton Deutsch / Corbis Historical (c). **25 Getty Images:** Buyenlarge / Archive Photos (tr); Museum of Science and Industry, Chicago / Archive Photos (crb). **26 Bridgeman Images:** Museo Nacional de Arqueologia y Etnologia, Guatemala City / Jean-Pierre Courau (ca). **Getty Images:** DEA / G. Dagli Orti (bc). **26-27 Alamy Stock Photo:** Photo Researchers / Science History Images. **28 Getty Images:** Hulton Archive. **29 Getty Images:** Culture Club / Hulton Archive (tl); Zangl / Ullstein Bild (tr); The Print Collector / Hulton Archive (br). **30-31 Getty Images:** Popperfoto. **32 Getty Images:** Parameswaran Pillai Karunakaran / Corbis Documentary (t). **Rex Shutterstock:** Indian Photo Agency (br). **33 123RF.com:** Nikola Volrábová (ca). **Alamy Stock Photo:** Lebrecht Music and Arts Photo Library (bl). **Getty Images:** BSIP / Universal Images Group (tr). **34 iStockphoto.com:** Gameover2012 (crb); Elena Rui (t). **35 Getty Images:** DEA Picture Library / De Agostini. **36 Alamy Stock Photo:** Tim Gainey (l). **Getty Images:** Hulton Deutsch / Corbis Historical (br). **37 Getty Images:** Sergio Bellotto / DigitalVision Vectors (cra). **38 Getty Images:** Ullstein bild Dtl. (clb). **Mary Evans Picture Library:** (ca). **39 akg-images:** Pictures From History. **40 Alamy Stock Photo:** Dan Leffel / Age Fotostock. **41 Bridgeman Images:** Purix Verlag Volker Christen (br). **42-43 123RF.com:** Andreyoleynik. **44 Alamy Stock Photo:** Interfoto (bl). **Getty Images:** DEA / G. Dagli Orti / De Agostini (cb); Bettmann (br). **45 123RF.com:** Actionsports (cb). **Getty Images:** Richard du Toit / Gallo Images (bl). **iStockphoto.com:** Aluxum (br). **46 Bridgeman Images:** Bibliotheque des Arts Decoratifs, Paris, France / Archives Charmet (ca). **46-47 Getty Images:** Martin Barraud / OJO Images. **47 Getty Images:** API / Gamma-Rapho (bl). **48 Getty Images:** Keystone-France / Gamma-Rapho. **49 Alamy Stock Photo:** Vintage Images (tl). **Bridgeman Images:** American School, (19th century) / Private Collection / Peter Newark American Pictures (crb). **Getty Images:** Foodcollection (bc). **50 Getty Images:** ZU_09 / DigitalVision Vectors (tr); Pete Mcbride / National Geographic (cra). **Mary Evans Picture Library:** Grosvenor Prints (bc). **51 Mary Evans Picture Library:** Grenville Collins Postcard Collection. **52 Getty Images:** Universal Images Group / Hulton Fine Art / Hulton Fine Art Collection. **53 Getty Images:** China Photos (bl); Florilegius / SSPL (tr). **54 Dreamstime.com:** Nicku (cra). **Getty Images:** Alinari Archives / Alinari (clb). **55 Dreamstime.com:** Mark Hammon. **56-57 Getty Images:** Keren Su / China Span. **56 Alamy Stock Photo:** Jennifer Booher (tr). **57 Alamy Stock Photo:** World History Archive (cla). **58-59 Getty Images:** Mint Images - Art Wolfe / Mint Images RF. **60 Alamy Stock Photo:** World History Archive (bl). **Depositphotos Inc:** AndreaA. (tr). **Getty Images:** Michael Maslan / Corbis Historical (ca). **61 Aléxandros Bairamidis**. **62 Depositphotos Inc:** Anjela30 (tr). **National Geographic Creative:** Jules Gervais Courtellemont (bl). **63 akg-images**. **64 Dorling Kindersley:** University of Pennsylvania Museum of Archaeology and Anthropology (br). **64-65 CIP International Potato Center**. **65 Alamy Stock Photo:** Chronicle (clb). **Bridgeman Images:** Bibliotheque des Arts Decoratifs, Paris, France / Archives Charmet (br). **66 Getty Images:** Jim Heimann Collection / Archive Photos (cr); Universal History Archive / Universal Images Group (tl). **67 Bridgeman Images:** Bastien-Lepage, Jules (1848-84) / National Gallery of Victoria, Melbourne, Australia / Felton Bequest (b). **Dreamstime.com:** Sarah2 (tc). **68-69 Alamy Stock Photo:** Charles Phelps Cushing / ClassicStock. **70 Getty Images:** DEA / G. Dagli Orti / De Agostini. **71 Getty Images:** © Vincent Boisvert, all right reserved / Moment (tc); DEA / G. Dagli Orti / De Agostini Picture Library (cr); Thepalmer / Digitalvision Vectors (bc). **72 Bridgeman Images:** Biblioteca Medicea-Laurenziana, Florence, Italy (bl). **72-73 Getty Images:** Lew Robertson / Stone. **74 Alamy Stock Photo:** Artokoloro Quint Lox Limited. **75 Getty Images:** Duncan1890 / Digitalvision Vectors (crb); De Agostini / Biblioteca Ambrosiana / De Agostini Picture Library (tr); Universal Images Group / Hulton Fine Art (bl). **76 akg-images:** (clb). **Getty Images:** Fred Tanneau / AFP (tr). **77 Getty Images:** Swim Ink 2 Llc / Corbis Historical (ca). **Zeki Yavuzak:** (b). **78 Bridgeman Images:** Basilius Besler's 'Florilegium,' published at Nuremberg in 1613. / Photo © Granger. **79 Alamy Stock Photo:** Karl Newedel / Bon Appetit (tr). **Bridgeman Images:** © Look and Learn / Rosenberg Collection (c). **80-81 Getty Images:** Luis Marden / National Geographic. **80 Alamy Stock Photo:** Ed Darack / RGB Ventures / SuperStock (bl). **Getty Images:** GraphicaArtis / Archive Photos (tc). **82 iStockphoto.com:** Pixhook (tl). **82-83 Getty Images:** Print Collector / Hulton Archive. **83 Alamy Stock Photo:** Patrick Guenette (bc). **Getty Images:** Ullstein Bild Dtl. / Ullstein Bil (tl); Transcendental Graphics / Archive Photos (cra). **84-85 Alamy Stock Photo:** H. Armstrong Roberts / ClassicStock. **86 123RF.com:** Robyn Mackenzie (cra). **86-87 Depositphotos Inc:** Vadim Vasenin. **87 123RF.com:** Luisa Vallon Fumi (tc). **Bridgeman Images:** Collection of the New-York Historical Society, USA (tr). **88 Bridgeman Images**. **89 akg-images:** Erich Lessing (cra). **Getty Images:** Ilbusca / Digitalvision Vectors (bc). **90 Getty Images:** De Agostini / Biblioteca Ambrosiana / De Agostini Picture Library (tl). **90-91 Getty Images:** Larigan - Patricia Hamilton / Moment Open. **91 Getty Images:** Rykoff Collection / Corbis Historical (cr); Bildagentur-Online / Universal Images Group (tc). **92-93 123RF.com:** Andreyoleynik. **94 Getty Images:** Universal History Archive / Universal Images Group (bl, br). **National Geographic Creative:** H. M. Herget (cb). **95 Getty Images:** Giorgio Conrad / Alinari Archives (crb); Stock Montage / Archive Photos (clb); Universal Images Group (bc). **96 123RF.com:** Patrick Guenette (cra). **akg-images:** Glasshouse Images (bl); Gilles Mermet (tr). **97 Getty Images:** Bettmann. **98 Getty Images:** Richard du Toit / Corbis Documentary. **99 Alamy Stock Photo:** Artokoloro / Artokoloro Quint Lox Limited (tc). **Getty Images:** Glasshouse Images / Corbis (crb). **Mary Evans Picture Library:** Maurice Collins Images Collection (bc). **100-101 akg-images:** Roland and Sabrina Michaud. **100 123RF.com:** Alex74 (crb). **Alamy Stock Photo:** Shawshots (clb). **101 Depositphotos Inc:** Valentyn Volkov (c). **Getty Images:** Jennifer Kennard / Corbis Historical (cb). **102 Getty Images:** Bettmann (ca); Clu / Digitalvision Vectors (bl). **102-103 Alamy Stock Photo:** Chronicle (t). **500px:** Marja Schwartz / www.marjaschwartz.com (b). **104-105 Getty Images:** Hulton-Deutsch Collection / Corbis Historical. **106 500px:** Basel Almisshal. **107 Alamy Stock Photo:** Historical Images Archive (cr); Kiyoshi Togashi (tr). **108 Spring 1904 / W.N. Scarff (Firm); Scarff, W. N; Henry G. Gilbert Nursery and Seed Trade Catalog Collection / New Carlisle, Ohio : W.N. Scarff**. **109 Getty Images:** Minnesota Historical Society / Corbis Historica (br). **naturepl.com:** MYN / David Hunter (cra). **110-111 Getty Images:** Broadcastertr / Moment Open. **110 Getty Images:** Found Image Holdings / Corbis Historical (tr). **111 Dover Publications, Inc. New York:** (crb). **Getty Images:** Planet News Archive / SSPL (tr). **112 Getty Images:** Creativ Studio Heinemann. **113 Getty Images:** Gamma-Rapho / API (bl); Boyer / Roger Viollet (cra). **114 Alamy Stock Photo:** Michael Seleznev (cr). **iStockphoto.com:** Ermingut (tr). **114-115 Getty Images:** James G. Welgos / Archive Photos. **116-117 Getty Images:** The Print Collector / Hulton Archive. **118-119 Alamy Stock Photo:** Lloyd Sutton. **119 Alamy Stock Photo:** Jim Engelbrecht / DanitaDelimont.com (tr); Granger Historical Picture Archive (ca). **120 Getty Images:** Nastasic / DigitalVision Vectors (ca); Paul Popper / Popperfoto (bl). **120-121 Dreamstime.com:** Rutchapong Moolvai. **121 Getty Images:** Evans / Three Lions / Hulton Archive (br). **122 Sandro Vannini / Laboratoriorosso**. **123 Getty Images:** De Agostini / Archivio J. Lange / De Agostini Picture Library (ca). **Mary Evans Picture Library:** Grenville Collins Postcard Collection (br). **124 Getty Images:** Anadolu Agency (bc); John Greim / LightRocket (tr). **125 akg-images:** Francis Dzikowski. **126 akg-images:** (cl). **The New York Public Library:** Abbott, Berenice / Federal Art Project (New York, N.Y.) (bc). **126-127 The Regents of The University of California / Online Archive of California:** Riverside Public Library (t). **128 Getty Images:** Universal History Archive / UIG (bc). **128-129 akg-images:** Arkivi. **129 Getty Images:** Heritage Images / Hulton Archive (tl). **130-131 Getty Images:** John W Banagan / Photographer's Choice. **132-133 Getty Images:** DEA / G. Dagli Orti / De Agostini Editorial (c). **132 123RF.com:** Yauheniya Litvinovich (cra). **Bridgeman Images:** Private Collection / Photo © Christie's Images (bl). **133 500px:** Art911 (cra). **134-135 Getty Images:** Universal History Archive / UIG. **134 Getty Images:** Transcendental Graphics / Archive Photos (br). **135 Dover Publications, Inc. New York:** (cl). **Dreamstime.com:** Felinda (bc). **Getty Images:** Amana Images Inc (cr). **136 Getty Images:** Print Collector / Hulton Archive (cl). **137 Alamy Stock Photo:** Muhammad Mostafigur Rahman (cra). **Getty Images:** Stockbyte (l). **iStockphoto.com:** Blackred (clb). **138-139 123RF.com:** Andreyoleynik. **140 Alamy Stock Photo:** North Wind Picture Archives (clb). **Bridgeman Images:** Egyptian 6th Dynasty (c.2350-2200 BC) / Saqqara, Egypt (bc). **Getty Images:** DEA / Archivio J. Lange / De Agostini (br). **141 Getty Images:** Martin Harvey / Photolibrary (clb); The Print Collector / Hulton Archive (bc); Universal Images Group (crb). **142 Getty Images:** Heritage Images / Hulton Archive (clb). **142-143 Getty Images:** Universal History Archive / Universal Images Group. **143 Getty Images:** Historical / Corbis Historica (tr). **144-145 Getty Images:** Bettmann. **146 akg-images:** Erich Lessing (c). **Getty Images:** Alinari Archives / Alinari (bl); Universal History Archive / Universal Images Group (tr). **147 Getty Images:** Hulton Deutsch / Corbis Historical. **148 Getty Images:** Print Collector / Hulton Fine Art Collection (bl); Ilbusca / E+ (ca). **148-149 Alamy Stock Photo:** MCLA Collection (t). **150 Getty Images:** Bloomberg (bl); Nastasic / DigitalVision Vectors (cra). **151 Getty Images:** Barbara Singer / Hulton Archive. **152 Getty Images:** Creativ Studio Heinemann (bl); Universal History Archive / Universal Images Group (tr). **153 Getty Images:** Mondadori Portfolio / Hulton Fine Art Collection. **154 Alamy Stock Photo:** Emilio Ereza (bl). **Getty Images:** DEA / L. Pedicini / De Agostini Editorial (ca). **154-155 Getty Images:** Florilegius / SSPL. **155 Getty Images:** Stefano Bianchetti / Corbis Historical (br). **156 Getty Images:** Transcendental Graphics / Archive Photos (clb). **156-157 Bridgeman Images:** Jean Leon Gerome (1863-1930) / Private Collection. **157 Getty Images:** DEA / Bardazzi / De Agostini Picture Library (cra); Topical Press Agency / Hulton Archive (bl). **158 Alamy Stock Photo:** Novo Images / Glasshouse Images (cr). **Dover Publications, Inc. New York:** (ca). **Wikipedia:** Science and Mechanics magazine in October 1911 (bl). **159 Getty Images:** DEA / G. Dagli Orti / De Agostini Picture Library. **160-161 Getty Images:** Fine Art / Corbis Historical. **162 Getty Images:** Evans / Three Lions, MPI / Archive Photos (tr). **Rex Shutterstock:** Granger (b). **163 Dover Publications, Inc. New York:** (bc). **Getty Images:** Flemish School (cr). **164 Alamy Stock Photo:** Emilio Ereza (cr). **164-165 Getty Images:** De Agostini Picture Library / De Agostini. **165 Getty Images:** De Agostini / Biblioteca Ambrosiana / De Agostini Picture Library (tr). **166-167 123RF.com:** Andreyoleynik. **168 Getty Images:** Sissie Brimberg / National Geographic (clb); 3LH-Fine Art / SuperStock (br). **169 Getty Images:** Peter Essick / Aurora (bc); Popperfoto (clb); Arctic-Images / Photolibrary (br). **170 Getty Images:** Popperfoto. **171**

Dreamstime.com: Irina Iarovaia (tc). **Getty Images:** MPI / Archive Photos (crb); Werner Forman / Universal Images Group (bc). **172 Getty Images:** Found Image Holdings Inc / Corbis Historical (bc); Fox Photos / Hulton Archive (tl). **172-173 Getty Images:** Beth Wald / National Geographic. **173 Getty Images:** Historical / Corbis Historical (br). **174 123RF.com:** Patrick Guenette (cra). **Getty Images:** Universal History Archive / Universal Images Group (bl). **175 Dorling Kindersley:** Durham University Oriental Museum (t). **Getty Images:** Museum of East Asian Art / Heritage Images / Hulton Archive (br). **176 Getty Images:** Encyclopaedia Britannica / Universal Images Group (ca); Universal History Archive / Universal Images Group (bl). **176-177 Getty Images:** Nigel Pavitt / AWL Images. **178 akg-images:** Jh-Lightbox_Ltd. / John Hios (cr). **Getty Images:** Historical Picture Archive / Corbis Historical (ca); Kip Ross / National Geographic (b). **179 Getty Images:** De Agostini Picture Library / De Agostini (clb). **Los Angeles County Museum Of Art:** Gift of Carl Holmes (M.71.100.154) (tr). **180 Getty Images:** Rykoff Collection / Corbis Historical (bl). **iStockphoto.com:** AdShooter (cra). **181 Bridgeman Images:** Private Collection / © Look and Learn. **182-183 Alamy Stock Photo:** Carl Simon / United Archives GmbH. **183 Alamy Stock Photo:** Stefan Auth / Imagebroker (bc); Ivan Vdovin (tl). **184 Getty Images:** Buyenlarge / Archive Photos (crb); James P. Blair / National Geographic (bl). **185 Getty Images:** Universal History Archive / Universal Images Group (bl). **iStockphoto.com:** PicturePartners (tr). **186 Alamy Stock Photo:** Granger, NYC. / Granger Historical Picture Archive (bl); Helen Sessions (tl). **186-187 Alamy Stock Photo:** The Keasbury-Gordon Photograph Archive / KGPA Ltd. **188-189 Bridgeman Images:** Bry, Th. (1528-98), after Le Moyne, J.(de Morgues) (1533-88) / Service Historique de la Marine, Vincennes, France. **190 123RF.com:** Anthony Baggett (cra). **Getty Images:** Universal History Archive / Universal Images Group (bl). **190-191 Getty Images:** Florilegius / SSPL. **192 Getty Images:** Hulton Deutsch / Corbis Historical. **193 Getty Images:** Bettmann (bc); Moodboard / Cultura (tr); De Agostini / Biblioteca Ambrosiana / De Agostini Picture Library (bc). **194-195 Getty Images:** Epics / Hulton Archive (b); Science & Society Picture Library / SSPL (t). **194 akg-images:** Universal Images Group / Universal History Archive (b). **195 akg-images:** Florilegius (br). **Getty Images:** Ilbusca / Digitalvision Vectors (ca). **196-197 Getty Images:** Penny Tweedie / Corbis Historical. **196 Getty Images:** IGFA / Getty Images Sport (bl); Universal History Archive / Universal Images Group (cra). **198 Getty Images:** Juan Carlos Muñoz / Age Fotostock (bl); Raphael Gaillarde / Gamma-Rapho (ca). **198-199 Getty Images:** Mauricio Handler / National Geographic. **200 Bridgeman Images:** Private Collection / © Look and Learn (bl); Mieris, Willem van (1662-1747) / Private Collection / Johnny Van Haeften Ltd., London (tr). **201 Bridgeman Images:** Hiroshige, Ando or Utagawa (1797-1858) / Blackburn Museum and Art Gallery, Lancashire, UK. **202 Getty Images:** Universal History Archive / Universal Images Group (bl). **iStockphoto.com:** Siscosoler (tr). **203 Bridgeman Images:** Hiroshige, Ando or Utagawa (1797-1858) / Minneapolis Institute of Arts, MN, USA / Bequest of Louis W. Hill, Jr. (t). **Getty Images:** B. Anthony Stewart / National Geographic (br). **204 Getty Images:** Christophe Boisvieux / Corbis Documentary (tr). **204-205 Getty Images:** DEA / M. Seemuller / De Agostini. **205 Getty Images:** Bettmann (tr). **206-207 Getty Images:** Photo Josse / Leemage / Corbis Historical. **208 Getty Images:** Fine Art / Corbis Historical (cra). **TopFoto.co.uk:** Ullsteinbild (b). **209 Image from the Biodiversity Heritage Library:** Kunstformen der Natur / Leipzig und Wien,Verlag des Bibliographischen Instituts,1904 / Haeckel, Ernst, 1834-1919. **210 iStockphoto.com:** Duncan1890 (clb). **210-211 Getty Images:** PHAS / Universal Images Group. **211 Getty Images:** Bettmann (bl). **212-213 naturepl.com:** MYN / Piotr Naskrecki. **212 Alamy Stock Photo:** Artokoloro Quint Lox Limited (tr). **213 Getty Images:** Duncan1890 / DigitalVision Vectors (br). **214 Alamy Stock Photo:** Patrick Guenette (tr). **214-215 Getty Images:** Print Collector / Hulton Archive. **215 Dreamstime.com:** Eyewave (ca). **Getty Images:** Keystone-France / Gamma-Keystone. **216-217 123RF.com:** Andreyoleynik (b). **218 Alamy Stock Photo:** Zev Radovan / BibleLandPictures / www.BibleLandPictures.com (clb). **Getty Images:** De Agostini Picture Library / De Agostini (crb); DEA / G. Dagli Orti / De Agostini (tl). **219 Alamy Stock Photo:** Mireille Vautier (br). **Getty Images:** Popperfoto (br); UniversalImagesGroup / Universal Images Group (l). **220 500px:** Sasin Tipchai. **221 Getty Images:** Danita Delimont / Gallo Images (cra). **iStockphoto.com:** Professor25 (tr). **222-223 Bridgeman Images:** Chinese School, (18th century) / Private Collection / Archives Charmet. **222 Alamy Stock Photo:** Alan King engraving (tl). **223 Getty Images:** Jialiang Gao / Moment (tc). **224 Alamy Stock Photo:** Chronicle (br); Quagga Media (tr). **Getty Images:** DEA / G. Nimatallah / De Agostini (cr). **225 Alamy Stock Photo:** Granger Historical Picture Archive. **226 Bridgeman Images:** Schlesinger Library, Radcliffe Institute, Harvard University (bl). **226-227 akg-images:** Ullstein Bild. **227 iStockphoto.com:** AntiMartina (tr). **228 Dreamstime.com:** Igor Sokolov / Breeze09 (cla). **228-229 Bridgeman Images:** Underwood Archives / UIG. **229 Bridgeman Images:** Castello del Buonconsilio, Torre dell'Aquila, Italy (tc). **Dover Publications, Inc. New York:** (c). **230 Getty Images:** Hulton-Deutsch Collection / Corbis Historical (bl); Lew Robertson / Photodisc (ca). **230-231 Getty Images:** Haeckel Collection / Ullstein Bild / Premium Archive. **231 iStockphoto.com:** Pidjoe (br). **232-233 Alamy Stock Photo:** Gonzalo Azumendi / Age Fotostock. **234 Alamy Stock Photo:** Jean Cazals / Bon Appetit (tl). **234-235 National Geographic Creative:** Paul De Gaston. **235 Alamy Stock Photo:** ART Collection (tc). **236 Benmokhtar Mohamed. 237 Bridgeman Images:** Radiguet, Maximilien (1816-99) / Bibliotheque des Arts Decoratifs, Paris, France / Archives Charmet (br); Algerian School, (20th century) / Musee des Arts d'Afrique et d'Oceanie, Paris, France / © Heini Schneebeli (tr). **238 Alamy Stock Photo:** Wildlife GmbH (br). **Getty Images:** Yann Arthus-Bertrand (tr); World History Archive (br). **239 Alamy Stock Photo:** Patrick Guenette (tr); World History Archive (br). **240 Getty Images:** Bartosz Hadyniak / Photodisc. **241 Bridgeman Images:** Museum of Fine Arts, Boston, Massachusetts, USA / Harvard University —Boston Museum of Fine Arts Expedition (bl). **Rex Shutterstock:** Granger (br). **242 Getty Images:** De Agostini Picture Library (cl); Nastasic / DigitalVision Vectors (br). **242-243 Rex Shutterstock:** Granger. **243 Getty Images:** Photo12 / Universal Images Group (tc). **244-245 iStockphoto.com:** Busypix. **244 Alamy Stock Photo:** Alberto Masnovo (cb). **245 Getty Images:** GraphicaArtis / Archive Photos (cl); Bettmann (br). **246-247 The Sikh Foundation:** The Camp of Bhai Vir Singh / Kapany Collection. **248 Alamy Stock Photo:** Dr. Wilfried Bahnmüller / Imagebroker (cr). **249 Getty Images:** Christopher Pillitz / Stone. **250 Getty Images:** Daily Herald Archive / SSPL. **251 Alamy Stock Photo:** Gameover (cra). **Image from the Biodiversity Heritage Library:** Description des plantes potagères / Vilmorin-Andrieux et cie. 1856 (c). **252 Getty Images:** Angelika Antl (tl). **253 Getty Images:** Sue Kennedy / Corbis Documentary (b). **iStockphoto.com:** Kudou (cra). **254 akg-images:** (bl). **Getty Images:** DEA / G. Cigolini / De Agostini (cra). **254-255 Getty Images:** Bloomberg. **255 Alamy Stock Photo:** Glasshouse Images / Corbis. **256-257 Bridgeman Images:** Galleria Palatina & Appartamenti Reali di Palazzo Pitti, Florence, Tuscany, Italy. **256 The Metropolitan Museum of Art, New York:** Gift of Mr. and Mrs. Nathan Cummings, 1964 (bl). **258 Getty Images:** Alinari Archives / Alinari (bl); Nastasic / DigitalVision Vectors (tr). **259 Getty Images:** Ullstein Bild Dtl. / Ullstein Bild. **260-261 123RF.com:** Macrovector. **262 Alamy**

Stock Photo: North Wind Picture Archives (bc). **Getty Images:** Print Collector / Hulton Archive (clb); Mondadori Portfolio (tr). **263 Getty Images:** Paul Cowell / Moment (br); Universal History Archive / Universal Images Group (bl); Jeff Goode / Toronto Star (tr). **264 Alamy Stock Photo:** David Keith Jones / Images of Africa Photobank (bl). **264-265 Getty Images:** Universal History Archive / Universal Images Group. **265 Getty Images:** Culture Club / Hulton Archive (tl); Nastasic / DigitalVision Vectors (tr). **266 The Metropolitan Museum of Art, New York:** Gift of The American Society for the Exploration of Sardis, 1914 (tr). **266-267 Getty Images:** Gavin Quirke / Lonely Planet Images. **267 Alamy Stock Photo:** Giuseppe Anello (crb). **Getty Images:** Swim Ink 2 Llc / Corbis Historical (tr). **268 123RF.com:** Patrick Guenette (bl). **Getty Images:** De Agostini Picture Library (ca). **268-269 Alamy Stock Photo:** ART Collection. **269 Getty Images:** Transcendental Graphics / Archive Photos (tr). **270-271 Getty Images:** Remie Lohse / Condé Nast Collection. **272 Alamy Stock Photo:** Kpzfoto (bc). **Getty Images:** Print Collector / Hulton Archive (tr). **272-273 Getty Images:** DEA / G. Dagli Orti / De Agostini. **273 Getty Images:** Nicoolay / E+ (tr). **274 Bridgeman Images:** La Societe / LeMonnier, Henry (1893-1978) / Private Collection. **275 Getty Images:** M&N (bl). **iStockphoto.com:** Floortje (tr). **276 Alamy Stock Photo:** Martin Baumgärtner / Mauritius Images Gmbh (cra). **Getty Images:** Print Collector / Hulton Archive (tr). **278 Getty Images:** De Agostini Picture Library (tr). **The Metropolitan Museum of Art, New York:** Harris Brisbane Dick Fund, 1953 (bc). **278-279 123RF.com:** Macrovector. **279 123RF. com:** Sergey Pykhonin (Honey dipper). **280 akg-images:** Album / Oronoz (clb). **Getty Images:** DEA / M. Seemuller / De Agostini (bc); Christophel Fine Art / Universal Images Group (cb). **281 Getty Images:** Print Collector / Hulton Archive (tr); DEA Picture Library / De Agostini (clb); Dinodia Photos / Hulton Archive (crb). **282 Alamy Stock Photo:** Art Collection 3 (br); Hristo Chernev (bc). **282-283 Claire Ingram. 284-285 Getty Images:** Universal History Archive / Universal Images Group. **284 Getty Images:** Marilyn Angel Wynn / Nativestock (crb). **285 Alamy Stock Photo:** The Granger Collection (br). **286 Bridgeman Images:** Straet, Jan van der (Giovanni Stradano) (1523-1605) (after) / Private Collection / The Stapleton Collection (bc). **286-287 Getty Images:** Universal History Archive / Universal Images Group (cl, tr). **287 Bridgeman Images:** Engelbrecht, Martin (1684-1756) / Bibliotheque des Arts Decoratifs, Paris, France / Archives Charmet. **288 Alamy Stock Photo:** Lucie Lang (tl). **288-289 Bridgeman Images:** Newbould, Frank (1887-1951) / Manchester Art Gallery, UK. **289 Getty Images:** Transcendental Graphics / Archive Photos (crb); Universal History Archive / Universal Images Group (tr). **290-291 123RF.com:** Zenina. **292 Getty Images:** DEA / G. Dagli Orti / De Agostini (bc); Albert Moldvay / National Geographic (clb); Richard T. Nowitz / Corbis Documentary (crb). **293 Alamy Stock Photo:** Jose Peral / Age Fotostock (bc). **Getty Images:** Keystone-France / Gamma-Keystone (clb); Heritage Images / Hulton Fine Art Collection (tl). **294-295 Bridgeman Images:** Straet, Jan van der (Giovanni Stradano) (1523-1605) (after) / Private Collection / The Stapleton Collection. **294 Getty Images:** PHAS / Universal Images Group (crb). **295 Getty Images:** De Agostini / Archivio J. Lange / De Agostini Picture Library (tr). **Rex Shutterstock:** Granger (tc). **296 Alamy Stock Photo:** Chronicle (tl). **Getty Images:** Owen Franken / Photographer's Choice (tr). **297 Bridgeman Images:** Huile d'olive de Nice / Photo © CCI. **298 Alamy Stock Photo:** All Canada Photos (cra). **298-299 Alamy Stock Photo:** Anca Emanuela Teaca. **299 Alamy Stock Photo:** Gameover (cb). **Getty Images:** Bettmann (tc). **300-301 Alamy Stock Photo:** SSPL / Hulton Archive. **302 Getty Images:** Dea / M. Seemuller / De Agostini. **303 Bridgeman Images:** Photo © CCI (tr). **Getty Images:** Zhang Peng / LightRocket (crb). **304 Getty Images:** DEA / E. Lessing / De Agostini (cra); DEA / C. Sappa / De Agostini (bc). **304-305 Getty Images:** Imagno / Hulton Archive. **305 Getty Images:** Universal History Archive / Universal Images Group (br). **306 Getty Images:** Print Collector / Hulton Archive (tl). **306-307 Getty Images:** Laura Grier / Robertharding. **307 Getty Images:** Christopher Pillitz / Corbis Historical (tc). **308-309 Kikkoman Corporation. 308 Dreamstime.com:** Winfish (crb). **309 Manhhai:** (br). **The Metropolitan Museum of Art, New York:** The Cesnola Collection / Purchased by subscription / 1874–76 (c). **310-311 123RF.com:** Marina99. **312 Getty Images:** DEA / J. E. Bulloz / De Agostini (crb); Culture Club / Hulton Archive (bc). **Mary Evans Picture Library:** J. Bedmar / Iberfoto (bl). **313 Getty Images:** Print Collector / Hulton Archive (clb, bc); Ian Cumming / Perspectives (tr). **314 akg-images:** Alinari Archives, Florence (tl). **315 Rex Shutterstock:** Amoret Tanner Collection (tr). **316 Getty Images:** Florilegius / SSPL (tr); Tetsuya Tanooka / A.collectionrf (bl). **317 Getty Images:** Rosemary Calvert / Photographer's Choice RF (bc). **Mary Evans Picture Library:** Medici (tr). **318 Getty Images:** Heritage Images / Hulton Archive (tl); Laurence Mouton / Canopy (cra). **319 Bridgeman Images:** Italian School, (14th century) / Osterreichische Nationalbibliothek, Vienna, Austria / Alinari (tl). **500px:** Vladislav Nosick (br). **320 Bridgeman Images:** Italian School, (14th century) / Osterreichische Nationalbibliothek, Vienna, Austria / Alinari (bl). **Getty Images:** Halfdark (tl). **321 Getty Images:** Halfdark (r). **322 Alamy Stock Photo:** FirstShot (br). **Getty Images:** Sprint / Corbis (tc). **Photo Scala, Florence:** Ministero Beni e Att. Culturali e del Turismo (clb). **323 Alamy Stock Photo:** Tim Gainey (tl); Lee Hacker (r). **324 Getty Images:** Stefano Bianchetti / Corbis Historical (cr); Stockbyte / Stockbyte (bl). **326 Getty Images:** Three Lions / Hulton Archive (tr); Bibliotheque Nationale, Paris, France / De Agostini Picture Library / J. E. Bulloz (br). **327 iStockphoto.com:** Yawfren (tr). **328 Dreamstime.com:** Alfio Scisetti (tc). **328-329 National Mustard Museum. 329 Getty Images:** Florilegius / SSPL (br). **330-331 Magnum Photos:** Bruno Barbey. **332 123RF.com:** bthnronic (br). **Alamy Stock Photo:** Dinodia Photos (bl). **332-333 Getty Images:** Dinodia Photo / Passage. **333 123RF.com:** Sataporn Jiwjalaen (crb). **334 Alamy Stock Photo:** Florilegius (tl); Umiko (tr). **Getty Images:** William Turner / Stockbyte (cb). **335 Getty Images:** BSIP / Universal Images Group (tl). **336 Michael Sheridan. 337 akg-images:** Pictures From History (bl). **338-339 Bridgeman Images:** Pictures from History. **339 Dover Publications, Inc. New York:** (cr). **Getty Images:** DEA Picture Library / De Agostini (br). **340 Getty Images:** Bildagentur-Online / Universal Images Group (l). **iStockphoto.com:** KieselUndStein (tr). **341 akg-images:** Pictures From History (tl). **Alamy Stock Photo:** Julie Woodhouse f (tr). **342 Getty Images:** De Agostini Picture Library / De Agostini (cr); DEA / M. Seemuller / De Agostini Picture Library (bc). **342-343 Bridgeman Images:** Rijksmuseum, Amsterdam, The Netherlands. **343 Cynthia Hawthorne / www.etsy.com/shop/CynthiasAttic:** (cra). **344 Bridgeman Images:** Photo © Christie's Images (c). **Getty Images:** WIN-Initiative (bc). **345 500px:** Tony One. **346 Getty Images:** Leemage / Universal Images Group. **347 Getty Images:** David De Lossy / Photodisc (br); Diane Macdonald / Photographer's Choice RF (tl); Jean-Pierre Muller / AFP (clb). **iStockphoto.com:** Burwellphotography (cra). **348 akg-images:** Arkivi (clb). **Getty Images:** Smith Collection / Gado / Archive Photos (ca). **iStockphoto.com:** Ockra (tl). **349 Bridgeman Images:** © Purix Verlag Volker Christen

All other images © Dorling Kindersley
For further information see: www.dkimages.com